Seminars in Psychology and the Social Sciences

DATE DUE			

College Seminars Series

Series Editors

Professor Hugh Freeman, Honorary Professor, University of Salford, and Honorary Consultant Psychiatrist, Salford Health Authority

Dr Ian Pullen, Consultant Psychiatrist, Dingleton Hospital, Melrose, Roxburghshire

Dr George Stein, Consultant Psychiatrist, Farnborough Hospital, and King's College Hospital

Professor Greg Wilkinson, Editor, *British Journal of Psychiatry*, and Professor of Liaison Psychiatry, University of Liverpool

Other books in the series

Seminars in Basic Neurosciences. Edited by Gethin Morgan & Stuart Butler

Seminars in Child and Adolescent Psychiatry. Edited by Dora Black & David Cottrell

Seminars in Clinical Psychopharmacology. Edited by David King

Seminars in General Adult Psychiatry. Edited by George Stein & Greg Wilkinson

Seminars in Liaison Psychiatry. Edited by Elspeth Guthrie & Francis Creed

Seminars in Old Age Psychiatry. Edited by Rob Butler & Brice Pitt

Seminars in Practical Forensic Psychiatry. Edited by Derek Chiswick & Rosemarie Cope

Seminars in Psychiatric Genetics. By Peter McGuffin, Michael J. Owen, Michael C. O'Donovan, Anita Thapar & Irving Gottesman

Seminars in the Psychiatry of Learning Disabilities. Edited by Oliver Russell

Seminars in Psychology and the Social Sciences. Edited by Digby Tantam & Max Birchwood

Seminars in Psychosexual Disorders. Series editors: Hugh Freeman, Ian Pullen, George Stein & Greg Wilkinson

Forthcoming title

Seminars in Psychotherapy. Edited by Sandra Grant & Jane Naismith

Seminars in Psychology and the Social Sciences

Edited by
Digby Tantam & Max Birchwood

GASKELL

British Library Cataloguing-in-Publication Data
A catalogue record for this book is available from the British Library.

ISBN 1 902241 62 1

Distributed in North America
by American Psychiatric Press, Inc.
ISBN 0 88048 629 5

Gaskell is an imprint and registered trade mark of the Royal College of
Psychiatrists, 17 Belgrave Square, London SW1X 8PG
The Royal College of Psychiatrists is a registered charity, number 228636

The views presented in this book do not necessarily reflect those of the
Royal College of Psychiatrists, and the publishers are not responsible for
any error of omission or fact. College Seminars are produced by the
Publications Department of the College; they should in no way be
construed as providing a syllabus or other material for any College
examination.

Phototypeset by Dobbie Typesetting Limited, Tavistock, Devon
Printed by Bell & Bain Ltd, Thornliebank, Glasgow

Contents

Contributors

Dr E. Annandale, Lecturer, Department of Sociology, University of Warwick
Professor M. Birchwood, All Saints' Hospital, Birmingham
Professor J. Busfield, Department of Sociology, University of Essex
Dr L. A. Champion, Lecturer, Department of Psychology, University College
  London
Dr D. Cramer, Senior Lecturer in Social Psychology, Social Sciences
  Department, University of Loughborough
Dr B. J. Diamond, Department of Research, Kessler Institute of
  Rehabilitation, USA
Dr M. J. Eales, Consultant Psychiatrist, Tone Vale Hospital, Taunton,
  Somerset
Professor H. J. Eysenck, Professor Emeritus of Psychology, Institute of
  Psychiatry
Dr K. R. Fontaine, Lecturer in Psychology, Department of Psychology,
  University of Central Lancashire
Dr N. Frude, Senior Lecturer in Psychology, School of Psychology, University
  of Wales, College of Cardiff
Ms G. M. Goodall, Researcher, MRC Child Psychiatry Unit
Dr S. Hallett, Consultant Clinical Neuropsychologist, Coventry Consulting
  Rooms, Coventry
Dr T. A. Harley, Department of Psychology, University of Warwick
Dr G. Harris, Lecturer in Psychology, School of Psychology, University of
  Birmingham
Dr M. R. D. Johnson, Senior Research Fellow, Centre for Research in Ethnic
  Relations, University of Warwick
Dr S. B. G. MacAndrew, Lecturer in Psychology, School of Health and
  Social Sciences, University of Coventry
Dr G. Matthews, Senior Lecturer in Psychology, Department of Psychology,
  University of Dundee
Dr P. Mitchell, Lecturer in Psychology, School of Psychology, University of
  Birmingham
Professor R. Moore, Department of Sociology, Social Policy and Social
  Work Studies, University of Liverpool
Dr P. Reed, Department of Psychology, University College London
Dr G. Rippon, Lecturer in Psychology, Department of Psychology, University
  of Warwick
Professor D. Tantam, Department of Psychology, University of Warwick

Foreword

Series Editors

The publication of *College Seminars*, a series of textbooks covering the breadth of psychiatry, represents a new venture for the Royal College of Psychiatrists. At the same time, it is very much in line with the College's established role in education and in setting professional standards.

College Seminars are intended to help junior doctors during their training years. We hope that trainees will find these books useful, on the ward as well as in preparation for the MRCPsych examination. Separate volumes will cover clinical psychiatry, each of its subspecialties, and also the relevant non-clinical academic disciplines of psychology and sociology.

College Seminars will also make a contribution to the continuing medical education of established clinicians.

Psychiatry is concerned primarily with people, and to a lesser extent with disease processes and pathology. The core of the subject is rich in ideas and schools of thought, and no single approach or solution can embrace the variety of problems a psychiatrist meets. For this reason, we have endeavoured to adopt an eclectic approach to practical management throughout the series.

The College can draw upon the collective wisdom of many individuals in clinical and academic psychiatry. More than a hundred people have contributed to this series; this shows how diverse and complex psychiatry has become.

Frequent new editions of books appearing in the series are envisaged, which should allow *College Seminars* to be responsive to readers' suggestions and needs.

Hugh Freeman
Ian Pullen
George Stein
Greg Wilkinson

Preface

This is a book about basic science written for the clinical scientist, among whose number we include clinical psychology students, general practitioners, community psychiatric nurses, and social workers, as well as the main group for whom it is written, psychiatrists in training.

Psychiatrists are increasingly, and some would say belatedly, becoming cognisant of the twin roots of their speciality. One root taps into medicine and the biological sciences; the other draws nourishment from the social sciences and psychology. The Royal College of Psychiatrists has recognised this trend, and the revised qualifying examination usually contains a substantial number of questions on these subjects.

Editors of any book on basic science which is intended to be used by applied scientists face a dilemma. Should the book convey an accurate picture of recent developments in the basic science, or should it concentrate on those aspects of the basic science which have already found their way into an application, usually many years after they were first reported? This problem is especially acute in psychiatry. Social psychiatry often seems to be a discipline *sui generis*, having little or no relation to its basic science or even to the clinical application of that basic science, psychiatric social work. Even greater differences exist between psychological medicine and academic psychology, as we are in a position to know, both being clinicians, and both also having appointments in university departments of psychology.

Memory disorder provides a good illustration of the difficulties. It is, according to Lishman (1987) in his authoritative textbook on organic psychiatry, a "symptom of the utmost importance in psychiatric practice"; and it should be assessed by testing the ability to register, to retain, and to retrieve information, including information from the remote past, and to use this 'old knowledge'. This examination scheme will be familiar to all psychiatrists, and is based on what Lishman describes as a "somewhat arbitrary division", made "for purposes of clinical description . . . into 'immediate', 'recent', and 'remote' memory" (p. 27). Although Lishman does not put it in these specific terms, he uses a model of memory that MacAndrew & Matthews (Chapter 3) describe as 'modal'. According to this model, information has first to be registered and put into a short-term store (Lishman calls this 'immediate'). Registration is tested clinically by immediate recall from this short-term store. Information is retained, according to the modal model, if it is passed into a long-term store, and is recalled to mind from this long-term store by a further step, retrieval. When 'recent' memory is tested, and patients are required to learn information of little personal relevance, it is assumed that retention rather than retrieval is the limiting step. When 'remote memory' is assessed, the patient's recall of familiar information is tested, and since it is assumed that this information has been retained, at least at some stage, recall is limited by retrieval.

The chapters by MacAndrew & Matthews and MacAndrew & Harley in this book present a contrasting viewpoint. MacAndrew & Matthews consider that, although the "more useful constructs [of the modal theory] still dominate theorising", it fails to account for some instances of both normal and pathological memory. They emphasise a process model of memory and also consider aspects of memory that are often neglected by clinicians, such as procedural memory – how to do things, rather than what to do – and episodic memory – memory for events, rather than for semantically encoded information. MacAndrew & Harley introduce a third polarity, 'implicit' versus 'explicit' memory, which is of particular interest because implicit memory is much less impaired in patients with memory disorders.

The seven years since the second edition of Lishman's book was published have seen a considerable change in the way that psychologists understand the brain. Gone are the mental modules which were assumed to correspond to areas of brain and to function like processing modules in a (non-parallel) computer. They have been replaced by neural networks (see Chapter 5), whose processors are simpler and much less differentiated but whose connections to other processors are highly complex. This 'cognitive neuropsychological' perspective has been applied to amnesic subjects, as MacAndrew & Harley show in their chapter, but it has yet to penetrate deeply into psychiatric theories of brain dysfunction, which still draw heavily on the earlier, modal tradition of neuropsychology.

Cognitive neuropsychology seems to be more of a programme than a consistent theory at the moment, and is less immediately useful to the clinician than a theory which links disordered function to diseased parts of the brain, as the modal theory does. Even so, the cognitivist programme is likely to generate many useful hypotheses which will influence clinical practice in the future – indeed, the diminished importance of structure has already inspired clinical psychologists to undertake much more active memory retraining in patients with memory disorders associated with brain lesions.

Our editorial dilemma is, then, whether this book is to be an account of the psychology and social science that is familiar to clinicians, like the modal theory of memory? Or is it to be an account of new theories which have yet to make their way in clinical application? Our editorial solution has been to go unreservedly for reviews of the current state of the basic science, but in topic areas that are likely to be of clinical relevance. The chapters do not therefore provide a systematic review of the whole of social science and psychology, but only as these relate to mental health.

Nor, being a book about basic science, are there many explicit links between the subject matter and mental health issues. In fact, links between clinical practice and most of the recent theories considered in the book have yet to be made. What each chapter does provide is an up-to-date summary of topics that are likely to be of considerable interest to the clinician, written clearly and without jargon, but without simplifying the subject either. Consequently, although no formal training in psychology or social science is required to understand the book, it should still be of interest to those who have been so trained. Psychiatrists preparing for the examination for membership of their College will find it highly relevant to that examination, but we intend it to be more than a revision guide. We hope that it provides the material for at least some of its readers to stimulate the next generation of applications of psychological and social theory to mental health.

The success of this book will be due to its contributors much more than to its editors. We therefore wish to thank each of them. We would also like to thank Pat Scott for administrative assistance. And, as always, we are grateful to our families, who come last when we allocate our time even though they come first when we list our priorities.

Digby Tantam
University of Warwick, and Gulson Hospital, Coventry

Max Birchwood
All Saints' Hospital, Birmingham, and University of Birmingham

Reference

Lishman, W. A. (1987) *Organic Psychiatry. The Psychological Consequences of Cerebral Disorder* (2nd edn). Oxford: Blackwell Scientific.

Part I
Cognition and emotion

1 Cognitive development

Peter Mitchell

Piaget's stages of cognitive development • Criticisms of Piaget's theories • A theory of mind • Autism: a failure to acquire a theory of mind? • Conclusion

---

The study of cognitive development is concerned with how the quality of thought processes improves with experience and maturity. The central theorist on this is Jean Piaget, who first became interested in human intelligence when he worked in Paris at the beginning of the 20th century, with IQ pioneers Alfred Binet and Theo Simon. Piaget had the revolutionary idea that the development of cognitive abilities does not undergo a smooth progression through childhood, but rather that it is stage-like, as the child negotiates a succession of intellectual revolutions. Each quantum leap in cognition equips the child to relate to and understand the world more objectively. That is, development consists of a progression from subjective conception to the objective (Table 1.1) (Piaget & Inhelder, 1969).

Piaget's stages of cognitive development

1 – The sensorimotor stage

First comes the 'sensorimotor' stage, spanning from birth to 2 years, where, according to Piaget, infants' subjectivity is so profound that they are unaware of any existence other than their own. As such, the infant fails to distinguish between self and not self, with the implication that for the infant, out of sight quite literally is out of mind. That is, Piaget tells us that the infant cannot conceive of an object's existence once it is no longer immediately perceptible.

As evidence for this, Piaget demonstrates the 4–8-month-old's failure to retrieve a rattle covered with a cloth. The infant possesses the requisite dexterity to pull away the cloth and grasp the rattle, yet does not do so. We can assume that infants find the rattle highly interesting, because they grasp it when it is not covered. Once the rattle is covered, even though it is within easy reach, the infant will no longer show any interest and make no attempt at retrieval. The reason, according to Piaget, is that the infant is no longer able to conceive of the rattle once it is out of view, and therefore does not search for it.

3

Table 1.1 Piaget's stages of cognitive development

Age: years	Stage
0–2	Sensorimotor Difficulty conceiving objects not present Perception subordinate to action
2–7	Preoperational Distinguishes self and not self Egocentric Fails to recognise conservation of different quantities Non-logical thought
7–12	Concrete operational Logical reasoning
>12	Formal operational Hypothesising

At approximately eight months, the infant shows continued interest in the rattle even when it is covered, and will successfully retrieve it by first whisking away the cloth and then grasping the rattle. However, infants still have difficulty conceiving of objects not immediately perceptible, as shown by the finding that between 8 and 12 months they will commit the 'A–B place error'.

Initially we place two cloths on the table side by side, which we label A and B, and we deposit the rattle under cloth A on three successive trials. Each time the infant will whisk away the cloth and retrieve the rattle. Then, on the fourth trial, we deposit the rattle under cloth B. Surprisingly, despite having watched the hiding of the rattle, the infant will persevere in searching under cloth A.

According to Piaget, the infant fails to search under cloth B because, although she witnessed the rattle being hidden there, the infant's perception is subordinate to action. In other words, infants represent external reality in terms of their own actions rather than in terms of perceptual images which reality imposes on them. This, according to Piaget, is because the infant has little conception of reality as distinct from self. In this case, 'self' is defined in terms of own action. Towards the end of infancy, as children approach their second birthday, they begin to exhibit considerable proficiency in conceptualising hidden objects. At this time they are able to distinguish between self and not self. According to Piaget, children achieve this conception through a newly acquired mental imagery, which allows them to imagine the existence of objects not directly perceptible.

2 – The preoperational stage

Now the child enters an entirely new stage of cognition which Piaget calls the 'preoperational stage'. This spans from approximately two to seven years of age. The newly acquired facility of mental imagery brings with it both advantages and disadvantages. An advantage, as already mentioned, is that children can distinguish between self and not self. A disadvantage is that they are dominated by images in a way that hinders an objective conception of reality. In particular, children wrongly suppose that their images are all there is to reality. So, for example, they fail to recognise that another person might view reality differently if situated at a different vantage point.

Missing points of view

Piaget attempted to demonstrate this with the 'three mountains test'. He showed the child a model of three mountains positioned side by side, each with a distinctive feature at its summit; for example, a house on one, a snow cap on another, and a cross on the third. The child's task is to select from a collection of photos what the array looks like to another person who is sitting at the opposite side of the model. The correct choice is the photo which shows the mountains in left–right reversal. However, the characteristic error made by children in the preoperational stage is to choose the photo showing the child's own view.

This shows, according to Piaget, that the preoperational child is oblivious to the notion that one's view of reality is but one of many possible views. As a consequence, the child is ignorant of other people's points of view, both strictly and figuratively, and so, to use Piaget's terminology, the child is 'egocentric'.

Non-conservation

Another sign of the child's domination by appearances is evident in the phenomenon of non-conservation. We show the child two glass beakers of identical shape and size, and we fill each to the same level with coloured water. We then ask the child whether there is the same amount in the two glasses. Once the child has agreed, we pour the contents of one into a tall thin glass with a resultant raised water level in that glass. We then repeat the question, asking whether there is the same amount to drink in the remaining short wide glass as there is in the new tall thin glass. A typical six-year-old will wrongly judge that the tall glass has more in it, whereas a typical eight-year-old will correctly judge that there is just the same amount in each. As such, the older child recognises the irrelevance of pouring and the higher level of water, whereas the younger child appears to be seduced by the higher water level into judging that quantity has increased. Thus the child fails to mentally conserve the quantity of water through the irrelevant transformation of pouring from one glass to another.

Another conservation test involves number. We arrange two adjacent rows of six counters in one-to-one correspondence, and the child will agree that there is the same number of counters in each. We then spread out the counters in one of the rows, thus making it longer. The typical six-year-old will now give a non-conserving response, usually by judging that there are more counters in the longer of the rows.

Another manifestation of non-logical thought in the preoperational stage is the child's failure to make transitive inferences. Formally, these are: given that $A < B < C$, which is greater, A or C? We can deduce that $A < C$. Piaget presented an analogous problem to children involving two towers of slightly different height, and invited them to work out which was the taller. It was impossible to do this without measuring, since the towers were situated in different parts of the room and on different levels. Piaget issued the child with a measuring stick to determine which tower was the taller. Eight-year-olds promptly took the stick and put it up against each tower to discover that it was shorter than one of the towers but taller than the other. They then correctly judged that the tower which was taller than the stick was also taller than the other tower. In contrast, six-year-olds apparently had no idea what to do with the stick, and even when Piaget did the measuring for them, they judged just as often that the taller tower was taller as they judged that the shorter one was taller. As such, they seemed to be devoid of the logical capability required to make a transitive inference.

Lack of class inclusion

A final demonstration of the young child's deficient logic is evident in a failure of class inclusion. We show the child six counters – four green and two yellow. We ask how many green ones there are, and the child will correctly reply 'four'; we ask how many yellow, and the child will say 'two'; we ask how many altogether, and the child will say 'six'. Yet, remarkably, when we ask whether there are more green counters or more counters altogether, the typical six-year-old, but not an older child, will judge wrongly that there are more green counters. According to Piaget, this is because young children cannot mentally compare superclass (counters altogether) with subclass (green counters) because they do not possess a logic of class hierarchy. That is, the child fails to grasp that a counter can simultaneously be a member of the general class of counters and also a member of the class of green counters. Consequently, she focuses on two subclasses (green counters versus yellow counters) and judges wrongly that there are more green ones than there are counters altogether.

3 – Concrete operational stage

At approximately seven years of age, the child enters the 'concrete operational' stage, marked by the onset of logical reasoning. This newly acquired logic enables the child to make the correct judgements on all the tests described above. The child is no longer at the mercy of superficial images, but instead is able to conceive of an objective reality which underlies appearances. During this stage, children are no longer egocentric, and they can now recognise that their view of reality is but one of many.

4 – Formal operational stage

According to Piaget, the child achieves the pinnacle of human cognition, the stage of adult cognition, which is 'formal operational' reasoning, at around 11 or 12 years of age.

That the concrete operational child is deficient in certain aspects of reasoning is evident in Piaget's pendulum problem. Piaget explained to the child that he was to determine which of four possible factors was the most important in the speed of oscillation of a pendulum: weight of the suspended object; force of the initial swing; height from which the object is released; or length of the string. The important factor is length of the string, although Piaget was not so much concerned with children arriving at the correct answer as with how they tackled the problem.

Children in the concrete operational stage would approach the problem in a thoughtless, ad hoc manner, by changing the values of two variables simultaneously. For example, they may increase both weight and length of string, and then find that the pendulum swings more slowly. It would be impossible to say whether that was because of the change in length, the change in weight, or a combination of the two. In sharp contrast, formal operational children were systematic in their investigation, and held all variables constant except one, and then observed the effect of varying values of the remaining variable.

According to Piaget, this reveals that the formal operational child must have correctly hypothesised the necessary conditions for conducting an informative test. The key feature of this is engaging in the hypothetical before testing, something absent in the concrete operational child. Piaget claims that the concrete operational child, although in possession of logical thought processes, is unable to apply these to hypothetical situations, such as in hypothesising on the optimal conditions for an informative test.

Piaget's mechanisms of cognitive development

Piaget not only described development progressing through a series of stages, but he also attempted to explain the mechanism of development.

According to Piaget, human intelligence has its roots in the actions of the newborn child. The newborn child is endowed with a repertoire of reflexes Piaget called motor 'schemes', which provide the foundations for subsequent cognitive feats. For example, infants have a grasping reflex, such that if we place a finger in the palm, they will clutch it, and so they possess a finger-grasping scheme.

In a process Piaget called 'assimilation', the infant will apply this scheme to novel problems, such as grasping a newly introduced rattle. The rattle is brought within the scope of the grasping scheme, but, incidentally, the infant has to adapt to the unfamiliar contours of the rattle in order to grasp it securely. Here the scheme is adapted to its new application, a process Piaget called 'accommodation'. In this way, assimilation and accommodation work together as complementary processes as the infant's repertoire of schemes becomes ever more generalised and refined.

Later on in development, the child acquires symbolic schemes, extending beyond the domain of action. For example, children will develop a scheme which informs them that tall means more. Consequently, when reasoning about conservation, the young child may regard the tall column of liquid as being more than the short one by virtue of its greater height. Problems arise for children's cognition when they also acquire a scheme which informs them that wide is associated with more. It will become apparent that this has happened when, on repeated presentation of the conservation test, the child vacillates, sometimes judging that the taller column contains more and sometimes that the wider one contains more.

This unsatisfactory state of internal cognitive conflict throws the child into a state of cognitive disequilibrium. Here we have two wrongs (wide is more and tall is more), and from these the child logically constructs a 'right': the extra tallness of one column is compensated for by the extra width of the other, cancelling out each other. Therefore, Piaget tells us, the child deduces conservation, that the two quantities are identical, and that the pouring and the deceptive appearance are irrelevant to this. Piaget refers to the process which eradicates the disequilibrium as 'equilibration', which has the potential to restructure the child's thinking through what amounts to an internal intellectual revolution, and so the child enters a higher stage of cognitive development. This higher stage will be more objective, less egocentric, and thus better adapted.

Criticisms of Piaget's theories

Piaget's interpretations of children's errors on his tests have been seriously challenged in recent years, which has resulted in a blurring of the boundaries between stages (Box 1.1). We shall now turn our attention to the arguments and findings of some of his most vehement critics, beginning with infancy.

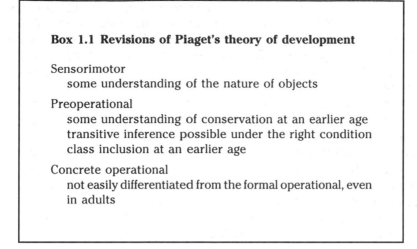

Box 1.1 Revisions of Piaget's theory of development

Sensorimotor
   some understanding of the nature of objects

Preoperational
   some understanding of conservation at an earlier age
   transitive inference possible under the right condition
   class inclusion at an earlier age

Concrete operational
   not easily differentiated from the formal operational, even
   in adults

Criticisms of the sensorimotor stage

Piaget claimed that the infant aged between four and eight months does not retrieve an object within easy reach covered by a cloth because of a failure to conceive of the object once it is hidden. This claim has been challenged by Bower (1982) in view of the findings of a study he conducted. Bower wired up three-month-old infants to apparatus which monitored various physiological functions, such as heart rate. He seated the infant in front of a table, on which he placed a rattle. Bower then lowered a screen, occluding the rattle in the process. After a short delay, he raised the screen to reveal either that the rattle was still situated on the table or that it had vanished. If the rattle was still present, infants showed no physiological reaction, but if the rattle had disappeared, heart rate increased. Bower attributed this to surprise, which he interpreted to mean that the infant expected the rattle to be on the table. He argued, therefore, that since infants apparently anticipated the presence of the rattle, they must have conceived of the existence of the rattle even in its perceptual absence.

Another recent study (Baillargeon, 1987) has yielded consistent results. Baillargeon exposed four-month-olds to the very realistically rigged illusion of one apparently solid object passing through another. Under a control condition, the two objects met each other and then became motionless. The infants stared at the objects under the illusion condition for much longer than under the control, which Baillargeon interpreted to be a sign that the infants were surprised. She suggested they were surprised because the event violated the normal principles of the behaviour of real objects, which shows, she argues, that they must have a fairly mature concept of object existence.

In that case, why do infants of the same age fail to retrieve an object covered by a cloth? Hood & Willatts (1986) explored the possibility that failure to search was a peculiarity of the mode of disappearance. They proceeded to make the rattle vanish from view by extinguishing the lights in the room, and found (with the help of infrared cameras) that infants reached out in the dark much more frequently to the location of the object than to an arbitrary control location. This finding suggests that young infants can search for a hidden object, providing the method of hiding does not involve covering it with another item. As such, coupled with the respective findings of Bower and Baillargeon, it seems that infants could know more about object existence than Piaget had given them credit for. Nonetheless, the observation that infants fail to retrieve an object covered by a cloth raises the possibility that their concept of object existence is somewhat immature.

Also, it seems that slightly older infants, aged between 8 and 12 months, really do tend to relate to objects in terms of their own previous actions. This was demonstrated neatly by Bremner & Bryant (1977). As mentioned above, the characteristic error of an infant this age is to search for a rattle under cloth A, where it had been located previously, rather than under cloth B, where the experimenter had just deposited it in full view of the infant. Bremner & Bryant questioned whether the infant's search was actually based on an inappropriate internal criterion of previously successful hand movement, or whether the infant was using an external criterion of associating the object with cloth A. To find out, they hid the rattle under cloth A for a series of trials, and the infant retrieved it each time, but then they moved the infant round to the opposite side of the table and deposited the rattle either under the same cloth or under cloth B. The findings were very clear: once on the other side of the table, the infants searched under B, whether correct or incorrect, thus executing the same hand action as in the preliminary trials where the object was hidden at A, even when the object was hidden yet again at A on the test trial. This shows conclusively that infants at this age have a strong tendency to code objects in terms of their previous action in connection with it. Once again, it seems that the infant conception of objects is rather immature, as Piaget had suggested.

Criticism of the preoperational stage

The naughty teddy controversy

Piaget has been the victim of a more scathing onslaught in connection with his interpretations of the errors children commit during the preoperational stage. One of his foremost critics in this respect is Margaret Donaldson (1978). With the help of colleagues, she has cast doubt on some of the fundamental Piagetian phenomena. For example, she points out that one would never ask the same question twice in a short period of time, unless a different answer was expected, yet that is exactly what Piaget did in the conservation test. She argues that on hearing the second presentation of the question, children would say to themselves, "I've already told him they're just the same, yet he's asking me again. He must want me to say something different. What shall I say? Well, this row of counters is longer now he's spread them out. He probably wants me to say that one has more."

In view of this, Donaldson, in collaboration with her colleague James McGarrigle (McGarrigle & Donaldson, 1975), sought to make the asking of the second question more sensible to children. They presented the conservation of number test both under a standard Piagetian condition and under a novel 'naughty teddy' condition. Under the latter, the spreading of the counters in one of the rows was effected by a delinquent teddy, who, so children were told, was bent on 'messing up the game'. After teddy had effected the transformation of one of the rows of counters, the experimenter then asked the second equality question, but this time the question seemed a perfectly sensible thing to ask, according to Donaldson, on the grounds that experimenter and child wished to establish whether teddy had succeeded in his endeavour of spoiling the game. As Donaldson had predicted, very many more five-year-old children made a correct, conserving judgement when the transformation to one of the rows was effected by teddy rather than directly by the experimenter, as in the standard procedure.

This finding led Donaldson to claim that non-conservation is more to do with the way a young child wrongly interprets certain questions in context than with a preoperational stage of thinking.

However, the facilitation under the naughty teddy procedure begins to look more apparent than real when we consider the findings of Moore & Fry (1986). They questioned whether the naughty teddy actually unmasked competence in conservation, or whether the procedure artefactually gave rise to equality judgements that the children did not really believe in. To find out, they repeated the naughty teddy procedure with the modification that teddy introduced an extra counter to one of the rows in his meddling. Under this condition, children still judged that the two rows had the same number of counters in each, whereas they (perhaps serendipitously) judged that a row with a counter added had more in it under a procedure which approximated to the standard Piagetian version. Clearly, then, the naughty teddy procedure was effective in eliciting judgements of equality from children, but there is no reason to suppose these judgements genuinely revealed any competence in conservation.

Another idea advanced about young children's difficulty with conservation takes on board the misleading cues arising from transformation (e.g. that when poured from a short wide glass into a tall thin one, a column of water does indeed look more), and that in order to understand non-conservation we ought to focus on ability to draw the appearance/reality distinction (Braine & Shanks, 1965).

Braine & Shanks found that at approximately five years of age, children come to distinguish between the apparent and the real in visual illusions. This ability precedes success on the conservation task by two years, and Russell & Mitchell (1985) supposed that might be because the standard conservation task does not employ appearance/reality wording which would alert children to focus on the distinction in question. Russell & Mitchell put matters right, and after transformation of pouring liquid from a short wide glass to a tall thin one, asked, "Do these two glasses look as though they have the same amount?" followed by, "Do they really have the same amount?" As many as 75% of a sample of five-year-olds correctly answered 'no' and 'yes', respectively, thus giving a conserving judgement, whereas only 25% judged equality under the standard procedure. This was not pseudo-conservation of the naughty teddy variety, since children correctly answered 'no' and 'no' to the appearance/reality questions when the transformation involved addition of water to one of the vessels. Russell & Mitchell went on to report a significant relation between children's success in distinguishing appearance from reality in visual illusions and success at conservation.

This is probably consistent with what Piaget would have predicted, given that he suggested children in the preoperational stage are dominated by surface appearances and overlook underlying reality. The problem it poses for Piagetian theory, and it may not be a serious one, is that his timetable is slightly wrong: it seems children know something about conservation at a younger age than Piaget had anticipated.

Some transitive inference

In contrast to young children's difficulty with conservation, it seems even children as young as four years can succeed at a modified version of the transitive inference test (Pears & Bryant, 1990). Recall that Piaget's test of this required the child to work out the relative heights of two towers by using a stick of intermediate height as a measuring device. Pears & Bryant showed children four towers, each made up of two coloured building blocks; for example, red on top of green, green on top of blue, blue on top of yellow, and yellow on top of white. The child's task was then to make a tower out of blocks of five different colours used in the sample towers: red, green, blue, yellow, and white. Pears & Bryant had previously trained the children to build towers maintaining the relationship between colour positions as presented in the sample towers. In other words, we can infer that the tower the child would have to construct would be red at the top, followed by green, blue, yellow, and finally white at the bottom. Therefore, we can make the transitive inference from the positions of colours in the sample towers that in the tower the child was to construct, green would be at a higher position than yellow.

Before allowing children to commence constructing the five-block tower, Pears & Bryant asked them which brick would be higher, the green or the yellow. Remarkably, a substantial majority of the children answered correctly with 'green', showing that under the right conditions they could perform a transitive inference. In that case, it seems Piaget's version of the test underestimated children's ability, and the reason might be, as Bryant & Trabasso (1971) suggest, that the task requires children to keep a considerable amount of information in their head all at the same time, which places too great a demand on the limited memory capacity of a young child. Pears & Bryant argue that, in contrast, the coloured-blocks version of transitive inference is far less demanding on memory and thus allows children to succeed.

Some class inclusion

Piaget argued that another manifestation of the preoperational child's deficient logic can be found in the class inclusion test. Once again, Donaldson (1978) makes the competing suggestion that children's failures on this test betray not a logical error but rather a misunderstanding of the experimenter's meaning. She points out that usually when adults direct questions at children, where alternatives are specified in the question these are mutually exclusive; for example, "Are you a boy or a girl?" A choice of one of these would necessarily rule out any consideration of the other, but in class inclusion a correct judgement of 'more counters altogether' requires the child to violate this pragmatic convention.

Yet again she calls upon the work of her colleague James McGarrigle to support her argument. McGarrigle set out to help children comprehend that the usual pragmatic convention of mutual exclusivity of alternatives did not apply in this game, by enabling them to get a visual grasp of the problem. He achieved this by laying out six counters in a line; he called these counters 'steps'. From left to right, the first four led to a chair, then a further two to the right of this led to a table. He then asked children, "Are there more steps to go to the chair or more to go to the table?", and found that two-thirds of six-year-olds gave a correct judgement of 'more to the table'. In making this correct judgement, children showed that they understood that steps to the table includes steps to the chair, and as such they succeeded at class inclusion at an earlier age than Piaget had supposed possible. However, it seems again that Piaget was only wrong about the developmental timetable, and that the phenomenon of failure at class inclusion is a characteristic associated with young children – but children aged five rather than six, contrary to Piaget's account.

The findings and arguments presented by Donaldson have made a great impact on the way in which we carry out research involving children as subjects, and nowadays we are much more conscious of the possibility that misleading cues inherent in our procedures could give rise to a distorted impression of children's cognition. Perhaps this has been Donaldson's most valuable contribution. She has also succeeded in some cases in showing that Piaget had underestimated young children's abilities. However, it now seems that Donaldson may have overestimated those very same abilities, with the implication that cognitive deficits do cause young children to make wrong judgements on certain tasks.

Differentiating the concrete operational from the formal operation stage

Piaget has also come under attack for his ideas about the fully fledged cognition which he claims first makes its appearance in adolescence as formal operational thinking. Piaget's theory is that formal operational thinking is liberated from the trammels of known reality, and therefore permits the individual comfortably to reason in the abstract. As such, reasoning processes are rule-bound and independent of content: a particular reasoning process can be applied generally, to various contexts, whether the content is familiar and concrete or abstract and hypothetical. However, research by Wason & Johnson-Laird (1972) shows that this description of adult cognition is far from the truth of things.

Wason & Johnson-Laird presented to undergraduates a test they devised now known as the 'selection task'. The subject sees four cards and is told that each has an alphabet letter on one side and a number on the other. The subject is able to see only one side of the four cards:

E   K   4   7

There is a rule which the subject has to test by turning over two of the cards:

If a card has a vowel on one side, then it has an even number on the other.

The great majority of subjects chose the apparently obvious, yet in fact incorrect, pair of E and 4. E is correct, but 4 is wrong, since if there was a consonant on the reverse side of 4, that would tell us nothing. The condition specified in the rule only pertains to what follows given a vowel, and it says nothing about what follows given a consonant. The correct pair is E and 7. If we turn over 7 and find a vowel, then this would show that the rule is wrong.

This error in people's reasoning does not in itself seriously damage Piaget's theory, but taken with the following finding it poses a considerable threat. The selection task is modified such that on one side of each card is the name of a city and on the other is a mode of transport:

Manchester   Leeds   Train   Car

and the rule to be tested is:

Every time I travel to Manchester I go by train.

The correct cards to turn over are Manchester and Car, and a good majority of undergraduate subjects successfully chose this pair. In that case, it seems Piaget was wrong to claim that adult reasoning processes are applied generally irrespective of content of the problem under consideration. Instead, people appear to be able to reason much better when the problem has a real-world concrete content (as in the travel version of the selection task) than when the problem has abstract content (as in the alphabet/ number version of the selection task).

Not only was Piaget wrong about the generality of reasoning processes, but the conditions under which people actually reason well and badly could also be informative. It looks as though adults are well suited to reasoning about problems with concrete content, but poor at reasoning on problems with hypothetical content, which makes their reasoning resemble that described by Piaget as being typical of the concrete operational child.

However, work subsequent to Wason & Johnson-Laird's suggests that adults do possess rule-based reasoning processes to a degree, but ones which are only applied in specific domains (Cheng & Holyoak, 1985). In other words, people do have rules for reasoning, as Piaget suggested, but these rules are not general and therefore cannot be applied to any suitable problem irrespective of content, contrary to Piaget's theory.

Conclusion

One effect of much of the work aimed at testing Piaget's findings and theory has been to blur the distinction between the stages he described, particularly in terms of the competence or otherwise of people who could be located within one or other of the stages. Specifically, the young child appears to be more competent than Piaget had supposed, and therefore has more in common with the child in the concrete operational stage than he had suspected. In contrast, the adult appears less competent than Piaget had thought, and so too has a considerable amount in common with the concrete operational child.

Additionally, developmentalists have begun to call into question the validity of the logic internal to Piaget's theory, and have concluded that there could be some serious inconsistencies in Piaget's thinking (e.g. Braine & Rumain, 1983). As a consequence, for example, not only is there a lack of evidence for an underlying cognitive deficit in the form of egocentrism in early childhood, but the diverse phenomena Piaget reported as manifestations of egocentrism do not form any logically coherent pattern.

In sum, Piaget's description of stages sometimes seems to be wrong, as does his theory which was advanced to explain those stages. However, it does not follow that cognitive development is a continuous process. For instance, it seems to be the case that there is indeed a stage of non-conservation, and nobody can claim to have eradicated this phenomenon no matter how child-based the procedure they have developed. As such, it seems that in some aspects of cognitive development children do progress through stages, but perhaps not at the ages or for the reasons stated by Piaget.

A theory of mind

Much recent research into cognitive development has turned away from testing Piaget's theory as such, but nonetheless has its roots in Piaget's ideas. Piaget's claim was that children below approximately seven years know little about others' points of view and intentionality. In other words, they know little about others' minds. An exciting and burgeoning area of interest is research into what the child knows about the mind, with the supposition that with increasing age the child comes to formulate a 'theory' of mind. It is a theory the child holds in the sense that the child hypothesises about a person's unseen mental constructs (which may have no immediate counterpart in reality) and is able to predict the behaviour of the person in question on the basis of these constructs. An example of this can be found in the 'deceptive box task', where a four-year-old child correctly predicts another person's behaviour by taking into account a false belief which the child supposes the other person entertains.

The deceptive box task

The deceptive box task typically involves a tube of sweets (Smarties) with the unexpected content of pencils. The experimenter invites the child to say what is inside, and the child will typically judge 'Smarties' on recognising this familiar product. Then the experimenter opens the lid to reveal the pencils. After the child has acknowledged these as the true content, the experimenter returns them to the tube and closes the lid, and then asks what the child thinks the next child, who has never seen the tube before, will say is inside when that child first sees it. A good majority of four-year-olds correctly predict that the next child will say the tube contains Smarties. This shows that they hold a 'theory' about the next child's false belief, and that they can predict the next child's behaviour on the basis of this theory. In other words, when predicting another person's behaviour, they do not refer to the present state of reality (that there are pencils in the tube), but instead refer to their hypothesis about the other person's belief (that the next child will believe there are Smarties in the tube).

All this is not very surprising, and is little more than spelling out what we all knew anyway. However, when we present the deceptive box task to a younger child, aged three years, now we find the child predicting that the next child will say the tube contains pencils. We can state that the four-year-old has a concept of false belief and therefore has a fundamental basis for the possession of a theory of mind, but the evidence for the three-year-old's theory of mind capability is not forthcoming.

Given the three-year-old's failure, some (e.g. Perner, 1991) have argued that they lack a fundamental requisite for possession of a theory of mind. Apparently, they do not understand that behaviour is governed by one's beliefs, and as such have difficulty in differentiating between mind and world. However, their deficiency is not so profound as first thought, as demonstrated by Wellman & Estes (1986). They asked three-year-olds to imagine a bicycle, and then proceeded to ask whether they could ride this imaginary bicycle, whether they could put it away until tomorrow, and whether they could let a friend play with it. Even these very young children judged correctly that they could not ride it, or keep it until tomorrow or let a friend have a go. As such, they could distinguish between imagination and reality, and therefore succeeded to an extent in drawing the mind–world distinction.

Returning to the deceptive box task, in wrongly judging that a person will act according to reality rather than according to a belief about reality, superficially the three-year-old appears egocentric in the sense in which Piaget used this term. It looks as though the concept is the same (failure to appreciate other's belief as distinct from own belief), except that the test is different (deceptive box rather than three mountains), as is the age of success (four years rather than seven years). However, closer inspection reveals that the concept of egocentrism is not appropriate for explaining young children's difficulty with false belief, as I explain below.

We can introduce the following variation so that children are invited to judge about their own belief rather than another child's. Having initially shown the Smarties tube, revealed the true content of pencils, and then returned them to the tube, we ask children what they had thought was in the tube when they first saw it. Three-year-olds will wrongly answer 'pencils', just as they give an inappropriate, 'realist' response when required to predict what another person will think is in the tube (e.g. Mitchell & Lacohee, 1991). In that case, it seems young children lack a conception of false belief, whether their own or another person's. So it is not the case that they know their own mind but fail to apply this knowledge to others in order to understand their minds, as the concept of egocentrism would imply. Instead, it might be that young children have to develop a theory of how the mind represents things (as distinct from reality), whether the particular mind in question is their own or someone else's (Perner, 1991). According to Perner, the development in question progresses in a stage-like manner.

Inferring colours

Another 'theory of mind' test shows more directly that young children's problem is not primarily one of egocentrism. Sodian & Wimmer (1987) demonstrated 4–5-year-olds' failure to attribute knowledge where inference could have served as a source of information. They introduced children to another person (Susie) and to a red ball and a blue ball. They then placed the red ball in an opaque container in full view of the child, but out of sight of Susie. Finally, they allowed Susie to see the remaining blue ball and asked the observing children whether Susie knew the colour of the ball in the container.

It is appropriate to judge that Susie does know the colour of the ball in the container on the grounds that she could have inferred it from the colour of the ball left out of the container. However, very many 4–5-year-olds judged wrongly that Susie did not know. Although we can say such a judgement is incorrect, it also shows that children are not egocentric, given that they themselves know the colour of the ball in the container yet are willing to deny that Susie knows. As such, we can suppose that young children's difficulty with the deceptive box test is not primarily the product of failure to differentiate between own and other's belief. Rather, it seems more likely that the child is deficient in grasping that beliefs can misrepresent reality.

The postbox response

Despite all that, it now seems that three-year-olds do have some notion of misrepresentation, but are predisposed to attend to reality at the expense of focusing on belief. This is suggested by the findings of Mitchell & Lacohee (1991), who endowed three-year-olds' false belief with a reality status when they asked the child to post a picture of Smarties into a special postbox when they initially saw the tube. By posting a picture of Smarties, children committed their belief to a reality which resided in the postbox, out of view. Subsequently, having seen the true content of pencils, the experimenter asked children what they had thought was in the tube at the moment they posted their picture. Children were much more likely to give a correct answer of 'Smarties', compared with the standard procedure as described previously. In this case, children were simultaneously able to focus on reality (the picture of Smarties in the postbox) and contemplate false belief, an ability which successfully revealed developmentally early false belief reasoning.

Conclusion

The general picture to emerge from such research into theory of mind is that three-year-olds are in a stage of development during which they have difficulty differentiating belief from world, and thus fail to acknowledge false belief. As such, they predict behaviour according to reality rather than according to a hypothesis they could have formulated regarding another person's belief. According to Perner (1991), children's transition to the higher stage of understanding the belief/reality distinction is the product of a cognitive revolution and expansion which takes place in the child's mind at approximately four years of age.

Autism: a failure to acquire a theory of mind?

In view of the above, it seems we are not born with all the necessary faculties for formulating a theory of mind, and that the acquisition of these depends critically on a cognitive metamorphosis at the age of four years. In that case, might it follow that there are some unfortunate people who fail to shift into the new stage, owing to a specific retardation in cognitive development? If so, what would these people be like? According to Frith (1989), these people would have the characteristics of autism, because autism, so she claims, largely amounts to a deficiency of a theory of mind.

Support for this claim was provided by Baron-Cohen *et al* (1985), who found that children with autism typically failed to acknowledge false belief, just as normal three-year-olds fail, and this was not simply because of their limited verbal intelligence. All their subjects had a verbal mental age above four years, so their belief reasoning appeared specifically retarded. That is, children's errors were not due to general intellectual immaturity.

According to Frith, there is reason to suppose that autism can be traced to an organic cause, and so the question arises as to whether anybody with intellectual retardation resulting from physiological brain abnormality would struggle to acknowledge false belief. If so, failure is not specific to autism, and therefore not a distinguishing feature of this syndrome. To check this, Baron-Cohen *et al* (1985) tested a sample of Down's syndrome children with learning difficulties. These were children who had a known physiological brain abnormality resulting in intellectual retardation, yet they passed the false-belief test with no difficulty. This was despite the fact that these children on average had inferior intellectual abilities of a general nature compared with the children with autism. This led Frith to claim that, specifically, a retarded theory of mind is the central feature in autism. Frith (1989) argues that retarded acquisition of a theory of mind is largely responsible for many of the difficulties children with autism have in relating to others. For example, children with autism are unable to empathise, or go beyond literal message meaning, because they fail to conceive of people as creatures with minds.

Conclusion

The shift in emphasis in research on cognitive development away from testing Piaget's theory to theory of mind has proved to be highly profitable and exciting. Now we tend to look at more circumscribed aspects of cognition, thereby avoiding all the ungainly theoretical and overly complex accessories of Piagetian theory. Findings on the distinctive way in which children reason about the mind are highly replicable, and what is more they seem eminently relevant to the condition of autism. Work on this area is expanding at an exponential rate as researchers look at communication, deception, pictorial representation, inference, memory, and many other phenomena within a theory-of-mind framework. The next decade promises some important breakthroughs in our understanding of the development of children's minds in this respect.

Further reading

Donaldson, M. (1978) *Children's Minds*. Glasgow: Fontana/Collins.
Frith, U. (1989) *Autism: Explaining the Enigma*. Oxford: Basil Blackwell.
Mitchell, P. (1992) *The Psychology of Childhood*. London: Falmer Press.

References

Baillargeon, R. (1987) Object permanence in 3½- and 4½-month-old infants. *Developmental Psychology*, **23**, 655–664.
Baron-Cohen, S., Leslie, A. M. & Frith, U. (1985) Does the autistic child have a 'theory of mind'? *Cognition*, **21**, 37–46.
Bower, T. G. R. (1982) *Development in Infancy* (2nd edn). San Francisco: W. H. Freeman.
Braine, M. D. S. & Shanks, B. L. (1965) The conservation of shape property and proposal about the origin of conservation. *Canadian Journal of Psychology*, **19**, 197–207.
—— & Rumain, B. (1983) Logical reasoning. In *Handbook of Child Psychology: Vol. 3. Cognitive Development* (eds J. H. Flavell & E. M. Markman). New York: Wiley.
Bremner, J. G. & Bryant, P. E. (1977) Place versus response as the basis of spatial errors made by young infants. *Journal of Experimental Child Psychology*, **23**, 162–171.
Bryant, P. E. & Trabasso, T. (1971) Transitive inferences and memory in young children. *Nature*, **232**, 456–458.
Cheng, P. W. & Holyoak, K. J. (1985) Pragmatic reasoning schemas. *Cognitive Psychology*, **17**, 391–416.
Donaldson, M. (1978) *Children's Minds*. Glasgow: Fontana/Collins.
Frith, U. (1989) *Autism: Explaining the Enigma*. Oxford: Basil Blackwell.
Hood, B. & Willatts, P. (1986) Reaching in the dark to an object's remembered position. *British Journal of Developmental Psychology*, **4**, 57–66.

McGarrigle, J. & Donaldson, M. (1975) Conservation accidents. *Cognition*, **3**, 341–350.

Mitchell, P. & Lacohee, H. (1991) Children's early understanding of false belief. *Cognition*, **39**, 107–127.

Moore, C. & Fry, D. (1986) The effect of the experimenter's intention on the child's understanding of conservation. *Cognition*, **22**, 283–298.

Pears, R. & Bryant, P. (1990) Transitive inferences by young children about spatial position. *British Journal of Psychology*, **81**, 497–510.

Perner, J. (1991) *Understanding the Representational Mind*. London: MIT Press.

Piaget, J. & Inhelder, B. (1969) *The Psychology of the Child*. London: Routledge & Kegan Paul.

Russell, J. & Mitchell, P. (1985) Things are not always as they seem: the appearance/reality distinction and conservation. *Educational Psychology*, **5**, 227–236.

Sodian, B. & Wimmer, H. (1987) Children's understanding of inference as a source of knowledge. *Child Development*, **58**, 424–433.

Wason, P. C. & Johnson-Laird, P. N. (1972) *The Psychology of Reasoning: Structure and Content*. London: Batsford Press.

Wellman, H. M. & Estes, D. (1986) Early understanding of mental entities: a reexamination of childhood realism. *Child Development*, **57**, 910–923.

2 Learning theory: the determinants of conditioned responding

Phil Reed

Association formation • Acquiring associations • Language • Social learning • Summary

---

Learning theory represents an attempt to account for behavioural change by reference to a limited set of principles, mostly derived from studies of animals. The aim of the present chapter is to show that these same principles apply to human behaviour, and to illustrate how putatively complex determinants of human behaviour (e.g. control of behaviour and behavioural change following observation of others) can be understood through learning theory. Establishing that human behaviour is influenced by learning, and an understanding of how important determinants of human behaviour (such as language and social learning) operate, gives a strong base from which to explore therapeutic intervention.

Association formation

Behavioural change may be understood in terms of developing an association between mental representations of events and actions, that is, learning. Learning may be about relationships between stimuli (usually studied through use of classical conditioning procedures) or about the consequences of actions (commonly studied by use of instrumental conditioning procedures). Classical (or Pavlovian) and instrumental conditioning represent two fundamental procedures under which associations are formed.

Classical conditioning

A widely cited demonstration of the power of classical conditioning comes from a study reported by Watson & Rayner (1920). A child ('little Albert') was presented with a rat (the conditioned stimulus, or CS), which had previously evoked no signs of fear in the child. Then, when the child

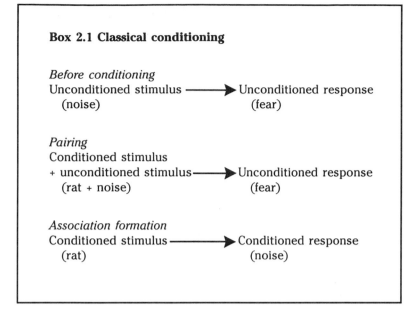

Box 2.1 Classical conditioning

Before conditioning
Unconditioned stimulus ⟶ Unconditioned response
   (noise)   (fear)

Pairing
Conditioned stimulus
+ unconditioned stimulus ⟶ Unconditioned response
   (rat + noise)   (fear)

Association formation
Conditioned stimulus ⟶ Conditioned response
   (rat)   (noise)

approached the rat, a metal bar was struck with a hammer just behind the child's head. This unpleasant auditory stimulus (the unconditioned stimulus, or US) elicited a withdrawal response and signs of distress. Subsequent pairings of the rat and noise led to the sight of the rat eliciting some signs of fear, previously elicited by the noise. Thus, a previously neutral stimulus (a rat) came to evoke a response (withdrawal) associated with an aversive event (a loud noise). The amount of overt behaviour (e.g. withdrawal) shown by the child is taken to be an index of the strength of the association formed between the representations of the rat and noise (see Box 2.1).

Instrumental (or operant) conditioning

An experiment by Keehn (1967) illustrates some of the principles of instrumental conditioning. College students were informed that pressing a button (the response) could earn them points which could subsequently be exchanged for money (the reinforcer). At a point during the experiment, unknown to the subjects, earning points (i.e. reinforcement) became dependent upon a blink response of the student. The rate of blinking increased from about 13 to 30 a minute, despite the fact that the students were apparently unaware that the blink response was involved. This experiment exemplifies the basic principle of instrumental conditioning; that is, making reinforcement contingent upon a response increases the rate of emission of that response.

Acquiring associations

The conditions under which stimulus–stimulus associations in classical conditioning and action–outcome associations in instrumental conditioning are acquired are thought to be similar (see Mackintosh, 1983). Many factors have been identified as important for establishing these associations (see Mackintosh, 1983, for a fuller treatment of these factors in associative learning experiments that use animals). Two of these factors deserve special attention:

(1) the temporal contiguity of events
(2) the degree to which one event predicts the occurrence of the other.

As two events become less temporally contiguous, behaviour resulting from pairings of these events becomes less pronounced, and this is taken to reflect the formation of a weaker association between them. Similarly, as one event becomes a poorer predictor of a second, behaviour that results from pairings of these events becomes less pronounced, and this is taken to reflect a failure to form an association between them.

The aim of the following sections is twofold: to illustrate the above conditioning principles; and to show how they apply to human behaviour.

Temporal contiguity: drug–drug conditioning

Injections of two drugs in sequence may be considered to be a Pavlovian pairing of one drug as a conditioned stimulus and the second drug as an unconditioned stimulus. Over the course of repeated pairing of the two drugs, the second drug may come to alter the effect of the first, sometimes to the extent of producing the opposite reaction to that normally associated with the first drug.

For example, Revusky *et al* (1989) changed the effect of pentobarbital on heart rate by injecting it into rats 30 minutes before an injection of amphetamine. After only three to five such pairings, injection of pentobarbital produced a higher heart rate than in a control condition in which the pentobarbital/amphetamine injections were given 24 hours apart. In Pavlovian terminology, the effects of pentobarbital provided the conditioned stimulus, those of amphetamine provided the unconditioned stimulus, and the increased heart rate normally associated with amphetamine (the unconditioned stimulus) became the conditioned response.

A variety of drug–drug intervals were tested during this experiment, and it was found that, as long as sufficient time was allowed for pentobarbital to be absorbed, the longer the pentobarbital–amphetamine interval, the weaker the change in conditioned responding – that is, the less did heart rate increase.

The claim that the effects produced by drug–drug pairings are the result of conditioning, rather than a simple pharmacological interaction, is supported by the wide variety of drug–drug combinations that will produce similar effects (see Revusky *et al*, 1982). Revusky & Reilly (1991) investigated the effect that pentobarbital would have on heart rate, given a variety of drugs administered as the unconditioned stimulus. Increased heart rate following pentobarbital injection, relative to control conditions, was found with d-amphetamine and nicotine sulphate as the unconditioned stimulus, but no such effect was noted with atropine, caffeine, lithium chloride, or footshock as the unconditioned stimulus. Although amphetamine and nicotine increase heart rate through different pharmacological mechanisms, the similarity in the relationships of delay between administering either drug and the pentobarbital to elevated heart rate was striking, and suggests that a common conditioning mechanism is operative.

That the action of one drug administered after another can alter the effect of the first drug has clinical implications. For example, the action of diazepam can be changed if it is prescribed with chlorpromazine (which is sometimes the case): diazepam's efficacy as a relaxant is reduced, while its capacity to reduce anxiety is increased, if followed by chlorpromazine (Taukulis & Brake, 1989). There is no reason to suppose that alteration of the effects of a drug by pairings with a second drug is limited to pentobarbital and amphetamine. As Revusky & Reilly (1991) have suggested, if the therapeutic effects of other drugs (especially sedatives) can be altered by nicotine, and this change can be effected with as few pairings as demonstrated in the laboratory rat, then the effect of heavy cigarette smoking may be to alter and potentially reduce the therapeutic value of such prescribed drugs.

Relative temporal contiguity: taste aversion in cancer patients

A further area in which associative learning has been found to provide a good account of the action of stimuli on human behaviour is the effect of chemotherapy on the production of taste aversions in cancer patients. A noxious stimulus experienced after consumption of a flavour can lead to subsequent aversion to that flavour. In classical conditioning terms, the subject has learned a flavour–illness association which modifies the reaction to the flavour. This phenomenon is well documented in rats, and the factors that influence the development of taste aversions have been found to be similar to those which influence the development of other stimulus–stimulus associations (e.g. Logue, 1981).

Berrnstein (1978) has noted a similar effect in people undergoing chemotherapy. Paediatric cancer patients were given an ice-cream before chemotherapy. Some time after the chemotherapy, they were given a choice between the ice-cream and the opportunity to play with some toys.

More chose toys than ice-cream, compared with a group not given the ice-cream before chemotherapy. Moreover, those who had had an ice-cream before chemotherapy and who chose the ice-cream after chemotherapy ate less than children not given the ice-cream before chemotherapy.

This procedure also allows a demonstration of the effect of relative temporal contiguity between events. In the experiment by Bermstein (1978), children who had had a strongly flavoured sweet after the ice-cream and before chemotherapy chose the ice-cream at test as often as subjects who had not had the ice-cream. Although the ice-cream and the sweet were both paired with the illness produced by the chemotherapy, the sweet, perhaps by virtue of its slightly closer temporal proximity, entered into an association with illness in preference to the ice-cream.

Contingency: depression

A number of authors have suggested that contiguity alone is not sufficient to produce conditioning (see Mackintosh, 1983, for a review). Rather, for an association to be formed between two events, those events must be contingent, one upon the other. That is, there must be a stronger correlation between the two events than between any other event and the US. For example, if humans are presented with pairings of a stimulus (e.g. a tone or light) with a mild puff of air into the eye, an increase in the amount of blinking (eyelid response) during the stimulus is noted. This is taken to indicate the formation of an association between stimulus and air puff.

In an analogue of an experiment on rats first conducted by Kamin (1968), Martin & Levey (1991) presented stimulus–air-puff pairings to humans, until a blink response developed. In a second phase of training, a simultaneous presentation of the original stimulus and a novel stimulus was paired with the air puff. Then, when this novel stimulus was presented alone, a much lower rate of blinking was produced in the above group than in a group of subjects who had only received a pairing of the two stimuli and the air puff, but who had not received the initial training with only one stimulus. Thus, although the novel stimulus was contiguous with the reinforcer, no learning occurred. This phenomenon is referred to as 'blocking' (Box 2.2). The previously established relationship between one stimulus and the US had prevented the formation of an association between the novel stimulus and the US.

Seligman (1975) (see also Abramson *et al*, 1978) has applied such effects to produce a model of depression ('learned helplessness'). The learned helplessness model involves exposure to conditions in which responding has no effect on whether reinforcement occurs subsequently. It is hypothesised that this reduces the ability to learn about relationships between responses and reinforcement in general (Maier & Seligman, 1976). For example, if subjects are given a mild electric shock which they can do nothing to avoid (i.e. there is no connection between a response and

---

Box 2.2 Blocking

Blocking group

Phase 1	Phase 2	Test
$CS_1 \longrightarrow$ US	$CS_1 + CS_2 \longrightarrow$ US	$CS_1 \longrightarrow$ CR
(tone) (airpuff)	(tone + light) (airpuff)	(tone) (blink)
		$CS_2 \longrightarrow$ no CR
		(light) (no blink)

Control group

–	$CS_1 + CS_2 \longrightarrow$ US	$CS_1 \longrightarrow$ CR
	(tone + light) (airpuff)	(tone) (blink)
		$CS_2 \longrightarrow$ CR
		(light) (blink)

Learned helplessness

Phase 1	Phase 2
Context $\longrightarrow$ US	Context + response $\longrightarrow$ US

Context is thus associated with US, whereas response is not associated with US

---

the reinforcement of not receiving the shock), then those subjects have difficulty in forming other response–reinforcer associations. This could be caused by the subject learning in the first phase of the study (where responses had no effect on receiving reinforcement) that events other than the response are correlated with the occurrence of the reinforcer (e.g. the stimuli provided by the context in which conditioning occurs). These stimuli may subsequently 'block' learning about a contingent response–reinforcer association.

The state of helplessness is taken to be analogous to that of depression, since the behaviours characteristic of the two are similar. According to Seligman (1975) there are at least six clear parallels between helplessness and depression:

(1) both result in lowered levels of voluntary behaviour
(2) both produce a negative cognitive set
(3) both have a similar time course of persistence
(4) both produce lowered levels of aggression
(5) both produce a loss of appetite
(6) both produce biochemical changes, such as norepinephrine depletion and cholinergic overactivation.

An experimental demonstration of such contingency learning in humans is provided by Hiroto (1974) (see also Ford & Neale, 1985; Hiroto & Seligman, 1975). Subjects were randomly assigned to one of three groups:

one group could neither avoid nor escape an aversively loud tone; the second group could escape the tone; and the third group were not exposed to the tone. In a subsequent test, in which the subjects could perform a response to escape the tone, subjects previously exposed to the inescapable tone took longer to perform the escape response than subjects in either of the other two groups, and subjects in the escape and non-exposure groups took the same time to escape the tone.

Extinction of responding: phobias

Extinction refers to the decrease in conditioned responding noted if reinforcement is discontinued. For example, if reinforcement has been made contingent upon a response, the level at which the response is emitted will increase (instrumental conditioning). When reinforcement is no longer obtained as a result of emitting the response, the level of responding declines (i.e. extinction has occurred) (Box 2.3).

It is important to show that putatively conditioned behaviour in humans is subject to such an extinction effect. If behaviour believed to be the result of association formation did not extinguish, then the role of association formation in generating that behaviour would come into question.

Examination of this topic allows an introduction to the literature on the treatment of situational phobias (e.g. of spiders, snakes, and flying) in humans, which relies on the technique of extinction. The experiment by Watson & Rayner (1920), reported above, may be taken as an example of

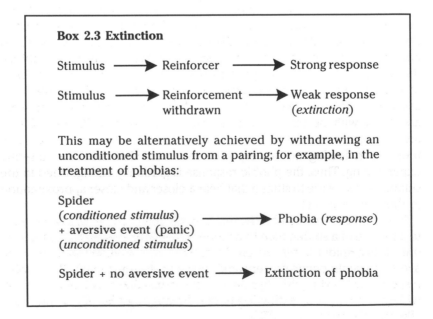

Box 2.3 Extinction

Stimulus ⟶ Reinforcer ⟶ Strong response

Stimulus ⟶ Reinforcement withdrawn ⟶ Weak response (*extinction*)

This may be alternatively achieved by withdrawing an unconditioned stimulus from a pairing; for example, in the treatment of phobias:

Spider
(*conditioned stimulus*)
+ aversive event (panic)
(*unconditioned stimulus*) ⟶ Phobia (*response*)

Spider + no aversive event ⟶ Extinction of phobia

how a phobia (in this case of a rat) could be acquired through classical conditioning. Although this interpretation of the acquisition of many common situational phobias such as those concerned with spiders and snakes is not universally accepted (see Rachlin, 1976), some experiments have demonstrated that classical conditioning could generate phobias (Sidman, 1960) and fetishes (Rachman, 1966). If the phobia is produced by pairings of the phobic stimulus (the conditioned stimulus) with an unconditioned aversive event (the unconditioned stimulus), then an obvious therapeutic approach is to extinguish the phobic response (the conditioned response) by presenting the phobic stimulus in the absence of an aversive event.

There are a number of different therapies which could be classified as using extinction procedures:

(1) massing and flooding (Malleson, 1959)
(2) implosion therapy (Stampfl & Levis, 1967)
(3) systematic desensitisation (Wolpe & Lazarus, 1966).

Extinction of a conditioned phobic response may be achieved by sustained and repeated exposure to the phobic object (referred to as massing or flooding). Miller & Levis (1971) demonstrated an increased tendency to approach a snake in a group of snake-phobic girls exposed to a snake for 15, 30, or 45 minutes. There is some evidence that the greater the length of exposure, the greater the tendency to approach the phobic object (see Wolpin & Raines, 1966).

An approach that avoids exposure to the phobic object initially (and, hence, may be associated with less anxiety for the phobic) is systematic desensitisation (Morganstern, 1973). The phobic person is asked to construct a ranked list of events or stimuli, linked to the phobic object, that produce anxiety (i.e. the phobic response). The subject is then exposed to each of these events or stimuli in turn, starting with the stimulus associated with the least anxiety and then moving on to the stimulus associated with the next lowest level of anxiety, and so on. Phobic subjects are not exposed to the next anxiety-producing situation in the list until they report feeling no anxiety from the event that they are currently experiencing. Thus, the phobic response is gradually extinguished in the subject by exposure to stimuli that bear a closer and closer approximation to the phobia object.

In the case of spider phobia, this may be achieved by initial exposure to a picture of a spider, then to a model of a spider, then to a dead spider, until a live spider is placed on the subject. It is assumed that since no aversive events occur on repeated exposure to the stimuli, the phobic response will extinguish. Systematic desensitisation has been the most widely used type of extinction-based therapy, and is one of the most effective (Morganstern, 1973).

Language

The above sections have illustrated some of the important concepts in contemporary associative learning, and also that principles of associative learning, developed from animals, can be applied to humans. However, although it may be possible to apply conditioning principles to explain phenomena such as taste aversion in cancer patients (e.g. Berrnstein, 1978), depression (Maier & Seligman, 1976), and even aspects of drug addiction (e.g. Siegal, 1984), the ability of associative principles of learning to encompass behavioural change in humans in a wider variety of settings is not clear. In particular, the fact that human behaviour can be affected by instructions, and by observation of other people's behaviour, has been given little attention by contemporary associative theorists. Indeed, the fact that verbal instructions can modify conditioned responding has often been taken to damage the claims for the generality of associative learning in humans (e.g. Brewer, 1974). How the principles of associative learning can accommodate instructional control of behaviour (and social learning) is outlined here; in doing so it is hoped to illustrate another important concept in the contemporary associative analysis of behaviour: the occasion-setting stimulus.

The assumption that conditioning (i.e. associative learning) occurs in humans does not mean that similar patterns of responding will be observed in humans and animals. A crucial variable that may produce different patterns of conditioned responding is the existence of a complex set of linguistic cues. The task for theorists who wish to argue that conditioning occurs in humans is to show that such cues can be dealt with within the framework of associative learning (see Box 2.4).

Effects of instructions on conditioning

The effects of instructions on human conditioning are striking. In classical conditioning studies, simply informing the subject of the relationship between the conditioned and unconditioned stimulus, without actually pairing the two stimuli, can produce immediate, apparent conditioned responding (e.g. Dawson & Grings, 1968). Informing the subject that the conditioned stimulus will no longer be paired with the unconditioned stimulus can produce a rapid decline in conditioned responding (e.g. Koenig & Castillo, 1969). Subjects instructed to withhold the conditioned response with continued pairings of conditioned with unconditioned stimuli can reduce the magnitude of that response (e.g. Swensen & Hill, 1970). Such evidence highlights the important role of instructions in human classical conditioning.

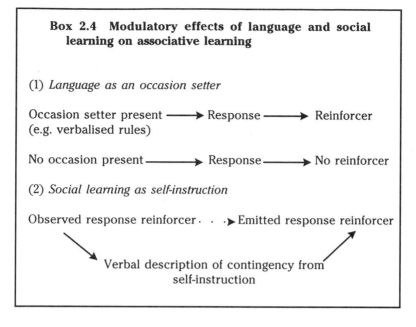

Box 2.4   Modulatory effects of language and social learning on associative learning

(1) *Language as an occasion setter*

Occasion setter present ——→ Response ——→ Reinforcer
(e.g. verbalised rules)

No occasion present ——→ Response ——→ No reinforcer

(2) *Social learning as self-instruction*

Observed response reinforcer · · ·▶ Emitted response reinforcer

Verbal description of contingency from
self-instruction

Schedules of reinforcement

The importance of the influence of instructions and language on human conditioned responding has been studied intensively in relation to instrumental performance, and particularly with respect to performance on 'schedules of reinforcement'. A schedule of reinforcement is a procedure which allows a reward to be made contingent upon a response. There are a number of ways in which this can be achieved. A reward can be made dependent upon the emission of a number of responses (e.g. a reward could be delivered for every five responses emitted); such a schedule is termed a 'ratio' schedule. Alternatively, a reward can be made contingent upon a response being emitted after a period of time (e.g. the first response made after ten seconds could be reinforced); such schedules are termed 'interval' schedules. The various schedules have pronounced and well-documented effects on the rate and pattern of behaviour of animals (Zeiler, 1977).

Associative learning in young children is typical of that observed in animals. Lowe *et al* (1983) exposed young children to a fixed-interval (FI) schedule (a schedule that reinforces the first response, such as pressing a button to gain access to a toy, after a constant period of time). Following reinforcement there was a pause from responding followed by an increase in response rate as the time for the next reinforcement approached. This pattern of responding is typical of animals.

Lippman & Meyer (1967) (see also Lowe, 1979) found a different pattern of responding in adults. Some subjects responded at high rates throughout the interval, and others paused for almost the entire interval and made only a few responses at the end. Such differences in performance were highly correlated with different verbal descriptions of the schedule contingencies. High-rate responders usually described the FI schedule in ratio terms (i.e. as involving the emission of a number of responses), whereas low-rate responders often described the schedule in terms of time (see also Harzem *et al*, 1978; Lowe, 1979; Wearden & Shimp, 1985). This pattern of results implies that the rule generated by the subject, rather than the schedule of reinforcement, is the primary source of behavioural control in these settings.

The transition between typical animal and adult performance has been noted to occur around the age of four to five, when children begin to develop a functioning linguistic capacity (Bentall *et al*, 1985; see also Chapter 1 for an account of cognitive changes at this age). It should be mentioned that the results of a study by Pouthas *et al* (1990) suggest that the development of language is not sufficient to explain these changes in performance. Children who could speak about the contingencies they experienced did not necessarily perform on the basis of their reports, but rather appeared to perform according to the relationship between responses and reinforcer that actually obtained. Thus, it may be that children have to learn that the verbal stimuli (overtly or covertly produced) can aid them in solving a particular problem before performance comes under the control of verbal rules (cf. Luria, 1961).

The importance of the ability to formulate a verbal rule about the contingency can be illustrated further by the finding that a verbal description of the relationship between response and reinforcer can determine performance. Hayes *et al* (1986) (see also, Shimoff *et al*, 1986) examined human schedule performance on a fixed ratio (FR; a schedule that delivers reward after a fixed number of responses have been emitted, e.g. every five responses) and a differential reinforcement of low rate (DRL) schedule (this schedule presents a reinforcer only if responses are separated by a specified minimum time). Some subjects received no instructions regarding the appropriate rates of responding, other subjects received instructions to respond either slowly or rapidly, and some subjects were told the circumstances in which it was better to respond either slowly or rapidly. After establishing performance on the two schedules, it was noted that the pattern of responding was appropriate (i.e. high in the FR and low in the DRL schedule) only in the conditions where no instructions were given or instructions to respond at both fast and low rates were given. However, on termination of the reinforcement (i.e. extinction), responding declined only in the conditions in which explicit instructions had not been given. In other words, the instructions given by the experimenter had overridden the effect of ceasing to deliver reinforcement.

This study demonstrates that behaviour in adult humans which appears to resemble that of animals (such as in the subjects instructed to respond at both high and low rates) may be under the control of a different set of mechanisms (i.e. instructions rather than reinforcement), since during the extinction test, the behaviour of the subjects in this condition did not resemble that of animals.

Language as an occasion setter

There are, in fact, many possible interpretations of the role of language in conditioning. One view suggests that humans do not display conditioning in the absence of adequate verbal descriptions of the contingencies, and require such descriptions for the genesis of conditioned behaviour (e.g. Brewer, 1974). Another potentially important function of language, which forms a parallel with explanations given for animal performance, concerns the role of verbal descriptions of schedules or contingencies as an 'occasion-setting' stimulus (see also Chapter 4). The view of instructions as occasion-setting stimuli suggests that the role of language in conditioning is modulatory, governing the expression of conditioned responding rather than its initial acquisition.

Under some conditions, stimuli have been found to modulate the expression of behaviour learned as the result of pairings of another stimulus (or response) and reinforcer. Such stimuli are variously termed 'facilitators' (Rescorla, 1985), 'occasion setters' (Holland, 1985), or 'discriminative stimuli' (Skinner, 1953). Ross & Holland (1981) presented rats with a tone followed by food only if the tone was preceded by a light; when the tone was not preceded by the light, food was withheld. The rats came to respond differentially to the tone, depending on whether it was preceded by the light. The light 'set the occasion' for the emission of the conditioned response to the tone. Similar results have been observed in other classical conditioning paradigms (e.g. Terry & Wagner, 1975), and in instrumental conditioning in which a stimulus signals when a response will, or will not, be reinforced (Bonardi, 1988). Loosely expressed, the occasion-setting stimuli inform the subject when a particular relationship between the stimulus (or response) and reinforcement will be operative.

It might be that verbal descriptions of a contingency, whether provided by the experimenter or generated by the subject, serve a similar role. In the study by Hayes *et al* (1986), described above, the instruction to respond quickly or respond slowly depending on the circumstances certainly seems to convey the same type of information as occasion-setting stimuli in animal experiments: it informs the subject when a particular relationship will hold between responding and reinforcement.

The view of verbal descriptions of contingencies or instructions as modulatory rather than essential to conditioned responding is not novel.

Kaufman *et al* (1966) (see also Lippman & Meyer, 1967; Skinner, 1969) suggested that the instructions given to subjects at the beginning of the session do not (usually) indicate the rate or pattern of responding to be emitted, but merely under what circumstances a reinforcer will appear. Thus, instructions do not lead to the detailed pattern of responding observed under some circumstances in humans, but rather provide a higher-order control over whether or not responding occurs. It is possible that instructions provide information regarding what responses are to be emitted and, thus, have an additional role to that as occasion-setting stimuli, but this is not to detract from their function as occasion setters.

In order to support the assertion that verbal descriptions of contingencies function as occasion setters, it would be necessary to show at least that they result in behavioural patterns similar to those typically found in animal experiments, and can be found as the product of the effect of the occasion-setting stimuli (e.g. a light or tone). In fact, such a demonstration is available. Wanchisen *et al* (1989) compared the performance of rats exposed to an FI schedule with that of rats exposed to an FI schedule after exposure to a variable ratio (VR) schedule (a schedule which delivers reward after a varying number of responses have been emitted). The stimulus conditions were not altered between exposure to the VR and FI schedules; that is, the stimuli that set the occasion for VR responding were still present during training with the FI schedule. Those rats not previously exposed to a schedule of reinforcement displayed the typical 'scalloped' pattern of responding on exposure to the FI schedule (subjects initially respond at low rates followed by an increase in rate of response as the time for the next reinforcement comes closer). In contrast, rats previously exposed to the VR schedule displayed either very high or very low rates of response during exposure to the VR schedule. This behaviour is typical of adult human performance under an FI schedule of reinforcement.

Summary

These findings suggest that language is critical in controlling human behaviour during conditioning tasks. However, the fact that a highly sophisticated language is uniquely human does not necessitate a view that it represents any deviation from the processes of associative learning. It is possible that one of the many functions of language in controlling behaviour is that of an occasion-setting stimulus. Thus, although conditioning principles extracted directly from experiments on animals often do not seem to apply to humans, if the influence of stimuli present in the human experimental context is appreciated, the apparent discrepancies may be resolved.

Social learning

As with language, contingencies related to social interactions can produce powerful controlling cues in human behaviour that are not often present in animal conditioning studies. Moreover, a view of learning based exclusively on classical or instrumental responding does not appear, at first view, to offer many insights into important processes such as socialisation. To accommodate such criticisms, some have suggested that observational learning is a powerful mechanism in shaping human behaviour (e.g. Bandura, 1977). The subject observes another person model some behaviour and imitates the model's behaviour; thus, the subject acquires responses (see also Chapters 8 and 14).

Vicarious reinforcement

The prototypical observational learning experiments were conducted by Bandura (1965, 1986) in which nursery-school children watched a film that depicted an adult displaying aggression towards a large rubber doll. There were different endings to the film. Some children saw a second adult reward the aggressor; some saw a second adult punish the aggressor. A third group of children saw an adult in the room with the doll but did not see any aggression towards the doll. On later testing, the children who had seen aggression being rewarded displayed more aggression towards the doll than those who had seen no aggression. Those children that had watched the film in which aggression had been punished avoided the doll. However, it should be noted that when these children were offered a reward for playing with the doll they were aggressive towards it. Standard conditioning explanations of this effect are given in terms of vicarious reinforcement: observing a response and its outcome strengthens behaviour despite the subject not personally experiencing the outcomes for that behaviour (Bandura, 1986).

The explanation of observational learning given in terms of vicarious reinforcement is not, however, particularly compelling. In the above study, observation of punished actions should not have produced a tendency to display the action, as was the case when the children who observed the punished aggression were persuaded to play with the doll. More damaging to an explanation involving vicarious reinforcement are the results from the group of children who observed the aggressive acts but saw no reward or punishment. These children also displayed more aggressive acts than children who observed no violent interactions. It should further be noted that, as an explanatory mechanism, vicarious reward is at best incomplete, since other factors such as the perceived status of the model (e.g. whether the observer likes the model) will exert an influence over whether observational learning occurs (Bandura, 1977; Mussen & Eisenberg-Berg, 1977).

Understanding contingencies through self-instruction

The shortcomings of vicarious reinforcement, however, do not mean that associative principles cannot be used to explain social learning. There is an alternative explanation available for such phenomena that relies on self-instruction to generate the appropriate occasion-setting stimuli for the manifestation of learned behaviour. A subject may observe a model perform a task and verbalise the relationship between what the model does and the outcome. This verbal description of the contingencies can then come to control the subject's own performance, as any other verbal instructions in conditioning experiments come to control performance. Under these circumstances social learning may be seen as an indirect method by which to bring behaviour under the control of self-instruction. That these verbal descriptions have a modulatory role (i.e. influence whether already established behaviour will be performed) rather than a generative role (i.e. enable the subjects to behave in ways they have never behaved before) can be shown by a number of findings. It is rare to observe completely novel behaviour being produced by observational learning: imitated behaviours do not conform precisely to those behaviours which have been modelled (see Yando *et al*, 1978, for a review); and there is evidence that responses not represented in a person's behavioural repertoire will not be formed through modelling (e.g. Hayden *et al*, 1976; Schloss, 1986). Thus, it appears that observational learning is largely concerned with producing rules regarding the appropriateness of behaviour under different circumstances.

Although few (if any) studies have been conducted which would directly test this notion, two lines of evidence support the view that one of the critical features that determines the extent to which social learning will occur is the degree to which the subject is given explicit instructions about the behaviour observed. In most subjects, verbalisations (overt or covert) about the observed task and consequences may occur simultaneously with observation.

Some patients who are incapable of forming such descriptions provide an opportunity to test the notion that this ability is important for observational learning to occur. Appropriate experiments have been conducted (although not for the above reason) using subjects with a variety of problems, including children with impulsive aggressive/behaviour problems (Meichenbaum & Goodman, 1971; Douglas *et al*, 1976) and schizophrenia (Lowe & Higson, 1981). In a study by Lowe *et al* (Lowe, 1979), schizophrenic patients performed poorly on a task that they had seen modelled by an experimenter. However, subjects who observed the experimenter performing a task accompanied by the experimenter giving appropriate verbal descriptions of the contingencies of the task, and who were taught how to produce such verbal descriptions of the task, performed more accurately than those who had observed the task and received the same experimenter attention, but who had not been taught to verbalise the relationship between action and outcome. This seems to indicate that the formation and use of appropriate verbal descriptions of the contingencies are important to the success of observational learning.

A second line of evidence has been produced from studies of non-clinical populations. Berry (1991) (see also Berry & Broadbent, 1984; Stanley *et al*, 1989) showed that merely observing another perform a decision-making task did not facilitate subsequent performance of that task: only when the subject actively participated in the task was learning subsequently improved. However, when the processes necessary for successful completion of the task were quite obvious (the subjects could explain what they had observed), performance was improved by observation alone. This suggests that if a subject can describe performance of a task through observation of another, then observational learning will occur, but if this verbal description or rule formation is difficult, then observational learning will be less likely to occur.

These studies do not show that social or observational learning is only achieved through verbal mediation. Demonstrations of observational learning in animals (e.g. Heyes & Dawson, 1990) suggest that there must be at least some mechanisms that lead to observational learning in the absence of the generation of self-instructions. The above experiments do, however, highlight the importance of language in observational learning. The role of language in social learning has received scant attention, but the explanation offered by associative learning principles, coupled with a view of language as an occasion setter, appears to be worth pursuing.

Summary

The present limited review of the relevance of contemporary learning theory to human behaviour suggests that association formation is an important source of behavioural change in humans. The view of conditioning as an automatic process that occurs without the awareness of the subject is inappropriate as a characterisation of associative learning. Contemporary learning theory stresses the importance of predictiveness as well as contiguity, and also highlights a further role for stimuli in modifying behaviour, that of occasion-setting stimuli.

The apparent differences between the results from animal and human subjects might be explained by the influence of instructions on human performance, but there is no strong reason to assume that these verbal cues function in any way not explicable in terms of associative learning. The importance of language was also highlighted in social and observational learning paradigms. A unified approach to explaining behavioural change, such as that provided by associative learning, at least provides the scaffolding around which an understanding of how behavioural change (through various techniques such as behaviour modification, instructional control, or modelling) occurs.

Acknowledgements

Thanks are due to Lisa Osborne, Steve Reilly, and Celia Heyes, who all read earlier versions of this chapter.

Further reading

Many of the issues in associative learning are dealt with in greater detail by Mackintosh (1983). Davey (1981) and Davey & Cullen (1988) deal with many of the therapeutic applications of conditioning principles to humans. More detailed expositions of the role of language in human conditioned responding can be found in the chapter by Wearden (1988).

References

Abramson, L. Y., Seligman, M. E. P. & Teasdale, J. D. (1978) Learned helplessness in humans: critique and reformulation. *Journal of Abnormal Psychology*, **97**, 443–447.

Bandura, A. (1965) Influence of a model's reinforcement contingencies on the acquisition of imitative responses. *Journal of Personality and Social Psychology*, **1**, 589–595.

—— (1986) *Social Foundations of Thought and Action: A Social Cognitive Theory*. Englewood Cliffs, NJ: Erlbaum.

—— (1977) *Social Learning Theory*. Englewood Cliffs, NJ: Prentice-Hall.

Bentall, R. P., Lowe, C. F. & Beasty, A. (1985) The role of verbal behavior in human learning: II. Developmental differences. *Journal of the Experimental Analysis of Behavior*, **43**, 165–181.

Berrnstein, I. L. (1978) Learned taste aversions in children receiving chemotherapy. *Science*, **200**, 1302–1303.

Berry, D. C. (1991) The role of action in implicit learning. *Quarterly Journal of Experimental Psychology*, **43A**, 881–906.

—— & Broadbent, D. E. (1984) On the relationship between task performance and associated verbalizable knowledge. *Quarterly Journal of Experimental Psychology*, **36A**, 209–231.

Bonardi, C. (1988) Associative explanations of discriminative inhibition effects. *Quarterly Journal of Experimental Psychology*, **40B**, 63–82.

Brewer, W. F. (1974) There is no convincing evidence for operant or classical conditioning in adult humans. In *Cognition and the Symbolic Processes* (eds W. B. Weimer & D. J. Palermo), pp. 1–42. Hillsdale, NJ: Erlbaum.

Davey, G. (1981) *Applications of Conditioning Theory*. London: Methuen.

—— & Cullen, C. (1988) *Human Operant Conditioning and Behavior Modification*. Chichester: Wiley.

Dawson, M. E. & Grings, W. W. (1968) Comparison of classical conditioning and relational learning. *Journal of Experimental Psychology*, **76**, 227–231.

Douglas, V., Parry, P., Marton, P., *et al* (1976) Assessment of a cognitive training program for hyperactive children. *Journal of Abnormal Child Psychology*, **4**, 389–410.

Ford, C. & Neale, J. (1985) Helplessness and judgment of control. *Journal of Personality and Social Psychology*, **49**, 1330–1336.

Harzem, P., Lowe, C. F. & Bagshaw, M. (1978) Verbal control in human operant behavior. *Psychological Record*, **28**, 405–523.

Hayes, S. C., Brownstein, A. J., Haas, J. R., *et al* (1986) Instructions, multiple schedules, and extinction: distinguishing rule-governed behavior from schedule controlled behavior. *Journal of the Experimental Analysis of Behavior*, **46**, 137–147.

Heyes, C. & Dawson, G. R. (1990) A demonstration of observational learning in rats using a bidirectional control. *Quarterly Journal of Experimental Psychology*, **42B**, 59–71.

Hiroto, D. S. (1974) Locus of control and learned helplessness. *Journal of Experimental Psychology*, **102**, 187–193.

—— & Seligman, M. E. P. (1975) Generality of learned helplessness in men. *Journal of Personality and Social Psychology*, **31**, 311–327.

Holland, P. C. (1985) The nature of conditioned inhibition in serial and simultaneous feature negative discrimination. In *Information Processing in Animals: Conditioned Inhibition* (eds R. R. Miller & N. E. Spear), pp. 267–297. Hillsdale, NJ: Erlbaum.

Kamin, L. J. (1969) Predictability, surprise, attention, and conditioning. In *Punishment and Aversive Behavior* (eds B. A. Campbell & R. M. Church), pp. 279–296). New York: Appleton-Century-Crofts.

Kaufman, A., Baron, A. & Kop, R. M. (1966) Some effects of instructions on human operant behavior. *Psychonomic Monograph Supplements*, **1**, 243–250.

Keehn, J. D. (1967) Experimental studies of "the unconsciousness": Operant conditioning of unconscious eyeblinking. *Behavior Therapy*, **5**, 95–102.

Koenig, K.P. & Castillo, D. D. (1969) False feedback and longevity of the conditioned GSR during extinction: some implications for aversion therapy. *Journal of Experimental Psychology*, **74**, 505–510.

Lauria, A. (1961) *The Role of Speech in the Regulation of Normal and Abnormal Behaviors*. New York: Liveright.

Lippman, L. G. & Meyer, M. E. (1967) Fixed-interval performance as related to the subject's verbalizations of the reinforcement contingencies. *Psychonomic Science*, **8**, 135–136.

Logue, A. (1981) The generality of the laws of learning. *Psychological Review*, **88**.

Lowe, C. F. (1979) Determinants of human operant behavior. In *Advances in the Analysis of Behaviour, Vol. 1: Reinforcement and the Organization of Behaviour* (eds M. D. Zeiler & P. Harzem), pp. 159–192. Chichester: Wiley.

—— & Higson, P. J. (1981) Self-instructional training and cognitive behavioral modification: A behavioral analysis. In *Applications of Conditioning Theory* (ed. G. Davey), pp. 162–188. London: Methuen.

——, Beasty, A. & Bentall, R. P. (1983) The role of verbal behavior in human learning. Infant performance on fixed interval schedules. *Journal of the Experimental Analysis of Behavior*, **39**, 157–164.

Mackintosh, N. J. (1983) *Conditioning and Associative Learning*. Oxford: Clarenden Press.

Maier, S. F. & Seligman, M. E. P. (1976) Learned helplessness: theory and evidence. *Journal of Experimental Psychology: General*, **105**, 3–46.

——, —— & Soloman, R. L. (1969) Pavlovian fear conditioning and learned helplessness: effects on escape and avoidance behavior of (a) the CS-US contingency and (b) the independence of the US and voluntary responding. In *Punishment and Aversive Behavior* (eds B. A. Campbell & R. M. Church), pp. 299–342. New York: Appleton-Century-Crofts.

Malleson, N. (1959) Panic and phobia. *Lancet, i,* 225–227.

Martin, I. & Levey, A. B. (1991) Blocking observed in human eyelid conditioning. *Quarterly Journal of Experimental Psychology,* **43B,** 223–256.

Meichenbaum, D & Goodman, J. (1971) Training impulsive children to talk to themselves: a means of developing self control. *Journal of Abnormal Psychology,* **77,** 115–126.

Miller, B. V. & Levis, D. J. (1971) The efficacy of varying short visual exposure times to a phobic test stimulus on subsequent avoidance behaviour. *Behaviour Research and Therapy,* **9,** 17–21.

Morganstern, K. P. (1973) Implosive therapy and flooding procedures: a critical review. *Psychological Bulletin,* **79,** 318–334.

Mussen, P. H. & Eisenberg-Berg, N. (1977) *The Roots of Caring.* New York: Freeman.

Pouthas, V., Droit, S., Jacquet, A-Y., *et al* (1990) Temporal differentiation of response duration in children of different ages: developmental changes in relations between verbal and nonverbal behavior. *Journal of the Experimental Analysis of Behavior,* **53,** 21–31.

Rachlin, H. (1976) *Behavior and Learning.* San Francisco: Freeman.

Rachman, S. (1966) Sexual fetishism: an experimental analogue. *Psychological Record,* **16,** 293–296.

Rescorla, R. C. (1985) Conditioned inhibition and facilitation. In *Information Processing in Animals: Conditioned Inhibition* (eds R. R. Miller & N. E. Spear), pp. 299–326. Hillsdale, NJ: Erlbaum.

Revusky, S., Coombes, S. & Pohl, R. W. (1982) Pharmacological generality of the Avfail effect. *Behavioral and Neural Biology,* **34,** 240–260.

——, Davey, V. & Zagorski, M. (1989) Heart rate conditioning with pentobarbital as a conditioned stimulus and amphetamine as an unconditioned stimulus. *Behavioral Neuroscience,* **103,** 296–307.

—— & Reilly, S. (1991) Drug–drug heart rate conditioning in rats: Effective USs when pentobarbital is the CS. (Submitted for publication.)

Ross, R. T. & Holland, P. C. (1981) Conditioning of simultaneous and serial feature positive discriminations. *Animal Learning and Behavior,* **9,** 293–303.

Schloss, P. J. (1986) Sequences of direct instructions activities for hearing-impaired learners. *Journal of the British Association of Teachers of the Deaf,* **10,** 45–50.

Seligman, M. E. P. (1975) *Helplessness: On Depression, Development and Death.* San Francisco: Freeman.

Shimoff, E., Mathews, B. A. & Catania, A. C. (1986) Human operant performance: sensitivity and pseudosensitivity to contingencies. *Journal of the Experimental Analysis of Behavior,* **46,** 149–157.

Sidman, M. (1960) Normal sources of pathological behaviour. *Science,* **132,** 61–68.

Siegal, S. (1984) Pavlovian conditioning and heroin overdose: reports by overdose victims. *Bulletin of the Psychonomic Society,* **22,** 428–430.

Skinner, B. F. (1953) *Science and Human Behavior.* New York: Macmillan.

—— (1969) *Contingencies of Reinforcement.* New York: Appleton-Century-Crofts.

Stampfl, T. G. & Levis, D. J. (1967) Essentials of implosive therapy: a learning theory-based psychodynamic behavioural therapy. *Journal of Abnormal Psychology,* **72,** 496–503.

Stanley, W. B., Mathews, R. C., Buss, R. R., *et al* (1989) Insight without awareness: on the interaction between verbalization, instruction, and practice in a simulated process control task. *Quarterly Journal of Experimental Psychology,* **41A,** 553–577.

Swensen, R. P. & Hill, F. A. (1970) Effects of instruction and interstimulus interval in human GSR conditioning. *Psychonomic Science*, **21**, 369–370.

Taukulis, H. K. & Brake, L. D. (1989) Therapeutic and hypothermic properties of diazepam altered by a diazepam chlorpromazine association. *Pharmacology, Biochemistry and Behavior*, **34**, 1–6.

Terry, W. S. & Wagner, A. R. (1975) Short-term memory for "surprising" vs "expected" unconditioned stimuli in Pavlovian conditioning. *Journal of Experimental Psychology: Animal Behavior Processes*, **1**, 122–133.

Thorndike, E. L. (1911) *Animal Intelligence*. New York: Macmillan.

Wanchisen, B. A., Tatham, T. A. & Mooney, S. E. (1989) Variable ratio conditioning history produces high- and low-rate fixed-interval performance in rats. *Journal of the Experimental Analysis of Behavior*, **52**, 167–179.

Watson, J. B. & Raynor, R. (1920) Conditioned emotional reactions. *Journal of Experimental Psychology*, **3**, 1–14.

Wearden, J. H. (1988) Some neglected problems in the analysis of human operant behavior. In *Human Operant Conditioning and Behavior Modification* (eds G. Davey & C. Cullen), pp. 197–224. Chichester: Wiley.

—— & Shimp, C. P. (1985) Local temporal patterning of operant behavior in humans. *Journal of the Experimental Analysis of Behavior*, **44**, 315–324.

Wolpe, J. & Lazarus, A. A. (1966) *Behaviour Therapy Techniques: A Guide to the Treatment of Neuroses*. New York: Pergamon Press.

Wolpin, M. & Raines, W. (1966) Visual imagery, expected roles and extinction as possible factors in reducing fear and avoidance behaviour. *Behaviour Research and Therapy*, **4**, 25–37.

Yando, R., Seitz, V. & Zigler, E. (1978) *Imitation: A Developmental Perspective*. Hillsdale, NJ: Erlbaum.

Zeiler, M. (1977) Schedules of reinforcement: the controlling variables. In *Handbook of Operant Behavior* (eds W. K. Honig & J. E. R. Staddon). New York: Prentice-Hall.

3 Attention and memory

Siobhan B. G. MacAndrew
& Gerald Matthews

The aims of attentional theory • Stage models of selective attention • Divided and sustained attention • Control processes in perception and attention • Connectionist approaches • Capacity models • Levels of control models • Concluding remarks on attention • Models of memory • What factors make for good memory? • What factors make for poor memory? • Computer simulations of memory • Concluding remarks on memory

---

The aims of attentional theory

Like many psychological terms, 'attention' has several connotations. One of these is the selection of information. Our senses provide far more information than the mind can fully apprehend, so we may ask how the mind chooses which sensory data are to be analysed, and which perceptions are permitted to govern response and action. A second aspect of attention is that it is intensive. When we have to concentrate hard on an activity, how do we maximise the efficiency of concentration? Selective and intensive aspects of attention may be interrelated: sometimes we have to make an effort to select information, when listening to a telephone call on a noisy line, for example.

Psychologists investigate the nature of attention through several distinct types of experiment.

(1) In experiments on *focused attention*, the person must attend to one type of information, while ignoring additional, potentially distracting information. The classic instance is the 'cocktail party effect', which describes the ability to pick out a single voice from a babble of voices.

(2) In studies of *divided attention*, the person must attend to two or more sources of information, like a taxi driver simultaneously conversing with a passenger and following traffic movements. In fact, the performance of two simultaneous tasks is often inefficient, even when the tasks are apparently quite different, like talking and driving. This loss of performance is termed 'dual-task interference'. Flexibility of divided attention is actually quite a reliable predictor of a person's likelihood of being in a vehicle accident (Arthur *et al*, 1991).

(3) Research on *sustained attention* requires monitoring of the environment for long periods of time. Real-world examples include radar watching and inspection for faulty components on a production line; often performance deteriorates over time on such tasks.

Hence, theories of attention must explain how we can focus, divide, and sustain our attention, and the circumstances under which these abilities break down. It is often suggested that the mind can be likened to a computer, which processes information from the senses, and formulates appropriate actions.

Beyond this point there is considerable disagreement. The first source of contention is the architecture of the system. If, as in selective attention, irrelevant sensory input is discarded at some stage of processing, we need to know the structure of the processing components of the system to account for the loss of irrelevant information. For example, we can ask whether information is processed one step at a time serially, or can the cognitive system run multiple, simultaneous analyses – that is, parallel processing? A second issue is whether the system has capacity limitations over and above those of its constituent processes. A third issue is the scope of voluntary control over attention, and how it should be characterised. Finally, there is debate over the role of consciousness in attention. It is evident that not all processing is conscious – we have no awareness of how we detect elementary features such as edges from the pattern of light falling on the retina, for example. More interestingly, perception may be affected by the meanings of 'subliminal' signals, which are too weak to reach awareness. For example, taboo words and other threatening stimuli tend to be more difficult to perceive, as though the material were being suppressed unconsciously (Dixon, 1981).

The significance and scope of the demarcation between conscious and non-conscious processing remain uncertain. We examine attention by looking at the various theoretical approaches to the topic, and describing examples of the application to the principal areas of empirical research: focused, divided, and sustained attention.

Stage models of selective attention

One of the simplest applications of the computer metaphor is to suppose that sensory input undergoes a series of analyses, eventually leading to a response (e.g. Sternberg, 1969). Each type of analysis, such as extracting perceptual features from sensory data, or selecting a response, constitutes a separate stage of processing.

For example, experiments on perception have shown how basic visual information can be computationally transformed into a series of increasingly complex representations, culminating in object recognition (see Humphreys & Bruce, 1989). One stage is the grouping together of stimulus features on the basis of their perceptual organisation. These processes can be described in terms of the 'Gestalt' principles: for example, features which are close together tend to be analysed as part of a single perceptual object. This kind of processing is said to be 'pre-attentive'.

Stage models of attention suggest that selectivity can be modelled in terms of a 'bottleneck' in the later stages of processing. At the bottleneck, some of the available information is discarded, and fails to feed forward to the next stage of processing.

Auditory selective attention

Locating the attentional bottleneck

The location of the attentional bottleneck has been investigated with the 'shadowing' task, a laboratory analogue of the cocktail party. The subject wears headphones, and listens to two spoken messages, one delivered to each ear. Normally, the subject is asked to attend to a particular ear (left or right), and repeat out loud the message heard. The efficiency of selection is then tested by assessing how much information from the other, unattended ear the subject picks up.

Early studies suggested that such information was limited to fairly simple physical properties of the unattended stimulus, such as its pitch and whether or not it was a human voice. Word meanings appeared to be largely inaccessible.

Early selection

Data of this kind generated early selection or filter theories of attention (Broadbent, 1958). All information receives some pre-attentive perceptual analysis, so that simple physical features are identified. The person can then choose to attend only to information possessing a single feature, such as being presented to the right ear, and filter out all other information. Most sensory information is lost at an early stage of processing.

It has been suggested that people with non-paranoid schizophrenia have difficulty in maintaining filtering: some studies show that they are more easily distracted during dichotic listening (e.g. Dykes & McGhie, 1976). Inefficiency of filtering may perhaps contribute to a schizophrenic person's disordered cognition.

Leakage versus late selection

Later research showed that under some circumstances word meaning was extracted from the unattended message in the shadowing task. For example, people often perceive their own name. More strikingly, people sometimes

(a) Early selection

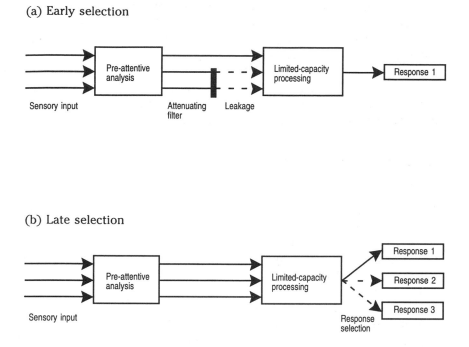

(b) Late selection

Fig. 3.1. Early and late selection models of attention. Contemporary models allow greater flexibility of selection

spontaneously follow a message which unexpectedly switches from ear to ear, showing that they can pick up information about the meaning of the unattended message, even if that information is not consciously accessible.

Evidence of this kind prompted two diverging interpretations. First, the perceptual filter may weaken rather than eliminate the unattended message, so there is some leakage of information through the filter (Treisman, 1964). *Late selection* theorists (e.g. Deutsch & Deutsch, 1963) made a radically different proposal. They suggested that all sensory data were fully analysed, in parallel, and selection took place only at the response stage, in choosing an appropriate action (Fig. 3.1). The implication is that our conscious experience of ignoring much of the sensory environment is misleading – we have access to much more information than we realise.

It has proved surprisingly difficult to choose between these two alternatives, perhaps because attentional selection is flexible. Yantis & Johnson (1990) suggested that selection may work in both fashions, depending on the person's aims, and on the ease with which early selection can operate in the particular situation.

Visual selective attention

Studies of visual attention to a location or area in space show how early and late selective mechanisms may be integrated. Eriksen & Yeh (1985) propose that selective attention is like the zoomlens of a camera. The person can either focus intensively on a small area of space, or attend to a wider area, with lower 'resolving power'. The focus of attention depends partly on the person's voluntary intent, and partly on the early, involuntary stages of attention, in that salient physical features (like a sudden change in brightness) tend to draw the focus of attention. Information within the attended area must be processed, as in late selection theory.

It has also been shown that distracting stimuli may elicit muscular activity even when the person successively ignores them, showing that selection occurs shortly before response. Information outside the attended area appears to receive only the analysis of physical properties associated with early, parallel processing.

Divided and sustained attention

Similar considerations apply to divided attention. We may again ask whether there is a bottleneck stage which can only process information from one task at a time, or whether attention is easily divided, and dual-task performance breaks down only when both tasks require similar responses (McLeod, 1978).

Yet another possibility is that divided attention is difficult not because of a bottleneck in attention, but because the cognitive system loses track of which information goes with which task, and fails to segregate the two streams of processing efficiently (Hirst, 1986).

Again, compromise positions were reached. Pashler (1989) suggests that there may be dual-task interference at both perceptual and response selection stages of processing. Broadbent (1971) has proposed that sustained attention also reflects information-processing structure: performance declines because the selective filter has an increasing tendency to switch attention from the task to other aspects of the environment.

Control processes in perception and attention

Simple stage models assume that processing is data driven: the output from each stage of processing depends only on its input. However, this assumption is invalid even for the early, perceptual stages of processing. Computer simulation studies show that passive reliance on inflexible, pre-programmed methods of stimulus analysis leads to perceptual ambiguities, where the object perceived cannot be recognised. Perception must make use of information about the expected nature of likely objects. We actively interrogate the sensory environment through memory-driven processing, to test whether the sensory data match our expectations of what should be perceived.

Experimental psychology provides many examples of how perception is guided and biased by its general context. For example, we can tamper with recordings of speech, by removing some of the speech sounds, or replacing them with brief tones. Generally, people fail to notice the alterations: the mind 'fills in' the missing speech sounds from its knowledge of what should be there.

Context effects in perception are largely unconscious and involuntary. Later in processing, the person has more voluntary control over attentional selection, so that context effects may reflect the person's deliberate intentions, as well as unconscious biases. In a complex environment, with several sources of information, a subject must develop a deliberate strategy for sampling the various available sources or channels of information. Generally, important and rapidly changing information sources are sampled more frequently. Hence a driver will spend more time looking at the road ahead than at the fuel gauge, although obviously the latter must also be checked occasionally.

Efficient sampling depends both on knowledge of the statistical properties of the environment, such as the probability of an event on any given channel, and the ability to use this knowledge to optimise sampling strategy. Old people sometimes show poorer visual attention because they have difficulty in using their knowledge of channel properties (Rabbitt, 1979).

Changes in sampling may also explain why it is sometimes difficult to sustain attention over time. To monitor a radar screen, for example, it is said that the person must actively make a series of observations, such that the rate of observation depends on the frequency of events. If event frequency is low, sampling will be infrequent, and the person may miss events. If so, their estimate of event frequency will decline, leading to a vicious circle where observation rate and performance become progressively lower.

Connectionist approaches

As we have seen, the majority position is that both voluntary and involuntary processes contribute to attention. However, theories which posit control processes have been criticised because they fail to specify how these controlling processes work in detail (Allport, 1980). It is almost as though there were a resident homunculus deciding which stimuli were to be selected, which is obviously an unsatisfactory state of affairs.

Such considerations have stimulated 'connectionist' models of information processing and attention (this topic is discussed in more detail below, and in Chapter 4). The basic assumption is that the cognitive system can be modelled by a network of very many individual, interconnected processing units, working in concert to process information, with few constraints on the flow of information between units. Modelling attention requires that the activity of units is affected by the person's goals, which may actually be represented as network units themselves, obeying exactly the same rules as other units (Allport, 1980). We might expect that the activation of goal units is related to the person's conscious intentions, but there are some philosophical difficulties in conceptualising such relationships. These ideas find their expression in computer simulations of attention.

Phaf *et al* (1990) modelled attention to perceptual attributes of stimuli, such as colour and position. Their simulation contains separate processing units associated with early perceptual information, and with particular attributes. Phaf *et al* showed that experimental data on selective attention to colour could be modelled simply by increasing the overall activity of colour-processing units in the network. A more complex simulation would achieve this by having the colour units connected to goal units (see Cohen *et al*, 1990).

Connectionist modelling of attention is still in its infancy, but, in principle, it may be applied to the whole range of attentional phenomena.

Capacity models

A radically different presumption is that performance is limited not just by the underlying structure of the computational machinery, but also by some kind of mental capacity. If the capacity of the system is limited, then performance will deteriorate if the demands for capacity made by processing exceed the capacity available. Capacity models accept that performance is limited by the structural properties of the cognitive architecture as well as by capacity, particularly for early, perceptual processing, which requires relatively little capacity. In addition, the allocation of resources to specific tasks or processes is at least partially under voluntary control.

Capacity theory has been formalised within a variety of detailed theories of attentional resources. The most contentious problem dividing these theories is whether resources are unitary or multiple. Originally, capacity theorists proposed a single resource, which could be allocated to a wide range of types of processing. More recently, it has been suggested that there may be different kinds of resource for qualitatively different kinds of processing. For example, rapid throughput of information requires one resource, whereas short-term retention of information requires a second resource.

Divided attention

The major application of capacity theory has been to divided attention (Wickens, 1970). Dual-task interference is attributed to the total demands of both tasks exceeding the amount of capacity available. It is often observed that similar tasks interfere with each other more than dissimilar tasks. One explanation is that similar tasks draw on similar processing structures, so that performance reflects limitations of the individual elements of the processing architecture as well as capacity limitations. Dissimilar tasks may be relatively easy to combine because they draw on different multiple resources.

Sustained attention

Capacity theory has also been applied to sustained attention. Parasuraman *et al* (1987) suggested that capacity may become depleted over time, so that eventually it becomes inadequate for efficient performance.

Experiments do indeed show that perceptual efficiency often declines if the task is particularly demanding. On undemanding tasks, however, there may be a performance decrement because people may tend to become reluctant to respond, as time goes on, whereas in fact their perceptual sensitivity does not change (Davies & Parasuraman, 1982).

Levels of control models

Several theorists have attempted to integrate information processing and capacity models, by proposing that there are two qualitatively different processing systems. A 'lower level' system works something like a connectionist network, and is used primarily for well-learnt, routine processing. Network activity is automatically triggered by stimulus input, and requires little or no attentional capacity, so that processing is largely involuntary, effortless, and unconscious.

When processing is particularly demanding, or when novel information is input, the second, 'upper level' system is called into operation (Fig. 3.2). This system allows the person to implement a voluntary strategy under conscious control. However, processing here is serial rather than parallel, and therefore slower and capacity demanding.

Normally, the control of processing shifts back and forth between the two levels, allowing a fast response to familiar stimuli, and a more flexible, considered response in demanding and unfamiliar situations.

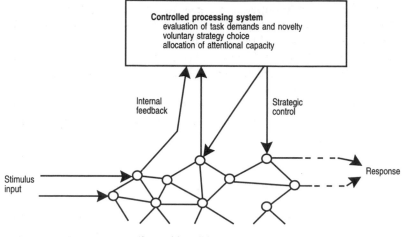

Fig. 3.2 Upper and lower levels of control of attention. Only a small part of the lower level parallel processing network is shown

Levels of control in visual search

Levels of control theory has been applied to the selection problem of searching an area of space for a particular target object or stimulus surrounded by irrelevant distractors. For example, a person might be searching a supermarket shelf for a can of tomato soup (the target) with other flavours of soup as distractors.

Shiffrin & Schneider (1977) have proposed that visual search works at two levels. If the target is sufficiently distinctive, with respect to distractors, automatic, parallel processing is sufficient for detection. Subjectively, the target just 'pops out' of the visual field. Automatic detection develops with practice, provided that fixed sets of targets and distractors are used. But if targets and distractors are easily confused, or frequently interchanged, the person must carry out a slower, voluntarily controlled serial search, comparing each stimulus with a representation in memory of the target. People may have to choose a strategy for controlled search, such as using familiar 'landmarks' to guide search.

Levels of control of divided and sustained attention

Levels of control theory has also been applied to divided attention. One of the difficulties for conventional capacity theory is that sometimes people are remarkably good at dual-task performance. For example, competent pianists can sight-read music while simultaneously following English prose, using the shadowing procedure previously described. Fisk & Schneider (1983) have shown that automatic processing tasks require less capacity than controlled processing tasks, and, in addition, dual-task performance may become more automatic with practice. Thus the skilled pianists required relatively little capacity for the (automatic) sight-reading task, and had enough left over to perform the shadowing task efficiently. The role of practice has been shown experimentally by Spelke *et al* (1976), who demonstrated that after 85 hours of practice two college students had learnt to read silently while simultaneously writing to dictation without loss of performance, although the two tasks were initially difficult to combine. Scerbo & Fisk (1987) suggest that controlled processing is harder to sustain over time than automatic processing, because attentional capacity becomes depleted.

Concluding remarks on attention

We have seen that there are a variety of approaches to understanding attention, and some sharp theoretical disagreements, particularly over the stage of attentional selection, and the existence and nature of attentional capacity. In general, the dominant approach to attention is to see it as a distinct mechanism for selection and for maintaining performance efficiency under demanding conditions.

From this perspective, there is a reasonable consensus that there are two domains of processing. Sensory data are initially processed unconsciously and in parallel, allowing analysis of simple physical properties. Information from this first domain feeds into the second, in which processes are more sensitive to voluntary strategy, more capacity limited, and more consciously accessible. Attention is a property of the second domain, with various functions, including the control of the flow of information between domains.

The contrasting view, exemplified by connectionist theories, sees attention as an effect rather than a cause. Here, the underlying information processing system is argued to be so structured that people's intentions simply bias or prime them towards processing task-relevant stimuli, thus eliminating the requirement to postulate a separate attentional selector.

The two views diverge most strongly on the nature of voluntary control of attention, which is an essential causal influence in conventional theories, but a by-product of more fundamental low-level processes in connectionist theory.

A final point is that both approaches may neglect the real-life context and adaptation of attention. Neisser & Becklen (1975) have criticised traditional theories of selective attention on the grounds that real-life selection is often guided by complex aims and contexts, rather than abstract stimulus properties. They showed that subjects could select between two games, superimposed on the same video film, in spite of the complexity of the visual field. Likewise, Duncan (1984) suggests that visual attention is designed to select objects, rather than abstract perceptual properties. Progress in attention research may require the integration of information-processing theories with an understanding of the evolutionary design of the system.

Models of memory

The simplest traditional model of memory is the modal model (Atkinson & Shiffrin, 1968). It developed from the tradition of describing cognition in terms of 'boxes and arrows', and its more useful constructs still dominate theorising. Memory was described as consisting of two basic elements: a short-term store (STS), and a long-term store (LTS). Information was argued to be processed in STS before being passed to LTS. While information is held in the STS, it is described as short-term memory; once it resides in the LTS, it is termed long-term memory.

The two memory stores were originally distinguished on the basis of the following characteristics. First, they had differing capacities. The STS can be said to hold information for several seconds, and the LTS several years. The STS can be demonstrated to have a capacity limited to '7 plus or minus 2' items, which can be digits, letters, or 'chunks' of two or three letters or digits. LTS seemed to have no such limitations. They were claimed to have different types of encoding: acoustic and phonological for STS, and semantic for LTS, and possibly different representational systems. Finally, some amnesic patients demonstrated double dissociation: they could remember information learnt pre-traumatically but could learn no new information (Milner, 1968), or, conversely, some had normal short-term memory skills but grossly defective long-term memory (Baddeley & Warrington, 1970). (Note at this point that 'short-term memory' is frequently misapplied in everyday conversation, such as "My problem is, I have a very short-term memory" – the speaker more precisely means an inefficient long-term memory.)

Later research showed that most of these hypotheses proved unsatisfactory (Baddeley, 1990). For example, Shallice & Warrington (1970) reported a patient with a drastically reduced short-term memory span, which means the capacity of the patient's STS was much less than '7 plus or minus 2'. However, the patient had a normal long-term memory capacity. This is a problem for the modal model of memory, since information was argued to be processed first in the STS before being sent on to the LTS. If the STS was disrupted, how were stable long-term memories being brought about? Empirical emphasis then turned to process-oriented models, rather than 'box and arrow' formulations. (Supporters of process-oriented models would claim that they were interested in the 'operational contents' of the boxes, rather than in constructing flow diagrams.)

In this tradition, *Levels of Processing* (Craik & Lockhart, 1978) was an approach which suggested that what was important was the degree to which information was processed. The suggestion was that:

(1) superficial sensory processing resulted in relatively short-lived memory traces

(2) phonological processing gave slightly more durable traces

(3) deep semantic processing resulted in the most stable encodings of all.

This account relied on two types of process, with self-explanatory names: maintenance rehearsal and elaborative rehearsal. Maintenance rehearsal, for example, 'repeating' to oneself, is sufficient to transfer a telephone number to LTS. The more sophisticated elaborative rehearsal takes care of more complex information.

Later, Baddeley (1986) developed his theory of attention and 'working memory', which is his more sophisticated formulation of the STS. Working memory consists of a modality-free central executive controlling an articulatory loop where information is encoded in a phonological form, and a sketch pad which handles visuospatial information.

Finally, there are theoretical distinctions of a qualitative nature which have guided and provoked memory research. For example, Anderson (1983) drew attention to the contrast between procedural knowledge (e.g. ability to perform a skilled task – 'knowing how') and declarative knowledge (e.g. knowing factual information which can be easily articulated – 'knowing what'). Anderson proposed these were acquired, processed, and represented differently.

Tulving (1983) makes another distinction, between episodic memory, which includes stored information about events like today's car parking location, and semantic memory, which refers to stored factual knowledge (such as the capital city of Scotland). This author has contributed a vast body of memory research, full discussion of which is beyond the scope of this chapter. However, a brief account of a controversy which he provoked serves to illustrate how theories of memory are developed in psychology.

The encoding specificity principle

Tulving's model of memory operation focused on the efficacy of various types of retrieval cues in long-term memory. Tulving and his colleague Thomson gave a challenging demonstration of recall which was superior to recognition. (Here 'recall' refers to a subject generating previously presented items for a memory test, while 'recognition' involves looking at lists of the previously presented words alongside distractors and deciding which of the words were in the experimental list.) From these and other data Tulving formulated the encoding specificity principle.

In effect, Tulving's theory explains why it helps to be given a 'clue' or cue, when trying to recall something. He looked at the efficacy of different types of cue and deduced what predicted their success. He concluded that the probability of an item's retrieval given a specific cue depends on that retrieval cue being incorporated into the memory during encoding. In other words, a cue is only going to help if the subject has somehow 'built-in' the nature of the cue when formulating the original memory trace. For example, suppose a subject is trying to recall the word 'tangerine' from the word pair 'tangerine – airplane'. It is simply no use cueing with 'Remember – it went with airplane' if the subject did not fully encode these items as components of a pair. In their experiment, Tulving and Thomson had manipulated the presence or absence of the retrieval cue at encoding; in other words, when the subject was learning the material in the first place. By a complex means of analysis they were thus able to demonstrate these seemingly counterintuitive results. They are counterintuitive because it might be thought that under normal circumstances it would be much harder to do free recall, than simply to pick out the targets from among distractors. This was not the case in this particular study. In summary, these authors showed that the difficulty of a memory task depends on the extent to which the encoding (i.e. learning) and retrieval contexts match.

Described so simply, this statement appears self-evident. However, it revolutionised the concept of a memory trace and ran counter to the then current 'generate and recognise' model of retrieval. That theory claimed that experimental list learning involved attaching a 'tag' to an item's representation in memory. Retrieval was getting access to this word's representation and then evaluating the evidence on the 'tag' to determine membership of the experimental list.

This assumed the 'trans-situational identity' of a memory trace. For example, suppose we taught our long-suffering memory test subject a long list of words which contained among them the word 'bear'. This word would be characterised as a passive unchanging representation, with information concerning its inclusion in the experimental list somehow associated to it. In Tulving's radical alternative there was no unchanging representation of 'bear'. Instead, as a result of encountering 'bear' in the experimental list, a cluster of 'bear features' was activated. The sum of these amount to the representation paraphrased by 'the word "bear" as encountered in this psychology experiment'. Next time the subject remembered this concept out of the laboratory, an entirely different trace might result; for example, 'the cuddly companion of my childhood'.

In contrast, in the 'generate and recognise' model, memory as a whole consisted of passive collections of concepts stored away, collecting 'tags' each time they were activated which could then be used in retrieval. Thus, in the example above, our subject would access the self-same 'bear' trace twice, reading the experiment 'tag' the first time, and a 'my childhood toy' tag the second time. For Tulving, there was no such repository of traces. On the contrary, clusters of features became instantiated on demand to deal with specific retrieval events (hence 'encoding specificity theory'). Thus Tulving's work heralded the development of more dynamic accounts of retrieval, and more distributed accounts of representation and storage.

What factors make for good memory?

There are scores of arcane details concerning verbal memory as practised in the laboratory. Here are but a few:

(1) in memory for word lists, memory for the first items is facilitated (primacy), as are the last items (recency)
(2) distributed practice makes for better learning
(3) semantic processing results in stable long-term traces
(4) the capacity of the STS can be enhanced by 'chunking'; for example, grouping long numbers into sets of three, or letters into trigrams.

What general principles for good memory have emerged?

Organisation

Categorising learned information greatly enhances retention, even if the instructions to group the material occur after presentation. Using 'pegs' to arrange incoming material also aids retrieval. This can be done by the ancient 'method of loci', and imagining the items displayed at points around a familiar scene, or by associating them with a heavily overlearned rhyme (Box 3.1). Research with waiting and bar staff showed it helps to connect the new material meaningfully with information already known, and to rely less on internal rehearsal and more on external cues. For example, the waiter can design a letter mnemonic to remember the order, assign each customer to it, and then make up a word to remember the whole table order. Thus 'SMOLK' may mean one order each of *s*teak (*m*edium), *o*melette, *l*asagne, and chicken *k*iev.

Elaboration

When items to be recalled are processed semantically, or elaborative operations are employed upon them, memory is enhanced. For example, asking subjects to solve riddles, the answers to which are the target items, requires them to encode the targets semantically and improves retrieval. Also, forming a complex image of groups of to-be-remembered items interacting also enhances memory (e.g. a *caterpillar* wearing a *jacket* and driving a *lorry* filled with *eggs*).

Box 3.1   Using a peg-word rhyme to recall Saturday-morning tasks

This method employs most of the factors which promote good memory. Simply form the mental images and, at retrieval, recite the rhyme and 'read' the images to cue recall of the list of tasks.

Peg word rhyme	Items to recall	Mental image
One is a bun	Get a newspaper	Bun with newspaper filling
Two is a shoe	Post letter	Shoe with letter inside
Three is a tree	Meet Judith for coffee	Judith waving from treetop
Four is a door	Collect jacket from cleaners	Door wearing dirty jacket
Five is a hive	Go to Presto's music shop to collect order	Hive made of piled compact discs with striped, winged letter P's instead of bees
Six is a brick	Buy a birthday card for Mark	Brick with 'Happy Birthday' written upon it and a smudge mark on its envelope
Seven is heaven	Go to Sainsbury's	Flocks of angels pushing shopping trolleys
Eight is a gate	Buy bread	A garden gate made of baguettes
Nine is wine	Buy lightbulbs	Champagne bottle with lightbulb instead of cork
Ten is a hen	Buy washing-powder	Hen taking a bath in the washing-machine

Integration

Retention is facilitated if the learner can attach incoming information to previously learned information. This proposal has a long history among educators and students alike, and it became important to experimental psychology with the work of Bartlett (1932). It was the powerful ability of memory to impose structure on incoming information, the 'effort after meaning', that led this pioneering memory researcher to propose the concept of a 'schema'.

Today this theoretical construct is brought up to date by artificial intelligence and mathematical modelling techniques, but its general character is still recognisable. The notion has been applied to many domains, from knowledge in human skills to the more abstract level of concept formation.

Schemata

In general terms, schemata are active recognition devices, or organising structures, which consist of slots or variables. These collect information relevant to their defining set and may either be filled with relevant information (instantiated), or left unspecified when input is irrelevant. Not all slots need to be filled to activate a schema – they may filled with a default value (which amounts to simple inference). To give a crude example, to activate a school schema, information concerning lesson and teacher may suffice. Once activated, the schema itself sketches in pupils by default. Schemata are vital in the efficient operation of both memory and comprehension. This can more easily be seen in the context of experiments.

Anderson & Pichert (1978) showed subjects a passage describing the activities of some boys playing truant from school. The passage contained various details about a house in which they were hiding. The subjects were asked to read the passage from the point of view of either a house purchaser or a burglar. Then they were later asked to recall the material. What they found was that the 'home buyers' could recall lots of the relevant information of that defining set, but did not spontaneously retrieve 'burglar' information. On the other hand, when the 'home buyers' were subsequently asked to think over the passage again, and try to recall information relevant to a burglar, they could retrieve new information not formerly accessible to them. The same pattern of recall was seen in the 'burglar' group. This shows that the schema used could actually affect retrieval, even when not activated at encoding. Bransford *et al* (1972) studied the effects of schemata on comprehension and had subjects listen to sentences of the following types:

either   *Three turtles rested on the floating log and a fish swam beneath them.*

or   *Three turtles rested beside a floating log and a fish swam beneath them.*

When tested for recognition of the sentences three minutes later, those subjects who had previously heard the first sentence type falsely recognised the following sentence:

Three turtles rested on the floating log and a fish swam beneath it.

This was because those subjects made the reasonable inference that if the fish swam beneath the turtles, it must also swim beneath the log. This mis-remembering did not occur in the group presented with the second sentence form, where the turtles were resting *beside* the log. Here we see the operation of a schema concerning spatial relations in the world affecting memory for the sentence and sketching in details by default which were not in the original stimulus.

Another demonstration of instantiation of information by default is seen in the experiments of Sulin & Dooling (1974). They asked subjects to read a passage about a girl who was a 'problem child'. She was violent and unmanageable, and the child's parents worried about her mental health. Some subjects were told the child was 'Carol Harris'; others, 'Helen Keller', the famous multiply disabled author. The subjects in the Helen Keller condition then later falsely recognised sentences such as 'she was deaf, dumb, and blind' as having been in the passage. This phenomenon was even observed in a condition where subjects read the passage as being about Carol Harris and were only *later* told it was really about Helen Keller. As can be seen above, the background knowledge represented in schemata helps us to maintain our comprehension. Imagine the results in situations where the default information is damaging or negative – here schemata may also underlie our prejudices.

Supermemory

Among the most fascinating findings in the study of human memory are those concerning the extraordinary feats of mnemonists. These people use the strategies described above to their fullest extent, resulting in excellent retrieval from memory. For example, Luria's subject Shereshevskii had perfect recall for anything he needed to remember, including both verbal and non-verbal information. He could even retrieve material in reverse order to that in which it was presented, and his memory endured for years (see Baddeley, 1982). Shereshevskii made important use of imagery, and was also able to associate images in one sensory modality, such as vision, with another sensory modality, such as sound. This is known as synaesthesia. Baddeley provides some fascinating examples. For instance, when Shereshevskii was presented with a stimulus tone of 2000 cycles per second to remember, he said the sound was like fireworks tinged with a red hue which had an ugly taste like a briny pickle!

These findings are not simply entertaining peripheral issues. Studies of supermemory have also informed and provoked theoretical debate. For instance, we know that the average short-term memory has a digit span of '7 plus or minus 2'. Chase & Ericsson (1981) have shown that, with practice, even ordinary subjects can increase their digit spans by orders of magnitude. Indeed, they argue that there is no good evidence that exceptional ability is more than just extensive practice effects.

On the other hand, Thompson *et al* (1991) report evidence that their subject (the fourth author of the paper) does show signs of an innate superior faculty. This is because, among other things, he has a digit span of up to 60 digits, yet does not seem to employ any kind of meaningful encoding, elaboration, or imagery. The authors argue that therefore he is not simply someone who has practised to have an efficient memory – he simply has an innate exceptional capacity.

A review of mnemonists in general is provided by Brown & Deffenbacher (1988).

What factors make for poor memory?

Early theories of forgetting involved a debate about the relative contributions of 'trace decay' in which the corruption of memory is caused by the passage of time only, and 'interference', where there is confusion of memory owing to interpolated events and new memories.

Investigation of the former mechanism proved difficult, as it was awkward to produce circumstances wherein subjects were having no interpolated activity. An early series of experiments provided some evidence that there was more forgetting in a group of active mobile cockroaches than in a group which spent that same intervening period comatose.

Interference

In general it was found to be much easier to investigate interference and thus most research into verbal memory of the 1950s and '60s concerns this topic. The experiments themselves involved learning successive lists of words or pairs of words, or perhaps groups of letters. Occasionally subjects were required to do distractor tasks such as mental arithmetic. Two main types of interference were distinguished: retroactive interference and proactive inhibition.

Retroactive interference (RI) is described as the deleterious effect of new learning upon retrieval of old information. Slamecka (1960) asked subjects to learn complex sentences. He varied the number of presentations of the sentences and then gave subjects either a rest period, or a new set of sentences to learn. He showed that the amount of learning depended on the number of learning trials, whereas the amount of forgetting depended on the number of interpolated and interfering new sentences.

Proactive inhibition (PI) is the inhibitory effect of previously learned information upon new learning. Among others, Wickens (1970) showed that if subjects were given successive lists from the same category, for example letters, their recall would gradually deteriorate. However, if after a number of trials the material was changed to numbers, then recall performance would suddenly improve. This phenomenon is release from proactive inhibition, and it can also be demonstrated with any category shift of information; for example, from lists of birds to lists of flowers.

It was argued that performance worsened because the similarity of the successive lists of materials produces excessive interference, which is overcome by a change to more distinctive information. This was cleverly emphasised by Gardiner *et al* (1972), who used lists of flowers in their study of PI. A change in material from cultivated to wild flowers was not discerned by their subjects, who accrued PI in recall as usual. However, if they were told after presentation, but before recall, that this subtle change in list had occurred, their recall improved and showed the classic release effect. The authors argued that the interference has most effect at retrieval, and the provision of distinctive cues at this point can overcome it.

Interference has been shown to play a major part in everyday memory failures. Jones (1990) investigated subjects' memory for the design on British pennies. Recall was on occasion significantly less than that expected if his participants had been in a state of complete ignorance of the visual appearance of the coins. He was able to show that the subjects used misleading background information which made performance worse than if they were guessing. For example, their memory of the orientation of the Queen's head was dominated by the head's opposite orientation on British stamps (see Fig. 3.3).

The effect of attention

An important factor in the quality of memory performance is the role of attention. Clearly, dividing a subject's attention will impair performance, but this is not the whole story. A subject's ability to engage in multiple tasks depends in part on the nature of the competing tasks as well as on their attentional resources. Thus, for example, if the memory part of their workload is semantic in nature and the competing tasks also reflect this, we cannot expect good recall. However, if the tasks are sufficiently dissimilar, or the subject is highly skilled through practice, several tasks may be efficiently and accurately performed.

Capacity

So far mention has been made of operational constraints on memory performance. There are also architectural limitations, such as the limited capacity of working memory. If a task places demands which exceed the

Fig. 3.3 'Head' and 'tail' of the current British penny (a), with the features likely to be recalled (b); reprinted with kind permission of G. V. Jones

capacity of working memory, then correspondingly less can be registered in long-term memory.

Context-dependent forgetting

Memory is sensitive to the circumstances of both learning and retrieval, and is particularly impaired when these are incompatible. An aspect of this is the influence of context-dependent forgetting.

Godden & Baddeley (1975) showed this by teaching deep-sea divers lists of words either onshore or underwater. Similar amounts of learning ensued in each case, but performance was drastically reduced if the learning and testing were carried out in different locations; for example, when divers tried to recall onshore words learnt underwater, or vice versa. The effect can even be shown with movement between rooms having differing décor or ambient music.

State-dependent forgetting

Many will be familiar with the domestic expression of a related phenomenon, state-dependent forgetting, experienced 'the morning after' alcohol. This can also be shown to operate on information learnt while smoking marihuana and tested much later. It is also demonstrated by depressive patients, who typically suffer impaired memory. These impairments are overlaid by a state-dependent component, and their recall of information presented while depressed is very poor if they are tested while they are not depressed and vice versa.

Mood can exert a profound effect on memory performance. For example, we know that depressed patients recall unpleasant memories more easily than pleasant memories, a factor which obviously interacts with their state, as they may then become still more depressed and resistant to therapeutic suggestions.

Misleading information

Memory is also affected by the nature of the material to be learnt, and is poor when this is unpredictable, chaotic, or beset with ambiguity or inconsistency. Misleading information has been shown to exert a powerful influence on eyewitness testimony in an important series of experiments by Loftus and her colleagues (e.g. Loftus *et al*, 1978). Her technique involved inserting incorrect information into her questions of experimental 'witnesses' who had seen slides showing the process of an accident. In one study she asked some of her subjects at what speed a car had been moving when it passed the 'yield' sign. In fact, the sign in the slide was a 'stop' sign, but this did not prevent 41% of those subjects who had been asked the misleading question from falsely recognising a slide depicting the car at a 'yield' sign. The misleading question had actually 'created' a memory for an item which did not feature in the original incident.

Computer simulations of memory

Some of the earliest computer simulations of cognition were applied to the operation of memory. Schank & Abelson (1977) developed a computer program called SAM (Script Applier Mechanism), based on scripts which are equivalent to schemata. SAM is capable of answering questions about a variety of stories, and also knows about how to behave in a restaurant. Anderson (1983) describes his program, ACT*, which encapsulates his theory of cognition, including a theory of declarative, procedural, and semantic memory.

Connectionism, which has already been mentioned as an approach which has proved fruitful in research on attention, has also contributed to memory research. Formerly, simulations used explicit localised symbols to represent concepts, and all relevant operations and rules were written into the program. Connectionism rejects symbol manipulation as a model for cognition. Concepts are instead represented by patterns of activation distributed across networks of nodes. The network itself develops its behaviour by the operation of mathematical evaluations, and there are no explicit rules or operations written into the program.

There are many types of connectionist model, some specialising in recognition, some remembering, and some even learning. An example of a connectionist model of recall is shown by McClelland (1981). He created

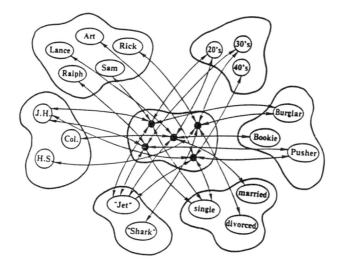

Fig. 3.4 Schematic representation of the Jets and Sharks program. Some connections are omitted for clarity. Reprinted with kind permission of J. L. McClelland. (J. H. = Junior High; Col. = College; H. S. = High School.)

a program which operates on information concerning two rival gangs, the Jets and the Sharks. The program knows the life history, age, and occupation of each gang member, and, given cues, can retrieve information. Each item of information is a node and all nodes are interlinked by connections. Related nodes have excitatory links, and mutually exclusive nodes – inhibitory links. So in Fig. 3.4 we can see that the nodes representing 'single' and 'married' are mutually inhibitory. The links between nodes representing 'Sam', who is a single Bookie, will be so arranged to excite those three nodes, but inhibit other marital statuses and occupations. The final output is thus achieved by a combination of competition between rival nodes and excitation among related nodes. For example, the program can tell us which Shark is in his 20s and went to high school. It can also generalise spontaneously. For example, it can tell us what people in their 40s with a high school education are like – they tend to be Sharks who are married.

Concluding remarks on memory

This section has described the development of theories of memory from those focusing on multiple stores to those stressing processing requirements. Qualitative issues have also been reviewed, and it has been noted that there are several types of memory which may be stored and processed differently. Similarly, we have seen that the nature of the to-be-remembered material itself influences the structure of memories.

Acknowledgements

The first author is employed on a grant funded by the ESRC/MRC/SERC Initiative on Cognitive Science/HCI, no. SPG 9018232. The authors would like to thank Trevor Harley and Gregory Jones for their helpful comments on this chapter. Figures 3.3 and 3.4 are reproduced by kind permission of the Psychonomic Society, Inc., and MIT/Bradford Books, respectively.

Further reading

A good general text of cognitive psychology is Eysenck & Keane (1990). A useful companion to this is Smyth *et al* (1987), which puts laboratory findings in an everyday context. Reviews of current work on attention are provided by a series of monographs called *Attention and Performance* (e.g. Coltheart, 1987). Work on attentional and other cognitive disorders is found in Ellis & Young (1988) and is essential reading for anyone interested in the effects of brain damage on cognition. Wells & Matthews (1994) and Williams *et al* (1988) provide reviews of the effects of emotional disorders on cognition. Everyday memory is an important area not covered in this chapter; therefore, Cohen (1989) is recommended. Finally, Loftus & Doyle (1987) give a detailed account of memory research, aimed at lawyers, jurors, or expert witnesses, and as a consequence this study is very readable.

References

Allport, D. A. (1980) Patterns and actions: cognitive mechanisms are content-specific. In *Cognitive Psychology: New Directions* (ed. G. Claxton). London: Routledge.

Anderson, J. R. (1983) *The Architecture of Cognition*. Cambridge, MA: Harvard University Press.

Anderson, R. C. & Pichert, J. W. (1978) Recall of previously unrecallable information following a shift in perspective. *Journal of Verbal Learning and Verbal Behaviour*, **17**, 1–12.

Arthur, W., Jr, Barrett, G. V. & Alexander, R. A. (1991) Prediction of vehicular accident involvement: a meta-analysis. *Human Performance*, **4**, 89–106.

Atkinson, R. C. & Shiffrin, R. M. (1968) Human memory: a proposed system and its control processes. In *The Psychology of Learning and Motivation: Advances in Research and Theory, Vol. 2* (ed. K. W. Spence). New York: Academic Press.

Baddeley, A. D. (1982) *Your Memory; A Users' Guide*. Harmondsworth: Penguin.

—— (1986) *Working Memory*. Oxford: Oxford University Press.

—— (1990) *Human Memory: Theory and Practice*. Hove: Lawrence Erlbaum.

—— & Warrington, E. K. (1970) Amnesia and the distinction between long- and short-term memory. *Journal of Verbal Learning and Verbal Behaviour*, **9**, 176–189.

Bartlett, F. C. (1932) *Remembering*. Cambridge: Cambridge University Press.

Bransford, J. D., Barclay, J. R. & Franks, J. J. (1972) Sentence memory: a constructive versus interpretive approach. *Cognitive Psychology*, **3**, 193–209.

Broadbent, D. E. (1958) *Perception and Communication*. London: Pergamon.

—— (1971) *Decision and Stress*. London: Academic Press.

Brown, E. & Deffenbacher, K. (1988) Superior memory performance and mnemonic encoding. In *The Exceptional Brain* (eds L. K. Obler & D. Fein). New York: Guilford Press.

Chase, W. G. & Ericsson, K. A. (1981) Skilled memory. In *The Psychology of Learning and Motivation* (Vol. 16) (ed. G. H. Bower). New York: Academic Press.

Cohen, G. (1989) *Memory in the Real World.* Hove: Lawrence Erlbaum.

Cohen, J. D., Dunbar, K. & McClelland, J. L. (1990) On the control of automatic processes: a parallel distributed processing account of the Stroop effect. *Psychological Review*, **97**, 332–361.

Coltheart, M. (ed.) (1987) *Attention and Performance XII: The Psychology of Reading.* Hove: Lawrence Erlbaum.

Craik, F. I. M. & Lockhart, R. S. (1978) Levels of processing: a framework for memory research. *Journal of Verbal Learning and Verbal Behaviour*, **11**, 671–684.

Davies, D. R. & Parasuraman, R. (1982) *The Psychology of Vigilance.* London: Academic Press.

Deutsch, J. A. & Deutsch, D. (1963) Attention: some theoretical considerations. *Psychological Review*, **70**, 80–90.

Dixon, N. F. (1981) *Preconscious Processing.* London: Wiley.

Duncan, J. (1984) Selective attention and the organization of visual information. *Journal of Experimental Psychology: General*, **113**, 501–517.

Dykes, M. & McGhie, A. (1976) A comparative study of attentional strategies of schizophrenic and highly creative normal subjects. *British Journal of Psychiatry*, **128**, 50–66.

Ellis, A. W. & Young, A. W. (1988) *Human Cognitive Neuropsychology.* Hove: Lawrence Erlbaum.

Eriksen, C. W. & Yeh, Y-Y. (1985) Allocation of attention in the visual field. *Journal of Experimental Psychology: Human Perception and Performance*, **11**, 583–597.

Eysenck, M. W. & Keane, M. T. (1990) *Cognitive Psychology: A Student's Handbook.* Hove: Lawrence Erlbaum.

Fisk, A. D. & Schneider, W. (1983) Category and word search: generalizing search principles to complex processing. *Journal of Experimental Psychology: Learning, Memory, and Cognition*, **9**, 177–195.

Gardiner, J. M., Craik, F. I. M. & Birtwhistle, J. (1972) Retrieval cues and release from proactive inhibition. *Journal of Verbal Learning and Verbal Behaviour*, **11**, 778–783.

Godden, D. R. & Baddeley, A. D. (1975) Context-dependent memory in two natural environments: on land and underwater. *British Journal of Psychology*, **66**, 325–332.

Hirst, W. (1986) Aspects of divided and selective attention. In *Mind and Brain* (eds J. Ledoux & W. Hirst). New York: Cambridge University Press.

Humphreys, G. W. & Bruce, V. (1989) *Visual Cognition.* Hove: Lawrence Erlbaum.

Jones, G. V. J. (1990) Misremembering a common object: when left is not right. *Memory and Cognition*, **18**, 174–182.

Loftus, E. F. & Doyle, J. M. (1987) *Eyewitness Testimony: Civil and Criminal.* New York: Kluver Law.

—— , Miller, D. G. & Burns, H. J. (1978) Semantic integration of verbal information into a visual memory. *Journal of Experimental Psychology: Human Learning and Memory*, **4**, 19–31.

McClelland, J. L. (1981) Retrieving general and specific information from stored knowledge of specifics. *Proceedings of the Third Annual Meeting of the Cognitive Science Society*, 170–172.

McLeod, P. (1978) Does probe RT measure central processing demand? *Quarterly Journal of Experimental Psychology*, **30**, 83–89.

Milner, B. (1968) Visual recognition and recall after right temporal-lobe excision in man. *Neuropsychologia*, **6**, 191–209.

Neisser, U. & Becklen, R. (1975) Selective looking: attending to visually specified events. *Cognitive Psychology*, **7**, 480–494.

Parasuraman, R., Warm, J. S. & Dember, W. N. (1987) Vigilance: taxonomy and utility. In *Ergonomics and Human Factors: Recent Research* (eds L. Mark, J. S. Warm & R. L. Huston). New York: Springer.

Pashler, H. (1989) Dissociations and dependencies between speed and accuracy: evidence for a two component theory of divided attention in simple tasks. *Cognitive Psychology*, **21**, 469–514.

Phaf, R. H., Van der Heijden, A. H. C., Hudson, P. T. W. (1990) SLAM: a connectionist model for attention in visual selection tasks. *Cognitive Psychology*, **22**, 273–341.

Rabbitt, P. (1979) Current paradigms and models in human information processing. In *Human Stress and Cognition: An Information Processing Approach* (eds V. Hamilton & D. M. Warburton). Chichester: Wiley.

Scerbo, M. W. & Fisk, A. D. (1987) Automatic and control processing approach to interpreting vigilance performance: a review and reevaluation. *Human Factors*, **29**, 653–660.

Schank, R. C. & Abelson, R. P. (1977) *Scripts, Plans, Goals, and Understanding: An Inquiry into Human Knowledge Structures*. Hillsdale, NJ: Lawrence Erlbaum.

Shallice, T. & Warrington, E. K. (1970) Independent functioning of verbal memory stores: a neuropsychological study. *Quarterly Journal of Experimental Psychology*, **22**, 261–273.

Shiffrin, R. M. & Schneider, W. (1977) Controlled and automatic human information processing: II. Perceptual learning, automatic attending, and a general theory. *Psychological Review*, **84**, 127–190.

Slamecka, N. J. (1960) Retroactive inhibition of connected discourse as a function of practice level. *Journal of Experimental Psychology*, **59**, 104–108.

Smyth, M. M., Morris, P. E., Levy, P., *et al* (1987) *Cognition in Action*. Hove: Lawrence Erlbaum.

Spelke, E. S. Hirst, W. C. & Neisser, U. (1976) Skills of divided attention. *Cognition*, **4**, 215–230.

Sternberg, S. (1969) The discovery of processing stages: extensions of Donders' method. *Acta Psychologica*, **30**, 276–315.

Sulin, R. A. & Dooling, D. J. (1974) Intrusion of a thematic idea in retention of prose. *Journal of Experimental Psychology*, **103**, 255–262.

Thompson, C. P., Cowan, T., Frieman, J., *et al* (1991) Rajan: a study of a memorist. *Journal of Memory and Language*, **30**, 702–724.

Treisman, A. M. (1964) Verbal cues, language, and meaning in selective attention. *American Journal of Psychology*, **77**, 206–219.

Tulving, E. (1983) *Elements of Episodic Memory*. Oxford: Oxford University Press.

Wells, A. & Matthews, G. (1994) *Attention and Emotion: a Clinical Perspective*. Hillsdale, NJ: Lawrence Erlbaum.

Wickens, D. D. (1970) Encoding categories of words: an empirical approach to meaning. *Psychological Review*, **77**, 1–15.

Williams, J. M. G., Watts, F. N., McLeod, C., *et al* (1988) *Cognitive Psychology and Emotional Disorders*. Chichester: Wiley.

Yantis, S. & Johnson, D.N. (1990) Mechanisms of attentional priority. *Journal of Experimental Psychology: Human Perception and Performance*, **16**, 812–825.

4 Language and thought

Trevor A. Harley

Introduction: the approach from linguistics • The function of language • Modern psycholinguistics • The relationship between language and thought • Mental representation • Word meaning and concept acquisition • New directions – the interdisciplinary approach

---

Introduction: the approach from linguistics

For most of us, the abilities of language and thought are two of the most important which set us apart from other animals, and of these two faculties, it is language which we think of as that which makes humans special. Animals do communicate with each other: for example, it is well known that bees can indicate the location of rich sources of nectar by means of a stylised 'dance', and the richness of the communication systems of dolphins is still a matter of some debate. However, naturally occurring animal communication systems are very limited in their scope and in the nature of the information they can convey. There have been attempts to teach other primates human-like languages. One of the earliest such attempts was by Gardner & Gardner (1969), who taught a chimpanzee called Washoe American sign language. There have been many criticisms of this type of work, ranging from methodological to interpretational, and it is still not clear whether or not apes can be taught a communications system with the same underlying richness as human language. Most would agree that primates can be conditioned to learn a sizeable vocabulary and some simple rules for ordering those words, but the ability to use a rich syntactic system as do human children and adults seems beyond them.

Chomsky

Language, then, does appear to be a uniquely human ability. Indeed, the American linguist Noam Chomsky has argued that aspects of language, in particular the *grammar* that enables us to acquire syntactic rules, are innate and species-specific. It is difficult to overestimate the influence of Chomsky in the history of the study of language and thought. In his earlier work, Chomsky was particularly concerned with the form of the mental representation underlying language, or the rules of grammar. Linguists have traditionally divided the study of language into four main components:

(1) *semantics* (the study of the meaning of language)
(2) *phonology* (the study of the basic sounds of particular languages)

(3) *pragmatics* (how we use language)

(4) *syntax* (the rules whereby words are ordered to form sentences).

Chomsky argued that to account for both the creativity of language – that is, that we can produce and understand sentences no one else has produced before – and our intuitions concerning the underlying structure of language, we must use a particularly powerful syntactic system called 'transformational grammar'.

For example, we can analyse the underlying syntactic structure of the sentence "The dog chases the cat" in terms of 'phrase structure rewrite rules' which rewrite more complex units, such as a sentence, in terms of

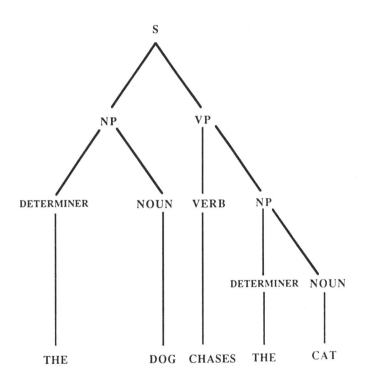

Fig. 4.1. A parse tree for the sentence "The dog chases the cat". This shows how this sentence's constituent structure, or 'phrase marker', is composed of lower-level structural units or grammatical categories, and also the relationship between these structural units:

Sentence —> NP + VP (noun phrase plus verb phrase)

NP —> Determiner + Noun

VP —> Verb + NP

Determiner —> the

Nouns —> dog, cat

Verb —> chases

simpler units, such as noun phrases and verb phrases. Phrases can then be rewritten as simpler units until we reach the component words of the sentence. This scheme has the desirable characteristic of describing the underlying syntactic structure of our language, in that it shows how the words of a sentence are related to each other. In particular, it emphasises the hierarchical nature of our language (see also Fig. 4.1).

Furthermore we can derive a new sentence from this basic underlying form by applying different types of transformation. For example, the 'question transformation' enables us to say "Does the dog chase the cat?", and the passivisation transformation enables us to produce "The cat was chased by the dog".

According to the earlier versions of Chomsky's theory, these sentences are first formulated in their root or kernel form in what was called 'deep structure'; the transformation is then applied to give their actual syntactic form in 'surface structure'. Chomsky further argued that at some very deep syntactic level, all languages have a great deal in common, and this makes the task of a child learning a particular language easier. One of the goals of modern linguistics is to discover such 'linguistic universals' and hence describe the nature of this underlying 'universal grammar'.

Chomsky stressed the point that he was concerned with studying our idealised linguistic *competence*: that is, explaining both how children can acquire language, and our knowledge of our language. It is important to distinguish competence from *performance*. Performance concerns how we actually produce and understand language, with the limitations of limited time and short-term memory; performance is very non-ideal. For example, spoken language contains many hesitations, slips of the tongue, simplified structures, false starts, and so forth. The study of linguistic performance – that is, the study of how we actually produce, understand, and remember language in real time – is called 'psycholinguistics'.

Early psycholinguistic experiments started with the natural assumption that there was a straightforward, simple relationship between performance and competence, as conceptualised by Chomsky (for a review of these experiments, and also for a more detailed exposition of the earlier version of Chomsky's theory, see Green, 1972). These experiments soon showed that this was not the case. For example, tests of the competence notion of the 'autonomy of syntax' (which states that syntactic processes can be considered independently of others) showed that the situation was much more complex. For example, syntactic decoding of sentences is affected by semantic considerations.

The function of language

There has been a strong linguistic tradition concerned both with studying the functions of language and with how language achieves these functions in use. The primary purpose of language is to communicate. Indeed, some linguistic exchanges serve no function other than to communicate for the sake of preserving communication – so-called 'phatic' exchanges (Lyons, 1977). Ethnomethodologists have focused upon the structure and nature of linguistic exchanges in a number of real-world settings. Some settings are very stylised and have a rigid structure (e.g. a debate); others are less formal but still have a more rigid structure than everyday conversation (e.g. seminars).

Conversation

In particular, the structure of everyday conversations has been examined in detail in both normal and abnormal settings (Labov & Fanshel, 1977). It has been proposed that conversations have a very clear structure in terms of conversational 'turns'. We do not normally speak at the same time, and there are clear turn-governing mechanisms which ensure this. The most obvious is when we ask a question, or use a stereotypical sequence such as 'hello'. We can convey our readiness to 'yield the floor', as it is called, by our intonation. We fill our pauses with 'ums' and 'ahs' when we wish to continue speaking (Petrie, 1987). Finally, the direction of our gaze is a very good indicator of our readiness to yield the floor; if we wish to carry on speaking we usually look away from the speaker.

The cooperative principle

Many of these considerations merge into those of pragmatics. For example, Grice (1975) argued that in conversation speakers assume – often implicitly – that other participants are collaborating to make the interaction coherent and meaningful by adhering to what he calls the 'cooperative principle'. He specified how this operates in more detail by postulating four 'conversational maxims', namely

(1)   quantity (saying no more or less than is required)
(2)   quality (telling the truth)
(3)   relevance (making one's contribution relevant to the current topic)
(4)   manner (avoiding ambiguity and obscurity).

If one of these maxims appears to have been disobeyed, the listener will attempt to draw an inference or 'conversational implicature' which will enable the sense of the conversation to be maintained. Sperber & Wilson (1986) argue that the maxim of relevance is by far the most important of these maxims.

Comprehension and inference

There are other types of inference we make routinely in language comprehension. Among the most studied by psycholinguists is 'anaphoric reference'. This is deciding which nouns attach to which pronouns.

Consider the sentence "He used the knife to cut the bread, but it was blunt". We normally infer that it was the knife that was blunt – that is, that 'knife' is the antecedent of the pronoun 'it' – with such ease that we are not even aware that cognitive processing has taken place. Nevertheless, the task is actually a complex one and sensitive to syntactic, semantic, and pragmatic factors. This work is reviewed in detail in Garnham (1985), and deficits involving reference are often important in schizophrenic speech.

Austin (1975) proposed that our speech achieves its purpose at a number of levels of analysis, through what he called 'speech acts'. The literal meaning of what we say conveys the *locutionary force*. Many utterances convey an intended meaning through the non-literal meaning of the utterance; this is its *illocutionary force*. For example, when we say "Can you shut that door?", we are not really asking about the listener's ability to shut the door; it is actually an indirect request for the listener to shut the door. Utterances also have effects upon the listener, which comprise the *perlocutionary force* of the utterance. Some effects may, of course, be unintentional; for example, by my tone of voice I may indicate that I am exceptionally tired.

This work was greatly extended by Searle (1969) in his analysis of indirect speech acts. These are utterances, such as "Can you shut the door?", which achieve their purpose through other than their literal meaning. (For some work on deficits of planning language in schizophrenia, see Hoffman (1986) and Schwartz (1982).)

Modern psycholinguistics

Modern psycholinguistics studies how we produce (by speaking and writing), store, and comprehend (spoken and written) language. However, for reasons to do with how easy it is to study these processes, the great majority of research has been upon how we recognise individual words, understand sentences, or produce simple speech. In a brief review such as this it is impossible to do justice to all the research which has been carried out in this area. To illustrate how experimental psycholinguistics operates, I will consider a recurring modern-day theme. This is the extent to which different types of language processes interact with one another.

Context

To some extent this is a legacy of the early days of psycholinguistics, when the autonomy of syntax was in vogue. A modular system, one in which different types of processes operate at different times, is also conceptually simpler than a non-modular one. Let us take the example of word recognition. At what stage does context (such as your expectations of what the next word is going to be) operate? It has been known for some time that prior context can speed up processing. For example, in an experiment using the lexical decision task, where subjects are shown a string of letters and have to decide whether or not they form a word, subjects respond more quickly if the target word to which they have to respond (e.g. NURSE) is immediately preceded by a semantically related word, or prime, such as DOCTOR, than when it is preceded by a semantically unrelated item, such as BREAD (Meyer & Schvaneveldt, 1971). (Priming appears to be abnormal in schizophrenic speakers.) Now consider, for example, a sentence which begins

> "In the morning, on the train, all the businessmen sit quietly and do their . . . ."

You may well have some idea of what the next word in this sentence is going to be. If asked to guess you might say "crosswords". Hence the context of the sentence is providing some clue as to what item comes next, yet this is not cued by any individual word in the sentence.

The central question tackled by psycholinguists is: when does this contextual information operate? Does it operate so early that it can be used by the perceptual system to assist in the actual identification of the word? Or does it affect processing only after perceptual identification has occurred – for example, does it merely speed up some checking process? The former type of model is an example of an interactive model (see, for example, the logogen model of visual word recognition of Morton (1969) and the *cohort* model of spoken word recognition of Marslen-Wilson & Tyler (1980)), while the latter type of model is a modular one (see, for example, the serial search model of word recognition of Forster (1979)). This topic is still being debated.

Comprehension

Similar issues have been raised in the study of sentence comprehension. Consider a sentence such as

> "The horse raced past the barn fell."

This is called a *'garden path'* sentence, because the human sentence parser (or syntactic analyser) is normally misled on hearing the first few words of such a sentence into expecting a particular syntactic structure. In actual fact, the expected structure is inappropriate because the sentence should actually be analysed in some other way. In this situation the parsing mechanism has to backtrack and reparse the sentence. (The garden path sentence is actually grammatical, but a little reflection might be necessary to arrive at the correct interpretation, which can be paraphrased as "The horse which was raced past the barn fell down".) How does the hearer resolve this temporary ambiguity? Again, there is still no agreement in the psycholinguistic literature, but the same basic concerns apply: is semantic information used to assist parsing, or are these processes independent? (For a recent review of this work, see Altmann (1989).)

Errors in speech production

Another example of interaction between processes may be seen in speech production. When we speak, we make occasional mistakes, or 'slips of the tongue'. Freud (1901) proposed an explanation for these errors which has passed into folk psychology: they are 'Freudian slips', in which the speaker's true, repressed intention is revealed.

However, modern theories view the great majority of speech errors as the consequence of transient processing difficulties in the speech production system alone. For example, simple word substitutions (such as saying 'old' when you mean to say 'young') are failures of lexical access.

The lexicon is the hypothesised mental construct resembling a dictionary: when we hear or read a word, we access it to obtain the meaning and pronunciation of a word; when we speak, we access a word's sound or phonology given its meaning.

Fay & Cutler (1977) and Garrett (1980) have argued that word substitution errors can arise at one of two stages:

(1) when moving from the underlying semantic to an abstract lexical representation of a word, giving a semantic word substitution (such as 'dog' for 'cat')
(2) when moving from the lexical to the phonological representation, giving a phonological word substitution, or malapropism (such as 'eucalyptus' for 'ukulele').

These two stages were argued to be independent. However, word substitutions where the target and error items are both semantically and phonologically related (such as saying 'head' for 'hat') occur far more than would be expected by chance. Hence Dell (1986), Harley (1984), and Stemberger (1985) have all argued that semantic and phonological processes interact in speech production, and have proposed models where interaction between different knowledge sources is central. Similar errors are numerous in fluent aphasic speech subsequent to damage to Wernicke's region of the brain (see Chapter 5).

Modular versus connectionist processing

The trend over the last few years has been towards accepting such interactive models of both language comprehension and production. This has culminated in widespread interest in the highly interactive models of cognitive processing called connectionist or parallel distributed processing models of cognition (Rumelhart *et al*, 1986, and see below). Nevertheless, it would be a mistake to assume that it has been unanimously agreed that interactive models are preferred to independent, modular models.

The relationship between language and thought

What, then, is the relationship between language and thought? Logically, a number of positions are possible, and each of these has been proposed at some time.

Independence of language and cognitive development

Chomsky argued that language has its own, separate, genetic roots in an innate 'language acquisition device' (Piattelli-Palmarini, 1980), and develops independently of other non-linguistic cognitive processes. One consequence of this is that language development will proceed normally in spite of more general cognitive impairments, such as those resulting from blindness (Cromer, 1991).

Later interaction between language and cognitive development

The influential Russian psychologist Vygotsky proposed a more complex position. He suggested that language and thought have distinct roots. In early childhood, linguistic and cognitive development proceed independently, but interact later. Vygotsky noted that very young children make great use of monologues: they talk a great deal, apparently to themselves, as their speech serves no obvious social function. At an important juncture in development, these monologues are internalised to become internal speech.

The famous developmental psychologist Jean Piaget (see Chapter 1) argued that cognitive development was primary, in that it provides a capacity for symbol formation and rule manipulation upon which language is based. Workers in the same tradition as Piaget have detailed this cognition hypothesis (Cromer, 1991).

Language as a determinant of thought

The final position is known as the Sapir–Whorf hypothesis, after an American anthropologist and an insurance agent who were primarily responsible for its development, as a result of studying the speech of native Americans. They maintained that language determines thought. In fact, there are two closely related ideas here: linguistic relativism states that the speakers of different languages dissect or perceive the world in different ways; linguistic determinism states that language determines the form of thought.

There is something of a hotchpotch of rather weak supporting evidence. For example, in problem-solving tasks the phenomenon of functional fixedness, whereby problem solvers become fixated upon the primary function of an object, because of its name, suggests that language use can certainly influence problem solving (for a review, see Eysenck & Keane, 1990).

The strongest evidence comes from studies of colour coding. Early evidence (Brown & Lenneberg, 1954) suggested that memory for colours is determined by the availability of colour names. However, more recent evidence about the use of colour terms across cultures (Berlin & Kay, 1969; Rosch, 1975) suggests that the structure of the human colour vision system influences our choice of colour names (see Clark & Clark (1977) and Cromer (1991) for reviews, and Bernstein (1973) for some possible further but controversial applications to education).

Conclusion

There is probably no simple relationship between language and thought. Cognitive, linguistic, and even perceptual factors interact with each other in a complex fashion.

Mental representation

If we cannot conclude that the development of language and thought are related in any simple way, how do they interact in normal cognitive processing? Does all thought have to be linguistic in form, for example? There is certainly much more to thought than language or internal speech.

People with aphasia who, as a consequence of brain damage, either have lost language totally or have major language impairments, can nevertheless usually perform well on other cognitive tasks such as reasoning, object recognition, and memory.

Fodor (1976) has argued that there is indeed a language of thought which bears a very close relationship to the external form of our language, possessing a complex syntax which operates upon internal mental symbols. (There are also other types of representation; for example, we can represent complex motor sequences and images.)

This leads to the question of whether we need different representations or *codes* for storing, on the one hand, pictures or images (sometimes called spatial representations) and, on the other, linguistic materials, such as words and sentences (sometimes called linear representations). One major theory, the dual-code theory (Paivio, 1971; Bower, 1972) states that these types of information are indeed representationally distinct and therefore need different cognitive processing systems. However, this hypothesis has received mixed experimental support.

On a related point, there is much evidence that while the left hemisphere of the brain (at least in the great majority of right-handed people) is specialized in linguistic, analytic processing, the right is primarily concerned with spatial and imaginal processing (Kolb & Whishaw, 1990).

A closely related problem involves determining the representation underlying mental images. A series of experiments by Kosslyn (1980) has shown that mental images behave in many ways like percepts of the external world. For example, it takes longer to scan between two points in the mental image of a fictitious mental map the further these points are apart. There is similar evidence from the work of Shepard (1978), who used a mental rotation task. In this task subjects have to rotate a mental image of an object (such as the letter 'R'). He showed that there was a linear relationship between the angle through which subjects had to rotate the image, and how long it took them to do it. This and similar results were used to argue that the manipulation of mental images involved processes which are similar to those involved in visual perception.

Propositions

There has been much debate, however, on the underlying representation of imagery. Anderson (1978) pointed out that any one type of representational system can formally be made to mimic any other, while Pylyshyn (1981) has also proposed that it is not necessary to hypothesise an independent imagery representation system to explain these findings. Instead, it is argued that all forms of mental representation are coded in terms of propositions. Propositions are simple, abstract, modality-independent units of meaning. Pylyshyn shows how experimental findings, such as those of Kosslyn (1980) and Shepard (1978), can be explained in propositional terms.

Propositions are also useful for representing the meaning of sentences (Anderson & Bower, 1973; Anderson, 1983, 1990). Networks of propositions are particularly useful and economical when representing the meaning of connected sentences in the form of text or discourse, and they form the basis of theories of text comprehension, such as that of Kintsch & van Dijk (1978). Figure 4.2 shows how propositional networks might represent the very simple story

"The man will give the woman a present. It will be a dog."

in terms of labelled connections.

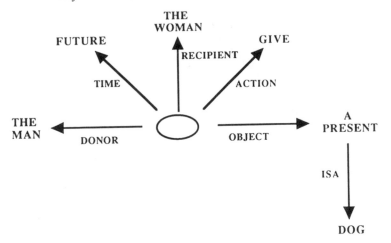

Fig. 4.2. A simple propositional network for the simple story "The man will give the woman a present. It will be a dog." This shows how the meaning of complex sentences and the relationship between them can be represented by connections between atomic units of meaning or 'propositions'. An abstract propositional node represents an 'event', and different components of the event are linked to the event node by relationships which are labelled so as to show how these sentences specify those components.

Connectionism

The situation has become even more complicated, however, with the advent of connectionism (see below). According to this approach, cognitive and linguistic processing occurs by the action of many simple processing units. Connectionism emphasises the importance of subsymbolic processing which lies beneath the explicit rule-based level of traditional cognitive theories. Doubtless many advances will be made in this area in the near future.

Word meaning and concept acquisition

A more specific problem concerns how we represent the meanings of words. The simplest idea is probably that we define word meaning in terms of simple units of meaning. This 'decompositional' view maintains that the meaning of words consists of a number of semantic features. For example, the meaning of the word 'dog' might be a list of the features: 'four legs', 'barks', 'eats meat', and so on. There have been sophisticated theories which attempt to relate semantic decomposition to perceptual processing (Miller & Johnson-Laird, 1976; see also Johnson-Laird, 1983).

A contrasting view (Fodor *et al*, 1980) argues that decomposition does not occur, and that instead word meanings are mentally represented as

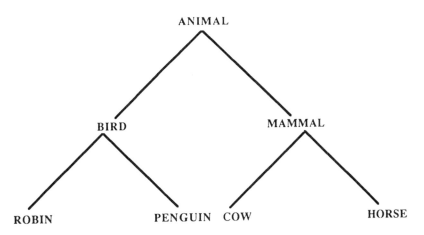

Fig. 4.3. A simple example of a semantic hierarchy showing the relationship between some natural kind terms

unitary wholes. Some years ago this led to vigorous debate among the major protagonists (see, for example, Fodor (1981)).

Semantic networks

Part of the problem with semantic decomposition theories is that it is not always obvious how the meanings of words should be decomposed. Indeed, it is often extremely problematic to give simple definitions of words. Therefore a number of alternative theories have been proposed. One of the most superficially attractive of these is the idea of a semantic network. Here the meanings of words are interconnected, so that the meaning of a word is given by its position in the network.

One of the earliest network theories was proposed by Collins & Quillian (1969). In this scheme, the meaning of words is represented hierarchically. Collins & Quillian tested their model by a task known as the sentence verification task. According to their model, it should take longer to verify the sentence "A robin is an animal" than the sentence "A robin is a bird", because to check the first sentence you have to travel higher up the hierarchy than for the second sentence (see, for example, Fig. 4.3). This is indeed what they found. The further you have to travel through your semantic network, the longer your response time.

A number of problems soon emerged with the earliest form of this theory (see Baddeley (1990) for a more detailed review). In particular, not all items at the same level in the hierarchy were treated alike. Hence subjects find it easier to verify the sentence "A robin is a bird" than the sentence "A penguin is a bird". There have been three main responses to these problematic findings.

The first was to modify the original semantic network idea, so that connections were no longer all identical (Collins & Loftus, 1975). At the same time the concept of spreading activation was introduced, which can be conceptualised as energy flowing along the connections. In many ways this can be thought of as a precursor of the later connectionist models, which make use of many of these concepts.

Semantic features

The second alternative was to take the idea of semantic features further, and to make a distinction between essential or defining features, and characteristic features which are not part of the strict definition (Rips *et al*, 1973). For example, it is a defining feature of 'bird' that it lays eggs, but only a characteristic feature that it flies.

Semantic prototypes

The third hypothesis is that such concepts are stored as idealised forms, or prototypes (Rosch, 1978). For example, the prototypical bird might be shaped like a sparrow, be small and brown, sing, and fly. Sentence verification occurs by reference to the prototype, so that the closer the test item is to the prototype, the faster is the response. Hence, as a robin is very close to the prototype, "A robin is a bird" is verified very quickly;   as "ostrich" is not very close to our prototypical bird, "An ostrich is a bird" is verified rather more slowly.

The prototype theory also addresses the issue of concept acquisition. Prototypes are acquired across time by abstracting the central tendency (the prototype) from a large number of exposures.

Conclusion

There has been some debate on the extent to which network and feature theories are actually distinguishable (Hollan, 1975), and the experimental evaluation of each of these theories is complex (Eysenck & Keane, 1990).

New directions – the interdisciplinary approach

In the last few years there have been two major advances in the study of language and thought. The first of these is progress in our understanding of normal linguistic and cognitive processing as a result of cognitive neuropsychology (Chapter 5). The second is the advent of what is known as connectionism, or parallel distributed processing. The impact of this has been so marked as to earn connectionism the accolade of being a 'paradigm shift' in cognitive science, and its influence has been particularly strong on language processing.

Connectionism represents a move away from the traditional model of the mind as a symbol-processing system, which had been idealised in the computational metaphor, where the mind is seen as acting like a traditional serial computer (Neisser, 1967; Johnson-Laird, 1983). Instead, connectionism views cognitive processing as arising as a result of the cumulative action of a large number of very simple elements. It is in much the same tradition as earlier neural network theories.

Processing is seen as highly interactive, and is not governed by the application of explicit rules; instead, rule-like behaviour emerges from the complex interaction of the large number of units. Such models are said to be subsymbolic.

Much emphasis is now placed upon learning. There are a number of different breeds of connectionism, including the 'interactive activation'

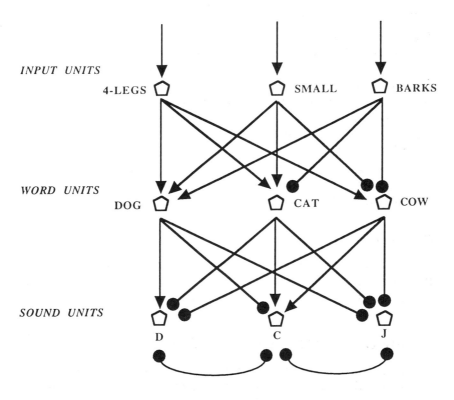

Fig. 4.4. Part of a connectionist network. This is an example of a three-level interactive activation network, the purpose of which is to output the initial letter of a word given an input semantic representation.
Connections along which excitatory activation flows are labelled with an arrow; inhibitory connections with a filled circle. See the text for further details.

model of letter identification and visual word recognition (Rumelhart *et al*, 1986), the Boltzmann machine (based on physical theories of statistical thermodynamics), and, most influential of all, back-propagation. Back-propagation systems learn merely by repeated exposure to input–output pairs. It is been applied to many psychological phenomena, including the pronunciation of printed words (Seidenberg & McClelland, 1989), the order of acquisition of irregular past tenses by children (but see Fodor & Pylyshyn, 1988; Pinker & Prince, 1988), speech production, visual object recognition, and many other topics (Bechtel & Abrahamsen, 1991; Quinlan, 1991).

The interactive activation network

Figure 4.4 illustrates how one type of connectionist system operates. In particular, this is an example of a part of an interactive activation network. Its purpose is that, when given an input representing the meaning of a word – a *semantic representation* – the net will correctly output the letters of that word. This is a net showing how the first letter is output.

In this very simple network there are three input units, each one of which corresponds to a semantic feature or component of meaning of a word. Suppose we wish to activate the word 'dog'. We then supply an input or 'activation' to all three semantic units. These are connected to the word units by appropriately weighted connections, so that activating all three semantic units ('has four legs', 'is small', and 'barks') has the consequence of activating the word unit corresponding to 'dog' most, 'cat' an intermediate amount (because it shares some semantic features with 'dog'), and 'cow' least of all (because it has only one active input unit).

Activation continues to flow to the letter level. 'Dog' excites the letter 'd' but inhibits 'c' and 'j'; 'cat' and 'cow' excite their first letter, 'c', but inhibit 'd' and 'j'. To speed up processing there are inhibitory connections between the output letter units so that when 'd' starts to be activated, it quickly wins out against its competitors. It is possible to add other types of connections (for example, McClelland & Rumelhart (1981) used more within-level inhibitory connections and also had feedback connections between levels) as well as other levels of processing. McClelland & Rumelhart used a three-level network comprising letter feature, letter, and word units to model word identification given a visual input.

Conclusion

The recent trend has been to integrate a number of approaches – linguistic, experimental, computer science, philosophical, and even anthropological – when studying language and thought, and the relationship between them. Indeed, for modern cognitive science this interdisciplinary approach to the topic is central.

Acknowledgements

The author's research is supported by grant no. SPG 9018232 from the ESRC/MRC/ SERC Initiative on Cognitive Science/HCI. I am grateful to Siobhan MacAndrew for comments on a draft of this chapter.

Further reading

There are a number of texts which cover psycholinguistics in more detail. Some of the more recent ones are Garnham (1985), Garman (1990), and Taylor & Taylor (1990). For a specific review of the area of pragmatics, see Levinson (1983), and for a specific review of gaze, gestures, and non-verbal communication, see Beattie (1983). There is an even larger number of general texts covering cognitive psychology, including Anderson (1990), Cohen (1983), and Eysenck & Keane (1990); Cohen also has a good section on animal cognition and language. An up-to-date coverage of connectionism is provided by Quinlan (1991). Borsley (1991) is a recent introductory text on modern syntactic theory.

References

Altmann, G. T. M. (ed.) (1989) *Parsing and Interpretation*. Hove: Erlbaum.

Anderson, J. R. (1978) Arguments concerning representations for mental imagery. *Psychological Review*, **85**, 249–277.

—— (1983) *The Architecture of Cognition*. Cambridge, MA: Harvard University Press.

—— (1990) *Cognitive Psychology and its Implications* (3rd edn). New York: W. H. Freeman.

—— & Bower, G. H. (1973) *Human Associative Memory*. Washington, DC: Winston.

Austin, J. L. (1975) *How to do Things with Words* (2nd edn). Oxford: Oxford University Press.

Baddeley, A. (1990) *Human Memory: Theory and Practice*. Hove: Erlbaum.

Beattie, G. (1983) *Talk: An Analysis of Speech and Non-verbal Behaviour in Conversation*. Milton Keynes: Open University Press.

Bechtel, W., & Abrahamsen, A. (1991) *Connectionism and the Mind*. Cambridge, MA: Blackwell Scientific.

Berlin, B. & Kay, P. (1969) *Basic Color Terms: Their Universality and Evolution*. Berkeley, CA: University of California Press.

Bernstein, B. (1973) *Class, Codes, and Control (Vol. 1)*. St Albans: Paladin.

Borsley, R. D. (1991) *Syntactic Theory: A Unified Approach*. London: Edward Arnold.

Bower, G. H. (1972) Mental imagery and associative learning. In *Cognition in Learning and Memory* (ed. L. Gregg). New York: Wiley.

Brown, R. & Lenneberg, E. H. (1954) A study in language and cognition. *Journal of Abnormal and Social Psychology*, **49**, 454–462.

Clark, H. H. & Clark, E. V. (1977) *Psychology and Language*. New York: Harcourt Brace.

Cohen, G. (1983) *The Psychology of Cognition* (2nd edn). London: Academic Press.

Collins, A. M. & Quillian, M. R. (1969) Retrieval time from semantic memory. *Journal of Verbal Learning and Verbal Behavior*, **8**, 240–247.

—— & Loftus, E. F. (1975) A spreading-activation theory of semantic processing. *Psychological Review*, **82**, 407–428.

Cromer, R. F. (1991) *Language and Thought in Normal and Handicapped Children*. Oxford: Blackwell Scientific.

Dell, G. S. (1986) A spreading-activation theory of retrieval in sentence production. *Psychological Review*, **93**, 283–321.

Eysenck, M. & Keane, M. (1990) *Cognitive Psychology*. Hove: Erlbaum.

Fay, D. & Cutler, A. (1977) Malapropisms and the structure of the mental lexicon. *Linguistic Inquiry*, **8**, 505–520.

Fodor, J. A. (1976) *The Language of Thought*. Hassocks: Harvester.

—— (1981) *Representations: Philosophical Essays on the Foundations of Cognitive Science*. Brighton: Harvester.

——, Garrett, M. F., Walker, E. C. T., *et al* (1980) Against definitions. *Cognition*, **8**, 263–367.

—— & Pylyshyn, Z. W. (1988) Connectionism and cognitive architecture: a critical analysis. *Cognition*, **28**, 3–71.

Forster, K. (1979) Levels of processing and the structure of the language processor. In *Sentence Processing* (eds W. E. Cooper & E.C. T. Walker). Hillsdale, NJ: Erlbaum.

Freud, S. (1901) *The Psychopathology of Everyday Life* (trans. (1975) A. Tyson). Harmondsworth: Pelican.

Gardner, R. A. & Gardner, B. T. (1969) Teaching sign language to a chimpanzee. *Science*, **165**, 664–672.

Garman, M. (1990) *Psycholinguistics*. Cambridge: Cambridge University Press.

Garnham, A. (1985) *Psycholinguistics: Central Topics*. London: Methuen.

Garrett, M. (1980) Levels of processing in sentence production. In *Language Production (Vol. 1: Speech and Talk)* (ed. B. Butterworth). London: Academic Press.

Green, J. (1972) *Psycholinguistics: Chomsky and Psychology*. Harmondsworth: Penguin.

Grice, H. P. (1975) Logic and conversation. In *Syntax and Semantics (Vol. 3: Speech Acts)* (eds P. Cole & J. Morgan). New York: Academic Press.

Harley, T. A. (1984) A critique of top-down independent levels models of speech production: evidence from non-plan-internal speech production. *Cognitive Science*, **8**, 191–219.

Hoffman, R. E. (1986) Verbal hallucinations and language production processes in schizophrenia. *Behavioral and Brain Sciences*, **9**, 503–548.

Hollan, J. D. (1975) Features and semantic memory: set-theoretic or network model? *Psychological Review*, **82**, 154–155.

Johnson-Laird, P. N. (1983) *Mental Models*. Cambridge: Cambridge University Press.

Kintsch, W. & van Dijk, T. A. (1978) Towards a model of text comprehension and reproduction. *Psychological Review*, **85**, 363–394.

Kolb, B. & Whishaw, I. Q. (1990) *Fundamentals of Human Neuropsychology* (3rd edn). New York: Freeman.

Kosslyn, S. M. (1980) *Image and Mind*. Cambridge, MA: Harvard University Press.

Labov, W. & Fanshel, D. (1977) *Therapeutic Discourse: Psychotherapy as Conversation*. New York: Academic Press.

Levinson, S. (1983) *Pragmatics*. Cambridge: Cambridge University Press.

Lyons, J. (1977) *Semantics (Vol. 1)*. Cambridge: Cambridge University Press.

McClelland, J. L. & Rumelhart, D. E. (1981) An interactive activation model of context effects in letter perception. Part 1: An account of the basic findings. *Psychological Review*, **88**, 375–407.

Marslen-Wilson, W. D. & Tyler, L. K. (1980) The temporal structure of spoken language understanding. *Cognition*, **8**, 1–71.

Meyer, D. E. & Schvaneveldt, R. W. (1971) Facilitation in recognizing pairs of words: evidence of a dependence between retrieval operations. *Journal of Experimental Psychology*, **90**, 227–235.

Miller, G. & Johnson-Laird, P. N. (1976) *Language and Perception*. Cambridge: Cambridge University Press.

Morton, J. (1969) Interaction of information in word recognition. *Psychological Review*, **76**, 165–178.

Neisser, U. (1967) *Cognitive Psychology*. New York: Appleton-Century-Crofts.

Paivio, A. (1971) *Imagery and Verbal Processes*. New York: Holt, Rinehart & Winston.

Petrie, H. (1987) The psycholinguistics of speaking. In *New Horizons in Linguistics (Vol. 2)* (eds J. Lyons, R. Coates, M. Deuchar & G. Gazdar). Harmondsworth: Pelican.

Piattelli-Palmarini, M. (ed.) (1980) *Language and Learning: The Debate Between Jean Piaget and Noam Chomsky*. London: Routledge & Kegan Paul.

Pinker, S. & Prince, A. (1988) On language and connectionism: analysis of a parallel distributed processing model of language acquisition. *Cognition*, **28**, 73–193.

Pylyshyn, Z. W. (1981) The imagery debate: analogue media versus tacit knowledge. *Psychological Review*, **88**, 16–45.

Quinlan, P. (1991) *Connectionism and Psychology*. Hemel Hempstead: Harvester Wheatsheaf.

Rips, L. J., Shoben, E. J. & Smith, E. E. (1973) Semantic distance and the verification of semantic relations. *Journal of Verbal Learning and Verbal Behavior*, **12**, 1–20.

Rosch, E. (1975) The nature of mental codes for color categories. *Journal of Experimental Psychology: General*, **104**, 192–233.

—— (1978) Principles of categorization. In *Cognition and Categorization* (eds E. Rosch & B. Lloyd). Hillsdale, NJ: Erlbaum.

Rumelhart, D. E., McClelland, J. L. & The PDP Research Group (1986) *Parallel Distributed Processing (Vol. 1. Foundations)*. Cambridge, MA: MIT Press.

Schwartz, S. (1982) Is there schizophrenic language? *Behavioral and Brain Sciences*, **5**, 579–626.

Searle, J. R. (1969) *Speech Acts*. Cambridge: Cambridge University Press.

Seidenberg, M. S. & McClelland, J. L. (1989) A distributed, developmental model of word recognition and naming. *Psychological Review*, **96**, 523–568.

Shepard, R. N. (1978) The mental image. *American Psychologist*, **33**, 125–137.

Sperber, D. & Wilson, D. (1986) *Relevance*. Oxford: Blackwell Scientific.

Stemberger, J. P. (1985) An interactive activation model of language production. In *Progress in the Psychology of Language (Vol. 1)* (ed. A. W. Ellis). London: Erlbaum.

Taylor, I. & Taylor, M. M. (1990) *Psycholinguistics: Learning and Using Language*. Englewood Cliffs, NJ: Prentice-Hall.

5 Cognitive neuropsychology

Siobhan B. G. MacAndrew
& Trevor A. Harley

Traditional neuropsychology and cognitive neuropsychology • Dyslexia
• Aphasia • Agnosia • Amnesia • New directions

Traditional neuropsychology and cognitive neuropsychology

Traditional neuropsychology

Neuropsychology is concerned with how the structure of the brain relates to human behaviour. As a discipline, it blends the approaches of neurology, physiology, psychology, and neuropsychiatry in studying the effects of various brain lesions on all human and animal functions. The subject matter of neuropsychology thus includes cognition, emotion, reproduction, motor function, sensation, sleeping, and eating (see Chapter 6).

Neuropsychology has tended to emphasise the importance of the localisation of function in the brain. Several techniques are used to achieve this. These include the study of basic neuroanatomy, neurochemistry, brain stimulation, recording the brain's electrical activity, and studying the effects of lesions upon the behaviour of brain-damaged people. In this chapter, we will concern ourselves with the last technique. The prototypical neuropsychological experiment compares the impaired function of groups of patients with a brain lesion in the same site with the intact function of groups of control subjects with no lesion.

Cognitive neuropsychology

Cognitive neuropsychology is a much more recent development, which claims to have changed the way in which we conceptualise the relationship between the brain and behaviour. Unlike traditional neuropsychology, it is concerned only with the *cognitive* human functions, such as language, reasoning, memory, and perception. While it shares fundamentals with traditional neuropsychology, it purports to depart from it in terms of research goals, methods, and theoretical background. For example, in contrast to traditional neuropsychology, there is much less emphasis on localisation of function in the brain. The techniques of cognitive neuropsychologists are primarily experimental tasks derived from those used in cognitive psychology, such as picture naming, sentence comprehension, and reasoning problems. The types of data may be response latencies, error rates, and speech errors.

Not everything about cognitive neuropsychology is new: several notions, such as the importance of single case studies, will be familiar to clinicians. What is new is the provision of a 'rallying flag' under which researchers from several disciplines and backgrounds have for the first time a common aim and framework in which to work.

In this chapter we give a short review of some neuropsychological data and the impact of modern cognitive neuropsychology on the field. We explain how cognitive neuropsychology differs from traditional neuropsychology, and the motivation for these differences. We shall then illustrate this with examples from language (dyslexia and aphasia), object recognition (agnosia), and memory (amnesia). Note that we do not claim here that the goals of cognitive neuropsychology are superior to those of traditional neuropsychology, but only that they are different.

In a major review of the theoretical basis of cognitive neuropsychology, Shallice (1988) argues that it is distinguished from traditional neuropsychology by its theoretical, methodological, and programmatic aspects.

(1) The *theoretical* advance it has made is in relating neuropsychological disorders to cognitive information-processing models.
(2) The *methodological* advance is in stressing the importance of the single case study.
(3) The *research programme* emphasises the importance of neuropsychological evidence for our understanding of normal function.

Shallice goes on to identify a position known as 'ultra-cognitive neuropsychology', which rejects three traditionally important sources of evidence as unimportant, or even dangerously misleading, when constructing theories.

First, ultra-cognitive neuropsychology deems that standard group studies cannot provide appropriate evidence for constructing models of cognition (for a detailed defence of this claim, see Caramazza (1986, 1991) and McCloskey & Caramazza (1988)). Averaging across a group of subjects can result in a pattern of performance not shown by any individual (the 'averaging artefact'). The use of a potentially functionally heterogeneous group also compromises the aim of establishing which parts of the cognitive system are damaged. Since the individuals concerned may be suffering damage to different functional components of the cognitive system, averaging across the group may obscure the correct interpretation of the data. Instead, single case studies are considered to be the *only* valid method of pursuing neuropsychological research.

Second, ultra-cognitivists claim that information on the localisation of function is irrelevant to our understanding of behaviour (Morton, 1984).

A third aspect, which is less frequently openly articulated within the cognitive neuropsychology community, is a tendency to undervalue traditional clinical information. Shallice (1988) argues that in these respects ultra-cognitive neuropsychology has "gone too far".

The status of syndromes

One consequence of the emphasis upon single case studies is that the status of *syndromes* has come into particular dispute. A syndrome is a broad co-occurrence of symptoms used to group patients and considered to have some explanatory force. Traditional examples include Broca's aphasia, Wernicke's aphasia, agrammatism, and deep dyslexia. The strongest claim was that if a patient has one particular symptom of the syndrome, he or she must also have the others, although there are weaker definitions, where symptoms merely cluster together.

Ultra-cognitive neuropsychologists such as Morton & Patterson (1980) reject the notion of a syndrome, arguing that it is useful only inasmuch as it provides the scientific community with convenient labels. Once again, this has the consequence of shifting the emphasis from the group study to the single case analysis.

Dyslexia

In some ways the cognitive neuropsychological approach to the acquired disorders of reading, the dyslexias, best exemplifies the approach as a whole. Note at this point that we are discussing reading disorders which occur as a result of brain damage in adults who formerly knew how to read, and not developmental dyslexia, which prevents the subject from learning to read effectively in the first place.

Traditional neuropsychological models of language emphasise the role of different brain structures. For example, Geschwind's (1972) neurological model of language provides an account of how different gross stages of language processing (such as 'read', 'hear and comprehend word') correspond to neural pathways.

The cognitive neuropsychology of reading, on the other hand, takes as its starting-point cognitive models of normal reading. Traditional psycholinguistic research proposed a 'dual-route' model of reading (Coltheart, 1978; Humphreys & Evett, 1985; Patterson & Coltheart, 1987).

(1) The lexical route

The direct or lexical route is used for reading words which have irregular spelling-to-sound correspondences. (The *lexicon* is our mental dictionary, where all our knowledge about word meaning, pronunciation, and use is stored – see Chapter 4.)

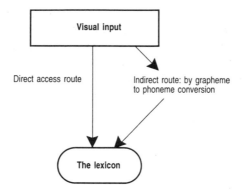

Fig. 5.1. The traditional psycholinguistic dual-route model of reading

There are many irregular words in English where the pronunciation of the 'graphemes' (the visual spelling units of a language, comprising letters or groups of letters) does not correspond to their regular or usual pronunciation. An example is STEAK; the grapheme EA is usually pronounced EE, as in BEAK, SNEAK, and CREAK. Hence the pronunciations of these irregular words cannot be simply derived from their constituent graphemes, and instead we must rely upon word-specific or lexical knowledge.

(2) The non-lexical route

The alternative, *non-lexical* route is used for assembling pronunciations out of individual letter-to-sound correspondences. This route is sometimes described as involving 'grapheme-to-phoneme' conversion, where *phonemes* are the units of sound of a language. Hence we can pronounce the non-word GAK correctly, even though it is a novel string of letters, by decomposing it into its constituent graphemes, 'G', 'A', and 'K', translating these into the appropriate sounds, and assembling a final pronunciation (see Fig. 5.1).

Types of acquired dyslexia

Different types of acquired dyslexia are hypothesised to correspond to various impairments of this model. In particular, distinct disorders arise as a consequence of damage to the lexical and non-lexical routes.

Case example 1. Phonological dyslexia
WB (Funnell, 1983) is a phonological dyslexic. He can read most words, but cannot read any non-words. Hence his lexical route has been left more or less intact, but his non-lexical route is damaged.

Case example 2. Surface dyslexia

Another patient, MP (Bub *et al*, 1985), is the opposite case; she shows normal performance on reading non-words, but has extreme difficulty reading irregular or exception words. Her non-lexical route is completely normal, but her lexical route was severely damaged. This is called surface dyslexia.

These two cases, however, are the most extreme cases yet reported (see Coltheart, 1985). It is more common to find patients who have great difficulty with irregular words but who also have some difficulty with non-words. (See Patterson *et al* (1985) for a discussion of many relevant case studies.)

Double dissociation and the modular system

Surface and phonological dyslexia taken together form a double dissociation. This is exemplified by the performance of two patients on two tasks, A and B. The first patient can perform task A perfectly but cannot do task B; the second patient performs perfectly task B but cannot do task A.

The notion of a double dissociation is an important one in cognitive neuropsychology, as it is taken as evidence for the 'modularity' of the functional architecture of the cognitive system. A modular system is one which comprises a number of independent processing units (Fodor, 1983). A further step is to reason that if lesions of different brain sites result in a behavioural double dissociation, then that cognitive system must be both physically and functionally modular (Shallice, 1988).

The problem of deep dyslexia

Another major type of acquired dyslexia does not correspond so simply to the above model. This is known as deep dyslexia. In many ways deep dyslexia resembles phonological dyslexia; for example, these patients have extreme difficulty with non-words. Deep dyslexia is characterised, however, by the presence of semantic reading errors, or 'paralexias'. Examples of this type of error include reading 'blowing' as 'wind', 'admiral' as 'ship', and 'sabre' as 'sword' (Coltheart *et al*, 1987). Patients who make semantic errors such as these typically also display the following additional symptoms: much better performance on reading concrete, imageable words (such as 'windmill') than abstract words (such as 'wish'); frequent visual errors (such as misreading 'signal' as 'single'), morphological errors (misreading 'courage' as 'courageous'); very poor reading of non-words; and visual-then-semantic errors (such as reading 'favour' as 'taste' via 'flavour').

Until very recently there were two very different interpretations of deep dyslexia. The standard cognitive neuropsychological approach viewed deep dyslexia as an attempt by a greatly damaged reading system to read normally. There have been more detailed explications of this, including hypothesised impairments of the grapheme–phoneme conversion route, plus an additional impairment of the semantic system, which deals with meaning.

The second interpretation instead views deep dyslexia as occurring because the normal reading route is damaged so much that an alternative mechanism involving reading via the right hemisphere comes into action (Coltheart, 1980; Saffran *et al*, 1980; Zaidel & Peters, 1981). This second interpretation is unpopular with cognitive neuropsychologists because if it is correct, then the study of deep dyslexia will tell us nothing about normal reading (Ellis & Young, 1988; Shallice, 1988).

However, each of these approaches has its difficulties. Now, however, a third and very different approach results from lesioning connectionist networks (Hinton & Shallice, 1991; and see below). This approach has great promise. Furthermore, it perhaps points the way to the rehabilitation of the syndrome in cognitive neuropsychology, because it shows how apparently unrelated symptoms can co-occur as the result of a single lesion. For example, the lesion to the connectionist net which is responsible for the origin of semantic paralexias seems also to give rise necessarily to visual errors.

Peripheral dyslexias

Finally, there are other types of dyslexia which are hypothesised as deriving from damage to less central parts of the reading system. For this reason these are called the peripheral dyslexias. They include:

(1) neglect dyslexia, in which patients neglect one half of the visual field, and therefore make visual errors – for example, 'level' is read as 'novel', and 'milk' as 'chalk' (Riddoch, 1990)

(2) attentional dyslexia, in which patients can read whole words well but are poor at naming individual letters within words, tending instead to name other letters which should be ignored (Shallice & Warrington, 1977)

(3) letter-by-letter reading, in which words can be named only after individual letters have been spelt out (Patterson & Kay, 1982)

(4) visual dyslexia, in which one word is misidentified as another (e.g. 'lend' is read as 'land', and easel is read as 'aerial') (Marshall & Newcombe, 1973).

Aphasia

Cognitive neuropsychology also attempts to relate impairments of language production, the aphasias, to cognitive models of language production. As mentioned above, traditional neuropsychology stresses the study of syndromes. The most important of these include Broca's aphasia, which follows from damage to Broca's area, towards the front of the left hemisphere, and Wernicke's aphasia, which results from damage to more posterior regions of the left hemisphere.

There is a proliferation of terminology in aphasia research. For example, Broca's aphasia and Wernicke's aphasia have also been known as 'expressive' and 'receptive' dysphasia, or dysfluent and fluent aphasia, respectively. These have fallen from favour in the research community. In fact, cognitive neuropsychologists would even avoid the terms Broca's aphasia and Wernicke's aphasia. This is because of their dislike of the syndrome approach, and because they prefer to characterise patients according to their functional impairments. For present purposes, however, we shall use these terms as convenient descriptive shorthand.

Broca's aphasia

The speech in Broca's aphasia is slow, hesitant, laborious, and particularly marked by agrammatism. This means that the speech displays a profound lack of syntactic structure: words are produced one at a time, with no obvious sentence frame, there are few grammatical connectives or function words (such as 'because', 'the', 'which'), and few verb tense and noun number endings (such as 'kiss*es*', 'lov*ing*', and 'house*s*'), or inflections. However, their content words (which do the semantic work of the language, and include nouns, verbs, adjectives, and most adverbs) are largely preserved. Hence Broca's aphasics produce strings such as:

> Dad . . . er . . . hospital . . . and ah . . . Wednesday . . . Wednesday, nine o'clock
> . . . and oh . . . Thursday . . . ten o'clock, ah doctors . . . two . . . and doctors . . .
> and er teeth . . . yah.

This patient was describing a visit to the hospital for dental surgery (Goodglass & Geschwind, 1976).

Wernicke's aphasia

The speech of Wernicke's aphasics is rapid and fluent, with largely preserved syntax. There are marked impairments in semantic comprehension and in the correct use of content words. In the more extreme cases, known as jargon aphasia, speech is replete with word substitutions or paraphasias (e.g. producing 'queen' as 'keen'). Sometimes neologisms are found, where words are apparently made up. Such speakers produce strings such as:

I spo'li but the labor of the speaker down here in New York. (Christman & Buckingham, 1989)

Clearly, there is a pattern of dissociation between the primary characteristics of Broca's and Wernicke's aphasias: in the former, syntactic planning is impaired but the retrieval of content words is intact, while in the latter the reverse is the case. This has been used to argue for modularity in the speech production system, with different systems involved in syntactic planning and the transformation of the semantic representation of content words into sound.

Anomia

Similar to Wernicke's aphasia both anatomically and behaviourally is *anomia* (sometimes known as nominal aphasia). This is a particular difficulty in retrieving names; indeed, it used to be called 'word amnesia'.

Patients with word-finding difficulties may display a great deal of circumlocution as they 'talk around' the word they are trying to locate. Anomia can arise as a result of deficits at different stages of the word retrieval process.

> **Case example 3**
> Patient JCU (Howard & Orchard-Lisle, 1984) could name very few pictures of objects unaided, yet her performance improved dramatically if she was given the initial sound as a cue. Under certain conditions she made semantic naming errors to pictures (e.g. she would say 'lion' to a picture of a tiger), yet Howard & Orchard-Lisle were able to show that JCU's object recognition and comprehension processes were intact.

> **Case example 4**
> Patient EST, on the other hand (Kay & Ellis, 1987), showed perfectly intact semantic processes, but disrupted phonological processing. Unlike JCU, he did not make semantic errors.

JCU is an example of anomia arising at the semantic level of word retrieval; EST is an example of anomia arising at the phonological level. This dissociation supports what we know from psycholinguistic research on normal word production (see Chapter 4).

Category-specific anomia

One type of semantic anomia is particularly bizarre. This is known as category-specific anomia. Warrington & Shallice's (1984) patient JBR was much better at naming inanimate than animate objects. MD (Hart *et al*,

1985) had particular difficulties only with the specific categories of fruit and vegetables. Detailed examination of such patients should tell us more about the structure of semantic memory.

Evaluation of the contribution of cognitive neuropsychology to aphasia

The contribution of cognitive neuropsychology to our understanding of aphasia has been primarily twofold. First, in emphasising the importance of single case studies rather than group experiments, it has focused upon specific symptoms which are in need of explanation. As a result of this, the status of agrammatism as a syndrome has come under particular attack; for opposing views, see Badecker & Caramazza (1985, 1986), and Caplan (1986, 1991).

The central issue is that there appear to be patterns of dissociation *within* agrammatism. For example, there are dissociations between the loss of inflections and omission of function words, and the ability to construct sentence frames; and also between the degree of impairment of the production and comprehension of syntax.

Secondly, cognitive neuropsychology has striven for explanations of symptoms in terms of models of normal speech production, such as that of Garrett (1980). According to Garrett's model, speech production occurs via a number of independent stages, including formulating an abstract representation of the planned utterance, constructing a syntactic planning frame for the utterance, and retrieving the phonological forms of the content words (nouns, verbs, and adjectives) independently of the function or grammatical words and word endings (see Chapter 4). Deficits associated with what is traditionally referred to as Broca's-type aphasia are impairments of the processes involved in constructing the syntactic frame, whereas those of Wernicke's-type aphasia are primarily due to impairments of lexical access (Schwartz, 1987).

Agnosia

Agnosia is a deficit in object perception and comprehension, in the absence of general blindness or intellectual deficiency. This impairment can affect visual, auditory, or tactile faculties. The most studied form concerns visual perception.

One of the most influential theories of normal visual perception is that of Marr (1982). He argued that three basic stages were necessary for effective object perception. Grossly simplified, these are:

(1) the *primal sketch*, which analyses differences in stimulus intensity across the visual field; this enables edges and outlines to be detected, and initiates the computation of depth and location

(2) this information is passed on to the second stage, the *2½-D sketch*; a *viewer-centred representation* is assembled which describes the object specifically from that observer's viewpoint

(3) an *object-centred representation* integrates all previous information into three dimensions; this is of sufficient generality to describe the object independently of any specific encounter.

Marr's theory provides cognitive neuropsychology with an excellent framework for explaining agnosia. Deficits can be found at each level. First, there are patients whose deficit lies in the very early stages of sensory analysis. These patients are unable to process the visual features of objects, making recognising or copying drawings impossible. These people are aware the objects exist, however, and can name them by touch (Campion & Latto, 1985).

Next, there are people for whom this first stage of processing is intact, but who are unable to categorise objects perceptually. Ellis & Young (1988) suggest that for these patients there is an impairment of integrating the viewer- and object-centred representations. The effect of this is that patients cannot identify items seen in an unusual orientation (Warrington & Taylor, 1973). This notion was pursued by Humphreys & Riddoch (1984), who suggested that the problem may be twofold. Many unusual views involve foreshortening of the object's image on the retina of the eye. Marr (1982) proposed that the principal axis of elongation was a powerful characteristic feature of an object. Humphreys & Riddoch suggested that patients with a lesion in the right posterior parietal lobe were particularly disadvantaged by foreshortening, which disrupted the ability to compute object-centred representations. In contrast, their much documented patient HJA, who had suffered bilateral occipital lesions, had no difficulty with this.

Case example 5
HJA can negotiate the first stage of processing (outline detection). He can also copy a drawing of an item, so his viewer-centred representation is intact. He can identify a foreshortened view, and so his object-centred representation is not impaired. Moreover, he can define an object's meaning, and often even describe the visual appearance of an object; he simply cannot recognise and name it. Riddoch & Humphreys (1987) describe this deficit as an integrative agnosia. HJA perceives any item feature by feature, but is unable to consolidate this into a stable coherent cognition.

Prosopagnosia

Of particular interest are deficits associated with face recognition. The most striking disorder is the inability to recognise familiar faces, or prosopagnosia. In extreme cases patients are even unable to recognise their own faces in a mirror. It is possible to relate these disorders to a cognitive model of normal face recognition (Bruce & Young, 1986). Again the concept of a dissociation has been important. It is possible to find patients with deficits of face perception, name retrieval, expression analysis, and even lip-reading (Ellis & Young, 1988).

Conclusion

Research into agnosia exemplifies the advantages of cognitive neuropsychology (Shallice, 1988). First, an explicit cognitive theory is directing the research programme of neuropsychologists. Secondly, the cognitive theory finds support from data from brain-damaged individuals. Thirdly, this emphasises a profitable cross-talk between cognitive psychology and neuropsychology.

Amnesia

We end our review of neuropsychological phenomena with an area in which cognitive neuropsychology has only recently taken hold. Research on this topic illustrates the major advantages and disadvantages of traditional neuropsychology. There are problems peculiar to research in amnesia, and the cognitive neuropsychological approach has the potential to alleviate them.

A comprehensive definition of amnesia is difficult. We have already seen in Chapter 3 that even the most simplified model contends that memory consists of a complex system of interdependent processes operating on various types of representation.

Memory may be disordered in a variety of ways. Amnesia results in poor recognition of recently presented words, faces, and pictures, with virtually no recall. However, motor memory and memory for skills such as riding a bike are intact.

It is claimed that amnesia may occur in the absence of other cognitive deficits, although this has been challenged (Shallice, 1988; Bowden, 1990). With the exception of amnesia resulting from dementia, *semantic memory*, or memory for facts, is unimpaired, whereas *episodic memory*, or memory for events, is poor. It is often said that the *procedural memory* of amnesics is often spared, whereas their *declarative memory* is damaged. Finally, there is often retrograde amnesia both for personal and public events. This simplified picture of memory impairments is common to the majority of memory-disordered patients.

A central problem for traditional neuropsychology has been associating specific brain areas with the workings of the complex system of memory processes. This comprises two related questions.

(1) 'Where' in the brain does memory occur? This focuses on what might be called the *structural architecture* of the brain – which brain structures are damaged in amnesia and how they interconnect.
(2) Which functional impairments are responsible for causing amnesia? This focuses on the *cognitive* architecture of the brain – which component processes of memory are impaired in amnesia.

Traditional neuropsychology aimed to relate the structural to the cognitive architectures of the brain. In contrast, cognitive neuropsychologists are more concerned with working out which parts of the cognitive architecture have been damaged in amnesia. This enterprise is firmly based on normal models of memory. Indeed, it is argued that we may find out about the workings of normal memory by looking at amnesia.

In the popular imagination, amnesic people have 'lost their memory'. In practice, of course, they have not forgotten everything, and they do not all have the same problems. Neuropsychologists approach this state of affairs by comparing and contrasting the memory deficits caused by lesions in different sites. Cognitive neuropsychologists focus on interpreting the data in terms of the normal memory system. They argue that we need to distinguish which types of memory processes are intact and which are impaired, and which classes of information amnesic people find easy or difficult to handle.

Organic amnesia

Neuropsychological research has traditionally focused upon organic amnesia. This results from brain dysfunctions such as lesions or biochemical abnormalities. The impairment usually affects acquisition of new memories post-traumatically, which is known as 'anterograde amnesia'; the disruption of memories acquired pre-traumatically is called 'retrograde amnesia'. The resulting impairment may be global, where most memory operations are affected, or specific, where many memory operations are spared.

Non-organic amnesia

Non-organic amnesia includes *psychogenic amnesia*, which is loss of memory as a result of intense emotion or trauma. This is also associated with the 'fugue state', which is a loss of the sense of personal identity and autobiographical memory. The precipitating factors range from the stress of divorce or bereavement, to committing murder, or being at war. There is one type of non-organic amnesia which is suffered by all of us. This is childhood or infantile amnesia, and is our inability to retrieve memories before we are approximately two years old.

Little experimental work has been carried out on these phenomena, so it is not yet possible to say whether they share characteristics with the more commonly studied amnesias resulting from brain pathology.

Temporary amnesia

Temporary amnesia can result from electroconvulsive therapy (ECT), hypnosis, or simulation studies of drug-induced amnesia. These are not strictly pathological, and are not discussed here (see Mayes (1988) for a review).

Organic amnesia and dementia

Organic amnesia arises from a variety of conditions and lesions, and several areas of the brain have been implicated in memory processing. Patients may be left with a profound memory impairment after suffering herpes simplex encephalitis; the damage which results is mainly to the hippocampus and amygdala. The most famous and extensively studied amnesic patient is HM, who had a bilateral temporal lobectomy to relieve severe epilepsy. His case also stresses the importance of the hippocampus. These patients are thus often referred to as suffering temporal lobe amnesia.

In contrast, Korsakoff's syndrome, which arises as a result of alcoholism, is associated with damage to the diencephalon. In particular, there are lesions in the dorsomedial nucleus of the thalamus and mamillary bodies. Damage to the dorsomedial nucleus of the thalamus is also responsible for the memory impairment of another famous patient, NA, who suffered his head wound when a fencing foil penetrated his brain via his right nostril. These patients are therefore said to suffer diencephalic amnesia.

Amnesia is one early sign of senile dementia of the Alzheimer type (SDAT). In this condition neurofibrillary plaques accrue in the hippocampus and amygdala, and sometimes later in the frontal lobes, whereas tangles are found all across the cortex. In Huntington's chorea, a general atrophy starting with the caudate nucleus is seen along with abnormal neurochemistry (see also multiple sclerosis, p. 133).

Memory problems associated with diffuse degenerative disorders such as dementias are treated as a special case in memory research. This is partly because of the nature of the lesions involved, but mostly because the patients suffer cognitive impairments of more than simply memory. This requires careful research methods which can tease out the memory deficits from the overlying mental deterioration. A full discussion of the cognitive impairments of these degenerative disorders can be found in Mayes (1988).

Aetiological variation

Cognitive neuropsychologists would argue that aetiological variation in amnesia results in variation in functional deficits, and therefore amnesia is not a single unitary syndrome. For instance, strong claims have now been made that patients with Korsakoff's syndrome are distinct from other amnesic patients because of their subsidiary frontal lobe damage. This, being combined with their diencephalic lesions, results in a unique pattern of memory deficit (Squire, 1982).

Parkin (1984) agrees with Squire, but takes the argument still further, claiming that diencephalic amnesia is significantly different from temporal lobe amnesia. He concludes that it is therefore prudent to distinguish between people suffering from diencephalic amnesia, Korsakoff's syndrome, and temporal lobe amnesia. This is because they differ with respect to the extent of their retrograde amnesia, forgetting rate, frontal symptoms, and susceptibility to interference. There is also variation in the extent of their confabulation, or tendency to fabricate stories of varying plausibility in response to questions to which they do not know the answer. In contrast, Weiskrantz (1985) opposes the view that there are several types of amnesia. He proposes that there exists a 'core amnesia' shared by all amnesics of whatever aetiology.

Concern with functional and aetiological variation in amnesia has resulted in a trend towards using more single case studies. The typical cognitive neuropsychological case study is not merely a description but a series of detailed 'mini-experiments'. Good examples of this include Wilson & Baddeley's (1988) study of a patient developing amnesia after meningitis and Parkin *et al*'s (1988) study of an amnesic patient with a ruptured aneurysm of the anterior communicating artery.

Theories of amnesia

Consolidation

What kinds of theory have been put forward to explain amnesia? The earliest theory of amnesia is the consolidation hypothesis (Milner, 1968), which emphasises a storage, or registration deficit, in amnesia. It is based on Hebb's (1949) work on reverberating circuits. Hebb claimed that if particular neural circuits were repeatedly excited over time, a permanent structural change would occur. The longer the reverberation, the more stable the memory. Amnesic patients cannot learn any new information if there is any type of distraction, and it was claimed that the distraction was disrupting the necessary structural changes required to formulate a stable long-term memory. However, the time course for memory consolidation was never established, and the theory had difficulty in accounting for recovery from temporary amnesic states. Finally, it was difficult to explain retrograde amnesia, as this would mean that memories which had already been consolidated would have to have been retrospectively disrupted.

Retrieval theory

Others have favoured an approach which concentrated on the functional deficits associated with amnesia. Shallice & Warrington (1970) found evidence for the distinction between two memory stores, by showing double dissociation between short-term and long-term memory (see Chapter 3). Their data from amnesic patients were interpreted in terms of a model of normal memory, the aim being to identify which operations were intact and which were spared. Warrington's later work resulted in the development of a retrieval theory of amnesia, according to which amnesia involved increased amounts of interference at retrieval, and thus greater response competition. In other words, at the point of remembering, memories which share characteristics with the target (such as having been in a similar list) intrude and are output instead of the correct item. The work was based directly on experiments on the effects of interference in normal memory. Warrington and her colleagues were able to show that under circumstances where response competition was reduced, such as when good cues are given as prompts, the performance of amnesics was improved.

Encoding deficit

The encoding deficit theory (Butters & Cermak, 1980) was a rival approach which was also strongly related to experiments in normal memory. These researchers focused on levels of processing (see Chapter 3), claiming that amnesic patients habitually encoded only the surface, superficial characteristics of information. As a consequence, memory for that material was very poor, since stable long-term memory could only be achieved by deep semantic encoding.

Relationship to normal function

So it can be seen that the foundations of modern cognitive neuropsychology were apparent even in early work on amnesia. Why, then, has cognitive neuropsychology anything new to offer? First, although neuropsychological data were routinely interpreted in terms of normal cognition, neuropsychological findings did not in their turn inform theories of normal functioning. Since the emergence of cognitive neuropsychology as an identifiable research programme, this is no longer the case. Notably, the relationship between theories of normal and impaired memory has been strengthened. As Shallice (1988) points out, cognitive psychology books could formerly be written without a mention of data from brain-damaged subjects. Whereas early work stressed the quantitative elements of memory processing in amnesia, recent theories of amnesia have focused on qualitative factors.

The context memory deficit

The context memory deficit hypothesis suggests that in amnesia there is an impairment in the automatic processing of context, including temporal, frequency, modality, and spatial information. The claim is that it is the loss of this information which renders the subject unable to remember (Mayes *et al*, 1985). Although these factors were known to be effective in normal memory, their importance was underestimated. Recent amnesia work stresses that efficient processing of contextual information is critical in normal memory and needs further investigation.

Implicit and explicit memory

Further research shows that amnesic patients have intact implicit memory abilities but impaired explicit memory (Schacter, 1987). Explicit memory is described as a 'conscious' process requiring the intention to retrieve something from memory; for instance, the recall task of a verbal learning experiment. In contrast, implicit memory does not require an intention to interrogate the memory store; rather, it becomes apparent in its facilitation of performance of a task.

This is shown by amnesic patients in word-fragment completion tasks. A list of words is presented several times. The experimenter then either asks the patient to recall the list, or to complete, "with the first word which comes to mind", some word fragments which are the initial letters of the targets. In this paradigm the subject will show very little *explicit* memory for the list. In other words, the number of recalled words will be low. However, the patients will be able to complete the majority of the word fragments correctly, showing intact *implicit* memory. The amnesic has indirectly 'remembered' the material.

Schacter and his colleagues have identified an important domain of preserved function in amnesia, and have outlined the operation of these processes in normal memory. It would not be true to say that experiments on explicit and implicit memory in normal subjects were inspired by the findings from amnesia, but it is a good example of a symbiotic relationship developing between the two fields.

Advances with cognitive neuropsychology

The development of contemporary cognitive neuropsychology has clarified both theory and methodology in amnesia research. It has facilitated a flow of influence between researchers concerned with memory in both the normal and brain-damaged population. Cognitive neuropsychology has encouraged interdisciplinary work by formulating the parameters of the discipline more clearly. Finally, it has even resulted in the discovery of new phenomena, which were formerly obscured because of a concentration on group studies.

New directions

In this chapter we have briefly reviewed neuropsychological data and the development and contributions of cognitive neuropsychology. We have seen how cognitive neuropsychology has amplified our understanding of both normal and brain-damaged cognition. The approach is not without its critics, and Shallice (1988) warns against dangers of ultra-cognitivism. These are ignoring group studies and information from the localisation of function, and undervaluing the importance of clinical data. Seidenberg (1988) adds another criticism: the approach places too much emphasis upon discovering the functional architecture of the system; that is, how different components of the cognitive system relate to one another. This essentially involves constructing classical 'box and arrows' diagrams, showing how information flows through the processing system. Seidenberg (1988) stresses the importance of investigating the actual processing mechanisms and the types of knowledge representations involved. That is, it is important to look at what goes on inside these boxes.

One way in which this might be achieved is indicated by what is perhaps the most exciting recent development in the area, which is the intersection of connectionism and cognitive neuropsychology. Connectionism sees cognitive processing as occurring not through the explicit manipulation of symbols and rules, but emerging through the cooperation of a large number of massively interconnected, simple processing units (see Chapter 4).

Connectionism is initially attractive to neuropsychology because the simple processing units involved are based upon a neural metaphor. Furthermore, unlike conventional artificial intelligence (AI) systems, connectionist systems display 'graceful degradation' when damaged. That is, they do not cease functioning correctly altogether, but instead the amount of disruption which they display is proportional to the amount of damage which has been inflicted. Linguistic deficits which arise as a consequence of brain damage are explained by lesioning connectionist models. This involves destroying some of the connections in the models. In some circumstances the models (run as computer simulations), which had previously been producing correct output, then start behaving like, for example, a surface dyslexic patient (Patterson *et al*, 1989), or a deep dyslexic patient (Hinton & Shallice, 1991). This type of research is going to be of increasing importance over the next few years.

Acknowledgements

The authors' research is supported by grant no. SPG 9018232 from the ESRC/MRC/ SERC Initiative on Cognitive Science/HCI to the second author.

Further reading

A standard reference for cognitive neuropsychology is either Ellis & Young (1988) or Shallice (1988). These textbooks both explain the distinction between cognitive and traditional neuropsychology, and cover examples of the approach in considerable depth. A comprehensive textbook of general neuropsychology is Kolb & Whishaw (1990). A more anecdotal approach can be found in Sacks (1985).

References

Badecker, W. & Caramazza, A. (1985) On considerations of method and theory governing the use of clinical categories in neurolinguistics and cognitive neuropsychology: the case against agrammatism. *Cognition*, **20**, 97–125.

—— & —— (1986) A final brief in the case against agrammatism: the role of theory in the selection of data. *Cognition*, **24**, 277–282.

Bowden, S. C. (1990) Separating cognitive impairment in neurologically asymptomatic alcoholism from Wernicke–Korsakoff syndrome: is the neuropsychological distinction justified? *Psychological Bulletin*, **107**, 355–366.

Bruce, V. & Young, A. W. (1986) Understanding face recognition. *British Journal of Psychology*, **77**, 305–327.

Bub, D. N., Cancelliere, A. & Kertesz, A. (1985) Whole-word and analytic translation of spelling to sound in a non-semantic reader. In *Surface Dyslexia* (eds K. E. Patterson, J. C. Marshall & M. Coltheart), pp. 15–34. Hove: Erlbaum.

Butters, N. & Cermak, L. S. (1980) *Alcoholic Korsakoff's Syndrome: An Information-Processing Approach to Amnesia*. New York: Academic Press.

Campion, J. & Latto, R. (1985) Apperceptive agnosia due to carbon poisoning: an interpretation based on critical band masking from disseminated lesions. *Behavioural Brain Research*, **15**, 227–240.

Caplan, D. (1986). In defense of agrammatism. *Cognition*, **24**, 263–276.

—— (1991) Agrammatism is a theoretically coherent aphasic category. *Brain and Language*, **40**, 274–281.

Caramazza, A. (1986) On drawing inferences about the structure of normal cognitive systems from the analysis of patterns of impaired performance: the case for single-patient studies. *Brain and Cognition*, **5**, 41–66.

—— (1991) Data, statistics, and theory: a comment on Bates, McDonald, MacWhinney, and Applebaum's "A maximum likelihood procedure for the analysis of group and individual data in aphasia research". *Brain and Language*, **41**, 43–51.

Christman, S. S. & Buckingham, H. W. (1989) Jargonaphasia. In *The Characteristics of Aphasia* (ed. C. Code), pp. 111–130. London: Taylor & Francis.

Coltheart, M. (1978) Lexical access in simple reading tasks. In *Strategies of Information Processing* (ed. G. Underwood), pp. 112–174. London: Academic Press.

—— (1980) Deep dyslexia: a right hemisphere hypothesis. In *Deep Dyslexia* (eds M. Coltheart, K. E. Patterson & J. C. Marshall), pp. 326–380. London: Routledge and Kegan Paul.

—— (1985) In defence of dual-route models of reading. *Behavioural and Brain Sciences*, **8**, 709–710.

——, Patterson, K. & Marshall, J. C. (eds) (1987) *Deep Dyslexia* (2nd edn). London: Routledge & Kegan Paul.

Ellis, A. W. & Young, A. W. (1988) *Human Cognitive Neuropsychology*. Hove: Erlbaum.

Fodor, J. A. (1983) *The Modularity of Mind*. Cambridge, MA: MIT Press.

Funnell, E. (1983) Phonological processes in reading: new evidence from acquired dyslexia. *British Journal of Psychology*, **74**, 159–180.

Garrett, M. F. (1980) Levels of processing in sentence production. In *Language Production, Vol. 1: Speech and Talk* (ed. B. Butterworth), pp. 177–220. London: Academic Press.

Geschwind, N. (1972) Language and the brain. *Scientific American*, **226**, 76–83.

Goodglass, H. & Geschwind, N. (1976) Language disorders (aphasia). In *Handbook of Perception, Vol. 7: Language and Speech* (eds E. C. Carterette & M. D. Friedman), pp. 389–428. New York: Academic Press.

Hart, J., Berndt, R. S. & Caramazza, A. (1985) Category-specific naming deficits following cerebral infarction. *Nature*, **316**, 439–440.

Hebb, D. O. (1949) *The Organization of Behaviour*. New York: Wiley.

Hinton, G. E. & Shallice, T. (1991) Lesioning an attractor network: investigations of acquired dyslexia. *Psychological Review*, **98**, 74–95.

Howard, D. & Orchard-Lisle, V. (1984) On the origin of semantic errors in naming: evidence from the case of a global aphasic. *Cognitive Neuropsychology*, 1, 163–190.

Humphreys, G. W. & Riddoch, J. (1984) Routes to object constancy: implications from neurological impairments of object constancy. *Quarterly Journal of Experimental Psychology*, **36A**, 385–415.

—— & Evett, L. J. (1985) Are there independent lexical and nonlexical routes in word processing? An evaluation of the dual-route theory of reading. *Behavioural and Brain Sciences*, **8**, 689–740.

Kay, J. & Ellis, A. W. (1987) A cognitive neuropsychological case study of anomia: implications for psychological models of word retrieval. *Brain*, **110**, 613–629.

Kolb, B. & Whishaw, I. Q. (1990) *Fundamentals of Human Neuropsychology* (3rd edn). New York: Freeman.

McCloskey, M. & Caramazza, A. (1988) Theory and methodology in cognitive neuropsychology: a response to our critics. *Cognitive Neuropsychology*, **5**, 583–623.

Marr, D. (1982) *Vision*. San Francisco: W. H. Freeman.

Marshall, J. C. & Newcombe, F. (1973) Patterns of paralexia: a psycholinguistic approach. *Journal of Psycholinguistic Research*, **2**, 175–199.

Mayes, A. R. (1988) *Human Organic Memory Disorders*. Cambridge: Cambridge University Press.

——, Meudell, P. R. & Pickering, A. (1985) Is amnesia caused by a selective deficit in remembering contextual information? *Cortex*, **21**, 167–202.

Milner, B. (1968) Preface: Material specific and generalised memory loss. *Neuropsychologia*, **6**, 215–234.

Morton, J. (1984) Brain-based and non-brain based models of language. In *Biological Perspectives in Language* (eds D. Caplan, A. R. Lecours & A. Smith). Cambridge, MA: MIT Press.

—— & Patterson, K. E. (1980) A new attempt at an interpretation, or, an attempt at a new interpretation. In *Deep Dyslexia* (eds M. Coltheart, K. E. Patterson & J. C. Marshall), pp. 91–118. London: Routledge and Kegan Paul.

Parkin, A. J. (1984) Amnesic syndrome: A lesion-specific disorder? *Cortex*, **20**, 479–508.

——, Leng, N. R. C. & Stanhope, N. (1988) Memory impairment following ruptured aneurysm of the anterior communicating artery. *Brain and Cognition*, **7**, 231–243.

Patterson, K. E. & Kay, J. (1982) Letter-by-letter reading: psychological descriptions of a neurological syndrome. *Quarterly Journal of Experimental Psychology*, **34A**, 411–441.

——, Marshall, J. C. & Coltheart, M. (eds) (1985) *Surface Dyslexia*. Hove: Erlbaum.

—— & Coltheart, V. (1987) Phonological processes in reading: a tutorial review. In *Attention and Performance XII: The Psychology of Reading* (ed. M. Coltheart), pp. 421–448. Hove: Erlbaum.

——, Seidenberg, M. S. & McClelland, J. (1989) Connections and disconnections: acquired dyslexia in a computational model of reading processes. In *Parallel Distributed Processing: Implications for Psychology and Neurobiology* (ed. R. G. M. Morris), pp. 131–181. Oxford: Clarendon Press.

Riddoch, J. (1990) Neglect and the peripheral dyslexias. *Cognitive Neuropsychology*, **7**, 369–389.

—— & Humphreys, G. W. (1987) A case of integrative visual agnosia. *Brain*, **110**, 1431–1462.

Sacks, O. (1985) *The Man Who Mistook His Wife For a Hat*. London: Picador.

Saffran, E. M., Bogyo, L. C., Schwartz, M. F., *et al* (1980) Does deep dyslexia reflect right-hemisphere reading? In *Deep Dyslexia* (eds M. Coltheart, K. E. Patterson & J. C. Marshall), pp. 381–406. London: Routledge and Kegan Paul.

Schacter, D. L. (1987) Implicit memory: history and current status. *Journal of Experimental Psychology: Learning, Memory, and Cognition*, **13**, 501–518.

Schwartz, M. (1987) Patterns of speech production deficit within and across aphasia syndromes: application of a psycholinguistic model. In *The Cognitive Neuropsychology of Language* (eds M. Coltheart, G. Sartori & R. Job), pp. 163–199. London: Erlbaum.

Seidenberg, M. S. (1988) Cognitive neuropsychology and language: the state of the art. *Cognitive Neuropsychology*, **5**, 403–426.

Shallice, T. (1988) *From Neuropsychology to Mental Structure*. Cambridge: Cambridge University Press.

—— & Warrington, E. K. (1970) Independent functioning of verbal memory stores: A neuropsychological study. *Quarterly Journal of Experimental Psychology*, **22**, 261–273.

—— & —— (1977) The possible role of selective attention in acquired dyslexia. *Neuropsychologia*, **15**, 31–41.

Squire, L. R. (1982) Comparisons between forms of amnesia: some deficits are unique to Korsakoff syndrome. *Journal of Experimental Psychology: Learning, Memory, and Cognition*, **8**, 560–571.

Warrington, E. K. & Taylor, A. M. (1973) The contribution of the right parietal lobe to object recognition. *Cortex*, **9**, 152–164.

—— & Shallice, T. (1984) Category specific semantic impairments. *Brain*, **107**, 829–853.

Weiskrantz, L. (1985) Issues and theories in the study of the amnesic syndrome. In *Memory Systems of the Brain* (eds N. M. Weinberger *et al*). New York: Guilford.

Wilson, B. & Baddeley, A. (1988) Semantic, episodic, and autobiographical memory in a postmeningitic amnesic patient. *Brain and Cognition*, **8**, 31–46.

Zaidel, E. & Peters, A. M. (1981) Phonological encoding and idiographic reading by the disconnected right hemisphere: two case studies. *Brain and Language*, **14**, 205–234.

6 Neuropsychology and psychometry

Steve Hallett

The psychometric approach • Validity and reliability • Common psychometric procedures in clinical practice • Clinical use of psychometric tests • Psychometry and neurology • Summary

---

Neuropsychology is concerned with understanding the relationship between brain structure and human function (cognition, perception, sensation, emotion, and behaviour), in the 'normal' person, the brain-damaged person, or those with formal psychiatric disturbance (see also Chapter 5).

One key aim of the neuropsychologist is to diagnose brain damage by quantifying the cognitive or intellectual status of an individual and interpreting these changes in terms of a model of brain function.

In addition, the neuropsychologist may be asked to assess and quantify the precise characteristics of the consequences of brain damage, for the following specific reasons:

(1) to determine the strengths and weaknesses of an individual's abilities and to institute a rehabilitation programme to remedy disability
(2) to determine change of function over time as a consequence of treatment or injury
(3) to discriminate between the neurological and psychiatric consequences of brain injury.

Why such questions require formal assessment becomes clear if we look at some examples.

One might be to determine the precise nature and characteristics of short-term memory loss following a road traffic accident in which someone incurred a closed head injury. The individual may have, for example, experienced a concussion, or may be suffering psychological changes associated with post-traumatic anxiety, or both. In principle both processes may be expected to exert an adverse effect on an individual's concentration and short-term memory, and it may not be possible to discriminate cause purely on the basis of observation or interview. In such an instance, formal neuropsychological assessment may quantify the nature and extent of cognitive change by the use of psychometric procedures which are highly sensitive to the effects of brain damage.

Thus, by interpreting the pattern and intensity of memory loss, the clinician is in a better position to discriminate between the roles that organic and psychological factors may play in the perceived memory loss.

A second example would be determining the likely cortical site of damage on the basis of reported disturbance of function.

Formal assessment can determine the precise weaknesses in the complex cognitive processes involved in memory, and the additional use of tests which are regionally sensitive (that is, are able to assess specific functions known to be subserved by, for example, temporal or frontal systems) is central to such discrimination.

It is not suggested that neuropsychological assessment is the only way of quantifying the effects or presence of brain damage, nor that assessment is required with everyone, but that, used in skilled hands, it is an invaluable tool for diagnostic, prognostic, and therapeutic decision making.

The psychometric approach

The process of neuropsychological assessment is not a uniform one across patients or presenting problems, and the psychometric approach should be seen as one method within this process.

The psychometric approach may be viewed as both a perspective and a method.

The psychometric perspective

As a perspective, the psychometric approach states that brain function can be understood as arising from the action of key anatomical sites of processing. In many ways it can be seen to parallel the view expressed by some personality theorists who argue for the presence of key traits or characteristics (e.g. Kline, 1980).

The heart of this approach lies in terms of the understanding of brain function and hence brain damage. Function can be seen as being subserved by demarcated areas of cortical and subcortical tissue; for example, intelligence within the frontal lobes, or language within the left cerebral hemisphere.

This view arose because of the success in, for example, delimiting the processes of vision and visual perception to certain areas within the occipital and temporal lobes, and it has been tempting to assume that this is also true of other functions.

This 'localisationist' approach initially arose from studies of people with known brain damage who had related changes in cognitive function. Thus the observations of Broca, Dax, and Wernicke in the 19th century of identifiable and differential disturbance of language function in relation to specific damage from closed and penetrating head injury led to the attractive view that certain gross features of language were clearly localised.

Thus the psychometric approach in neuroscience is founded on the concept that brain damage, and more importantly its effects, is a unitary, singular process. This, in turn, led to the need to find methods of assessing brain function and the effects of brain damage which could be relied upon to give accurate descriptions of dysfunction which would point to localised and localisable disturbance of the central nervous system (CNS)

The psychometric method

There are certain key elements in the methods of testing that arise from this approach.

(1) Tests are administered in a standard way

This means that there are inflexible guidelines for the instructions and presentation of stimulus material for testing. Such instructions are invariant across clinicians and patients, irrespective of individual differences. Within this approach there is no manoeuvre for modifying the administration to take account of the individual client or to test an individual's function to its limits.

(2) Similar guidelines are offered for the scoring of individual test items

The administration of lengthy and protracted tests is therefore reducible to the recording of numbers.

(3) All test items are administered

All test items within a battery are administered regardless of individual need, since the interpretation of the scores ultimately rests on complete administration.

(4) Test batteries or items incorporate a statistical heritage

The value of batteries or items is determined by administration to a large number of the population to determine the variability of test scores within the general population, the variation across and between sexes, and which items are useful in the discrimination of certain pathological states. In addition, such tests achieve their discrimination by a statistical elimination process whereby performance on certain tests is numerically compared in known clinical populations (be this for disease processes, such as dementia, or for localisable insults, such as temporal or frontal damage).

Those tests able to discriminate at an accepted level of statistical accuracy are retained, and those that cannot are removed.

(5) Interpretation is statistically assisted

On the basis of item 4 above, the interpretation of a test battery is statistically assisted. Thus, a person's score and score variation, when corrected for age or education, are compared against the scores and variation for identifiable pathological groups and the normal population.

Advantages of the psychometric approach

The psychometric or test battery approach is the simplest and probably the most cost-effective method for neuropsychological assessment, especially if assessment is carried out by inexperienced practitioners (Box 6.1). Its reliance on a standardised format and normative data makes it an easy tool for diagnosis and discrimination.

There are certainly other advantages to such an approach beyond simplicity and cost effectiveness. Thus the emphasis on standardisation and normative data means there is less emphasis on clinical intuition. Additionally, psychometric procedures are attractive tools for comparative research.

Test batteries, by virtue of assessing a broad range of cognitive function, tend to focus on individual strengths and weaknesses, although such qualities are not exclusive to this approach. In a similar fashion the broad assessment of behaviour makes it unlikely that significant cerebral functions will remain unmonitored and hence this increases the probability of correct diagnosis.

Finally, it may be noted at this stage that at a scientific as well as clinical level the psychometric approach is more likely to be amenable to statistical analysis, and hence it is possible to determine and to monitor such important factors as Reliability and Validity (see below).

Box 6.1 The advantages of the psychometric method

Simplicity
Cost-effectiveness
Reliance on standardised, normative data
Objectivity
Focus on the individual
Aid to correct diagnosis
Amenability for statistical analysis
Allows monitoring of reliability and validity

Box 6.2 The disadvantages of the psychometric approach

It is atheoretical

It lacks a driving theory of cognition

Its reliance on global measures and statistical guidelines hinders the elucidation of the relationship between CNS structure and function

The time taken to administer some test batteries is too long; sometimes redundant information is produced

Allows the misconception that it is easy to assess brain function

---

Disadvantages of the psychometric approach

There are, however, a number of weaknesses to this approach and these may be outlined as follows (see also Box 6.2).

The major disadvantage of the test battery approach is that it is atheoretical and hence lacks a driving theory of cognitive function. This means it is not always possible to translate the test results into inferences as to how the brain actually works, or what aspects of cognitive processing may be dysfunctional.

A quantitative approach which relies on global measures and statistical guidelines cannot in a real sense elucidate the relationship between individual CNS structure and function. As such, the application of percentile scores or standard scores does not in itself contribute to the understanding of the underlying deficits in brain dysfunction. This aspect is based upon the knowledge, experience, and skill of the clinician.

The inflexible and redundant nature of the administration of psychometric test batteries may unselectively focus on irrelevant areas, at the expense of time. Thus the Halstead–Reitan Battery (see, for example, Lezak, 1983) may take up to eight hours to administer when much of the information it gives, with some people, may be redundant to diagnosis.

Finally, the test battery approach gives rise to the misconception that it is easy to assess brain function and that interpretation is a relatively straightforward process. It fosters the idea that a poor score on a certain test is invariably related to specific damage.

Thus, it may be that individuals with, for example, temporal lobe lesions perform poorly on test 'A'. It is therefore tempting to interpret every subsequent poor performance on that test as being consistent with temporal lobe disturbance.

This stems from the attitude of this approach that brain function is easily localisable and it ignores the possibility that complex cognitive processing reflects networked interactions between separate cortical and subcortical sites as much as it reflects the operation of single sites.

There is, therefore, a growing awareness that in its clinical and research application, the psychometric approach must be tempered with more intuitive and hypothesis-driven methods (e.g. Gilandas *et al*, 1984).

Validity and reliability

In general, any attempt to measure human behaviour, cognition, and emotion needs to be able to do so according to certain criteria. These criteria, validity and reliability, are not the exclusive domain of psychometry, but psychometric testing is clearly amenable to the statistical manipulations necessary to determine these criteria.

Validity

Validity poses the fundamental question as to whether a specific method of measurement actually measures what it sets out to measure. It asks the question, for example, "does this assessment of extroversion actually measure extroversion?" This example was chosen (as opposed to, for example, language production) because it highlights a number of complexities:

(1) Is there such a process as extroversion, and, if so, what are its characteristics?
(2) Does the method of measurement we use assess this process?
(3) Does it measure all aspects of the process of extroversion or only certain key attributes?
(4) Does the method of measurement of extroversion and the resultant score tell us anything about the operation of extroversion in real life?
(5) Does the method of measurement of extroversion actually seem to measure this?

In other words, if we examine the assessment of extroversion, can we see that it measures this as opposed to any other process?

The above list outlines a number of types of validity which include conceptual validity (2 and 3), face validity (5), and ecological validity (4). It must be stated that not all tests do, or need to, fulfil all types of validity in order to be seen as useful tests.

Validity is statistically determined in a number of ways. One such method would be to determine the closeness of correlation between a putative test of a function and other known tests of the same function. A second method would be to determine the discriminative accuracy of certain aspects of the test, retaining those which add to accuracy and removing those which detract from it. A final method is that of factor analysis to determine the underlying structure of tests in terms of their purity, or lack thereof, in assessing a specific attribute.

In addition to the above, one must raise the issue of conceptual validity or perhaps ontological validity – namely, does the process we seek to assess actually exist? This may seem a little odd to raise. But, for example, we might draw an analogy from a different sphere to illustrate the need for raising such an issue at this stage.

In the realm of subatomic physics the massless, chargeless neutrino was invoked to balance the logical and mathematical equation of radioactive decay. The quark was invoked to encapsulate theory concerning the constituent aspects of electrons, protons, and neutrons, in order to arrive at a hypothesis defining the consistency and similarities between fundamental units of matter. Both types of particle could not be directly observed: both gave a cohesiveness to quantum theory, but only by virtue of their mathematical sense.

Invoking the terms 'neutrino' and 'quark' was an epistemological convenience and not an ontological reality. In a similar way, if we had discovered quantum mechanics before classical mechanics, then the terms 'mass', 'weight, and 'charge' would be meaningless, and yet we use them as if they are real attributes.

This raises the real possibility that certain procedures and tests may act as highly valid and reliable measures of convenient labels rather than actual properties.

Reliability

Reliability refers to the degree to which a given test is able to show an aspect of repeatability. Thus one type would be referred to as test–retest reliability – examining the consistency of scores on tests within the same person over time.

While this may seem easy to determine, such reliability needs to be offset against the reactive process of the 'practice effect', and clearly needs to be determined in an unvarying population in which it would not be expected that a cognitive function will change in and of itself over time.

A second aspect of reliability would be defined as inter-rater. This may refer to the reliability of assessing a particular function in terms of its administration by two independent administrators (using the standardised assessment guidelines), or may refer to the scoring of particular items and the degree to which this may be consistent across raters.

Reliability is most often statistically determined either by reliability coefficients (that is, correlational methods) or by use of the standard error of measurement (which may be defined as the band of error which is around a person's theoretical true score; it is an estimate of the standard deviation of the score on a test if that person could be assessed a large number of times without the intervening factors of fatigue and practice).

Reliability and validity in practice

Clearly, a test or battery can be highly reliable as a procedure with exceptionally low statistically determined validity and obviously the reverse is also true (a valid but unreliable indicator).

One of the criticisms of a number of psychometric tests is that they have acceptably high inter-rater and test–retest reliability but low conceptual, face, or ecological validity, and this relates to some of the disadvantages outlined earlier in terms of interpreting the results of neuropsychological tests in respect of brain dysfunction.

An example of good validity

If we take a relatively discrete process such as primary visual perception, then it is possible to manufacture certain procedures which assess particular aspects of this process and no other. By using normal populations and those with definable organic impairment it may prove possible to modify the procedure to the point where it is extremely accurate at describing the perceptual correlates of impaired visual processing and clearly separating this impairment from the normal variation in perception in non-injured populations. Administration of the same test to those who have a variety of other cognitive disturbances which exclude the above may also determine the accuracy of the test in identifying only central aspects of visual perception as opposed to other types of processing, thus reducing the chances of misidentification.

The processes involved in visual perception are among the most researched in neuropsychology and allied fields, to the point where it is possible to localise the processes to certain specific and discrete areas of cortical tissue within the occipital areas and even down to certain types of neuron. There are, therefore, a number of anatomical and electro-physiological methods for localising the relationship between certain disturbances and damage to the occipital cortex. Such methods are safe for clinical use and provide a way of determining the reliability of the performance task.

The process then of determining the reliability and validity of such a test of visual perception is relatively straightforward.

An example of questionable validity

At the other extreme we may take the case of a standard assessment of intellectual function such as the Wechsler Adult Intelligence Scale – Revised (WAIS–R; Wechsler, 1981).

Reliability such as inter-rater and test–retest are straightforward to demonstrate and, if this is not too tautological a statement, the essence of psychometric tests at a methodological level is the ease of demonstrating such reliability by virtue of their rigid guidelines for administration and scoring.

Addressing the issue of validity is much more hazardous. The manual to the WAIS–R addresses the issue of the validity of the test in two specific ways.

Firstly, it raises the issue of high intercorrelation with other tests of intelligence such as the WAIS and Wechsler–Bellevue Scale, both predecessors of the WAIS–R. These procedures are themselves derived from an amalgamation of individual test items which were considered to assess intelligence in educational practice.

The second aspect of statistical validity is in terms of the factor analytical structure; that is, statistically determining common denominators of processing across separate subtest components. What this tells us (and importantly so) is the need to measure verbal and non-verbal intellectual skills separately, rather than treat intelligence as a single, global process.

Omitted from any description of validity in such manuals is a real determination of the existence of intelligence as a complex cognitive process. This is not the place to enter into a central debate as to the existence of intelligence as a definable and meaningful complex cognitive action, or of the existence and value of the measurable IQ, but this is raised to illustrate certain issues.

It has to be said, for example, that the WAIS–R is an extremely robust tool for assessing certain definable cognitive processes, and it epitomises the qualities and strengths of the psychometric approach.

It also exemplifies the weaknesses of that approach in terms of understanding the significance of performance on such tests, the degree to which it measures a meaningful and identifiable cognitive process, and the degree to which that process might be localisable (even in a loose sense of the word) to the CNS.

Common psychometric procedures in clinical practice

There are literally hundreds of psychometric tests available which assess different facets of cognitive function. To acquaint the reader with psychometric procedures, however, it is useful to concisely describe some of the more commonly used tests.

(1) Wechsler Adult Intelligence Scale – Revised (WAIS–R)

The WAIS–R is probably the most universally used assessment of intelligence. While it was devised as an 'IQ', test it should also be viewed as a broad-spectrum assessment of cognitive function. The test comprises 11 individual subtests, six of which assess verbal skills, and five of which are described as performance or non-verbal tests. In addition to this broad verbal/non-verbal distinction, it is worth noting that four of the five performance subscales require a motor output.

Briefly, the subtests may be described as follows.

Verbal Scale

Vocabulary – assesses a person's ability to define correctly words of increasing complexity.

Arithmetic – simple arithmetic calculation and reasoning ability.

Comprehension – verbal problem solving, practical reasoning, and social understanding.

Information – general knowledge.

Digit span – immediate attentional span; sequencing ability.

Similarities – verbal reasoning (concept formation), abstraction, and synthesis.

Performance Scale

Picture completion – visual recognition and organisation (recognition and naming of missing components of pictures of common scenes).

Block design – visuospatial organisation, constructional ability (reproduction of patterned designs).

Picture arrangement – visuospatial organisation, sequencing, and concept formation (correct ordering of picture story scenes).

Object assembly – visual organisation and concept formation ('jigsaw puzzle' construction).

Digit symbol – symbol substitution task assessing motor speed, attention, visual–verbal transformation.

The WAIS-R subtests are administered in a definable order with the subject's verbatim responses recorded. Precise guidelines are available for scoring of items within each subtest – the result being a series of raw score totals. These are converted to scaled scores which are then summated to arrive at verbal, performance, and full-scale (overall) scaled scores. The final procedure is to convert the three summated scaled scores to IQs.

Interpretation of the WAIS–R, beyond simple determination of IQs, is a complex process of statistical comparison both to population figures and within the subject's profile, and is also amenable to qualitative analysis.

(2) Wechsler Memory Scale – Revised (WMS–R)

The WMS–R provides a broad assessment of predominantly short-term memory and learning. Administration takes, on average, 45 minutes and comprises the following.

Information and orientation – simple assessment of autobiographical memory, spatial and temporal orientation.

Mental Control – rote memory for automatised sequences.

Figural memory – visual recognition memory.

Logical memory – immediate and delayed recall for stories.

Visual reproduction – immediate and delayed recall for designs.

Digit span – immediate auditory/verbal attention and sequencing.

Visual span – immediate visual/non-verbal attention and sequencing.

Paired associate learning – new verbal learning ability (incorporating a delayed recall trial).

Visual paired associates – new spatial learning (incorporating a delayed recall trial).

While no one test or battery may be seen to assess memory in all of its facets, the WMS–R may be seen as a robust general screen. Scores on each subtest are summated to provide indexes of general, visual, non-verbal, and delayed memory, as well as an attention/concentration index.

The WMS–R is an extremely useful diagnostic test which contains norms for discriminating between memory disturbance of organic and psychometric origin.

(3) The Halstead–Reitan Neuropsychological Battery (HRNB)

The HRNB is one of the most commonly used single batteries for diagnosing brain damage. This test was first developed in the USA and comprises 11 components, briefly described as follows:

(a) Wechsler Adult Intelligence Scale (see above)

(b) Minnesota Multiphasic Personality Inventory

(c) Trail Making Test (motor speed, visuo-motor coordination, number and letter sequencing, category alternation)

(d) Category Test (hypothesis formation and testing, planning, and organisation)

(e) Speech Sounds Perception Test (phonemic discrimination, attentional processing)

(f) Seashore Rhythm Test (rhythm and pitch discrimination, attention)

(g) Aphasia Screen (brief, broadly ranging assessment of language comprehension and production)

(h) Tactual Performance Test (spatial memory and learning, uni- and bimanual coordination)

(i) Finger Oscillation Test (pure motor speed of dominant and non-dominant hand).

(j) Dynanometer (dominant and non-dominant hand grip strength)

(k) Sensory Perceptual Examination (finger agnosia; finger tip number writing; astereognosis; visual, auditory, and manual suppressions).

This protracted battery may typically take about five hours to administer with a motivated subject. Its strengths lie in respect of robust normative data for normal, organic, and psychiatric populations and in an extremely high discriminative accuracy of about 85–90%.

(4) Rennick Repeatable Battery

The Rennick battery may be considered an offshoot of the HRNB and comprises a series of short tests which are sensitive to organic impairment as well as small but definable changes over time. The test comprises:

(a) the Trail Making Test
(b) the Dynanometer and Finger Oscillation Test
    (both from the Halstead–Reitan Battery)
(c) the Digit Symbol subtest from the WAIS or WAIS–R (this subtest being considered one of the most sensitive indicators of organic impairment on the Wechsler scale)
(d) the Visual Search Test (assessing visual scanning and visuoperceptual recognition and matching)
(e) the Colour Naming Test (colour hue discrimination and naming speed)
(f) the Digit Vigilance Task (sustained concentration)
(g) sentence writing.

The advantages of this battery are that it comprises a number of procedures which are sensitive to brain damage; the norms provide indices for severity of impairment (rather than just a single cut-off score) and finally that each test comprises five equivalent forms. This latter facility enables the same functions to be assessed in a repeatable fashion over a short period with negligible practice effect. As such, it is a reliable tool for assessing change of function over time as a consequence of, for example, deterioration, treatment, recovery from trauma, or fluctuation of emotional status.

(5) The Stroop Colour–Word Interference Test

This test is essentially a speed of naming assessment comprising three subtests:

(a) the subject reads out from a series of 100 colour-words (the words red, green, and blue repeated in a randomised fashion)
(b) the subject reads out a similar randomised format of colour hues
(c) the subject is presented with an interference process whereby the colour name (e.g. red) is written in a disparate colour hue (e.g. blue) with the subject instructed to read the colour hue only.

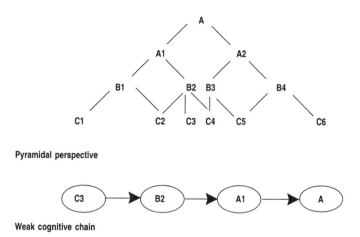

Pyramidal perspective

Weak cognitive chain

Fig. 6.1 In the pyramidal model, complex functions are seen to be divisible into simpler units (from level A to C) such that it is possible to assess which level and type of function may be impaired. This can be achieved either with tests which assess a single process or those in which it may be possible to rule out a single process (e.g. comparing tests which assess overlapping functions such as A1/B1/C1 and A1/B1/C2). In this fashion it may be possible to identify the path of weak cognitive chains.

Low scores across all three components (referred to as Word, Colour, and Colour-Word Series, respectively) are associated with lesions in the dominant hemisphere; selectively low colour and colour-word scores reflect lesions in the non-dominant hemisphere; a singular lowering of the colour-word series is mostly seen in cases of frontal damage.

This procedure benefits from speed and ease of administration, applicability across a wide age range (5–75 years), and ease of repeatability. The Stroop test exemplifies a group of easily administered test procedures which are sensitive to brain damage and, because of their speed of administration, can be used alongside more lengthy procedures.

Categorising psychometric tests

The above brief descriptions convey an impression of the types of procedures in common usage. There are a number of ways in which one might categorise psychometric tests in clinical usage.

The simplest categorisation is as follows, although there is clearly some overlap in function:

(1) organic batteries (conglomerate tests with highly accurate diagnostic ability)
(2) tests of global cognitive processing (general, broad-based procedures

which assess functional units such as language comprehension or global processes such as intelligence)

(3) organic screening tests (often easily administered tests with poor localisability but accurate discriminability)

(4) tests of individual functions (tests which assess specific and key aspects of global function such as short-term auditory/verbal memory; rate of learning and forgetting; visuospatial sequencing)

(5) neurological tests (tests of discrete sensory, motor, or perceptual function).

It is perhaps important to reiterate in conclusion that the presence of a plethora of tests should not imply a 'cook-book' approach to neuropsychological assessment. Instead, psychometric procedures should be visualised as the methods or tools whereby the neuropsychologist attempts to understand the person's cognitive strengths and weaknesses.

Assessment geared towards diagnosis is envisaged as the identification of weak links in an overall cognitive chain which is achieved by the testing of both global, or higher-order, cognitive functions and of the more discrete cognitive processes which may be visualised as 'simpler' subdivisions of these global abilities (see Fig. 6.1).

Clinical use of psychometric tests

In a chapter of this nature it would be inappropriate and nearly impossible to cover all of the major uses of psychometric testing as applied to clinical neuropsychology. The focus here, therefore, is on the strengths and weaknesses of psychometric decision making within psychiatry and neurology by the use of appropriate case examples.

Neuropsychology and psychiatry

The application of clinical neuropsychology to the psychiatric field lies chiefly in the ability to discriminate between known psychiatric disturbance and neurological deficits. Such decision making may assist diagnosis, the placement of a patient, and the selection of appropriate treatment regimens.

This decision-making process is, often, a difficult one, since current research strongly indicates that a number of psychiatric disturbances may reflect, at some level, a disturbance of CNS processing. Thus biological factors have been strongly implicated in the pathogenesis of schizophrenia, manic–depressive psychosis, endogenous depression, and certain types of hysteria (Yamamoto *et al*, 1987). In a similar mode there is sufficient evidence to suggest cognitive, electrophysiological, and biochemical changes in reactive depression and anxiety states (op. cit.). Indeed, neuropsychological assessment in its research capacity has often been a central component in the database which supports the hypothesis of organic determinants of some psychiatric disturbances.

Given this database, the determination of organic deficits by virtue of assessment is not, in itself, sufficient to allow for discriminative interpretations.

To exemplify this process, the following case examples are introduced.

Case example 1

A 53-year-old, right-handed woman had presented with a two-month history of sudden memory loss. Specifically, she was reported to have retained long-term memory while exhibiting short-term memory loss. After referral by her general practitioner she was admitted for psychiatric assessment, after which it was felt that her symptoms chiefly reflected the onset of depression. To clarify the nature of her memory loss, she was referred out of her health district for neuropsychological assessment.

Interview suggested a perceived sharp decline in short-term memory, especially for verbal material. Before this she reported no everyday difficulties in memory, nor any obvious cognitive disturbance. The decline in memory was not associated with any obvious precipitating factor, but since that time the client had needed to resort to the use of a diary and notebook to keep track.

The nature of the difficulties included problems in recalling the names of people she had known well, difficulties in recalling conversations, instructions and telephone numbers, and difficulties in retaining information after reading or watching the television. The client did not report any obvious difficulties in concentrating beyond the fact that interruption of a task produced subsequent difficulties in remembering, and that at times she had difficulty in concentrating on what other people were saying.

In addition, there were certain spatial difficulties such as misplacing objects and occasional disorientation in place. The client also reported a slowing of her mental speed of processing.

There was evidence from the interview to indicate symptoms of depression, which included loss of motivation, energy, and drive, bouts of unexplained tearfulness, and negative or self-depreciatory thoughts.

Within her personal and family history there was evidence of psychiatric disturbance in key relatives, although she had had no previous admissions or investigations. There was no relevant medical history in her own personal background but a close member of the family had suffered a cerebrovascular accident (CVA) many years before.

Initial assessment indicated that she was disoriented in both time and place. Her initial level of concentration, as assessed by digit span forward, was within normal limits, but her digits backwards were, by contrast, much lower (digits forward 7, digits backwards 3), suggesting difficulties in sequencing and manipulating information.

Assessment of her immediate memory for verbal material
suggested that she was able to retain only 20% of verbal material
and 36% of spatial material.

The major component of her assessment was by the Standardised
Luria–Nebraska Neuropsychological Battery (LNNB); before
discussing the results of this, it is useful to outline some of the major
characteristics of this assessment battery.

The LNNB

The LNNB was devised by Golden *et al* (1980) as a successful attempt to
standardise the qualitative assessment approach of A. R. Luria. It consists
of 279 test items which can, for convenience, be grouped into definable
clinical sections such as motor function, memory, and so on.

The test is a comprehensive assessment of fundamental and higher-
order cognitive function which provides a quantifiable description of
cognitive strengths and weaknesses; from this description, inferences as
to localisation of disturbance can be made. Each item is scored as normal
(0), probably organic (1), or definitely organic (2), and initial analysis
consists of summating the scores for each of 11 clinical scales and then
converting these scores into 'T' (or transformed) scores for easy
comparison.

The resultant profile (see Fig. 6.2) can be used to make initial
determinations of organicity. For assistance in interpretation, the scores
can be reordered and placed within a localisation profile (see Fig. 6.3).
This localisation chart is statistically, not empirically, determined, and
consists of those items which are statistically most commonly
underperformed in groups with definable and discrete damage to specific
areas of the neocortex.

This is not the forum to enter into a major discussion of the procedures
for analysis of the LNNB, but the fundamental aspects of interpretation are
discussed within the framework of the case under question.

Statistically, however, the LNNB is considered to be able to discriminate
accurately between organic and non-organic disturbance in approximately
86% of cases, and, as such, it may be seen as an extremely useful tool for
diagnosis, comparing extremely favourably with the diagnostic accuracy
of other methods, such as electroencephalography and computerised
tomography.

Case 1 *(continued)*
The initial interpretation of the LNNB is from the clinical scales shown
in Fig. 6.2. To arrive at an individual profile, a critical level is
constructed, based upon the person's age and educational
experience, this being set for T = 65 in this case. With normal subjects,
their T scores across the clinical scales are expected to be within
a narrow range below the critical level, in the order of T = 20 points.

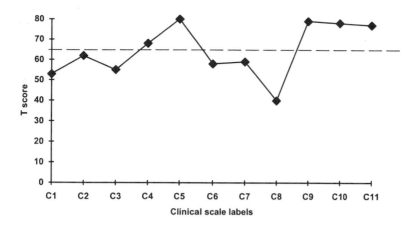

Fig. 6.2 Primary clinical scales of the LNNB (from case example 1, a woman who suffered a CVA): C1–C11 are, respectively, motor, rhythm, tactile, visual, receptive speech, expressive speech, reading, writing, arithmetic, memory, and intellectual processes. The dotted line indicates the critical level.

In this case, five of the clinical scales are elevated above critical level, and the overall spread of scores is 40 T points, strongly suggesting that the profile is consistent with organic impairment. Those scales above the critical level are visual processing (C4), receptive speech (C5), arithmetic (C9), memory (C10), and intellectual processes (C11). This profile is one which is inconsistent with the effects of anxiety and depression.

It should be noted that the labels of the clinical scales do not mean that the items that comprise a particular scale are purely tests of a single function. Rather it should be seen that there are certain common cognitive elements running through such tests which suggest a loading on a particular function, but that they are in other respects heterogeneous.

The further analysis of the test is executed by a finer-grained inspection of subscale elements. In this manner it was noted that the elevation on the arithmetic scale (which can often occur in people with poor educational experience) reflected poor abilities in sequencing and manipulation of material, as well as in extracting mathematical information from language-based problems (in other words, this latter problem reflected an aspect of language comprehension).

Closer inspection of the visual scale similarly indicated difficulties in manipulating and ordering of visually presented material. The patient's performance on the intellectual processes scale suggested that she had particular difficulties in higher-order reasoning and in items requiring planning and sequencing.

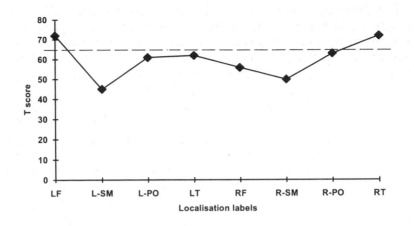

Fig. 6.3 Localisation profile from the LNNB (from case example 1): L, left; R, right; F, frontal; SM, sensorimotor; PO, parieto-occipital; T, temporal. The dotted line indicates the critical level.

Finally, her performance on the memory scale suggested both verbal and non-verbal memory difficulties, the former being more impaired.

The interpretation of these results was that they reflected possible discrete areas of disturbance in the dominant and non-dominant hemispheres. The inference from the data was of possible dominant frontal disturbance and an additional focus of disturbance in more posterior areas.

An additional non-dominant focus may be inferred from aspects of poor performance on spatial memory and visuospatial processing and the nature of the deficits would be consistent with a discrete non-dominant temporal lobe disturbance.

Inspection of the localisation profile (Fig. 6.3) confirms two discrete peaks above critical level in the left frontal and right temporal regions, with additional but lower peaks in the left temporal and parieto-occipital and right parieto-occipital areas.

The neuropsychological assessment would be interpreted as an organic impairment of a multifocal nature rather than suggesting that the patient's perceived memory disturbance reflected psychological disturbance. On the basis of this assessment, further investigations were requested.

At the end of the investigations, the cumulative medical data suggested a cerebrovascular disturbance and that the sudden onset of cognitive disturbance reflected a CVA. In fact this patient later succumbed to a second CVA, with the focus being the non-dominant middle cerebral artery.

The above case illustrates a number of the issues raised earlier in this chapter, and highlights the practical utility of neuropsychological assessment in such discriminations. This should not imply that such assessment ought to be a standard adjunct to other forms of investigative procedure, or that the psychometric qualities of neuropsychological assessment confer a simplicity of interpretation or a cookbook approach to diagnosis. The localisation chart above, for example, clearly concurs with the interpretation derived from individual test item indicators. Such clear profiles are not, however, the norm, and the key to interpretation lies in accounting for the pattern of the clinical and localisation charts in conjunction with fine-grained analysis of performance on individual test items.

Clearly, to illustrate some of the qualities of assessment and its use, a promising case example has been chosen. It must not be thought, however, that neuropsychological assessment is a panacea for all diagnostic ills, and in many instances it can be used not as a stand-alone system, but as an adjunct to other types of investigation.

It is, therefore, perhaps worth reiterating that psychometric assessment in neuropsychology is an assessment of cognitive process and not of brain integrity or brain damage *per se*. The ultimate qualities required for appropriate interpretation are understanding the uses and limitations of the tools, and using the right tool for the right job, but successful interpretation ultimately relies on the skill of the clinician.

The above case also highlights certain conceptual problems raised at the beginning of this section, namely the ability of psychometric procedures to distinguish organic from psychiatric disturbances in the face of evidence that certain types of psychiatric disturbance may have a biological basis.

In respect of depression, it is assumed that, at a general level, disturbance of mood, ideation, and psychomotor ability may have the effect of dampening a person's performance on tests. Thus it might be inferred that tests which have a principal motor component may be poorly performed by depressed subjects by virtue of psychomotor retardation. Tests which load heavily on initial and sustained concentration may also be poorly performed, by virtue of inappropriate and negative thinking and cognitive speed, reduced by the lowered energy, motivation, and drive in depression. The net effect of this would perhaps be to produce a general lowering of performance across a range of apparently dissimilar tests. The profile above is certainly not consistent with this generalised depression of performance.

More specifically, there is evidence that depression is associated with disturbances in non-dominant hemisphere function, and that mood disturbance is an emotional manifestation of dysfunction in spatial information-perceiving systems (Flor-Henry, 1983).

Figures 6.4 and 6.5 display, respectively, a clinical scale and localisation profile from a depressed person. There are a few essential features from these profiles which can be used in comparison with those of the previous case. First, the overall spread of scores across the scales of the clinical

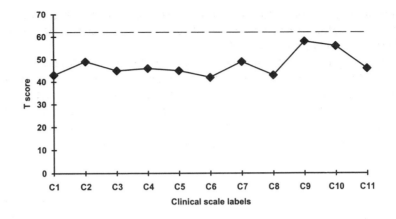

Fig. 6.4 Primary clinical scales of the LNNB, from case example 2 (a depressed man): C1–C11 are, respectively, motor, rhythm, tactile, visual, receptive speech, expressive speech, reading, writing, arithmetic, memory, and intellectual processes. The dotted line indicates the critical level.

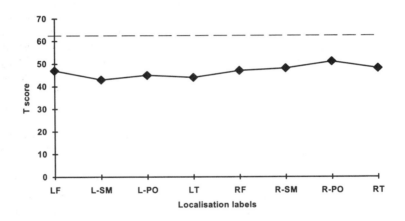

Fig. 6.5 Localisation profile from the LNNB (from case example 2): L, left; R, right; F, frontal; SM, sensorimotor; PO, parieto-occipital; T, temporal. The dotted line indicates the critical level.

profile is small, and the general elevation is low. All clinical scale items also lie below the individual's critical level.

The only relative peaks to emerge are on arithmetic and memory, and closer inspection reveals that this reflects spatial memory disturbance and certain spatial analytical difficulties on certain mathematical equations. The localisation profile is again quite flat, and the only relative peak is over the right parieto-occipital area. This profile accords well with the conclusions of research studies on depressed patients which report non-dominant parietal disturbances, perhaps reflecting spatial perceptual difficulties (Yamamoto *et al*, 1987).

The depressed profile contrasts with that of the case example, and this again fosters the view that the deficits perceived by the patient were not reflective of depression. While the neuropsychological research on depression is relatively sparce and it would not be possible to form firm conclusions, the data do point to the ability to achieve discriminations at a clinical level by psychometric assessment procedures.

Case example 2

A 61-year-old man was referred with poor memory, concentration, and problem-solving abilities following an accident in which he had been struck by a blunt object at work, some six months previously. He remembered all events up to and including the impact, and claimed to have been unconscious for five or so minutes.

Initial symptoms on arrival at hospital were headaches, unsteadiness, slow speech, and word-finding difficulties. Skull X-ray and computerised tomography scan were both normal.

At neuropsychological evaluation he reported that his speech difficulties had recovered within weeks of the accident, but that he had continued to experience difficulties with concentration, memory, and problem solving. He found it difficult to sustain an initially high level of concentration over time – he began to lose the thread after 10–20 minutes. His memory difficulties were characterised by poor short-term memory recall for verbal items such as conversations, instructions, and reading.

Finally his decline in intellectual skills manifested itself as slower ability in solving work and everyday problems and being "unable to think things through clearly".

Neuropsychological assessment comprised administration of the WAIS–R, the Adult Memory and Information Processing Battery (or AMIPB, a comprehensive battery of memory tests similar to the Wechsler Memory Scale) and organic screening tests (see previous section).

On the WAIS–R he emerged with an overall, verbal and non-verbal IQ within the superior range with no obvious scatter across subtests. His estimated premorbid IQ was also within the same range.

On the AMIPB the following emerged:

> verbal recall (immediate and delayed) – normal
> non-verbal recall (immediate and delayed) – normal
> verbal and non-verbal learning – normal
> motor speed – normal
> cognitive processing speed – low.

On the above test one feature of note beyond the selectively low processing speed is that his verbal recall was relatively lower than non-verbal recall.

Tests of concentration suggest that this man's low attentional span was within low but normal limits as was his ability to sustain concentration.

On all tests sensitive to brain damage, his performance was within the normal range.

Thus, the neuropsychological evaluation essentially revealed no objective absolute change in cognitive function consistent with brain damage. Instead it revealed a relative reduction in concentration, speed of processing, and initial verbal memory.

Interview revealed certain facts which helped in the evaluation of these results:

(1) he was alarmed by his early symptoms and became concerned and worried that the injuries he had sustained might lead to a type of dementia

(2) on return to work after four months he found the routine difficult and was unable to deal with the backlog of work

(3) his inability to meet his own criteria at work engendered frustration, anxiety, and irritability.

The interaction of these three factors led to a vicious circle, with anxiety and worry reducing concentration, which in turn would affect a number of cognitive tasks. Poor ability on the task in relation to his high expectation led to further anxiety, and so on.

The type of concentration difficulty seen above on neuropsychological assessment is fairly typical of the effects anxiety can produce on cognitive functions; anxiety produces a pattern of disturbance which is often confused with organic impairment.

Psychometry and neurology

Head injury

Neuropsychological evaluation in cases of head injury has a role in rehabilitative means, diagnosis, and differential discrimination.

The demand for assessment of cognitive, emotional, and behavioural changes consequent upon head injury has increased for a number of reasons.

One such morbid factor may well be the increasing number of people who can be expected to survive severe brain damage given the expertise of the neurosurgical profession.

A second factor may be a general and increasing awareness that more traditional methods, such as computerised tomography (CT), are of limited use in defining the long-term sequelae of head injury, except perhaps for a few very severe injuries; and that a large proportion of normal CT scans taken after trauma come from people who have severe cognitive disturbance and significant lesions undetectable by CT (Wilson, 1990).

A third factor probably reflects a growing awareness that the psychological and neuropsychological consequences of head trauma are as important as, if not more important than, physical disabilities, and that these psychological difficulties may be the most significant long-term disturbances for the individual. In clinical practice, many relatives of the victims of head trauma state that they are able to help the patient with the physical difficulties and how to come to terms with them, but that they find the changes in memory, intellect, and personality devastating.

Again, it has to be emphasised that neuropsychological assessment measures cognitive function, not brain damage. One of the misuses of assessment is to assume that every aspect of impaired performance reflects brain damage, as opposed to variable test application, psychiatric disturbance, fatigue, and poor motivation and, in relation to trauma, post-traumatic stress disorder, hysteria, or post-traumatic anxiety.

Determining the parameters of poor test performance relies on accurate understanding of the nature, characteristics, and consistency of measured cognitive disturbance and the relationship between this and a range of other factors such as:

(1) perceived disturbance of function
(2) location and nature of head injury
(3) factors associated with acute brain injury, such as post-traumatic amnesia, length and depth of coma, etc.
(4) premorbid characteristics of personality, and medical, educational, and vocational history
(5) presence of continuing psychological shock and trauma
(6) post-injury experiences.

The use of psychometric procedures

The value of psychometric procedures in cases of head injury is that they are able to document level of function in a quantifiable way, and their high reliability and acceptable validity, as well as discriminative ability, make them powerful tools in the documentation of disability.

In addition, a number of test batteries incorporate within them procedures for determining the likelihood that currently measured function represents a deterioration from a previously higher level.

In some instances, it is possible to be entirely confident that the accident was the main or sole contributor to a specific disturbance. Thus certain aspects of cognition and perception may be impaired only as a function of direct primary brain injury.

This is less easily determined with, for example, intellectual disturbance. There are only rare instances in which it will be possible to obtain relatively reliable measures of a person's premorbid intelligence for comparison with IQ after the injury. For a working adult, one cannot use school or college records except to achieve a very broad 'guesstimate'.

With tests such as the WAIS–R, however, it is possible to derive estimated measurements of premorbid IQ by pro-rating certain scales on the test which measure functions considered to be relatively resistant to the effects of brain injury (i.e. well- or overlearned skills).

Additionally, by virtue of their reliability over time, repeat administration of psychometric test procedures, with an appropriate intervening time period, may help to document change of function over time and therefore be particularly useful in addressing the issue of prognosis and the effects of intervention.

The normative data for specific tests can clearly be of use in determining the degree or intensity of disturbance. Thus it may be possible to assess whether a person's pattern of disturbance in cognitive function and the intensity of disturbance are consistent with the nature and severity of head injury as determined by other measures and estimates.

Thus it is possible to examine the interface between the organic and psychological factors which may be expected to exert an adverse effect on cognition and emotion.

Where the value of psychometric procedures may be limited is in terms of addressing equally important areas of a more ecological nature, such as driving competence, vocational ability, social judgement, activities of daily living, and management roles (e.g. managing finances in the home or at work).

This discussion covers only a few of the issues, strengths, and limitations of the value of psychometric assessment. The next case highlights some of these issues. The following account presents some of the neuropsychological data on a young man who received a closed head injury as a consequence of a road traffic accident. Some personal details are not vital for the discussion and are omitted to preserve anonymity. Rather, the aim is to detail certain of the implications of the neuropsychological data.

Case example 3

After the head injury this man was rendered unconscious for approximately 24 hours. He experienced a post-traumatic amnesia for six days. A CT scan taken on the day of the accident revealed a general swelling of the brain, with bruising to the left frontal lobe and an area of bleeding over the right parietal area.

Neuropsychological assessment was conducted approximately two years after the accident, at a time when the patient was complaining of continuing difficulties in speech production, reduced capacity for concentrating, diminished short-term memory function, especially for verbal material, and general slowing of cognitive speed.

Assessment of this man's intellectual capacity suggests a full-scale IQ within the low–average range. This comprises a verbal IQ in the average range of 100–109 and a non-verbal IQ within the mentally deficient range of 69 and below, a difference in IQ of some 45 points. Other aspects of his test performance are detailed below:

concentration: digits forward 3, digits backwards 2
immediate verbal memory: 15th percentile
delayed verbal memory: 1st percentile
immediate spatial memory: 2nd percentile
delayed spatial memory: 1st percentile
cognitive processing speed: impaired (for verbal and spatial material)
psychomotor speed: impaired
verbal fluency: impaired
word-finding ability: impaired
reading comprehension: impaired.

The facts to emphasise here are that, except for the IQ test, all measures of this person's performance were impaired, including measures of functions which he did not report as being problematic. In most instances, the impairment was considered to be severe enough for any deficits to be clearly observable in the man's natural environment by those around him and by himself. In respect of language comprehension, to take but one example, neither the client nor significant others reported any manifestation of such deficits.

Taken at its face value, the above data are consistent with a significant disturbance in non-verbal intellectual skills and with deficits in concentration and short-term memory, as well as certain deficits in language ability. Additional data would suggest a slowing of speed of cognitive processing and in psychomotor performance. However, some inconsistencies emerged:

(1) the observation of impaired performance on tests in the absence of noticeable manifestation in his environment
(2) the severity of impaired performance being inconsistent with the severity of head injury as ascertained closer to the accident
(3) the blanket reduction on most general cognitive measures but the clear and significant distinction between measured verbal and non-verbal IQ.

Additionally it has to be stated that attempts to determine whether he was dissimulating were negative; thus there was no psychometric reason to presume that there was any manipulation of the test data. Before unravelling some of the inconsistencies, I would note that inspection of the subtests which comprised the WAIS–R for this man indicate a wide spread of abilities. Thus although the verbal IQ emerges as being significantly higher than the non-verbal IQ, there is some considerable scatter among the verbal subtests.

Thus, using percentile scores to equate across subtests, one can contrast this person's score on the comprehension subtest (an assessment of general problem solving, reasoning, and social comprehension), which lies at the 91st percentile, with his performance on arithmetic, which lies at the 2nd percentile. Within the non-verbal subtests the range of abilities is much smaller and overall lower.

The common denominator of poor performance on the IQ test may be defined as poor sequencing, organising, and internal manipulation and rotation of data. Tests which load heavily in this area of cognitive processing are poorly performed, in contrast to reasonable performance on tests with minimal loading in such functions. In addition, the nature of the concentration and cognitive processing tasks is such that they load heavily on sequencing and rotating and, consequently, are poorly performed.

Although not all of the data are presented, this example is used because it raises some interesting complexities in interpretation.

The simplest overall interpretation rests at the level of the inconsistencies detailed above. As the interpretation of neuropsychological data is made in relation to site and intensity of injury, one might infer that the magnitude of deficit in this man is inconsistent with the mechanics of the head injury. In addition, the general nature of the deficits may be inconsistent with observation and the nature of deficits one might infer from the CT scan. As such, it might be inferred that the test data reflect an inappropriate exaggeration of disturbance, such as hysteria. The danger in such an inference is both that analysis of the data may terminate at the point of invoking hysteria as the generator of inappropriate responding, and that the determinants of the putative hysteria will not be investigated with the same degree of exactitude as one might discover the determinants of organic changes. It also raises the thorny issue of the precise nature of hysteria and the possibility that there may be an organic basis to this process (Lishman, 1987).

Determining the key cognitive processes which underlie apparently widespread changes of function and matching these to the types of difficulties one might expect to see in certain types of injury (left frontal and right parietal injury in this case) must be done before invoking hysteria; however, irrespective of method, the hypothesis one generates to account for change of function must be supported by all aspects of the test performance and history, and not be inferred by dissatisfaction or inability to account for inconsistencies.

In this case the common denominators of poor performance are quite specific, and their subelements are logically consistent with the known areas of damage sustained at the time of the injury. The intensity is, however, unusual, as is the disparity between observed and recorded deficits, and this may suggest psychological factors. The conclusion to such an interpretation should not be an 'either/or' one, but one which perhaps acknowledges the complex interaction of factors at the time of a traumatic head injury. The degree to which a purely psychometric approach can cope with this complexity alone is debatable.

Central degenerative neurological disorders

The final case example describes the neuropsychological evaluation of someone with multiple sclerosis (MS). This man had exhibited symptomatic MS for 14 years. Neuropsychological assessment was requested on the basis of gradual but inexorable change of personality over 18 months.

While MS is generally viewed as a demyelinating disease of the peripheral nervous system, there are relatively infrequent cases where demyelination may begin to exert an effect upon the CNS in the absence of advanced signs of peripheral disorder, resulting in both focal and diffuse effects.

Case example 4

At the time of neuropsychological assessment of this 50-year-old man his MS was in a phase of relative remission. He exhibited mild disturbance of balance and gait, with mild visual disturbance, minimised at that stage by astigmatic glasses.

Over the previous 18 months, relatives had noted the emergence of eccentricities in his behaviour and affect, such as inappropriate jocularity, manic–depressive mood swings, lack of concern over important family matters, and impulsiveness. Both he and his relatives reported that his cognitive abilities had declined.

This predominantly reflected reduction in concentration was coupled with high distractibility, confusion in his memory of past events, and short-term memory disturbance. The latter reflected both verbal memory deficits – difficulty in remembering the names of known people, forgetting what he was about to say or what others said to him – and spatial memory disturbance such as losing his way in familiar surroundings and inability to recognise old friends.

Both the client and his relatives felt that these difficulties reflected his instability in coping with the MS and its prognosis, and felt that any changes in his personality reflected extremities of his natural characteristics rather than novel additions to his behaviour.

Neurological investigation and CT imaging were unremarkable in terms of evaluating these alterations in cognitive, affective, and behaviour status.

The following results are derived from the general neuropsychological tests administered, most of which have been covered in the preceding section on commonly used tests:

(1) Stroop Colour Word Test:
    word series, normal
    colour series, normal
    colour/word series, impaired
This pattern was referred to earlier as one consistent with frontal impairment.
(2) Halstead–Reitan Category Test:
    errors = 125 (cut-off = 50)

This is consistent with organic impairment. The high error rate in conjunction with a high rate of perseverative error (42%) is again consistent with frontal impairment.

(3) Trail Making Test:
　　trail A, score = 60 seconds (cut-off = +39 seconds)
　　trail B, score = 171 seconds (cut-off = +91 seconds)

Both components are impaired and initially may reflect motor slowness and disturbed visuomotor coordination. Observation on trail B suggests that rigidity of cognitive processing is also present.

(4) Digit-Symbol Subtest:
　　Score = 28 items, in impaired range.

This confirms organic impairment.

(5) Recognition Memory Test:
　　Recognition of both faces and names was impaired.

(6) Wechsler Memory Scale:

The man was fully oriented in time and place with normal attentional span. By contrast, immediate and delayed recall of both verbal and spatial material was impaired. Learning of novel verbal information was normal for simple material but impaired for complex material.

The above results comprise a core of the full neuropsychological evaluation. They confirm organic impairment or brain damage. Other aspects of the evaluation suggest a specific decline in certain aspects of intellectual ability, such as reasoning and abstraction. Assessment of language function suggests intact comprehension skills but with errors in speech production indicative of paraphasia, reduced verbal fluency, and word-finding difficulties.

Overall the results do not suggest global or diffuse brain damage but rather indicate focal involvement. Features of the test profile suggest frontal damage to the dominant hemisphere and bilateral but discrete temporal lobe damage.

In conclusion, it may be noted that subsequent magnetic resonance imaging revealed focal central demyelination. In addition, follow-up assessment some six months later indicated improvement of function after intensive treatment with adrenocorticotrophic hormone.

Summary

This chapter has outlined the nature, strengths, and limitations of the psychometric approach. Neuropsychological assessment is often seen as synonymous with psychometric assessment, but this is incorrect (Incagnoli *et al*, 1986).

The strengths of the psychometric approach are readily seen, and there is little doubt that the application of psychometric methods to a number of subdisciplines within psychology have assisted in legitimising their worth. There has, however, been a negative result in that in some instances the subdiscipline has been equated with the method (or one of the methods) it employs. Within neuropsychology this has led to the view that assessment and its applications are simply a process of test administration and textbook interpretation, and we run the risk of losing sight of the role of hypothesis testing, deductive and inferential reasoning, and comprehensive interpretation.

An additional seduction of psychometry is the view that the ability to quantify and numerically compare confers, in and of itself, meaning, because this view must lead to a misrepresentation of the value and scope of psychometry. Simply stated, by way of conclusion, one must not lose sight of the fact that it is the neuropsychologist who assesses brain function, and not psychometric tests.

References

Flor-Henry, P. (1983) Mood, the right hemisphere and the implications of spatial information perceiving systems. *Research Communications in Psychology, Psychiatry and Behaviour*, **8**, 143–170.

Gilandas, A., Touyz, S., Beumont, P. J. V., *et al* (1984) *Handbook of Neuropsychological Assessment*. Sydney: Grune and Stratton.

Golden, C. J., Purisch, A. D. & Hammeke, T. A. (1980) *A Manual for the Luria–Nebraska Neuropsychological Battery*. Los Angeles: Western Psychological Services.

Incagnoli, T., Goldstein, G. & Golden, C. J. (1986) *Clinical Applications of Neuropsychological Test Batteries*. New York: Plenum Press

Kline, P. (1980) The psychometric model. In *Models of Man* (eds A. J. Chapman & D. M. Jones). Leicester: British Psychological Society.

Lezak, M. D. (1983) *Neuropsychological Assessment*. New York: Oxford University Press.

Lishman, W. A. (1987) *Organic Psychiatry* (2nd edn). Oxford: Blackwell Scientific.

Wechsler, D. (1981) *Manual for the Wechsler Adult Intelligence Scale – Revised*. New York: The Psychological Corporation.

Wilson, J. T. L. (1990) Significance of MRI in clarifying whether neuropsychological deficits after head injury are organically based. *Neuropsychology*, **4**, 261-270.

Yamamoto, T., Flor-Henry, P. & Gruzelier, J. H. (eds) (1987) *Laterality, Cerebral Dynamics and Psychopathology*. Amsterdam: Elsevier.

7 Emotion

Kevin R. Fontaine & Bruce J. Diamond

History of the emotion concept in the social sciences • Defining emotion • The cognition–emotion connection • The emotion process • Appraisal patterns and emotion • Physiological considerations • Social regulation and emotion • Conclusions

---

It is somewhat ironic that despite emotion's prominent place in our day-to-day lives, it remains one of the least understood aspects of our experience. This chapter highlights some of the relevant issues in the field, laying particular emphasis upon 'appraisal-based' theories of emotion which are currently dominating the field. Firstly, however, the history of emotion research is outlined in order to place in context the notion of 'cognitivism in emotion' which underlies much contemporary research.

History of the emotion concept in the social sciences

Although the study of emotion has evolved into an interdisciplinary field encompassing a broad range of seemingly diverse social and biological sciences (anthropology, psychology, sociology, neurophysiology, and so on), this has not always been the case.

In academic psychology, emotion was for many years discounted as a substantive area of inquiry (e.g. Duffy, 1941). This was largely due to the dominance of behaviourism with its strict adherence to simple linear stimulus–response (S–R) formulations. This empirical philosophy (often called logical positivism) maintains that phenomena are verifiable only if they can be observed directly via the senses. Hence, within that framework, the study of emotion was considered unscientific because emotion could only be inferred on the basis of what was observable (i.e. overt behaviour, physiological changes, and so on). Therefore, emotion was subsequently described by ostensibly more quantifiable explanatory concepts such as activation, motivation, and drives. In this way, emotion became synonymous with arousal or physiological mobilisation, a sort of phylogenetically inherited warning system which compelled an individual to 'fight or flight' from danger. In essence, emotion (most notably fear and anxiety), was seen as a noxious tension state, a motivator which urged or prompted the person into action in an effort to re-establish homeostasis.

This unidimensional drive-theory conceptualisation proved inadequate because viewing emotion merely as a state of arousal initiated by innate biological forces meant that emotion simply acted as an intervening variable. There was no coherent consideration of the richness and fluidity that appears to be the hallmark of emotion. Moreover, by focusing exclusively upon a narrow range of emotion states, such as anxiety and fear, whose survival value is presumably self-evident, this approach fails to consider other more complex emotional states whose adaptive function is less than obvious (guilt, pride, joy, love, and so on). Most importantly, strict adherence to an arousal or drive-focused theory in effect simplifies our emotions, in the sense that we are viewed simply as passive and reactive beings, driven by a series of 'hard-wired' biological instincts.

Freudian viewpoint

Not surprisingly, a similar stance on emotion was taken within clinical theories of emotional disturbances and psychopathology. For instance, Freudians considered anxiety to be a drive arising in early life as a result of childhood experiences. This anxiety would periodically re-emerge as a result of certain events in adult life which in some way triggered this deep-seated intrapsychic conflict buried within the unconscious. This anxiety was thought to motivate the subsequent use of mechanisms of defence which would attempt to reduce this drive tension by keeping the underlying conflict out of consciousness and therefore at bay. Hence, emotion is again seen as a noxious state which rather reflexively compels ameliorative action.

Behaviourist viewpoint

Not unlike the Freudian view, behaviourists espouse the notion that emotion is a conditioned response which results from previous learning. A given stimulus (e.g. an object or event) becomes associated with this noxious tension state so that any subsequent exposure to this stimulus (or something similar) elicits the same arousal state. Clinical interventions (e.g. systematic desensitisation) attempt to 're-expose' the individual to the anxiety-provoking event while simultaneously blocking or short-circuiting the tension state by teaching the person a response that runs counter to the arousal (e.g. progressive muscle relaxation).

Physiological viewpoint

Early conceptualisations of emotion were guided by mechanistic and reductive models which proposed that emotion was merely arousal or a state of activation which compelled any number of survival-related activities. Moreover, by equating emotion with arousal, this approach was further limited, insofar as the physiological correlates of arousal were viewed as responding in a uniform and undifferentiated manner. However, arousal as indexed by physiological measures does not appear to be undifferentiated. That is, physiological response systems may vary considerably (i.e. heart rate may decrease, displaying parasympathetic-like responses, while increasing skin conductance responses display sympathetic-like responses) when we become 'aroused'. Hence, the interpretation of physiological response patterns will be made more difficult by the tendency of individuals to display individual response specificity (i.e. exhibiting a particular pattern across various situations), and stimulus-response specificity (i.e., the tendency for a stimulus or situation to evoke a specific pattern of physiological response; Engel, 1960). Ax (1964) invoked the idea of motivational response specificity, which represented the interaction of these two factors.

Arousal is far more complex than was once believed. Because of this, its usefulness as a 'barometer' of emotion must be seriously questioned. The fact that 'states of arousal' are often associated with differentiated response indices across individuals indicates that a simple 'on–off' dichotomy with respect to arousal is inadequate. (This issue is described in greater detail later in this chapter.)

Cognitive viewpoint

In the 1960s and 1970s, as the cognitive movement began to take hold in psychology, there was a progressive shift away from unidirectional drive theories of emotion to a more sophisticated view; namely, that we actively construct our relationships with the environment, and that our evaluations have causal significance for our emotional responses. It is important to be aware of some of the difficulties inherent in providing an adequate definition of emotion, before theories of emotion are discussed.

Defining emotion

As with many other complex concepts in psychology (e.g. stress, intelligence, motivation), there is currently no universal definition of the term 'emotion'. Because emotion can be conceptualised as a stimulus, an intervening variable, or a response, it is extremely difficult, if not impossible, to develop a single definition. By far the most common definition has been to refer to an emotion as a response and hence to focus exclusively upon measurable psychological, social, or physiological indices that are thought to be the emotion. In short, given the multifaceted nature of emotion, one must resist the temptation to dilute the richness of the phenomenon by 'pigeon-holing' the concept into a series of mutually exclusive analytical categories which provide only selective and therefore incomplete understanding. Emotion is perhaps best thought of as a complex synthesis of cognitive, behavioural, and physiological activity. Any treatment of the topic therefore requires at least some attempt to integrate and explicate some of these diverse factors.

Distinguishing emotion from mood

An issue at least peripherally related to the definitional problems associated with emotion has been its relationship to the concept of mood. It has been traditional, especially in clinical settings, to distinguish between emotions and moods. Typically, emotions (even acute ones) are thought to be solely the product of a specific event or transient life circumstance. By contrast, moods have long been considered the dispositional tendencies of people to react in a certain characteristic way over a variety of situations (e.g. John is an angry person, Helen is carefree, and so on). The implication is that moods are pervasive, enduring 'styles' of expression in that they are the product of both the situation and what the person 'brings' to the encounter. For instance, someone who persistently displays a depressed mood is likely to view innocuous or even positive events in such a way as to perpetuate or sustain that mood. Hence, mood disorders may be thought of as the result of a long-standing maladaptive style of viewing the world and one's relationship to it. Beck's (1976) notion of the cognitive triad of depression is a prime example. In his view, people who are prone to persistent bouts of depression have a greater tendency to view themselves, their worlds, and their futures in a maladaptive and negative fashion. Moreover, these dysfunctional views are extremely resistant to alteration, even in the face of significant contradictory evidence.

In summary, an emotion is difficult to adequately define; however, it is generally regarded as a multifaceted response to an evaluation that a

---

Box 7.1 Distinctions between emotion and mood

Emotion
    the appraisal of a specific event
    cognitive, behavioural, and physiological activity
    intense
    time-limited

Mood
    the dispositional tendency to react over a variety of situations
    a long-standing maladaptive style of viewing the world
    less intense
    self-perpetuating

particular situation or event affects one's well-being; emotions also tend to be time-limited. By contrast, moods are generally less intense though more enduring in nature (Box 7.1). Moreover, moods tend to be displayed consistently across a range of experiences. Thus, many postulate that moods are the product of an inflexible style of perceiving and interpreting the world. The origins of these perceptual tendencies are not clear, although some theorists argue that they are undoubtedly the manifestations of one's personality and early life experiences.

The cognition–emotion connection

The notion that our thoughts significantly influence our emotional responses has gained almost universal acceptance among emotion researchers. The mechanism or mediator which translates these situational and personal variables into an emotion is called appraisal.

Appraisals

The concept of 'appraisal' (although not labelled as such) emerged initially out of research on 'war neuroses' (Grinker & Spiegel, 1945). It was later expanded to encompass the broader issue of emotion (Arnold, 1960). In essence, an appraisal is an evaluative process in which the individual judges whether or not a given circumstance or event is personally relevant or significant. Appraisal has been the linchpin of a host of cognitive theories of emotion for a number of years, although the concept has taken many different forms (Lazarus, 1966, 1991; Scherer, 1984; Smith & Ellsworth, 1985; Frijda, 1986). These so-called 'functional theorists' view emotion as a response which is coordinated or steered by the appraisals which emerge over the course of a given person–environment transaction. That is, our emotional lives are intimately tied to the evaluations we place on situations with respect to our well-being. In a sense, emotion is a multifaceted reaction to the meaning generated by appraisal.

Appraisal-based formulations were derived initially from Lazarus' laboratory experiments designed to investigate the influence of cognitive mediational processes (i.e. appraisal) upon psychological stress. In these studies (for reviews, see Lazarus, 1966; Lazarus & Launier, 1978) stress was induced by having subjects watch films depicting disturbing events such as woodworking accidents, while relevant stress-related responses were monitored (e.g. heart rate, galvanic skin response, subjective reports). In conjunction with viewing the films, subjects were instructed to 'appraise' the events in the film in a certain way. For instance, some subjects were instructed to remain detached, while others were requested to engage fully in the film. The manipulation of these so-called 'orientating' instructions proved to have a significant and systematic effect upon both the objective and subjective indices of stress. Specifically, detachment reduced stress responses, while engagement increased them.

These studies have shown that evaluative appraisal processes have a profound impact upon people's reactions to the events in their lives. Although this research centred upon stress experiences, Lazarus' theory has been progressively expanded to encompass the broader concept of emotion. Indeed, if one subscribes to the notion that appraisal has causal significance in reference to stress and its associated emotions (anxiety, fear, anger, sadness, disgust), then it seems theoretically feasible to contend that appraisal processes are also influential in all emotional experiences. Before we examine the specifics of appraisals, we need to review the broader theoretical perspective upon which Lazarus' appraisal-based theory of emotion rests.

The emotion process

As we have noted, one of the major drawbacks of a drive-theory formulation of emotion is that it conceptualises emotions as static, emerging primarily to mobilise survival-related activity. Such an approach fails to take account of the fact that person–environment relationships are in constant flux and the resultant emotions are reflections of this, changing from moment to moment as the conditions in our lives evolve. The notion that emotion is a process can be clearly seen by observing the ebb and flow of emotional reactions as a poignant play or movie is watched. Our emotions shift dramatically over the course of such an experience as we become increasingly involved in the plight of the main characters.

To address the fluidity of emotion, Lazarus (1991, p.39) has outlined a process-orientated approach by postulating five broad themes or principles which he believes to describe the inherent multicausal nature of emotion.

(1) *The systems principle.* This simply states that emotion is a complex and ever-changing phenomenon involving a configuration of a large number of variables (many of which have yet to be identified). This principle implies that emotion cannot be adequately described or understood by invoking explanatory models which emphasise single variables such as personality traits or stimulus properties.

(2) *The product of the process and structure principles.* Lazarus contends that emotions are the product of two separate yet interdependent principles, the process and structure principles. Process refers to the flux and change, prevalent in human emotion, while structure refers to the notion that there is a certain degree of stability in the ways people construe and react to their environments which results in recurrent patterns of emotion generation and expression.

(3) *The developmental principle.* Essentially this refers to the biological, cultural, and social influences on our emotional lives which are the products of our unique personal histories.

(4) *The specificity principle.* This contends that individual emotions (i.e. anxiety, guilt, sadness, joy, and so on) can only be understood in reference to the particular patterns of appraisal which emerge over the course of a given encounter.

(5) *The relational meaning principle.* This principle is a correlate of the specificity principle in the sense that it states that each emotion is defined by a unique and specific relationship between person and environment which is characterised by how the events are appraised with respect to their relevance to one's well-being. In this respect, emotion is seen as a reaction to personal meaning which is generated by appraisal.

In essence, the first three principles proposed by Lazarus are nothing more than guidelines which attempt to convey that human emotion is perhaps best thought of not only as a unitary static response, but also as a process of interacting systems whose confluence produces a given emotion. However, it must be noted that emotion affects subsequent appraisals, changing or revising them as the situation unfolds. Moreover, emotion can also serve to compel action directed toward eliminating or solving a problem that is thought to be causing the emotion (i.e. coping).

The final two principles attempt to translate the systemic perspective into a testable framework by proposing that appraisal processes mediate all relationships between the person and the environment. Hence, the study of the appraisals which emerge during encounters provides an avenue into the emotion process. The broader implication is that if certain emotions are consistently associated with certain appraisal patterns, then it should be possible to delineate these patterns in an effort to forge a greater understanding of the types of person–environment relationships which produce different emotions.

Appraisal patterns and emotion

By examining the patterns of appraisal retrospectively reported shortly after the experience of an emotion, it may be possible to identify the particular types of appraisals which affect the quality and intensity of emotion. Lazarus refers to these patterns as core relational themes. They represent the ongoing patterns of relationship between person and environment that are considered both necessary and sufficient to produce a given emotion (Lazarus, 1991, p. 22). There is some preliminary evidence (Smith & Ellsworth, 1985, 1987; Ellsworth & Smith, 1988; Manstead & Tetlock, 1989) supporting the contention that both negative and positive emotional experiences are related to distinct patterns of appraisal.

Lazarus has recently forged a cognitive-motivational-relational theory of emotion which attempts to differentiate emotions on the basis of the particular types and patterns of appraisal which emerge during a given encounter. In order to provide a detailed analysis of the appraisal–emotion relationship, Lazarus has divided appraisal into two interdependent components.

(1) *Primary appraisal.* This refers to the stakes one has in the outcome of the situation. It signifies what is important or significant to the person (i.e. whether it is harmful or beneficial). In order for a given encounter to be appraised as personally significant, it must, in some way, be relevant to one's goals. For instance, if an individual applied to medical school, but had no particular commitment or wish to be a doctor (perhaps he/she applied only to please his/her parents), then a failure to be admitted to the programme would not be likely to elicit any particularly strong emotions. However, if being a doctor was a goal relevant to the person, then a failure to gain admission would provoke negative emotions.

(2) *Secondary appraisal.* This concerns the options or prospects for managing a given encounter. It determines what, if anything, can be or needs to be done to cope with the situation.

The two forms of appraisal act interdependently in the sense that a primary appraisal that a situation is potentially harmful and thereby anxiety-provoking can subsequently be 'revised' if the person judges that he/she has the resources to manage the encounter. For example, people who fail to gain admission to medical school may not experience emotional distress if they judge that they can secure admission in the future if they simply work harder. In this way, the future expectancy embedded within secondary appraisal (i.e. "if I really work, I will get in next time") has reduced the threatening aspects of failure in this instance.

Distinguishing different emotions

In Lazarus' view, emotions can be distinguished from each other in terms of unique appraisal patterns which emerge over the course of encounters. In general, any emotion is generated as a result of the appraisal that a given situation is personally relevant or significant to one's well-being. What distinguishes between emotions (say anger and sadness) are the particular types of appraisals within the components that are 'activated' by the encounter.

For instance, in anger there is a strong theme of blame or accountability in the appraisal process. Someone other than oneself is appraised as responsible for the harmful actions; hence, anger is generated. On the other hand, sadness generally involves an appraisal of loss (either tangible or symbolic), although there is no blame or accountability. (For an account of the specific appraisal patterns thought to be associated with the various emotions, see Lazarus (1991).)

It is important to note that we rarely experience 'pure' emotions. Typically, our emotional lives are characterised by a blending of emotions (i.e. a mixture of even seemingly contradictory emotions). Because of this, it is somewhat artificial to speak of distinct appraisal patterns associated with distinct emotions.

Cognitive processes

We do not wish to imply that appraisals are always conscious and deliberate processes whereby the person rationally judges every encounter with respect to its personal significance. Indeed, it is highly probable that the vast majority of our appraisals are reflexive and automatic in nature. This may be especially the case when the event is unexpected or brief. For situations that are anticipated (e.g. an oral presentation scheduled in two weeks' time), the individual may engage in a more deliberate appraisal process which is in keeping with what Lazarus is postulating.

Lazarus' approach does have the potential of identifying the crucial elements of cognition which initiate and sustain the onset, course, and duration of emotional experiences.

Additionally, to the extent that such patterns of appraisal are generalisable, it may offer a useful means of conceptualising and structuring clinical interventions. In fact, to a certain extent, clinical endeavours have preceded empirical verification, in the sense that cognitively based means of influencing emotions have been practised intuitively by practitioners for a number of years (Beck, 1976; Meichenbaum, 1985).

Physiological considerations

Although we have taken pains to dispel the notion that emotion is best conceptualised simply as an arousal-driven somatic response, it is clear that emotions are associated with a series of physiological responses. Indeed, we have all experienced the sweaty palms and racing heart associated with certain emotional experiences. Hence, it is not surprising that, for many researchers, these physiological changes have represented their focus of inquiry. Perhaps the most interesting issue being addressed today by these physiologically-orientated emotion researchers is whether there is a uniform, undifferentiated somatic response common to all emotions or whether each emotion has its own 'specific' pattern of physiological activity. It is beyond the scope of this chapter to delve into the so-called 'generality–specificity' issue in any great depth; however, we have summarised some of the literature.

The generality–specificity issue

Arnold (1960) argued that different emotions have specific physiological response patterns. For example, she cites lust as a parasympathetic nervous system (PNS) phenomenon, and argues that the PNS is involved whenever we appraise something as good or pleasurable. Schachter (1957), in using multiple physiological measures, found that fear gave rise to an adrenaline-like effect, that pain gave rise to a noradrenaline-like effect, and that anger showed an indeterminate, mixed effect. Children have been found to show greater levels of skin resistance while watching sad scenes in a movie, and slower gastric peristaltic rates during happy scenes (Sternbach, 1962). The former was interpreted as representing an inhibition of sympathetic activity, and the latter a decrease in vagal activity. Furthermore, Averill (1969) found that in his subjects, sadness was accompanied by higher blood pressure, which he interpreted as indicative of increased sympathetic activity. Weerts & Roberts (1976) found that diastolic blood pressure could differentiate the emotions of anger and fear, when subjects invoked imagery of emotion-related scenes. In a similar vein, Ekman *et al* (1983) investigated the correspondence between emotional specificity and autonomic differences, and found that heart rate and finger temperature increased more with anger than with happiness.

As we have illustrated, it is now well documented that there is some physiological specificity in reference to the emotions of anger and fear. However, the evidence of specificity in other more complex emotions is less well established (see Wagner, 1989). It should be noted in passing that the notion of emotion-specific physiological activity is consistent with appraisal theories of emotion since they postulate that emotions (including any physiological manifestations) are systematically organised on the basis of the particular pattern of appraisals which emerge during a given encounter (Smith, 1989).

Social regulation and emotion

There is a body of opinion that argues that emotion is a social construction. In fact, it would be difficult to overstate the impact of these social factors, especially in reference to the appropriateness of particular emotional expressions. It is not surprising, then, that emotion has long been of interest to sociologists and anthropologists, who are concerned with social systems and cultural influences upon individual and group behaviour.

The notion that society helps to generate, sanction, and sustain the emotional life of the individual is the fundamental premise of social constructivist approaches to emotion (see Averill, 1980). Within this and related anthropological frameworks, social influence is divided into two broad and interdependent forms; culture and social structure. Culture refers to the shared meanings which people internalise over the course of their psychological development. It influences the ways in which we perceive, evaluate, and respond to the events in our lives. Social structure, on the other hand, refers to the immediate demands and constraints which operate in every encounter. Social structure helps define the various roles we play in our lives (e.g. student, brother, citizen, mother, and so on), and brings with it a host of pressures, expectations, and opportunities. In short, culture and social structure work together to influence the ways in which we appraise and respond to the events in our lives.

To examine these societal influences upon emotional experience and expression, Hochschild (1979) uses the term 'feeling rules'. Feeling rules refer to the overt manifestations of cultural and social influence upon the emotional life of the individual. For instance, in Japan it is considered dishonourable to display grief or despair in the face of a personal loss, since to do so is thought to burden others unduly. Hence in that culture, the feeling rule is quite clear: if you experience a loss your overt expression should be one of detachment. By contrast, in many European and North American cultures the expression of grief or sadness is not only sanctioned, but often encouraged. Within these social contexts grief is to be shared as a means of enhancing a sense of community and to relieve the burden upon the individual.

It seems reasonable to propose that emotional life is in no small way a function of society. The central premise of such an outlook is that a multitude of sociocultural factors have a sustained impact upon the emotion process, both in terms of how a given situation is appraised and how and when emotions are expressed.

In many ways investigating the effect of social influences on emotion represents the greatest challenge to researchers. This is because many of these influences are subtle and embedded within the developmental histories of the culture, the society, and the individual.

Conclusions

In this chapter we have outlined some of the issues and research directions which characterise contemporary research into emotion. The field has been characterised by predominantly fragmented studies of individual components or facets of emotion. The role played by cognitive, social, and physiological factors in mediating emotion is inadequately described by invoking unidimensional models of either emotion or arousal. Any valid and reliable assessment and interpretation of emotion must incorporate all of these factors into a highly integrated perspective (Box 7.2). This must take processes of appraisal into account, as well as the social context in which the appraisal occurs, and recognise the inherent variability (and even incongruities) among various physiological response modalities. Moreover, all of these factors are also superimposed onto a

---

Box 7.2 Cognitive, physiological, social, and behavioural factors of emotion

Cognitive – the appraisal (primary and secondary) of a situation

Physiological – hormonal accompaniments of emotion

Social – appropriateness of emotional expression within a society

Behavioural – conditioned response

---

rich tapestry of memories and experiences, which adds an additional dimension to this complex configuration that constitutes emotion.

Cognitive appraisal has emerged as a possible synthesising concept of emotion in that it seems to represent a common thread connecting socio-cultural, psychological, and physiological treatments of the subject. In this way appraisal may build a bridge across the interdisciplinary 'divide' and thereby encourage empirical efforts that are multidisciplinary in scope. It is clear that the production and generation of emotion is modulated by a combination of factors, the study of which requires the creative use of diverse disciplines and methods. Thus far, appraisal appears to be slowly fulfilling this promise.

Further reading

Arnold, M. B. (1960) *Emotion and Personality*. New York: Columbia University Press.

Averill, J. R. (1980) A constructivist view of emotion. In *Emotion: Theory, Research, and Experience, Vol. 1. Theories of Emotion* (eds R. Plutchik & H. Kellerman), pp. 305–339. New York: Academic Press.

Beck, A. T. (1976) *Cognitive Therapy and the Emotional Disorders*. New York: International University Press.

Lazarus, R. S. (1991) *Emotion and Adaptation*. New York: Cambridge University Press.

Wagner, H. (1989) The peripheral physiological differentiation of emotions. In *Handbook of Social Psychophysiology* (eds H. Wagner & A. S. R. Manstead), pp. 77–98. London: John Wiley and Sons.

References

Arnold, M. B. (1960) *Emotion and Personality*. New York: Columbia University Press.

Averill, J. R. (1969) Autonomic response patterns during sadness and mirth. *Psychophysiology*, **5**, 399–414.

—— (1980) A constructivist view of emotion. In *Emotion: Theory, Research, and Experience, Vol. 1. Theories of Emotion* (eds R. Plutchik & H. Kellerman), pp. 305–339. New York: Academic Press.

Ax, A. F. (1964) Goals and methods of psychophysiology. *Psychophysiology*, **1**, 8–25.

Beck, A. T. (1976) *Cognitive Therapy and the Emotional Disorders*. New York: International University Press.

Duffy, E. (1941) An explanation of "emotional" phenomena without the use of the concept "emotion". *Journal of General Psychology*, **25**, 283–293.

Ekman, P., Levenson, R. W. & Friesen, W. V. (1983) Autonomic nervous system activity distinguishes among emotion. *Science*, **221**, 1208–1210.

Ellsworth, P. C. & Smith, C. A. (1988) Shades of joy: patterns of appraisal differentiating pleasant emotions. *Cognition and Emotion*, **2**, 301–331.

Engel, B. T. (1960) Stimulus-response and individual-response specificity. *Archives of General Psychiatry*, **2**, 305–313.

Frijda, N. (1986) *The Emotions*. Cambridge: Cambridge University Press.

Grinker, R. & Spiegel, J. (1945) *Men Under Stress*. New York: McGraw-Hill.

Hochschild, A. R. (1979) Emotion work, feeling rules, and social structure. *American Journal of Sociology*, **85**, 551–575.

Lazarus, R. S. (1966) *Psychological Stress and the Coping Process*. New York: McGraw-Hill.

—— (1991) *Emotion and Adaptation*. New York: Cambridge University Press.

—— & Launier, R. (1978) Stress related transactions between person and environment. In *Perspectives on Interactional Psychology*, pp. 287–327. New York: Plenum Press.

Manstead, A. S. R. & Tetlock, P. E. (1989) Cognitive appraisals and emotional experience: further evidence. *Cognition and Emotion*, **3**, 225–240.

Meichenbaum, D. H. (1985) *Stress Inoculation Training*. New York: Plenum Press.

Schachter, J. (1957) Pain, fear and anger in hypertensives and normotensives: a psychophysiological study. *Psychosomatic Medicine*, **19**, 17–29.

Scherer, K. R. (1984) Emotion as a multicomponent process: a model with some cross-cultural data. In *Review of Personality and Social Psychology* (ed. P. Shaver), pp. 37–63. Beverly Hills, CA: Sage.

Smith, C. A. (1989) Dimensions of appraisal and physiological response in emotion. *Journal of Personality and Social Psychology*, **56**, 339–353.

—— & Ellsworth, P. C. (1985) Patterns of cognitive appraisal in emotion. *Journal of Personality and Social Psychology*, **48**, 813–838.

—— & —— (1987) Patterns of appraisal and emotion related to taking an exam. *Journal of Personality and Social Psychology*, **52**, 475–488.

Sternbach, R. A. (1962) Assessing differential autonomic patterns in emotions. *Journal of Psychosomatic Research*, **6**, 87–91.

Wagner, H. (1989) The peripheral physiological differentiation of emotions. In *Handbook of Social Psychophysiology* (eds H. Wager & A. S. R. Manstead), pp. 77–98. London: John Wiley and Sons.

Weerts, T. C. & Roberts, R. (1976) The physiological effects of imaging anger provoking and fear provoking scenes. *Psychophysiology*, **13**, 174.

Dr Elcock } 14/11/11 @ 1:30 pm
Dr Surtado }

Coming to assess Jistina Shaping
following referral

Linda - 01777 247699

Part II
Social psychology

8 Developmental psychology: infancy and attachment

Gillian Harris

The 'bonding' hypothesis • Neonatal behaviour • Attachment formation • Attachment figures • Measures of attachment • The effects of attachment • Conclusion

---

The nature of a child's early relationship with the parent is still accepted as being crucial in determining the subsequent socio-emotional well-being of the adult. Disruptions of such relationships are implicated in the development of many adult psychiatric disorders. However, few people are clear about what aspects of the formation of such early relationships are important, or how and when it is that such relationships develop.

The relationship in which we are interested is usually termed 'attachment' and is the first enduring relationship for a child. The attachment can be described either as that of the parent or parent substitute (the caregiver) to the child, or the attachment of the child to the caregiver. Therefore, the way in which we assess such an attachment will differ according to whether we are looking at the child or the caregiver. The strength of the attachment of caregiver to the child is usually measured in terms of observable parenting, or mothering, behaviour, or of verbal expressions of positive feelings towards the child. The attachment of child to caregiver is usually measured in terms of the child's proximity-seeking behaviour in times of distress or separation, and of approach behaviour towards other adults when the caregiver is present.

The 'bonding' hypothesis

Observations carried out by ethologists in the 1930s led to the concept of 'imprinting'; that is, a form of immediate and irreversible learning by which a newborn animal recognised, and attached itself to, the parent. This concept was generalised to the human infant, and it was thought that such immediate imprinting, or 'bonding', might occur between infant and mother, subsequent to birth. The emphasis was, however, changed in that it was thought that 'bonding' was primarily concerned with the formation of the attachment of the mother to her infant, rather than of infant to mother.

The main proponents of this hypothesis were Klaus & Kennel (1976), who felt not only that bonding did occur during the hours following birth, but that bonding could *only* occur during this time. The relationship between mother and child would therefore be determined by the availability of such early contact during the neonatal period. Mothers and infants who had not experienced early contact would be characterised by poor mothering and inter-relational problems. Support for such assumptions was found in the higher incidence of physical abuse observed between mothers and their low-birth-weight infants (Lynch, 1975). These infants would have experienced prolonged separation from the mother in the neonatal period.

Investigating bonding

Many of the early studies of the effects of early contact on the subsequent relationship between mother and infant were flawed by poor experimental design (Sluckin *et al*, 1984). There were also difficulties in that the studies based their measure of the relationship between infant and mother on behavioural definitions of 'mothering'; such definitions differed from study to study. Good mothering is difficult to define in absolute terms, because it is a culturally specific construct.

Later, more carefully controlled longitudinal studies do seem to reach a consensus (Carlsson *et al*, 1979; Svejde *et al*, 1980; Rode *et al*, 1981). Most studies found no difference in mothering behaviour as a result of extended physical contact between mother and infant. Those studies that did find differences in the early hours of interaction found that such differences disappeared by the time the child was a few weeks old. In addition, no direct relationship has been found between premature birth, early contact, and later abuse of the child (Egeland & Vaughn, 1981).

Shortcomings of the hypothesis

The consequences of the 'bonding' hypothesis were, however, far-reaching. Both term and concept are still used, among the general populace as well as health professionals. Mothers who do not immediately feel love for their infant feel guilty, although many do not feel such affection for their infant in the neonatal period.

From a sociobiological perspective, it is nonsense to assume that a relationship as crucial to the child as that between a helpless infant and the caregiver should be based upon contact between mother and child in the few hours after such a risky and dangerous procedure as giving birth.

A further implication of the bonding hypothesis is that an attachment can form only between an infant and the biological mother.

Neonatal behaviour

If we are to understand how and when first attachments might form between infant and caregiver, then we need to look at the development of social competence in the infant.

Social competence

The neonate is equipped with reflex responses which may either aid survival, or be residual from earlier evolutionary stages. The infant can suck and turn towards the food stimulus; it can grasp, show rudimentary stepping, avoid suffocation, and hold its breath under water. Such reflex responses usually disappear at the end of the second month, and during the third month truly intentional behaviour begins to appear. However, even in the early weeks, when reflex behaviour could be said to predominate, the infant gives the appearance of being socially aware.

Vision

The visual acuity of the neonate is poor. Adult levels of acuity are not attained until the infant is at least six months old. However, even though the infant might not see very well, it still has visual preferences. Infants prefer bright, high-contrast, complex stimuli, especially those stimuli which are face-like in configuration. They prefer to track face-type configurations from birth (Goren *et al*, 1975) and seem to show a preference for the mother's face when a few days old (Bushnell *et al*, 1989).

Hearing

Although they cannot hear very well, neonates also seem to prefer speech-type sounds, and will orient towards them (Hutt *et al*, 1969). They even show evidence of a preference for the mother's voice (De Casper & Fifer, 1980).

Eating

There is an innate preference for sweet tastes, and neonates show reflex facial expressions which denote disgust at sour or bitter tastes (Rosenstein & Oster, 1988).

Smiling

Any stimulus which is pleasing to the infant may elicit a smile, and such a smile may be observed soon after birth. The smile is fairly indiscriminate in the early months, but becomes more discriminating, and therefore more social in intent, from the third month onwards (Kaye & Fogel, 1980).

Imitation

Neonates also seem capable of a form of imitation of the facial expressions of others (Meltzoff & Moore, 1977). This is not, however, true imitation, in that the infant can as yet have no internal representation of self (Jacobson, 1979).

The pretence of social intent

The neonate, although not able to form an internal model of the mother or other caregiver, and having as yet no real concept of self and other, is still able rapidly to learn preferences for certain perceptual stimuli. The neonate can also respond positively to these stimuli by smiling, or orientating towards them. The function of such behaviour is to give the appearance of social intent – social behaviour intentionally directed towards another person. The mother, or caregiver, is made to feel that the infant is aware of her and feels and responds positively towards her. However, the neonate cannot really at this stage be said to be attached to the caregiver, for at this age the infant shows no distress at separation, and the seemingly social responses can be elicited by any positively active stranger.

Neonatal interactions

Neonatal behaviour seems to have evolved in such a way that the infant appears to be giving out social signals to the caregiver, signals which will draw the attention of others. The neonate also has facial features which adults find most appealing (Alley, 1981): large wide-set eyes, wide cheeks, short face. Once again, the function of these features is to draw attention to the infant's face. The neonate is therefore well set up to elicit in others that care-giving behaviour upon which its survival depends.

Caregivers also modify their behaviour in such a way that they too are most likely to gain the attention of the infant, and draw it into an interaction

The speech and behaviour, of both adults and children alike, are modified to some extent when they are talking or playing with an infant (Snow, 1977; Newport *et al*, 1977; Stern, 1977). These modifications are most noticable in use towards infants of about three months of age, but continue to be observed in use with children well into their second year.

Speech behaviour

The modifications of speech, usually termed 'motherese', show themselves in the use of exaggerations of speed and pitch, frequent repetitions, frequent questions, and short phrases. Any utterance that the infant might make is likely to be repeated and expanded upon.

Behaviour shows similar modifications, with exaggerations of facial expression, and the turning of face and body to maintain eye contact with the infant.

The conversational mode

These modifications do not serve to teach the infant language (Gleitman *et al*, 1984) but are thought to be used as a marker to cue infants to that speech which is being directed towards them. The frequent exaggerations of pitch and speed of speech, and of facial expression, are also thought to maintain the infant's attention upon the speaker's face. Thus the infant is drawn into a conversational mode of interaction. The 'turn-taking' aspect of this conversational mode is highlighted by the pauses which the adult leaves, between the speech bursts, for the infant's response, although none might occur. However, synchrony between adult speech and infant bursts of physical activity can be observed even in the early interactions of infants and adults (Condon & Sanders, 1974).

In the early months such interactions between infant and adult require sensitive monitoring by the adult to ensure that the infant is not overstimulated and that adult behaviour is appropriate to the competence of the infant.

Reciprocal behaviour

These interactions develop until, at the age of five or six months, truly reciprocal games emerge between the caregiver and the infant. The infant learns that certain behaviour can elicit pleasurable responses in others. In these learnt patterns of interaction, the subtle games of give and take, lie the roots of attachment.

Disruptions of attachment formation

The infant both responds to the initiations of others and elicits interactions from others. The nature of the relationship with the caregiver is affected therefore both by the state and temperament of the caregiver and by the state and temperament of the infant (Weber *et al*, 1986). A depressed mother will not interact with her child, or respond to elicitations from the child to play. A developmentally delayed or irritable child will not respond well to the overtures of the caregiver (Greene *et al*, 1983); a disfigured child might not be pleasing to look at.

We can see therefore how some children might not be socially rewarding to the caregiver. This would mean a decrease in the amount of stimulation directed towards the child, in turn affecting both the nature of the attachment and the child's future level of cognitive attainment. Similarly, some adults might not be sufficiently 'rewarding' to the child; if a mother is depressed and no response is forthcoming, the infant might give up trying to elicit such a response (Radke-Yarrow *et al*, 1985).

Attachment formation

The formation of an attachment between the infant and caregiver does not seem to rely on instant recognition or attraction, but rather on a building up of a gradual relationship over the first six months of life; this relationship is based upon reciprocal interaction rather than upon the meeting or satisfaction of physical needs. It is still true, however, that attachments can form between infants and caregivers where the relationship cannot be described as always pleasant or rewarding for both partners. Caregivers can become strongly attached to children whose level of handicap allows them to make but little response; children can become attached to parents who are frequently physically abusive.

The process of attachment usually takes place over the first six months of life if a continuous attachment figure is available to the child.

Object permanence

By the age of seven to eight months the infant will recognise the caregiver and show distress at his/her departure (Bower, 1974), for at this age infants begin to attain the concept of object permanence; that is, they begin to understand that objects still exist even though they may not be visible to the infant (Wishart & Bower, 1985). When this stage is attained, the infant cannot only distinguish the caregiver from strangers, but can also recall the caregiver when he or she is absent (Kagan, 1976). Only when infants reach this age can they be aware that the attachment figure has an existence separate from their own.

Box 8.1   The nature of attachment

Attachment is initially formed through reciprocal (reflex on the part of the infant) social interactions

Although there is generally a primary attachment figure, a heirarchy of attachment figures is formed

Primary attachments may be formed through to middle childhood

The primary attachment figure is not necessarily the biological mother

The pattern of early attachments seems to form a basis for later relationships and behaviour

---

The fear response

The attainment of this developmental stage must explain to some extent the onset of the fear response observed in some children towards strangers at the end of the first year (Sroufe, 1977). This response is more accurately described as wariness, or prolonged, sombre, inspection. It is not observed in all children and cannot therefore be seen as an invariate stage in development. It is, however, more likely to be observed when infants encounter 'strangers' least like the adults with whom they are familiar. The response will also be less marked where the stranger acts positively towards the child, or where the stranger is treated positively by the infant's parent (Feinman & Lewis, 1983). The fear response observed at this age is also confined to strange adults (Brooks & Lewis, 1976); the fear of strange children does not occur until the second year of life.

One of the more interesting explanations of this phenomenon is that of Kaye (1982), who suggested that, as infants learn styles of interaction specific to different family members, they also come to realise that they cannot predict how strangers might behave towards them. In simpler terms, infants remain wary until they are sure that the adult knows the rules of the game.

This explanation fits in with the lack of a fear response towards children; attachments to other children do not usually start to develop until the second year (Lewis *et al*, 1975). The explanation also accords with the hierarchy often observed in young children's fear responses. An adult who is known slightly by an infant might be avoided when familiar caregivers are present but used as a safe base when such caregivers are absent (Kaye, 1982).

Attachment figures

One of the drawbacks of the 'bonding' hypothesis is its implication that, because attachments are formed immediately after birth, only the biological mother can be a primary attachment figure for the child. If we assume that, although a child might form many attachments to others, only one of these attachments will achieve primacy (that is, there will be one figure to whom the child will preferentially turn in times of distress), then, if we are to accept the bonding hypothesis, we must also assume that the primary attachment figure must be the biological mother. This precludes strong and primary attachment to non-biological parents, or to the father.

Children, however, are luckily not confined to forming attachments solely to the biological mother. Such attachments can be formed with anyone with whom the child builds up a continuous reciprocal relationship. Attachment figures can be adults of either sex, or even other children (Stewart, 1983).

The primary attachment figure will not necessarily be the person who provides most physical care of the child. In a study by Schaffer & Emerson (1964) it was found that many children in urban Glasgow had a primary attachment figure who was not the biological mother, even though the mother might have provided most physical care for the child. In fact most children have more than one attachment figure, and such a hierarchy is beneficial to the child in that the distress at separation from, or loss of, one attachment figure is ameliorated by the presence of another attachment figure (Rutter, 1981).

The bonding hypothesis also assumes a critical period for the formation of attachments; for many years it was thought that strong attachments between child and caregiver could form only in the first two years of life. However, case studies of children who have suffered severe deprivation and isolation in early childhood (Clarke & Clarke, 1976), or who have been institutionalised and in the charge of multiple caregivers (Hodges & Tizard, 1989), show that such children can form stable attachments later in life.

These studies seem to suggest that if there is a critical period for attachment formation, after which time a child is no longer able to form stable and loving relationships, then this period extends well into middle childhood. Careful reading of the case studies, however, does usually reveal that there has often been the opportunity for isolated or institutionalised children to form relationships with other children, if not with other adults, during early life.

Animal studies have shown that the opportunity to interact with 'age-mates' has a protective effect against the absence of adult attachment figures, and is as important as attachment to adults for subsequent social functioning (Harlow & Harlow, 1962). These animal studies also show that the effects of even total isolation in early life may be reversed given the correct therapeutic environment (Novak, 1979). The necessity of a remedial environment in reversing the effects of early experience is also stressed by those studying the human infant (Clarke & Clarke, 1976).

Infants are therefore likely to form attachments to those children and adults with whom they come into daily contact. These attachments will form where the relationship between child and other continues over time and is based upon some form of reciprocal interaction. One of these attachment relationships is likely to have primacy, and the primary attachment figure will be the one to whom the child preferentially turns in times of distress.

However, the availability of a hierarchy of attachment figures has a protective function for the child. The child's first attachment relationship does not necessarily have to be formed in the first hours of life, or even in the first years of life, to ensure the subsequent socio-emotional well-being of the child.

Measures of attachment

Attachment, like any other form of love, is difficult to quantify. The attachment of parent to child is measured by verbal report, or by observed incidences of 'good' parenting behaviour, such as smiling, kissing, talking, touching. However, parenting behaviour is likely to vary according to the personality of the parent as well as with the temperament of the child, although parental temperament is the better predictor of the nature of the attachment between child and parent (Weber *et al*, 1986).

'Good' parenting behaviour is also culture specific; in some cultures it is not acceptable even to make eye contact with the child during the first year of life (Brazelton *et al*, 1969). Even the subjective measure of 'sensitive-responsiveness', a term which Ainsworth (1979) used to describe optimal parenting behaviour towards the child, is as much a measure of skill and experience as it is of attachment and love.

The strange situation

The attachment of child to caregiver is usually described by means of the Ainsworth 'strange situation' (Ainsworth *et al*, 1978). This is a measure of the behaviour shown by the child at separation from, and reunion with, the caregiver.

The procedure is carried out in a novel environment, and the manoeuvres involve the child's being left by the caregiver with a stranger in a strange environmment. With this procedure, behaviour falling into three categories (Table 8.1) was initially observed in a group of 14-month-old children's interactions with their mothers.

Twenty per cent of the children observed were deemed 'avoidant', category A. These children showed no distress at separation from the mother, and made no attempts to make contact or maintain proximity with the mother at reunion. The children in this category typically ignored the mother, and avoided interaction with her.

Table 8.1   Children's responses to the strange situation

Category	Proportion of children	Type
A	20%	Avoidant
B	66%	Securely attached
C	12%	Ambivalent

Most of the children, 66%, showed behaviour which fell into the second category, B. These children were described as 'securely attached'. Such children were happy to explore the environment when the mother was present, and at this time showed no proximity-seeking behaviour. They showed distress at separation from the mother, and during separation showed little exploratory behaviour. On reunion with the mother the children showed both pleasure and proximity-seeking behaviour.

The behaviour of the children in the third category, C, was deemed 'ambivalent'. This was the smallest group, comprising 12% of the children. These children showed anxious, proximity-seeking behaviour before separation. They were also extremely distressed at separation, but showed anger at reunion, and approach/avoidance behaviour rather than direct proximity seeking.

The amount of proximity-seeking behaviour observed does not, in Ainsworth's category system, directly correlate with strength of attachment. Although children showing no proximity-seeking behaviour, category A, are deemed to be insecurely attached, those children showing most proximity-seeking behaviour, category C, are also assumed to be insecurely attached. Where there is no attachment the child does not approach or interact with the mother. Where there is anxious attachment (category C), children do not feel secure enough in the relationship to move away from the mother and explore the strange environment, nor are they secure enough in the relationship to tolerate a brief separation with the expectation of reunion. Those children described as securely attached were able to explore the environment and to tolerate a short separation, showing positive proximity-seeking behaviour on reunion.

It has been suggested that the children's behaviour in the strange situation was a function of differences in child temperament (Kagan, 1984). Of course, if this were true, then children would behave towards all adult attachment figures in the same way in the same environment. However, children who showed insecurely attached behaviour with the mother did not necessarily show the same behaviour when observed with the father (Sroufe, 1985). It might be that some children show greater distress at separation from the mother as the primary caregiver, and that this variation in distress shown is due to differences in temperament. However, using measures of temperament, no one study has yet been able to explain the differences shown between children in the strange situation (Prior, 1992). These studies are further confounded by the fact that measures of infant temperament contain questions about infant attachment behaviour and fear of strangers.

We can perhaps assume, therefore, that the behaviour observed in the strange situation does in some way reflect the nature of the relationship between the child and the parent. But it is important to note that there are cross-cultural differences in the number of children within a normal sample whose behaviour would be described as falling into each category

(Grossman & Grossman, 1981). In addition, the group that is described as 'normative', category B, comprises only two-thirds of the population. This implies that one-third of the population might belong to a deviant group.

The home situation

In an attempt to explain the nature of the relationship between mother and child, children who had been observed in the strange situation were observed with their mothers at home (Ainsworth *et al*, 1978). In the home, few differences were observed between the behaviour of the category A and category C children.

Differences were observed, however, between the behaviour of the mothers. Category B mothers were described as 'sensitive' to their children's emotional and physical needs, responding appropriately and consistently, without over- or understimulation of the child. Category A mothers, however, were described as 'rejecting', in that they actively rebuffed their children's attempts to make physical contact. These mothers were also described as emotionally labile, with immobile and inexpressive faces. Category C mothers were seen to be 'insensitive'; their responses to the children were not consistent. Such mothers might hug the child at one approach and push them away at another. This behaviour meant that the child could not accurately predict what the mother's response was going to be. This led, understandably, to confusion and anger in the child.

The effects of attachment

The nature of the relationship between child and parent is thought by many to predict subsequent (adult) socio-emotional well-being. If we accept that the lack of opportunity to form a secure attachment with the mother in the first years of life will act detrimentally to the psychological well-being of the child, then we must also accept that one-third of all children appear to be at risk. However, children are able to form secure attachments with others within their environment; and such attachments continue to form throughout life. These secondary attachments might for some children give 'protection' against any possible adverse effects from the absence of a secure attachment to the primary caregiver.

In considering what the long-term effects of insecure primary attachments might be, we have to consider the function of attachment formation. In case studies, or in animal experimentation (Harlow & Harlow, 1962; Clarke & Clarke, 1976), it is difficult not to confound the effects of isolation from any social stimulation, or deprivation of all physical stimulation, with those of the lack of opportunity to form a stable attachment. It would be difficult to conceive of a situation in which a child receives adequate social and physical stimulation but without some continuity of care or companionship. It is also difficult to overcome the disconfounding effects of disturbances within the home environment and an inability to form an attachment to the parent.

Bowlby thought that a lack of opportunity to form an attachment to the mother caused later psychopathology (Bowlby *et al*, 1956). But such effects that he did observe are just as likely to have been caused by disharmony in the home, or other social factors (Quinton & Rutter, 1976).

The function of attachment

If we consider what happens during the formation of attachments, then we might have a better idea of the function of the attachment. Attachment formation is based, as we have seen, upon exposure, and upon reciprocal, predictable interactions. Infants learn the rules of the social 'game'. They also learn that they have the power to elicit specific patterns of interaction from others within the environment. The infant can therefore act upon the environment and receive a predictable response. We might also suggest that if others react to the infant pleasurably, then the infant will form an image of self as one who can give pleasure to others – a person of worth.

The infant would therefore come into the second year of life, if the first had seen the formation of a secure attachment to an adult, with an emerging image of self as competent and lovable. The child would also expect to be able to interact successfully with others. Their world would be predictable, safe, and consistent.

Peer-group interactions

Longitudinal studies carried out on children over the first years of life seem to confirm this model; children who were deemed securely attached at one year showed greater interpersonal competence with their peers at nursery school than did children deemed insecurely attached (Waters *et al*, 1979). Securely attached children also showed more curiosity in the school environment, and more self-directed behaviour.

If interactions between pairs of insecurely attached children are studied (Troy & Sroufe, 1987), we find that 'victimisation' is more likely to occur between such pairs than between pairs with at least one securely attached child. Category A, avoidant, children are most likely to behave as 'victimisers'; category C, ambivalent, children as 'victims'.

In these studies we see what might be the beginnings of habitual modes of interaction with others which might, without remedial experience, carry on into adult life.

There is even the suggestion that there might be a gender difference in the peer-directed social behaviour of insecurely attached children (Turner, 1991). Four-year-old boys judged insecurely attached to their mothers were more likely to show 'acting out' behaviour; to be aggressive, disruptive, assertive, controlling, and attention-seeking, than were securely attached boys. In contrast, four-year-old girls judged insecurely attached to their mothers were more passive-compliant, showing less oppositional behaviour but more positive expressive behaviour (such as smiling), than were securely attached girls.

We find, then, that these studies do confirm the idea that young children judged insecurely attached to their mothers do seem to carry patterns of behaviour into subsequent peer-group interactions, and that the patterns of behaviour that emerge are gender specific.

Other factors

We might once again ask whether or not these differences in behaviour that are observed in interactions both with the mother and with peers are enduring aspects of child temperament, rather than a function of insecure attachment. However, correlations between longitudinal measures of temperament in pre-school children are remarkably weak, and likely to be affected by environmental factors. Recent studies seem to stress the interaction between child temperament, maternal management, and later outcome (Prior, 1992), rather than to perceive temperament as a linear predictor.

The long-term consequences of insecure attachment

The effects on behaviour and peer-group competence of insecure attachment to the mother can be observed in the pre-school child. However, secure attachments can be formed in later childhood which might reverse the detrimental effects of early experience. How likely is it, therefore, that the effects of early insecure attachments will be carried on into adulthood?

One of the main problems in answering this question is that of methodology. To get an accurate answer, we would have to carry out large-scale longitudinal studies, such as that currently being undertaken by Tizard (Hodges & Tizard, 1989). Retrospective correlations, carried out on patient populations, are likely to give a distorted impression of the importance of early experience. All serial murderers may have had problematic childhoods; this does not mean that all children with problematic childhoods will become serial murderers – other factors have to be at work as well.

Given these reservations, studies carried out on adult patient populations could give some insight into how patterns of behaviour or thought might carry over from childhood to adulthood and affect adult functioning. We cannot, however, generalise from these studies and conclude that childhood patterns of behaviour will always carry over into adult life.

One such study has attempted to relate retrospective measures of security of attachment in childhood to diagnoses in adulthood of borderline personality disorder (Patrick *et al*, 1991). Such adults are described as showing "patterns of unstable and intense interpersonal relationships characterized by alternating between two extremes of overidealization and devaluation" (DSM–III–R; American Psychiatric Association, 1987). As compared with a patient group classified as dysthymic, the patients with borderline personality disorder reported attachments to the mother in childhood which were more frequently described as corresponding to category C , insecure–ambivalent, or category D, disorganised–disoriented (Main & Solomon, 1986). (The latter classification is one more recently devised to describe children severely traumatised by early experience or abuse.)

The early childhood pattern of anxious clinging, alternating with hostile avoidance, does seem, for this group of patients, to have been carried on into adult relationships. However, we must be cautious in this interpretation; the study was based upon retrospective data, and the nature of the disorder may in itself cause distortion of perceptions of past relationships. Neither can we be sure that the early patterns of interaction of children who are later to develop borderline personality disorders do not contribute to the formation of attachments that would, in retrospect, be described as insecure.

Conclusion

Attachments form in infancy as a function of exposure and reciprocal interaction. Such attachments are not based on an immediate emotional recognition, occurring soon after birth, but develop gradually during the first year of life. In fact infants are probably unable to form an attachment until they have reached a stage of being able to both recognise and recall the attachment figure, a stage achieved during the second six months of life. This does not mean that the first year is a critical period for such primary attachments to form; children who have had little or no opportunity to form attachments with a stable caregiver within the first years still seem able to form such relationships in later childhood. Nor is it, as has often been assumed, that the child must form a primary attachment with the biological mother. Attachments can be, and are, frequently formed with any adult or child with whom the infant has a continuing relationship. Most infants, by the end of the first year, have a hierarchy of attachment figures and each of these will have a 'protective' function against the loss or absence of other attachment figures.

As attachments form, they are based upon learned patterns of interaction; patterns of interaction that are specific to each infant–other dyad. The success of these patterns of interaction is reflected by the sensitivity of the 'other' to the infant's emotional and cognitive needs, and to the level of stimulation that is acceptable to the infant. Infants in turn learn that they can predictably elicit patterns of behaviour from others that are both consistent and pleasurable. The infant learns to act upon the world. If the 'other' also receives pleasure from the interaction, then by social referencing, the infant's image of self becomes that of one who is worthy of love. If the primary caregiver shows consistent sensitive-responsiveness, then the infant becomes secure enough to explore the environment, and take risks within that environment without undue anxiety. However, if the primary caregiver is either 'rejecting' or 'insensitive', then we might find differences in the infant's social behaviour which generalise from the primary caregiver to the infant's peer group. This may, in some children, set up modes of interacting with others and patterns of expectancies about the thoughts and behaviour of others that continue into adult life.

Further reading

Field, T. (1990) *Infancy*. Cambridge, MA: Harvard University Press.
Rutter, R. (1991) *Maternal Deprivation Reassessed*. Harmondsworth: Penguin.
Schaffer, H. R. (1991) *Making Decisions about Children*. Oxford: Blackwell Scientific.
Sluckin, W., Herbert, M. & Sluckin, A. (1983) *Maternal Bonding*. Oxford: Blackwell Scientific.

References

Ainsworth, M. D. S. (1979) Attachment as related to mother–infant interaction. In *Advances in the Study of Behaviour*, vol. 9 (eds J. S. Rosenblatt, R. A. Hinde, C. Beer, & M. Busnel). Orlando, FL: Academic Press.
——, Blehar, M., Waters, E., *et al* (1978) *Patterns of Attachment*. Hillsdale, NJ: Erlbaum.
Alley, T. R. (1981) Head shape and the perception of cuteness. *Developmental Psychology*, **17**, 650–654.
American Psychiatric Association (1987) *Diagnostic and Statistical Manual of Mental Disorders* (3rd edn, revised) (DSM–III–R). Washington, DC: APA.
Bower, T. G. R. (1974) *Development in Infancy*. San Francisco: Freeman.
Bowlby, J., Ainsworth, M., Boston, M., *et al* (1956) The effects of mother–child separation: a follow-up study. *British Journal of Medical Psychology*, **29**, 211–247.
Brazelton, T. B., Robery, J. S. & Collier, G. A. (1969) Infant development in the Zinacanteco Indians of southern Mexico. *Pediatrics*, **44**, 274–93.
Brooks, J. & Lewis, M. (1976) Infants' responses to strangers: adult, midget and child. *Child Development*, **47**, 323–332.
Bushnell, I. W. R., Sai, F. & Mullin, T. (1989) Neonatal recognition of the mother's face. *British Journal of Developmental Psychology*, **7**, 3–15.
Carlsson, S. G., Fagenberg, H., Horneman, G., *et al* (1979) Effects of various amounts of contact between mother and child on the mother's nursing behaviour: a follow-up study. *Infant Behaviour and Development*, **2**, 209–214.

Clarke, A. M. & Clarke, A. D. B. (1976) *Early Experience: Myth and Evidence*. London: Open Books.

Condon, W. & Sanders, L. (1974) Neonatal movement is synchronised with adult speech: interactional participation and language acquisition. *Science*, **183**, 99–101.

De Casper, A. J. & Fifer, W. P.(1980) Of human bonding: newborns prefer their mothers' voices. *Science*, **208**, 1174–1176.

Egeland, B. & Vaughn, B. (1981) Failure of bond formation as a cause of abuse, neglect and maltreatment. *American Journal of Orthopsychiatry*, **51**, 78–84.

Feinman, S. & Lewis, M. (1983) Social referencing at 10 months: a second-order effect on infants' responses to strangers. *Child Development*, **54**, 753–771.

Gleitman, L., Newport, E. & Gleitman, H. (1984) The current status of the motherese hypothesis. *Journal of Child Language*, **11**, 43–79.

Goren, G. C., Sarty, M. & Wu, P. Y. K. (1975) Visual following and pattern discrimination of face-like stimuli by newborn infants. *Pediatrics*, **56**, 544–549.

Greene, J. G., Fox, N. A. & Lewis, M. (1983) The relationship between neonatal characteristics and three-month mother infant interaction in high risk infants. *Child Development*, **54**, 1286–1296.

Grossman, K. & Grossman, K. (1981) Parent–infant attachment relationships in Bielefeld. A research note. In *Behavioural Development: The Bielefeld Interdisciplinary Project* (ed. K. Immelman). New York: Cambridge University Press.

Harlow, H. F. & Harlow, M. K. (1962) Social deprivation in monkeys. *Scientific American*, November.

Hodges, J. & Tizard, B. (1989) Social and family relationships of ex-institutional adolescents. *Journal of Child Psychology and Psychiatry*, **30**, 77–99.

Hutt, S. J., Lenard, H. G. & Prechtl, H. F. R. (1969) Psychophysiological studies in new-born infants. In *Advances in Child Development and Behaviour*, vol. 4 (eds L. P. Lipsitt & H. W. Reese). New York: Academic Press.

Jacobson, S. (1979) Matching behaviour in the young infant. *Child Development*, **50**, 425–430.

Kagan, J. (1976) Emergent themes in human development. *Scientific American*, **64**, 186–196.

—— (1984) *The Nature of the Child*. New York: Basic Books.

Kaye, K. (1982) *The Mental and Social Life of Babies*. London: Methuen.

—— & Fogel, A. (1980) The temporal structure of face-to-face communication between mothers and infants. *Developmental Psychology*, **16**, 454–464.

Klaus, M. H.& Kennel, J. H. (1976) *Parent–Infant Bonding*. St Louis: Mosby.

Lewis, M., Young, G., Brooks, J., *et al* (1975) The beginning of friendship. In *Friendship and Peer Relations* (eds M. Lewis & L. A. Rosenblum). New York: Wiley.

Lynch, M. A.(1975) Ill health and child abuse, *Lancet, ii*, 317–319.

Main, M. & Soloman, J. (1986) Discovery of an insecure disorganized attachment pattern. In *Affective Development in Infancy* (eds T. Brazelton & M. Yogman). New Jersey: Ablex.

Meltzoff, A.N. & Moore, M.K. (1977) Imitation of facial and manual gestures by human neonates. *Science*, **1998**, 75–78.

Newport, E., Gleitman, H. & Gleitman, L. (1977) Mother, I'd rather do it myself: some effects and non-effects of maternal speech style. In *Talking to Children* (eds C. Snow & C. Ferguson). Cambridge: Cambridge University Press.

Novak, M. A. (1979) Social recovery of monkeys isolated for the first year of life. *Developmental Psychology*, **15**, 50–61.

Patrick, M., Hobson, P., Castle, D., *et al* (1991) Patterns of relationship: associations among adult personality disorder, adult attachment classifications, and perceptions of early parenting. Paper given at the British Psychological Society, Developmental Section Conference: Cambridge.

Prior, M. (1992) Childhood temperament. *Journal of Psychology and Psychiatry*, **33**, 249–279.

Quinton, D. & Rutter, M. (1976) Early hospital admissions and later disturbances of behaviour: and attempted replication of Douglas' findings. *Developmental Medicine and Child Neurology*, **18**, 447–459.

Radke-Yarrow, M., Cummings, E. M., Kuczynski, L., *et al* (1985) Patterns of attachment in two and three year olds in normal families with parental depression. *Child Development*, **56**, 884–893.

Rode, S. S., Chang, P. N., Fisch, R. O., *et al* (1981) Attachment patterns of infants separated at birth. *Developmental Psychology*, **17**, 188–191.

Rosenstein, D. & Oster, H. (1988) Differential facial responses to four basic tastes in newborns. *Child Development*, **59**, 1555–1568.

Rutter, M. (1981) *Maternal Deprivation Reassessed*. London: Penguin.

Schaffer, H. R. & Emerson, P. E. (1964) Patterns of response to early physical contact in early human development. *Journal of Child Psychology and Psychiatry*, **5**, 1–13.

Sluckin, W., Herbert, M. & Sluckin, A. (1984) *Maternal Bonding*. Oxford: Blackwell Scientific.

Snow, C. (1977) The development of conversation between mothers and children. *Journal of Child Language*, **4**, 1–22.

Sroufe, L. A. (1977) Wariness of strangers and the study of infant development. *Child Development*, **48**, 1184–1199.

—— (1985) Attachment classifications from the perspective of infant–caregiver relationships and infant temperament. *Child Development*, **56**, 1–14.

Stern, D. (1977) *The First Relationship: Infant and Mother*. London: Fontana.

Stewart, R. B. (1983) Sibling attachment relationships: child infant interactions in the strange situation. *Developmental Psychology*, **19**, 192–199.

Svejde, M. J., Campos, J. J. & Emde, R. N. (1980) Mother–infant bonding: failure to generalize. *Child Development*, **51**, 775–779.

Troy, M. & Sroufe, L. A. (1987) Victimization among pre-schoolers: role of attachment relationship history. *Journal of the American Academy of Child and Adolescent Psychiatry*, **26**, 166–172.

Turner, P. J. (1991) Relations between attachment, gender and behaviour with peers in pre-school. *Child Development*, **62**, 1475–1488.

Waters, E., Wippman, J. & Sroufe, L. A. (1979) Attachment, positive affect and competence in the peer group: two studies in construct validation. *Child Development*, **50**, 821–829.

Weber, R. A., Levitt, M. J. & Clark, M. C. (1986) Individual variation in attachment security and strange situation behaviour: the role of maternal and infant temperament. *Child Development*, **57**, 56–65.

Wishart, J. G. & Bower, T. G. R. (1985) A longitudinal study of the development of the object concept. *British Journal of Developmental Psychology*, **3**, 243–258.

9 Personal relationships

Duncan Cramer

---

*Attraction and satisfaction • Similarity and complementarity •
Satisfaction with a relationship • Social exchange • Social interaction •
Beliefs and attributions • Conclusions*

Close or personal relationships play an important part in the lives of most people. For instance, about 67% of a representative sample of British adults interviewed in 1986 said that they were married and living with their spouse, while a further 4% reported that they were cohabiting with their partner (Jowell *et al*, 1987). Only about 20% stated that they did not have a steady partner. Excluding partners and family, about 86% said that they had a close friend and over 50% estimated that they saw their closest friend at least once a week.

Furthermore, how happy or unhappy we generally feel is most highly associated with how happy we are with our marital relationship. Surveys of married adults in the United States have found that overall happiness is more strongly related to marital happiness than to satisfaction with other aspects of life such as work, income, or leisure (Glenn & Weaver, 1981). Although most Americans say they are happy with their marriages, marital difficulties are the most common personal problem for which professional help is sought (Veroff *et al*, 1981): about 40% of people who sought expert help did so for marital difficulties. The breakup of a marriage can cause considerable emotional and financial hardship (Bloom *et al*, 1978; Spanier & Thompson, 1987).

While non-experimental findings such as these cannot establish whether marital happiness is the cause of psychological well-being, they do suggest that the causal nature of this association is worth exploring further. The ways in which supportive relationships may ameliorate both psychological and physical health is discussed elsewhere.

Perhaps the issue which is seen as central to the study of personal relationships and which has received the greatest attention is the development of such relationships, including their maintenance and dissolution. This chapter briefly outlines and evaluates some of the most important research carried out on personal relationships, as well as some of the main principles put forward to explain their growth (Box 9.1). The theoretical and methodological strengths and limitations of this work are also discussed.

**Box 9.1   Potential factors involved in the development
of personal relationships**

Physical attractiveness
Perceived acceptance
Similar attitudes on central issues
Less negative ways of resolving salient disagreements
Sexual attitudes
Emotional stability

Most of the research appears to have been done on romantic or marital heterosexual relationships rather than on friendships. Since many of the proposed theoretical principles are stated in such general terms that they can be seen as applying to most kinds of close relationship, it is more economical to discuss the research on these two kinds of relationship together rather than separately.

Attraction and satisfaction

Many theories of personal relationships suggest that the attraction felt towards someone or the satisfaction obtained from the relationship with that person is based on how rewarding the relationship is. For example, Byrne & Rhamey (1965) defined 'attraction' behaviourally as

> "the positive linear function of the sum of the weighted positive reinforcements associated with that person, divided by the total number of weighted positive and negative reinforcements associated with them."

Winch (1958), on the other hand, has described love more generally as the positive experience which results from the other person's fulfilling one's important needs and/or possessing desirable characteristics, while Thibaut & Kelley (1959) have stated that attractive or satisfactory relationships are ones in which the overall rewards or outcome are perceived as being greater than those experienced by themselves alone, or others.

Several attempts have been made to differentiate empirically various kinds of interpersonal attraction. A recurrent distinction is that between passionate and non-passionate attraction.

Differentiating love

Rubin (1970) developed two 13-item scales to measure loving and liking, which have been widely used. The liking scale may be more accurately described as assessing respect, since most of the items seem to be measuring this attribute.

The most highly differentiated conceptualisation of love has been put forward by Lee (1976). He described six main types of loving relationships, which were given Greek or Roman names and which were seen as having a predominant characteristic:

(1) eros (physical attraction)
(2) mania (possessive, dependent love)
(3) storge (friendship)
(4) pragma (rational, practical love)
(5) agape (altruistic love)
(6) ludus (non-committal love).

While Lee described his classification as a typology, it may be more precisely and economically regarded as a multidimensional scheme in which his six basic types constitute six dimensions along which love may vary. Six 7-item scales have been designed to measure these dimensions (Hendrick & Hendrick, 1986), although there is some disagreement about their construction (Feeney & Noller, 1990). Because of the atheoretical nature of these classificatory proposals, it is unclear whether these distinctions have implications for how interpersonal attraction is to be explained.

Desirable characteristics

One problem with defining attraction and satisfaction in terms of rewards is that no information is given as to what characteristics are seen as being rewarding. A simple method of initially trying to determine these qualities is to question people about what features in a person or relationship they find desirable.

When people are asked what makes for a successful or happy marriage, the characteristics which are most frequently mentioned imply mutual love and commitment. For instance, a representative British sample of adults chose faithfulness, mutual respect/appreciation, and understanding/ tolerance as the three most important qualities for producing a successful marriage from a list of 13 characteristics (Jowell *et al*, 1987). Love, trust, and mutual respect were judged by a random group of married Americans to be the most important of 32 listed factors in bringing about marital satisfaction (Sabatelli & Pearce, 1986), while the absence of these kinds of factors were most often cited as reasons for seeking divorce (Levinger, 1966). These kinds of factors have also been found to be highly related to marital satisfaction (Snyder, 1979).

While these findings are of some interest, their value in helping to identify rewarding features of relationships is limited in that the qualities most commonly mentioned are precisely those aspects of relationships that need to be explained. Consequently, it may be necessary to pay more attention to factors rated as being less important, such as having similar interests and attitudes. Indeed, the role played in close relationships by more specific characteristics such as physical attractiveness, attitudes, and personality have often been separately investigated.

A few studies, however, have simultaneously examined a variety of variables in a relatively large number of close relationships. The great advantage of this kind of research is that it shows which of many factors are most closely associated with such relationships, and which therefore may be most deserving of closer scrutiny. The earliest studies were carried out by Terman (1938), on 1133 married and 109 divorced couples living in California, and by Burgess & Wallin (1943) on 1000 engaged couples residing in Chicago. More recent studies have been conducted by Eysenck & Wakefield (1981), on 566 married couples in Britain, and Kandel (1978), on 1879 adolescent friendship pairs in New York State.

Similarity and complementarity

One method of exploring which factors are most strongly allied to interpersonal attraction is to choose those variables on which the two members of a relationship are most highly correlated. Eysenck & Wakefield (1981) found that the largest correlations were obtained (in decreasing order of size) for age, marital satisfaction, social attitudes, and sexual attitudes. There were also small, significant correlations for the personality variables of conscientiousness, neuroticism, and psychoticism (see Chapter 10). While the personality factor of neuroticism seems to reflect emotional instability, that of psychoticism may be more accurately described as representing lack of caring (Cramer, 1992). All these correlations were positive, indicating that like tends to marry like.

More recent studies have also noted that married couples tend to be similar in terms of education, intelligence, and some personality factors (Mascie-Taylor & Vandenberg, 1988; Phillips *et al*, 1988), together with physical characteristics such as height and weight (Harrison *et al*, 1976). However, it should be noted that the correlations for similar personality variables are not always significant. For example, while Eysenck & Wakefield (1981) obtained a significant correlation for neuroticism but not for extraversion, Mascie-Taylor & Vandenberg (1988) reported the reverse, and Harrison *et al* (1976) observed no significant correlations.

In another large study, which was primarily concerned with illegal drug use in adolescents, Kandel (1978) found that friends were most similar in drug use and academic activities, and less alike on other characteristics such as self-esteem or political orientation.

People may form close relationships with others because they share similar interests and attitudes. People with common concerns may spend more time together enjoying and exploring those interests, while having one's own views confirmed by those with similar attitudes may be reassuring. Indeed, the major component of one of the most widely used instruments of marital adjustment, the Marital Adjustment Test (Locke & Wallace, 1959), and of related questionnaires such as the Dyadic Adjustment Scale (Spanier, 1976), measures the extent to which partners agree on various issues. This factor has been reported to be strongly related to satisfaction, affection, and 'togetherness' (Spanier, 1976; Eysenck & Wakefield, 1981), implying that holding similar views on certain issues is associated with these other dimensions.

Similarity and the direction of causality

One problem with cross-sectional studies, in which the same variables are measured at only one point in time, is that the causal direction of the correlation between two variables cannot be ascertained. Four causal connections are possible for any observed association between two factors such as being attracted and having similar attitudes:

(1) we may like those who hold similar attitudes
(2) we may develop similar views to those of people we like
(3) both (1) and (2) may occur
(4) the association may be spurious and may result from other related factors, such as age or social class.

To determine whether people are attracted to those with similar attitudes, Byrne (1961, 1971) used a simple experimental paradigm in which subjects who had given their opinions on various topics were asked to form an impression of a stranger based on the stranger's supposed opinions on the same topics. The similarity of the non-existent stranger's answers to those of the subject were varied by the experimenter. Using this procedure, Byrne found that liking was a function not of the total number of similar attitudes, but of the proportion of similar to dissimilar attitudes, weighted in terms of their importance.

More recently, Condon & Crano (1988) have proposed that the reason for the similarity–attraction relationship is that we assume that people with similar views will like us, and that it is this positive inference which is responsible for the subject's favourable evaluation of the stranger. However, this interpretation seems to beg the question of why we should assume that similar others will like us.

These findings do not rule out the possibility that our views may become more similar to those we like. This idea does not seem to have been adequately tested. The observation by Eysenck & Wakefield (1981) that longer-married spouses were not generally more similar does not mean that no change in attitudes took place, since couples were only tested at one time. Furthermore, the attitudes may have become more alike during the courting, before marriage.

The attraction of dissimilarities

It has been suggested that for some characteristics, members of a close relationship may not be expected to be similar and may even be dissimilar. For example, a dominant person may prefer to interact with someone more submissive. Winch (1958), who proposed such a complementarity theory for the satisfaction of psychological needs, distinguished two types of need complementarity. In the first type, one partner is high on a need such as dominance, while the other is low on it. In the second type, one person is high on a need such as nurturance, while the other is high on a different but complementary need such as succour. Winch's work has stimulated substantial research, particularly on the first type of complementarity, which has generally not supported this notion (Murstein, 1976).

Satisfaction with a relationship

An alternative procedure for ascertaining which variables are most closely related to interpersonal attraction is to examine the correlation between these variables and satisfaction with the relationship. This approach was also used by Eysenck & Wakefield (1981), who found that marital satisfaction in both husbands and wives was most strongly associated with sexual satisfaction, certain sex-related behaviour (such as frequency of refusing sex and desiring sex with someone else), and psychoticism and neuroticism in both partners, although the correlation for the same variable in the partner tended to be slightly lower than that for the respondent. Those satisfied with their marriages reported more sexual satisfaction and positive sex-related behaviour but lower psychoticism and neuroticism. Moreover, Eysenck & Wakefield (1981) noted that the qualities themselves were more highly correlated with marital satisfaction than was how similar couples were in terms of these qualities.

Since two of the 22 items assessing marital satisfaction in this study referred to sex, the moderately large correlation between marital satisfaction and both sexual satisfaction and behaviour may have been partly due to this overlap in content between these measures. However, Snyder (1979) also found that global marital dissatisfaction (which did not refer to sexual activity) was moderately associated with sexual dissatisfaction, indicating that this relationship is not simply a function of any commonality of content.

Longitudinal studies

Inferring the causal direction of an observed association between two variables is not possible in a cross-sectional study. Although the most appropriate method for determining causality is a truly experimental design in which only the factors of interest are varied and participants are randomly exposed to these variations, this procedure is often difficult to implement in the study of personal relationships. A method which yields more information about the causal nature of an association than a cross-sectional investigation is the longitudinal study, in which people are tested on two or more occasions. If, for example, sexual satisfaction measured earlier on is found to be positively related to subsequent marital satisfaction, then, clearly, later marital satisfaction could not have been responsible for the earlier sexual satisfaction.

However, the relationship between prior sexual satisfaction and subsequent marital satisfaction may be mediated by other factors, particularly prior marital satisfaction. Consequently, in analysing such data, it is preferable that prior marital satisfaction be controlled statistically. Furthermore, in exploring the predominance, over time, of the two variables, it is advisable that the correlation of prior sexual satisfaction with subsequent marital satisfaction be compared with that between prior marital satisfaction and subsequent sexual satisfaction. If the former correlation is more positive than the latter, then this result implies that sexual satisfaction leads to marital satisfaction. An extended exposition of the rationale behind this approach to analysing longitudinal data is provided elsewhere (Cramer, 1990).

Nonetheless, longitudinal studies which do not incorporate these statistical refinements provide valuable information about the extent to which it is possible to predict marital compatibility. Two notable recent studies are those by Bentler & Newcomb (1978) and Kelly & Conley (1987).

Predicting compatibility

Bentler & Newcomb (1978) collected data on eight demographic features and 28 self-rated personality traits on 77 newly married couples followed up over four years, after which time 24 couples had separated or divorced. The still married group were significantly more similar than the separated group in age, attractiveness, interest in art, and extraversion only. About 46% of the variation in the marital adjustment for the couples was accounted for by ten characteristics. Higher scores for marital adjustment were found where the women had previously had children and were less ambitious

---

Box 9.2   A summary of factors underlying attraction

Similarity: both friends and romantic partners have been found
    to be similar in terms of various sociodemographic and
    psychological factors
Dissimilarity: people who differ psychologically are not particularly
    attracted to one another; there is no good evidence that
    complementarity (e.g. a dominant with a submissive partner)
    produces a good relationship
Psychological characteristics such as emotional stability
Sexual satisfaction

---

and intelligent but more objective, neatly dressed, and masculine, and
where the men were less flexible and orderly but more careful and thrifty.

This appears to be one of the few studies in which the predictive value
of psychological factors was examined with demographic ones such as
age, education, and occupation, although no direct attempt was made to
control the demographic variables statistically. Personality factors,
particularly of the women, made a greater contribution to predicting marital
adjustment than demographic ones. However, no conclusions can be
drawn about the predictive value of partner similarity on these
characteristics since, unlike Eysenck & Wakefield (1981), this measure
was not included in this analysis.

In the study by Kelly & Conley (1987), 300 couples who were engaged
in the 1930s were followed up for more than 40 years. Of these, 22 broke
their engagements and 50 were later divorced. In one analysis of 177
couples, about 20% of the variation in a composite measure of marital
compatibility (consisting of marital status and satisfaction) was accounted
for by five premarital characteristics. Greater marital compatibility was
associated with lower neuroticism and greater impulse control in the man,
and lower neuroticism, less sexual experience than the partner, and fewer
romantic involvements with others in the woman. The three personality
factors were the average ratings of five people who knew the person taking
part at the start of the study, while the measures of sexual and romantic
activity were based on retrospective reports made by the participants about
18 years later.

Emotional stability has been found to be positively related to marital
satisfaction in several longitudinal studies (Sears, 1977; Vaillant, 1978), as
well as cross-sectional ones (Burchinal *et al*, 1957; Zaleski & Galkowska,
1978).

Social exchange

A relationship must be mutually rewarding for two people to be attracted towards one another and to enjoy each other's company. The notion that satisfaction in a relationship depends on the extent to which the overall benefits to each member are maximised, or are expected to be maximised, is the basic assumption underlying what are collectively known as social-exchange theories (La Gaipa, 1977).

Equity

The social-exchange theory that has stimulated most research is equity theory (Walster *et al*, 1978), which consists of four propositions:

(1) people try to maximise their outcomes (where outcome equals rewards minus costs)
(2) groups will develop equitable systems of sharing outcomes which will maximise their collective outcomes
(3) inequity will cause distress, with greater inequity leading to more distress; the under-benefited will feel greater distress than the over-benefited
(4) people will attempt to reduce distress by restoring equity, with more distress resulting in greater efforts to reduce inequity.

The perception of equity in a relationship has been measured in terms of a single quality, different qualities taken together, and globally. Regardless of how it has been assessed, equity has generally been found to be associated with relationship satisfaction in cross-sectional investigations.

A longitudinal study by Van Yperen & Buunk (1990), of 171 Dutch couples followed up for one year, examined the causal relationship between satisfaction and equity evaluated globally and based on a series of factors. The results of this analysis suggested that equity, when measured globally, may lead to subsequent satisfaction only in the women. However, even this finding may come into question, since its interpretation is based on the unexamined assumption that the test–retest correlations of these measures did not differ.

Consequently, the causal relationship between equity and satisfaction is unclear. Furthermore, while global equity was positively related to later satisfaction, other longitudinal studies on student 'dating' relationships have noted no such association for either satisfaction with the relationship or its continued existence (Lujansky & Mikula, 1983; Cate *et al*, 1985; Berg & McQuinn, 1986).

The equity of attractiveness

While perceived equity has generally not been found to predict satisfaction, it is possible that matching takes place on certain desirable characteristics such as physical attractiveness. Although people prefer more physically attractive individuals (Walster *et al*, 1966; Byrne *et al*, 1970), romantic partners including married couples tend to be similar in terms of physical attractiveness as rated by themselves or others (Feingold, 1988). Furthermore, male friends are also rated as being similar in physical attractiveness.

There is little evidence, however, to suggest that women can trade their physical attractiveness for educational attainment in men, or that men can exchange their educational attainment for physical attractiveness in women (Stevens *et al*, 1990). Women with more attractive partners have been found to be less neurotic and have a better sense of humour than women with less attractive partners, while there were no such differences for men (Feingold, 1981).

Interdependence

Another social-exchange approach is interdependence theory (Thibaut & Kelley, 1959), which generally postulates that people will be more attracted to a person and will be more satisfied with that relationship if the outcome from it is more positive than anticipated (their comparison level). On the other hand, they will be dependent on that relationship if the outcome from it is greater than they expect to attain elsewhere (their comparison level for alternatives). In other words, interdependence theory distinguishes satisfaction from dependence.

Contrary to the theory, Michaels *et al* (1984) found that relationship satisfaction was more strongly related to actual than to anticipated outcome. They also noted that commitment (which is seen as being synonymous with dependence) was more highly associated with simple outcome than with other alternatives (Michaels *et al*, 1986).

More consistent with the theory was the finding that the breakup of marriages two years later was better predicted by marital alternatives than by marital satisfaction, although both variables explained only about 8% of the variation in marital stability (Udry, 1981).

The investment model

An extension of interdependence theory is the investment model (Rusbult, 1980), which proposes that commitment to a relationship will be stronger the better the outcome, the fewer the alternatives, and the greater the investment.

In a longitudinal study, 34 students who were dating were followed up over seven months, or less if their relationship had ended before then, as happened to ten of them (Rusbult, 1983). For those who stayed together, costs increased less and alternatives became less attractive, while rewards, satisfaction, investment, and commitment all increased more than for those who separated.

At least two other similar longitudinal studies on student romantic relationships have been reported. One study found that couples who remained together over four months, initially had both a higher comparison level and comparison level for alternatives than, but did not differ in rewards from, those who had broken up (Berg & McQuinn, 1986). The other study reported that partners who stayed together over two months, originally had greater satisfaction, investment, and commitment than those who split up (Hendrick *et al*, 1988).

Although the results of these three studies are generally consistent with the investment model, because the follow-up period in all of them was relatively short, it is unclear to what extent the social exchange variables simply described rather than predicted what happened in these relationships. Furthermore, in a cross-sectional study on a much larger number of couples, Sprecher (1988) found that commitment was largely associated with satisfaction and alternatives, and that when these two factors were taken into account, investments did not make a significant contribution.

Social exchange and dissatisfaction

Rusbult *et al* (1982, 1986) have suggested that how people react to an increase in dissatisfaction in a relationship also depends on satisfaction with the relationship, the investment in it, and the alternatives to it. Four major responses to such dissatisfaction were proposed:

(1) exit (leaving the relationship)
(2) voice (trying to resolve the problem)
(3) loyalty (acting positively while waiting for improvement without working to bring it about)
(4) neglect (ignoring the problem but behaving negatively).

Greater satisfaction and investment should lead to voice and loyalty rather than exit and neglect, while better alternatives should bring about voice and exit rather than loyalty and neglect. Several cross-sectional and experimental studies generally supported these propositions, although there was little consistent relationship between alternatives and voice or neglect.

The tautology in social exchange

One major problem with social-exchange constructs is that they are conceptually similar to the phenomena they are trying to explain and so may, in effect, be largely tautological. For example, admitting that there are more appealing alternatives to a current relationship might well be another way of saying that that relationship is not satisfactory and that the commitment to it is not high. Consequently, it would not be surprising if all three measures of alternatives, satisfaction, and commitment were moderately strongly intercorrelated, as has sometimes been noted (Sprecher, 1988). Moreover, many of these concepts are assessed by questionnaires with relatively few items, making it difficult to determine the reliability and validity of these measures.

Social interaction

Unhappy couples

Do couples in which one or both partners report being dissatisfied with their relationship actually behave differently from those who are satisfied? Several studies have found that when discussing issues (including marital ones) in a laboratory setting, unhappily married couples behave more negatively than happily married ones, as rated by outside observers (Gottman *et al*, 1977; Birchler *et al*, 1975; Billings, 1979; Gottman, 1979; Cousins & Vincent, 1983; Schaap, 1984). Moreover, the difference between unhappy and happy couples was greater for non-verbal than verbal behaviour (Gottman, 1979; Schaap, 1984).

However, Smith *et al* (1990) have reported that although negative behaviour observed in couples discussing a disagreement six weeks before the wedding was concurrently associated with relationship satisfaction, neither negative nor positive behaviour in this situation was related to marital satisfaction 6, 18, and 30 months after the wedding. On the other hand, while greater involvement in this discussion was not related to premarital satisfaction, it was associated with marital satisfaction at 18 and 30 months. In other words, predictors of marital satisfaction may differ from their current correlates.

Some other interesting findings were reported by Gottman (1979). Unhappy couples were more likely to reciprocate negative behaviour, to disagree than to agree, to use sarcasm, to express feelings negatively, to make attributions negatively, and to respond to a feeling about a problem with a feeling about the same problem or a different one, and not to agree with the feeling. In addition, unhappy spouses reacted more negatively than happy spouses to hypothetical remarks which they had to imagine as coming from their partner. However, contrary to the conclusion drawn by Gottman, this finding does not indicate that spouses' responses were more a function of their marital relationship than their general style of relating to others, since their behaviour to their partner was not compared with how they might have responded to comments made by someone other than their spouse, such as a close friend.

It was also noted that although dissatisfied couples do not vary from satisfied ones in terms of their perception of the intended effect of their own responses to their partner when discussing problems in a laboratory, they do evaluate the effect of their partner's response to them as being more negative than do satisfied couples (Gottman *et al*, 1976; Gottman, 1979). In a follow-up study of 26 couples intending to marry, these laboratory-based ratings of intended effects correlated moderately with marital satisfaction, not only two and a half years later (Gottman, 1979; Markman, 1979) but also five and a half years later (Markman, 1981), which was not the case for a relationship questionnaire (although Smith *et al* (1990) found that premarital satisfaction in more than 65 couples was generally most strongly and consistently related to marital satisfaction at 6, 18, and 30 months after the wedding).

The procedure used by Gottman and Markman cannot determine whether the responses were sent or were interpreted more negatively than was intended. Unhappily married husbands in particular have been found to be less accurate than happily married ones in both communicating and decoding affect non-verbally, although no affective bias was detected in the errors made (Noller, 1980). This suggests that the difference between happy and unhappy couples may lie in the verbal rather than the non-verbal content of the response. There was no difference between satisfied and dissatisfied couples in understanding the non-verbal intent of messages sent by strangers, implying that the difficulties of interpretation lay in the marital relationship and not in the general ability to decipher non-verbal affect (Noller, 1981). Sabatelli *et al* (1982), however, noted that the wife's ability to convey accurately her feelings facially was associated with greater marital satisfaction of her husband, and that the wife's ability to interpret her husband's poorly encoded facial expressions accurately was related to greater marital satisfaction of both herself and her husband.

Beliefs and attributions

Several investigators have suggested that beliefs about relationships may help determine the satisfaction felt with them. For example, believing that relationships should be equitable has been shown to be related to marital dissatisfaction (Murstein *et al*, 1977; Broderick & O'Leary, 1986). However, whether marital dissatisfaction was increased in couples with inequitable relationships was not investigated.

Eidelson & Epstein (1982) proposed that relationship satisfaction may be adversely influenced by the following five dysfunctional beliefs about relationships:

(1) disagreement is destructive
(2) mind-reading is expected
(3) partners cannot change
(4) sexual perfectionism
(5) the sexes are very different.

These beliefs, particularly that of disagreement being destructive, have been found to be correlated with current relationship dissatisfaction (Eidelson & Epstein, 1982; Kurdek & Schmitt, 1986; Epstein *et al*, 1987; Fincham & Bradbury, 1987), but not with marital dissatisfaction one year later by a composite belief measure (Fincham & Bradbury, 1987).

To whom or to what happily and unhappily married couples attribute various aspects of their marital relationship has been examined in a number of investigations, most of cross-sectional design (Bradbury & Fincham, 1990). Examples of such attributions include seeing the cause of the behaviour as being located in the other partner, as affecting other areas of the marriage, and as likely to recur.

In a longitudinal study of 34 married couples, Fincham & Bradbury (1987) found that causal and responsibility attributions about two marital difficulties and three negative spouse types of behaviour made one year earlier were very weakly related to subsequent marital satisfaction in the wife, but not the husband, when earlier marital satisfaction was taken into account. Initial marital satisfaction, however, was not associated with later satisfaction when earlier attributions were controlled for. Although the number of participants was too small to carry out the most appropriate statistical analysis for exploring causality (Cramer, 1990), the results suggest that, in wives at least, causal and responsibility attributions may lead to marital satisfaction. The causal attribution was based on belief that the origin of the problem lay in the spouse, affected other aspects of the marriage, and was likely to cause the same problem in the future, while the responsibility attribution reflected the view that the spouse should be blamed for the problem and that the behaviour was intentional and resulted from selfishness. Unfortunately, the extent to which these attributions may have been shared or justified was not determined.

Conclusions

Since most of the research has been cross-sectional in design, inference of the causal nature of the observed associations has not been possible. While the predictors used in longitudinal studies have largely differed, the amount of variation in marital compatibility accounted for seems promising and merits further investigation. At this stage, it may be useful to distinguish the following four aspects of personal relationships which may well be related and which need to be explained:

(1) the nature and strength of attraction towards the other person
(2) the satisfaction derived from the relationship
(3) the time spent together
(4) the desired or actual duration of the relationship.

The understanding of relationships is further complicated in that two people are involved, the two people may be of different sex, and the psychological demands on them may vary at different stages in their lifetime. Nonetheless, research to date suggests that the psychological factors which may be most directly implicated in the development of satisfactory romantic relationships include:

(1) the perception of being liked or loved
(2) similarity or agreement over central issues
(3) procedures for satisfactorily resolving salient disagreements
(4) sexual attitudes
(5) physical attractiveness
(6) emotional stability.

While this distillation of characteristics is undoubtedly a gross oversimplification of what is inevitably a complex process, its predictive value deserves to be ascertained.

Further reading

Brehm, S. S. (1992) *Intimate Relationships* (2nd edn). New York: McGraw Hill.
Duck, S. (1991) *Friends For Life: The Psychology of Personal Relationships* (2nd edn). Hemel Hempstead: Harvester Wheatsheaf.
Lauer, R. H. & J. C. Lauer (1991) *Marriage and Family: The Quest for Intimacy*. Dubuque, IA: Brown.

References

Bentler, P. M. & Newcomb, M. D. (1978) Longitudinal study of marital success and failure. *Journal of Consulting and Clinical Psychology*, **46**, 1053–1070.
Berg, J. H. & McQuinn, R. D. (1986) Attraction and exchange in continuing and noncontinuing dating relationships. *Journal of Personality and Social Psychology*, **50**, 942–952.
Billings, A. (1979) Conflict resolution in distressed and nondistressed married couples. *Journal of Consulting and Clinical Psychology*, **47**, 368–376.

Birchler, G. R., Weiss, R. L. & Vincent, J. P. (1975) Multimethod analysis of social reinforcement exchange between maritally distressed and nondistressed spouse and stranger dyads. *Journal of Personality and Social Psychology*, **31**, 349–360.

Bloom, B. L., Asher, J. A. & White, S. W. (1978) Marital disruption as a stressor: a review and analysis. *Psychological Bulletin*, **85**, 867–894.

Bradbury, T. N. & Fincham, F. D. (1990) Attributions in marriage: review and critique. *Psychological Bulletin*, **107**, 3–33.

Broderick, J. E. & O'Leary, K. D. (1986) Contributions of affect, attitudes, and behavior to marital satisfaction. *Journal of Consulting and Clinical Psychology*, **54**, 514–517.

Burchinal, L. G., Hawkes, G. R. & Gardner, B. (1957) Personality characteristics and marital satisfaction. *Social Forces*, **35**, 218–222.

Burgess, E. W. & Wallin, P. (1943) Homogamy in social characteristics. *American Journal of Sociology*, **49**, 109–124.

Byrne, D. (1961) Interpersonal attraction and attitude similarity. *Journal of Abnormal and Social Psychology*, **62**, 713–715.

—— (1971) *The Attraction Paradigm*. New York: Academic Press.

—— & Rhamey, R. (1965) Magnitude of positive and negative reinforcements as a determinant of attraction. *Journal of Personality and Social Psychology*, **2**, 884–889.

——, Ervin, C. R. & Lamberth, J. (1970) Continuity between the experimental study of attraction and real–life computer dating. *Journal of Personality and Social Psychology*, **16**, 157–165.

Cate, R. M., Lloyd, S. A. & Henton, J. M. (1985) The effect of equity, equality, and reward level on the stability of students' premarital relationships. *Journal of Social Psychology*, **125**, 715–725.

Condon, J. W. & Crano, W. D. (1988) Inferred evaluation and the relation between attitude similarity and interpersonal attraction. *Journal of Personality and Social Psychology*, **54**, 789–797.

Cousins, P. C. & Vincent, J. P. (1983) Supportive and aversive behavior following spousal complaints. *Journal of Marriage and the Family*, **45**, 679–682.

Cramer, D. (1990) Towards assessing the therapeutic value of Rogers's core conditions. *Counselling Psychology Quarterly*, **3**, 57–66.

—— (1992) *Personality and Psychotherapy: Theory, Practice and Research*. Milton Keynes: Open University Press.

Eidelson, R. J. & Epstein, N. (1982) Cognition and relationship maladjustment: development of a measure of dysfunctional relationship beliefs. *Journal of Consulting and Clinical Psychology*, **50**, 715–720.

Epstein, N., Pretzer, J. L. & Fleming, B. (1987) The role of cognitive appraisal in self–reports of marital communication. *Behavior Therapy*, **18**, 51–69.

Eysenck, H. J. & Wakefield, J. A., Jr (1981) Psychological factors as predictors of marital satisfaction. *Advances in Behaviour Research and Therapy*, **3**, 151–192.

Feeney, J. A. & Noller, P. (1990) Attachment style as a predictor of adult romantic romantic relationships. *Journal of Personality and Social Psychology*, **58**, 281–291.

Feingold, A. (1981) Testing equity as an explanation for romantic couples "mismatched" on physical attractiveness. *Psychological Reports*, **49**, 247–250.

—— (1988) Matching for attractiveness in romantic partners and same–sex friends: a meta–analysis and theoretical critique. *Psychological Bulletin*, **104**, 226–235.

Fincham, F. D. & Bradbury, T. N. (1987) The impact of attributions in marriage: a longitudinal analysis. *Journal of Personality and Social Psychology*, **53**, 510–517.

Glenn, N. D. & Weaver, C. N. (1981) The contribution of marital happiness to global happiness. *Journal of Marriage and the Family*, **43**, 161–168.

Gottman, J. M. (1979) *Marital Interaction: Experimental Investigations*. New York: Academic Press.

——, Notarius, C., Markman, H., *et al* (1976) Behavior exchange theory and marital decision making. *Journal of Personality and Social Psychology*, **34**, 14–23.

——, Markman, H. J. & Notarius, C. I. (1977) The topography of marital conflict: a sequential analysis of verbal and nonverbal behavior. *Journal of Marriage and the Family*, **39**, 461–478.

Harrison, G. A., Gibson, J. B. & Hiorns, R. W. (1976) Assortative marriage for psychometric, personality and anthropometric variation in a group of Oxfordshire villages. *Journal of Biosocial Sciences*, **8**, 145–153.

Hendrick, C. & Hendrick, S. (1986) A theory and method of love. *Journal of Personality and Social Psychology*, **50**, 392–402.

Hendrick, S. S., Hendrick, C. & Adler, N. L. (1988) Romantic relationships: love, satisfaction, and staying together. *Journal of Personality and Social Psychology*, **54**, 980–988.

Jowell, R., Witherspoon, S. & Brook, L. (1987) *British Social Attitudes Survey: The 1987 Report*. London: Gower.

Kandel, D. B. (1978) Similarity in real–life adolescent friendship pairs. *Journal of Personality and Social Psychology*, **36**, 306–312.

Kelly, E. L. & Conley, J. J. (1987) Personality and compatibility: a prospective analysis of marital stability and marital satisfaction. *Journal of Personality and Social Psychology*, **52**, 27–40.

Kurdek, L. A. & Schmitt, J. P. (1986) Relationship quality of partners in heterosexual married, heterosexual cohabiting, and gay and lesbian relationships. *Journal of Personality and Social Psychology*, **51**, 711–720.

La Gaipa, J. J. (1977) Interpersonal attraction and social exchange. In *Theory and Practice in Interpersonal Attraction* (ed. S. Duck), pp. 129–164. London: Academic Press.

Lee, J. A. (1976) *Lovestyles* (revised edn). London: Dent.

Levinger, G. (1966) Sources of marital dissatisfaction among applicants for divorce. *American Journal of Orthopsychiatry*, **36**, 803–807.

Locke, H. J. & Wallace, K. M. (1959) Short marital adjustment and prediction tests: their reliability and validity. *Marriage and Family Living*, **21**, 251–255.

Lujansky, H. & Mikula, G. (1983) Can equity theory explain the quality and the stability of romantic relationships? *British Journal of Social Psychology*, **22**, 101–112.

Markman, H. J. (1979) The application of a behavioral model of marriage in predicting relationship satisfaction of couples planning marriage. *Journal of Consulting and Clinical Psychology*, **47**, 743–749.

—— (1981) Prediction of marital distress: a 5–year follow–up. *Journal of Consulting and Clinical Psychology*, **49**, 760–762.

Mascie–Taylor, C. G. N. & Vandenberg, S. G. (1988) Assortative mating for IQ and personality due to propinquity and personal preference. *Behavior Genetics*, **18**, 339–345.

Michaels, J. W., Edwards, J. N. & Acock, A. C. (1984) Satisfaction in intimate relationships as a function of inequality, inequity, and outcomes. *Social Psychology Quarterly*, **47**, 347–357.

—— , Acock, A. C. & Edwards, J. N. (1986) Social exchange and equity determinants of relationship commitment. *Journal of Social and Personal Relationships*, **3**, 161–175.

Murray, H. (1938) *Explorations in Personality*. New York: Oxford University Press.

Murstein, B. I. (1976) *Who Will Marry Whom? Theories and Research in Marital Choice*. New York: Springer.

—— , Cerreto, M. & Macdonald, M. G. (1977) A theory and investigation of the effect of exchange–orientation on marriage and friendship. *Journal of Marriage and the Family*, **39**, 543–548.

Noller, P. (1980) Misunderstandings in marital communication: a study of couples' nonverbal communication. *Journal of Personality and Social Psychology*, **39**, 1135–1148.

—— (1981) Gender and marital adjustment level differences in decoding messages from spouses and strangers. *Journal of Personality and Social Psychology*, **41**, 272–278.

Phillips, K., Fulker, D. W., Carey, G., *et al* (1988) Direct marital assortment for cognitive and personality variables. *Behavior Genetics*, **18**, 347–356.

Rubin, Z. (1970) Measurement of romantic love. *Journal of Personality and Social Psychology*, **16**, 265–273.

Rusbult, C. E. (1980) Commitment and satisfaction in romantic associations: a test of the investment model. *Journal of Experimental Social Psychology*, **16**, 172–186.

—— (1983) A longitudinal test of the investment model: the development (and deterioration) of satisfaction and commitment in heterosexual involvements. *Journal of Personality and Social Psychology*, **45**, 101–117.

—— , Zembrodt, I. M. & Gunn, L. K. (1982) Exit, voice, loyalty, and neglect: responses to dissatisfaction in romantic involvements. *Journal of Personality and Social Psychology*, **43**, 1230–1242.

—— , Johnson, D. J. & Morrow, G. D. (1986) Determinants and consequences of exit, voice, loyalty, and neglect: responses to dissatisfaction in adult romantic involvements. *Human Relations*, **39**, 45–63.

Sabatelli, R. M., Buck, R. & Dreyer, A. (1982) Nonverbal communication accuracy in married couples: relationship with marital complaints. *Journal of Personality and Social Psychology*, **43**, 1088–1097.

—— & Pearce, J. (1986) Exploring marital expectations. *Journal of Social and Personal Relationships*, **3**, 307–321.

Schaap, C. (1984) A comparison of the interaction of distressed and nondistressed married couples in a laboratory situation: literature survey, methodological issues and an empirical investigation. In *Marital Interaction: Analysis and Modification* (eds K. Hahlweg & N. S. Jacobson), pp. 133–158. New York: Guilford Press.

Sears, R. R. (1977) Sources of life satisfaction of the Terman gifted children. *American Psychologist*, **32**, 119–128.

Smith, D. A., Vivian, D. & O'Leary, K. D. (1990) Longitudinal prediction of marital discord from premarital expressions of affect. *Journal of Consulting and Clinical Psychology*, **58**, 790–798.

Snyder, D. K. (1979) Multidimensional assessment of marital satisfaction. *Journal of Marriage and the Family*, **41**, 813–823.

Spanier, G. B. (1976) Measuring dyadic adjustment: new scales for assessing the quality of marriage and similar dyads. *Journal of Marriage and the Family*, **38**, 15–28.

—— & Thompson, L. (1987) *Parting: The Aftermath of Separation and Divorce* (updated edn). Newbury Park, CA: Sage.

Sprecher, S. (1988) Investment model, equity, and social support determinants of relationship commitment. *Social Psychology Quarterly*, **51**, 318–328.

Stevens, G., Owens, D. & Schaefer, E. C. (1990) Education and attractiveness in marriage choices. *Social Psychology Quarterly*, **53**, 62–70.

Terman, L. M. (1938) *Psychological Factors in Marital Happiness*. New York: McGraw-Hill.

Thibaut, J. W. & Kelley, H. H. (1959) *The Social Psychology of Groups*. New York: Wiley.

Udry, J. R. (1981) Marital alternatives and marital disruption. *Journal of Marriage and the Family*, **43**, 889–897.

Vaillant, G. E. (1978) Natural history of male psychological health: VI. Correlates of successful marriage and fatherhood. *American Journal of Psychiatry*, **135**, 653–659.

Van Yperen, N. W. & Buunk, B. B. (1990) A longitudinal study of equity and satisfaction in intimate relationships. *European Journal of Social Psychology*, **20**, 287–309.

Veroff, J., Kulka, R. A. & Douvan, E. (1981) *Mental Health in America: Patterns of Help-Seeking from 1957 to 1976*. New York: Basic Books.

Walster, E., Aronson, V., Abrahams, D., *et al* (1966) Importance of physical attractiveness in dating behavior. *Journal of Personality and Social Psychology*, **4**, 508–516.

——, Walster, G. W. & Berscheid, E. (1978) *Equity: Theory and Research*. Boston: Allyn and Bacon.

Winch, R. F. (1958) *Mate-Selection: A Study of Complementary Needs*. New York: Harper & Row.

Zaleski, Z. & Galkowska, M. (1978) Neuroticism and marital dissatisfaction. *Behaviour Research and Therapy*, **16**, 285–286.

10　Personality and temperament

Hans J. Eysenck

Trait measurement • Validity and reliability • The hierarchical model •
The genetics of personality • The biological basis of personality •
Psychiatric relevance • Conclusions

The terms 'personality' and 'temperament' are often used synonymously by psychologists, and in a sense not dissimilar to popular usage as defined in modern dictionaries. 'Personality' in the *Concise Oxford Dictionary* (6th edn, 1976) is defined as "distinctive personal character", and 'temperament' as "individual character of one's physical constitution permanently affecting the manner of acting, feeling, and thinking".

Given the biosocial nature of man (Eysenck, 1980), the suggested distinction (behavioural or biological) is often difficult to make (there is no behaviour without physiological, neurological, or hormonal antecedents), but some psychologists (e.g. Strelau, 1983) do insist on treating the terms as referring to different contexts.

In essence, the study of personality deals with non-cognitive individual differences, while the study of cognitive differences is more concerned with the study of intelligence and differential abilities, even though cognitive factors also emerge in the study of personality (Kreitler & Kreitler, 1990), but not in the form of differential ability.

In the study of personality, we are mainly concerned with aspects of behaviour (sociable, persistent, machiavellian, suggestible, anxious); these aspects are accompanied by cognitions of one kind or another which guide the expression of these divergent types of behaviour.

The study of personality may be divided into descriptive or taxonomic, on the one hand, and causal, on the other. A taxonomy of behaviour, however provisional, must precede any causal analysis, and psychology has followed in the footsteps of common sense by using the concept of traits as the major constituent of scientific description. There are thousands of trait names in the English language, in the form of nouns, adverbs, or adjectives; clearly, they cannot serve as the basis for any kind of scientific study.

We must try to establish a firm basis for conceptualisation and measurement; as Lord Kelvin said:

> "One's knowledge of science begins when he can measure what he
> is speaking about, and express it in numbers."

How can we transmute popular concepts into measurable quantities? There are many different ways of doing this, some better than others. All must be preceded by a proper conceptualisation of the traits to be measured; we must know what we are looking for if we are to have any hope of finding anything worthwhile.

Trait measurement

Self-rating

The old adage – if you want to know what a person thinks, ask him – can be translated into a more formal set of questions incorporated in a questionnaire. Let us say you are interested in the trait 'sociability'; you can pin down your conceptualisation in the form of a number of questions such as:

> "Do you like being with other people?"
> "Can you bring life to a boring party?"
> "Do you often speak first on meeting someone new?"

After each question you print 'Yes' and 'No' for the subjects of your study to underline, according to their own estimation; or you might also have a '?' between, to allow for people who are doubtful about their correct answer. Or you could have a graded response series, from 'Very much' or 'Very often' through 'Often' to 'Average', 'Seldom', and 'Very rarely'. Or you could print a line marked from 1 to 100, or from 0 to 10, with only the extremes carrying a descriptive wording, and perhaps 'Average' printed in the middle, inviting subjects to put a cross somewhere on the line to indicate their position.

Rating

We often try to estimate other people's personality, as in job interviews, getting to know possible marriage partners, or teachers trying to get to know the children they teach. Such ratings are usually implicit, global, and intuitive; psychologists make them explicit, specific, and conscious, by supplying the rater (who should be intimately acquainted with the subject) with a questionnaire asking for the frequency of specific types of behaviour, such as those listed above in relation to sociability (Davey & Harris, 1982).

Observation

A third method is controlled observation. If we are dealing with schoolchildren, say, we could observe their behaviour in the playground and place a tick in the appropriate place on a prepared sheet whenever a child behaved in a relevant manner; for example, approached another child to initiate a discussion, organised other children in a game, or stood alone in a corner. The observer would be well trained, and be asked to observe each child for a given time before switching to another designated child.

Miniature situation

The observational method could be made more specific by arranging a situation, identical for all subjects, which allowed for social behaviour. Subjects could be invited to come to the laboratory on some pretext, and would then encounter a confederate of the experimenter; the subject's behaviour would be filmed to allow ratings to be made by several independent judges. (The confederate would behave throughout in a manner planned by the experimenter.)

Experimental situation

Real-life

For many traits we can arrange real-life experiments to see how the subject behaves. If we were interested in, say, punctuality of college students, we could arrange a series of meetings, varying in importance, and check when they arrived – early, on time, late – and average their performance over all meetings.

In the laboratory

For some traits we could carry out laboratory experiments. Consider persistence as a trait. We could give our subjects certain tasks in the laboratory which call for persistence, and check their performance. Thus we might give them an IQ test and include an insoluble problem and see how long they persisted with it. Or we could give them a dynamometer to measure the strength of pull, and then ask them to go on pulling at two-thirds of their maximum power to see how long they persisted.

Projective tests

Some tests depend on the interpretations of test behaviour, such as the Rorschach inkblot test or the thematic apperception test. In the former, subjects have to say what they see in a standard series of black-and-white and coloured inkblots; in the latter, they are asked to write short stories on themes suggested by a standard series of drawings.

These tests are based on a fundamental fallacy. The major premise, namely that cognitive choices are determined by personality factors, may be true, but the minor premise, that interpretations can invert the process, is not. I may prefer a Jaguar car to a Mini, and there are undoubtedly good reasons for this. I may be a sporting type whom the image of the car fits; I may be a non-sporting type who wishes to give the image of a daredevil; I may judge on aesthetic grounds, because the Jaguar is such a beautiful car; I may be swayed by the economies of the case, such as getting a luxury car at a non-luxury price. There is an endless list of possible reasons for the choice, and the fact of the choice does not enable us to decide between them; we cannot argue backwards. Empirical study has shown the lack of validity of these tests (Zubin *et al*, 1965).

Expressive techniques

Of the many techniques falling under this heading, graphology (analysis of handwriting) is perhaps the best known. Unfortunately, there is little evidence for its validity: graphology, when tested, usually does better than chance, but not much – certainly not enough to be of any practical use. This is an interesting area for research, as is that of projective techniques, but not for serious application.

Psychophysiology

Behaviour is often mirrored in psychophysiological correlates, and these may be used for personality diagnosis. Thus, we may deduce evidence of anxiety by noting sympathetic activity in mildly anxiety-provoking situations. Differential activation betrays different degrees of anxiety, enabling us to grade persons as to their position on an 'anxiety' continuum (Zuckerman, 1991).

Choosing a technique

The above are the main varieties of techniques used by psychologists, in addition to interview procedures which can be controlled to a varying extent, from 'free' to simply asking a set of predetermined questions. In practice the technique is chosen which fits the requirements of the situation, the theory to be tested, and the type of subject tested. We cannot give a questionnaire to a two-year-old child; we have to rely on controlled observation or parental ratings, for instance. Best of all is usually a combination of methods to cross-validate the methods and obtain more reliable results.

Validity and reliability

This basic and abbreviated listing of methods of measurement will undoubtedly suggest many objections. Do subjects tell the truth? Indeed, do they know the truth about themselves? Do raters know the subject well enough to give a valid assessment? Does a person's behaviour in a laboratory situation tell us anything about his/her everyday behaviour? Cannot a person's behaviour change from day to day, so that no meaningful assessment can be made?

These and many other questions have engaged psychologists for many years, and the answers to most of them are known. We are concerned with two main questions. The first relates to validity: does our measurement really measure what it is supposed to measure? The second relates to reliability: carrying out our measurement several times, do we get similar answers? There are many ways of answering these questions, most of them involving statistical treatment of the data collected.

Suppose we have a 50-item questionnaire on sociability. We can correlate the sum of the 25 odd-numbered questions with the sum of the even-numbered questions; if the correlation is high (as it would be in any properly constructed questionnaire), then, clearly, the answers cohere together in a reliable fashion. Repeat the manoeuvre after six months, and correlate the scores for the two occasions; if the correlation is high, then, clearly, our measure is consistent over time.

A reliable measure is not necessarily valid. We might correlate our score on the questionnaire with the outcome of a rating experiment, or any of the other methods listed; if the outcome is positive, then several quite distinct methods agree on the outcome, suggesting validity. In fact the experiment has been done many times, usually with positive results: social behaviour, self-rated, correlates quite well with ratings given by friends. Agreement is less, although still positive, when less obvious types of behaviour are rated, such as anxiety.

In addition to testing reliability and validity, psychologists have invented techniques to trap subjects resorting to inaccurate or fraudulent reporting. Lie scales have been developed which ask questions which should be answered in a socially undesirable way by an honest subject; for example, "Do you never tell lies?" If a subject answers 'Agree', he is obviously trying to put himself in the best light. (One would not rely on just one question and answer for such a conclusion, but score a whole set of questions.) Some subjects show a 'yea-saying' tendency; that is, they answer 'Yes' much more frequently than 'No'. Hence, in most questionnaires, half the items are written in such a form that the trait-positive question demands an affirmative answer, and half a negative answer.

There are many such tricks to make sure that dishonest or false answers are caught; there is no absolute certainty, but, as we shall see, such questionnaires have been found to predict with considerable accuracy everyday behaviour in real life. Some critics have suggested that traits and their measurement may be pretty useless because human behaviour is situation-based (Mischel, 1968); in other words, it is the situation which determines what we do. We do not smoke on parade, we do not socialise

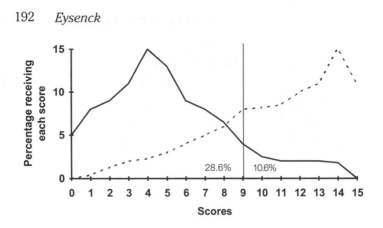

Fig. 10.1 Proportion of neurotics (solid curve) and normal subjects scoring at various levels of an anxiety scale.

in church during the sermon, we do not indulge in drunken driving under the eyes of the police. Such a criticism is mistaken because personality study is concerned with the differential behaviour of people in identical situations; of two people invited to a party, one accepts with joy, another refuses; the situation is identical, but one person is sociable, the other not (Eysenck & Eysenck, 1980).

It is impossible to list all the objections which can be (and have been) made to the use of the methods of measuring personality outlined above, or the answers made by exponents of the methods used to obviate relevant criticisms. A well-designed measure of personality must demonstrate reliability and validity before it is accepted by psychologists as a proper instrument which can be used in clinical, social, industrial, or research work; the standards recommended by professional bodies are high, and adherence is compulsory.

As an example of validation, consider Fig. 10.1, which shows the scores on an anxiety questionnaire filled in by 1000 neurotic and 1000 normal subjects. High scores are characteristic of neurotics, only 28.6% of whom score below nine points on the questionnaire; of the normal subjects, only 10.6% score above that point. Nor are all of these misclassified; it is usually considered that in a normal population, some 10% are in fact neurotic, but decline treatment. There is no one-to-one agreement, but the data show a clear differentiation between the groups.

The hierarchical model

The search for a reliable and valid measurement of personality traits is only a first step. The traits we find are not independent of each other: they correlate in certain patterns that suggest more complex entities that might

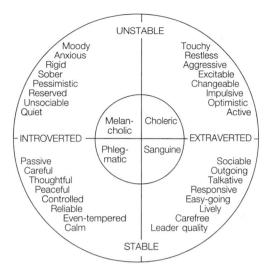

UNSTABLE

Moody
Anxious
Rigid
Sober
Pessimistic
Reserved
Unsociable
Quiet

Touchy
Restless
Aggressive
Excitable
Changeable
Impulsive
Optimistic
Active

Melan-
cholic
Choleric

INTROVERTED

EXTRAVERTED

Phleg-
matic
Sanguine

Passive
Careful
Thoughtful
Peaceful
Controlled
Reliable
Even-tempered
Calm

Sociable
Outgoing
Talkative
Responsive
Easy-going
Lively
Carefree
Leader quality

STABLE

Fig. 10.2 Two major dimensions of personality, the traits characterising extremes on each dimension, and the relation of the dimensions to the four ancient Greek temperaments (Eysenck, 1970)

be called 'types'. The search for such types, higher-order factors, or dimensions of personality, is usually conducted by means of factor analysis, a statistical technique designed to discover patterns in a table of intercorrelations. Two such patterns are

(1) extraversion–introversion (E)
(2) neuroticism–stability (N).

These two dimensions were anticipated in a rather primitive fashion by the ancient Greeks, in the form of their four 'temperaments'. Fig. 10.2 shows the traits which define E and N, and their relation to the four temperaments.

To illustrate briefly how such higher-order constructs originate, consider Box 10.1, which contains six E and six N questions, according to theory. These were administered to a large group of subjects, and answers were intercorrelated and factor analysed. Fig. 10.3 shows the outcome – two clear clusters of items, defining the two factors. Normally, we would of course intercorrelate whole scales, not single questions, but the logic is the same.

Exhaustive research in many parts of the world, and by many investigators, has shown that there are three major dimensions of personality which appear in practically any large-scale analysis, and in many different countries and civilisations (Eysenck & Eysenck, 1985). In

Box 10.1   Six typical extraversion and six typical neuroticism questions (Eysenck, 1970)

1. Do you sometimes feel happy, sometimes depressed, without any apparent reason?
2. Do you have frequent ups and downs in mood, either with or without apparent cause?
3. Are you inclined to be moody?
4. Does your mind often wander while you are trying to concentrate?
5. Are you frequently 'lost in thought' even when supposed to be taking part in a conversation?
6. Are you sometimes bubbling over with energy and sometimes very sluggish?
7. Do you prefer action to planning for action?
8. Are you happiest when you get involved in some project that calls for rapid action?
9. Do you usually take the initiative in making new friends?
10. Are you inclined to be quick and sure in your actions?
11. Would you rate yourself as a lively individual?
12. Would you be very unhappy if you were prevented from making numerous social contacts?

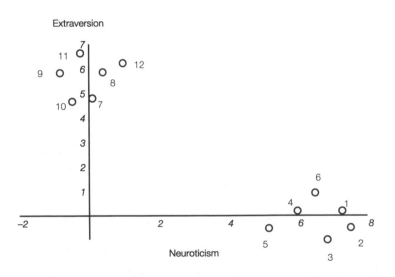

Fig. 10.3 Position of six extraversion and six neuroticism items on two factors derived from intercorrelations of items shown in Box 10.1

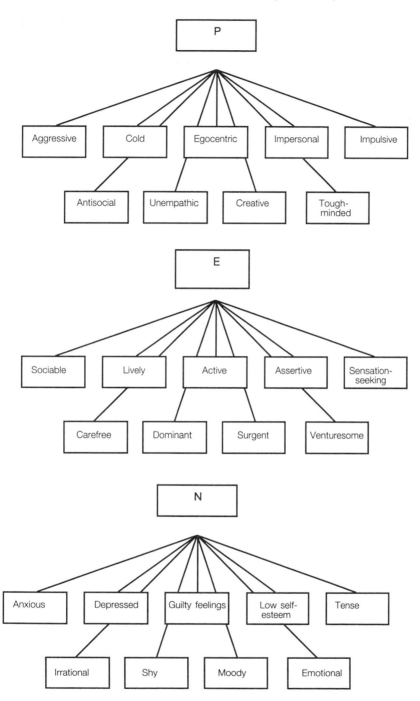

Fig. 10.4 Traits the intercorrelations between which give rise to second-order factors 'psychoticism' (P), 'extraversion' (E), and 'neuroticism' (N) (Eysenck & Eysenck, 1985).

addition to E and N, we have psychoticism–superego control (P), and Fig. 10.4 shows the traits whose intercorrelations establish these dimensions of personality as independent entities forming the centre of human personality.

It is important to distinguish between neuroticism and neurosis, and psychoticism and psychosis. The personality dimension measures a predisposition; the clinical entity an actual psychological disorder. The psychological variable constitutes the diathesis; under strong stress this diathesis can become a psychiatric illness (Claridge, 1985).

The genetics of personality

It is important to turn now to causal factors in the determination of personality differences, and of primary importance is the demonstration that genetic factors are as important as environmental ones; possibly, they are more important (Eaves *et al*, 1989). The evidence here is based on twin studies and adoption studies, often using groups of 12 000 and 15 000 pairs of twins, and complex modern methods of analysis which set up models of genetic and environmental action and interaction, and then test the adequacy of the models against the data obtained from the samples tested.

That genetic factors are the most important single determinants of differences in personality is perhaps not surprising; although long unpopular among psychologists, this fact has never been seriously denied.

What is probably more important is the finding that of the two major environmental influences (common environment or between-family influence, and specific environment or within-family influence), it is the latter that appears from the analyses to be important, not the former. In other words, the influence of the family is almost exclusively genetic; environmental influences come from events that happen to children and adolescents regardless of their family provenance; for example, having an especially good or bad teacher, having or not having an accident or illness, marrying a good or bad partner. This finding, replicated many times, goes counter to most psychological or psychiatric teaching, and illustrates the weak foundation on which most previous theories were constructed. Future theories will have to start *de novo*, and take into account these decisive findings (Loehlin & Nichols, 1976).

Certain consequences follow from these considerations. Psychiatrists are often faced with the question: "To what extent do (extreme) environmental experiences influence personality development?" Early sexual abuse, domestic violence, broken homes, deprivation, or being brought up in a home with parents showing neurotic or even psychotic symptoms may have some bearing on the development of personality, but there are two major problems in proving such theories.

In the first place, the influence may be genetic rather than environmental. Children who are frequently beaten by their parents often become aggressive and even sadistic, but it may be a case of sadistic children inheriting bad genes from sadistic parents (Eaves *et al*, 1989). Many prostitutes complain of early sexual abuse, but the correlation may not be environmental; sexual behaviour may be inherited (Eysenck, 1976). The evidence is inherently ambiguous, and investigations which neglect the possibility of genetic influences cannot be regarded as convincing. (See Chapter 8.)

In the second place, identical environmental conditions may have different and even contrary effects on children differing in genetically determined personality. "The flame that melts the wax tempers the steel." A poor environment may cause some children to give up and submit; others to fight against it and succeed. Again, no account which looks only at environmental effects can be regarded as sufficient.

We always deal with the interaction between nature and nurture, and our experiments have to be geared to that fact. Studies of criminality and antisocial behaviour illustrate the methods appropriate to such investigations (Eysenck & Gudjonsson, 1989). For a detailed discussion of the whole problem, Hoffman (1991) should be consulted; he tried to build a bridge between geneticity and developmental psychologists, and to indicate ways of resolving differences in methods and findings.

It follows from the fact that genetic factors are important in producing differences in personality that there must be observable physiological, neurological, and/or hormonal differences which can serve to mediate the genetic and behavioural sides; DNA cannot directly determine behaviour. This has led to the construction of theories which in turn have produced experimental studies to support or disconfirm theoretical predictions. These form an important part of the scientific study of personality because they enable us to test the validity of our measurements against experimentally testable predictions.

Consider the following chain:

(1) tests are constructed to measure various traits
(2) the traits intercorrelate to suggest a higher-order factor, e.g. E
(3) E is shown to be highly heritable
(4) a biological theory is suggested to account for extraverted behaviour in terms of certain testable physiological/neurological/hormonal factors
(5) experimental studies verify the theoretical predictions (Eysenck, 1967).

Such a progression would seem to give confirmation of the validity of our original measures, and their reliability, as well as the essential correctness of the theory; had the measures been unreliable, invalid, or both, the whole chain of arguments and demonstrations would have collapsed ignominiously.

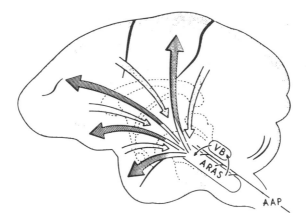

Fig. 10.5 Diagram of biological substrate of cortical arousal (Eysenck, 1967): VB, visceral brain; AAP, ascending afferent pathways; ARAS, ascending reticular activating system.

The biological basis of personality

There is now a huge literature on the topic (Zuckerman, 1991), and I will give only a very brief example of the logic in question. It has been suggested that extraverted behaviour is due to habitual low cortical arousal; extraverts need strong external stimulation to achieve a satisfactory level of arousal (Eysenck, 1967). Introverts on the other hand have a habitual high level of cortical arousal, and hence avoid such strong stimulation. Fig. 10.5 illustrates the theory: incoming ascending afferent pathways take information to the cortex but also send collaterals to the ascending reticular activating system, which in turn sends arousal messages to the cortex to enable it to deal properly with the incoming signals. Extraverts have a sluggish reticular formation, introverts have an overactive one, and ambiverts are in the middle. There are many additional features to this system, but in essence this is what it says.

Strelau & Eysenck (1987) have edited a book which summarises the empirical evidence to date, which is largely physiological (from electroencephalography, contingent negative variation, evoked potentials, positron emission tomography, electrodermal responses, etc.); the verdict is cautiously optimistic. Consider one study to illustrate modes of proof.

Wilson (1990) measured skin conductance in his subjects once every hour, and also got them to write down what they were doing at the time. (The measures were taken by the subjects themselves on a portable device.) It will be seen that throughout the day skin conductance, as a measure of arousal, is higher in introverts than in extraverts, by the age-corrected values (Fig. 10.6). The two scales come together late at night because

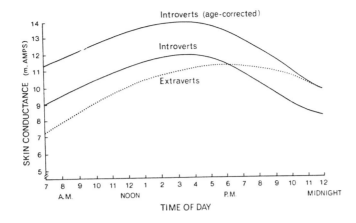

Fig. 10.6 Skin conductance level of extraverts and introverts throughout the day (Wilson, 1990).

extraverts resort to arousal-producing activities (parties, etc.) to increase their arousal, while introverts shun such activities, and resort to arousal-reducing activities such as reading or watching television.

This study is also important because it demonstrates the weakness of the Mischel situationist theory. People are not usually free during the working day to choose what they would like to do; choice is constrained, and hence arousal is determined by personality. But in the evening personality dictates the choice of situation; it is personality traits which select appropriate situations, not situations which determine conduct.

Psychiatric relevance

Psychiatrists may wonder what contributions psychological studies such as those outlined here can make to their concerns. A brief answer would be that there is both an important general contribution, as well as specific contributions.

Taxonomy is of great importance in psychiatry, yet such models as DSM–III are not based on research, but on committee resolutions corresponding to political compromises (Kirk & Kutchins, 1992). The most fundamental problem in any diagnostic scheme is whether we are dealing with a continuum or with categorical disease entities. DSM–IV did not even consider the first alternative but plumped for the second, although there is much psychological evidence to show the relevance of continua – such as stable–neurotic (Claridge, 1985). Eysenck *et al* (1983) have given a detailed criticism along these lines.

The authors of DSM–III have argued that their approach has greatly increased the reliability of diagnoses, but this claim is quite unsubstantiated; diagnoses are as unreliable as ever (Kirk & Kutchins, 1992), as unreliability is inherent in the erroneous choice of a categorical, disease-entity model. Much would be gained by using psychological techniques of analysis, and accepting the continua outlined in previous sections as basic to any proper taxonomy.

A specific example illustrating the application of such a principle is the following (Eysenck, 1987). Personality disorder is one of the most puzzling mental 'diseases' in DSM–III. According to DSM–III, personality disorders can be grouped into three clusters, which resemble quite closely the psychological personality dimensions of P, E, and N. The first cluster (P) includes paranoid, schizoid, and schizotypal personality disorders. The second cluster (E) includes histrionic, narcissistic, antisocial, and borderline personality disorders. The third cluster (N) includes avoidant, dependent, compulsive, and passive–aggressive personality disorders, members of the group often appearing anxious and fearful. Any particular person can be well and reliably diagnosed in terms of his/her standing on the three personality dimensions; forcing a person into a specific disease category (or into the fourth DSM–III category labelled 'atypical' or 'mixed') is inevitably a *pis aller*.

Much can be said in this controversy (Claridge, 1985), but the psychological approach using dimensions or continua has proved far more promising than the disease-entity model more properly belonging to physical medicine.

Conclusions

The study of personality and temperament has come a long way in the past 50 years, as a look at a modern *Handbook of Personality* (Pervin, 1990) will demonstrate. Its richness is suggested by the huge area covered, and by the amount of social behaviour it explains (Wilson, 1981). Large areas of psychiatry depend on personality theory and an accurate measurement of personality variables, and the scientific study of these fields has separated them most markedly from the former reliance on Freudian speculation and untestable interpretation. Studies of the genetic basis of personality, and of the biological intermediaries which translate DNA into behaviour, promise us increasingly precise information on the fundamental question of why we do what we do. Personality study and the investigation of temperament have finally come of age (Pervin, 1990).

Further reading

Pervin, L. A. (ed.) (1990) *Handbook of Personality: Theory and Research*. New York: Guilford Press.

This book provides a balanced account of the various current theories about personality. Situational and interactional theories of personality are given a full treatment, and are contrasted with the biologically oriented, trait approach summarised in this chapter.

References

Brengelmann, J. C. (1960) Expressive movements and abnormal behaviour. In *Handbook of Abnormal Psychology* (ed. H. J. Eysenck), pp. 62–107. London: Pitman.

Claridge, G. (1985) *Origins of Mental Illness*. Oxford: Basil Blackwell.

Davey, D. M. & Harris, M. (1982) *Judging People*. London: McGraw-Hill.

Eaves, L., Eysenck, H. J. & Martin, N. (1989) *Genes, Culture and Personality: An Empirical Approach*. London: Academic Press.

Eysenck, H. J. (1967) *The Biological Basis of Personality*. Springfield, IL: C. C. Thomas.

—— (1970) *The Structure of Human Personality*. London: Methuen.

—— (1976) *Sex and Personality*. London: Open Books.

—— (1980) The biosocial model of man and the unification of psychology. In *Models of Man* (eds A. J. Chapman & P. M. Jones), pp. 49–62. Leicester: British Psychological Society.

—— (1987) The definition of personality disorders and the criteria appropriate for their description. *Journal of Personality Disorders*, 1, 211–219.

——, Wakefield, J. & Friedman, A. (1983) Diagnosis and clinical assessment. The DSM–III. *Annual Review of Psychology*, 34, 167–193.

—— & Eysenck, M. W. (1985) *Personality and Individual Differences: A Natural Science Approach*. New York: Plenum Press.

—— & Gudjonsson, G. (1989) *Causes and Cures of Criminality*. New York: Plenum Press.

Eysenck, M. W. & Eysenck, H. J. (1980) Mischel and the concept of personality. *British Journal of Psychology*, 71, 191–204.

Hoffman, L. W. (1991) The influence of the family environment on personality: accounting for sibling differences. *Psychological Bulletin*, 110, 187–203.

Kirk, S. A. & Kutchens, H. (1992) *The Selling of DSM: The Rhetoric of Science in Psychiatry*. New York: De Gruyter.

Kreitler, S. & Kreitler, H. (1990) *The Cognitive Foundations of Personality Traits*. London: Plenum Press.

Loehlin, J. C. & Nichols, R. C. (1976) *Heredity, Environment and Personality: A Study of 850 Sets of Twins*. Austin: University of Texas Press.

Mischel, W. (1968) *Personality and Assessment*. London: Wiley.

Pervin, L. A. (ed.) (1990) *Handbook of Personality: Theory and Research*. New York: Guilford Press.

Strelau, J. (1983) *Temperament – Personality – Activity*. London: Academic Press.

—— & Eysenck, H. J. (eds) (1987) *Personality Dimensions and Arousal*. New York: Plenum Prss.

Wilson, G. D. (1981) Personality and social behaviour. In *A Model for Personality* (ed. H.J. Eysenck), pp. 210–245. New York: Springer-Verlag.

—— (1990) Personality, time-of-day and arousal. *Personality and Individual Differences*, **11**, 153–168.

Zubin, J., Eron, L. D. & Schumar, F. (1965) *An Experimental Approach to Projective Techniques*. London: Wiley.

Zuckerman, M. (1991) *Psychobiology of Personality*. Cambridge: Cambridge University Press.

11   Sex and gender differences: issues for psychopathology

Georgina Rippon

Sex and gender differences • Sex differences in psychopathology •
Conclusions

As Table 11.1 shows, one particular phenomenon that psychiatrists encounter is that there are apparently sex differences in the risk of psychopathological problems. Women predominate in particular categories of psychopathological disorders, such as depression, phobias, anxiety, and eating disorders (Briscoe, 1982), whereas there is a higher incidence among men of conditions such as alcoholism, sexual disorders, and criminal behaviour (Al-Issa, 1982). This is particularly true of the last category; its inclusion as a category of psychopathological disorders is a matter of debate which is outside the scope of this chapter.

Overall, the majority of adults in treatment for a psychological disorder are women. This is true for rates for admission to hospitals or clinics, community surveys, or treatment by general practitioners (Gove, 1979; Ussher, 1991, p. 165), and even if criminal behaviour is included. Although there are some areas where men are apparently more vulnerable, much research has concentrated on the greater vulnerability of women overall. Examination of this phenomenon could provide insight into the aetiology of psychological disorders by considering women as a high-risk group whose characteristics might indicate factors which increase a person's vulnerability to such problems.

Sex and gender issues in psychopathology have attracted comment on a range of fronts: historical (Showalter, 1987), feminist (Chesler, 1972), and sociological (Miles, 1988), as well as psychological (Ussher, 1991). This chapter considers the relevance of psychology to this debate, by outlining what psychologists have to say about sex and gender differences, both in terms of measurement and explanation, and of indicating how this has been applied in the study of psychopathology. The emphasis is on female psychopathology and psychology's attempts to explain women's apparently greater vulnerability.

It should be noted that the terms 'sex' and 'gender' are sometimes used interchangeably; that is, to refer to a person's biological sex, or differences between groups divided on the basis of their biological sex. The term 'sex differences' is therefore appropriately applied in those studies which attempt a biological explanation of psychopathological problems.

Table 11.1 Hospital admission for psychiatric illness in England (1986)

Diagnostic group	Rates per 100 000 population	
	Males	Females
All diagnoses	364	468
Schizophrenia, paranoia	66	58
Affective psychoses	35	68
Senile and presenile dementia	33	55
Alcoholic psychoses	2	1
Other psychoses (including drug psychoses)	32	44
Neurotic disorders	22	42
Alcohol-dependence syndrome	36	14
Nondependent abuse of alcohol	9	8
Drug dependency	6	3
Nondependent abuse of drugs	3	1
Personality and behaviour disorders	28	32
Mental retardation	1	1
Depressive disorders not elsewhere classified	51	97
Other psychiatric conditions	1	1
Mental illness – diagnosis not stated	–	–
Other conditions and undiagnosed cases	37	44

From DHSS (1987).

In some cases the term 'gender' has psychological or sociological connotations, and is taken, for example, to refer to the feeling of femininity or masculinity that a person has (as in 'gender identity') or to refer to the different roles that females and males have in society (as in 'gender roles'). The term 'gender differences' is therefore more appropriate in those studies which incorporate psychological or psychosocial explanations.

It is also important to note that one needs to take account of both real differences and stereotyped differences (i.e. beliefs that there are differences even if it can objectively be shown that there are none). This is because the power of stereotypes in determining how people will behave and what place in society they will occupy is as great (if not greater) than that of any real differences. Stereotypes can affect the expectations both of people for themselves and of others; if the expectations are negative, then the consequences may well be pathological. The operation of stereotypes can affect the diagnosis of psychopathological conditions, and can impose restrictive roles and inappropriate behaviour (Rothblum, 1973).

Sex and gender differences

Personality

Although much work has been done in psychology on female–male differences in cognitive processes (Halpern, 1986), it is the study of personality differences and of differences in social roles which is of most relevance to an understanding of sex differences in psychopathology. Personality characteristics (discussed in Chapter 10) can be defined as

> "the configuration of characteristic thoughts, feelings and behaviours that persists over time and situations and distinguish one person from another" (Hothersall, 1985).

Maccoby & Jacklin (1975) published an extensive review of research into psychological sex differences in order to clarify which were reliably demonstrated by the evidence and which were unsupported, or could at best be described as unproven. Where differences were shown they were small (less than one standard deviation) and the distributions of the scores from the two groups were overlapping (i.e. where girls were shown to have a higher overall mean on a particular task, not all girls will be superior to all boys, but more girls than boys were found among the high scorers and more boys than girls among the low scorers).

The only personality characteristic emerging from Maccoby & Jacklin's review that reliably differentiated males and females was that boys are more aggressive than girls. This applies to both physical and verbal aggression, and occurs from an early age.

Subsequent support for this has indicated that it is not a consistent difference. In a review of 72 studies comparing the aggressiveness of females and males, Frodi *et al* (1977) reported that more than 60% of the studies showed that aggression in males was specific to a given situation, and in many cases no sex differences in aggression emerged. Hyde (1984) carried out a meta-analysis of 143 studies and showed that differences in aggression were smaller in older children, and generally confirmed that, overall, the differences were small.

Contrary to stereotype, Maccoby & Jacklin's review found no evidence that girls are more social or more suggestible than boys, or that they have lower self-esteem and lack motivation to achieve. Subsequent studies have recast the latter concept as 'fear of success' (Horner, 1972) and have shown that in certain circumstances, such as when in competition with men, women may show a reluctance to succeed which could appear as a lack of motivation.

Other aspects of sex differences which they felt had to be left as open questions, because of ambiguous findings or too little evidence, included suggestions that girls are more timid or anxious than boys, that boys are more competitive than girls and display more dominance behaviour, and that girls are more compliant and more likely to display nurturant behaviour. Any differences that did emerge tended to be very specific to situation.

Stereotyping

Given that genuine differences between males and females are in fact few and small, it is necessary to gain an understanding of the stereotyping of sex and gender differences.

A study by Rosenkrantz *et al* (1968) generated a Stereotype Questionnaire which has been used in many subsequent studies on this issue. College students were asked to list the behaviours, attitudes and personality characteristics that they believed to be typically male or typically female. The 'typically female' characteristics were then grouped under one heading, and the 'typically male' under another. There were 41 items on which there was 75% or better agreement, and these were designated as the stereotypic items. The female items included descriptions of women as dependent, passive, and very emotional, while men were aggressive, self-confident, adventurous, and independent. An additional aspect of this study is that the stereotypically masculine traits were also perceived as more socially desirable.

Social roles

The above findings refer to concepts of masculinity and femininity. It is generally the case that male–female differences are taken to mean more than this, and to include differences in social roles. This refers both to what males and females hope to do and to what they actually do.

Archer & Lloyd (1982) report sex differences in career aspirations and career choice. There is differential representation of women and men in different types of employment (Hartnett & Bradley, 1986), and differential representation within different types of employment; representation of women in the higher categories within all occupations remain low (Equal Opportunities Commission, 1990).

Stereotyping

Sex stereotypes are found not only in beliefs about what is appropriate behaviour for males and females, but also in the belief that there are 'masculine' and 'feminine' careers, and 'masculine' and 'feminine' family responsibilities.

Hollin (1986) reviews the development of beliefs about sex roles in adolescents. Research has shown clear differences in the allocation of activities as 'only a woman's responsibility' (such as cleaning the house) or 'only a man's responsibility ' (such as 'earning salary to support family'). Adolescents also have clear ideas about what are appropriate careers for females and males, generally determined by perceptions of occupations as 'female' or 'male' dominated.

Explanations for the social differential

It is clear that psychological sex differences between men and women are actually few and small. Beliefs in these differences are, however, quite marked, particularly with reference to personality characteristics.

However, the social situation and status of women and men are different, as are the expectations that men and women have about their own roles. There are three main categories of explanation for this:

(1) psychological (e.g. in terms of a person's personality characteristics or learning experiences)
(2) psychobiological (e.g. in terms of the 'control' a person's biology may exert over behaviour or capabilities)
(3) psychosocial (in terms of the roles people play in society).

Psychological explanations

In terms of traditional psychological learning theory, girls and boys learn to behave differently because of differential reinforcement of their behaviour. This can refer to the acquisition of certain skills; for example, boys' superiority in spatial processing has been accounted for by the fact that they are encouraged from an early age to play with toys that involve the manipulation of shapes. It can also apply to patterns of behaviour which can be interpreted as personality characteristics. For example, if a boy behaves in a way which is deemed appropriate, then he is rewarded, his behaviour is shaped, and he is more likely to add that sort of behaviour to his repertoire. If he behaves in a way that is deemed inappropriate, he is either punished or unrewarded, and that sort of behaviour is less likely to occur (Lewis, 1986). What is deemed appropriate or inappropriate depends on the stereotypes that are used by the reinforcing agents, be they parents, peers, or teachers (Weitz, 1977).

An extension of this learning approach is that children will come to identify the sources of reinforcement and imitate their behaviour, shaping it in the face of further reward and reinforcement (Bandura, 1968). Kagan (1964) takes the modelling approach further, and suggests that children imitate the behaviour of 'significant' others not just to attract rewards, but also to identify with the positive qualities they perceive their model to possess.

What constitutes a 'significant' other is sometimes explained in psychoanalytical terms. Freud (1925) suggested that boys eventually come to identify with their fathers as an indirect way of possessing their mothers. 'Castration anxiety' prevents any direct attempt at such possession by the boy. A consequence of his identification with his father is that he acquires masculine behaviour and characteristics. The picture for girls was less well developed by Freud; girls identify with their mothers as a way of becoming love objects for their fathers; they thus acquire female behaviour and characteristics.

More contemporary psychological theories take account of cognitions, of internal perceptions of external realities, the way in which we interpret the world. Kohlberg (1966) has suggested that internalisations of sex occur at a very early age, and that it is these that guide the acquisition of sex-appropriate behaviour in the child. The action of these internal concepts can be seen by measuring activities such as toy choice, play interests, and so on (Ullian, 1976; Hargreaves, 1986). Cognitive behavioural models have also been applied to an understanding of how women (particularly) and men come to view themselves and their abilities, capacities, and status (Fransella & Frost, 1977).

Psychological explanations of the development and maintenance of sex and gender differences and the associated stereotypes would suggest that personality traits, behaviour patterns, and so on emerge through the learning experiences of the developing child, with behaviour differentially reinforced and the availability of different role models to copy and identify with. A purely behaviourist approach is rarely espoused now, but the emphasis on learning experiences is clear even in the more psychodynamic approaches. An extension of the psychological approach is in the cognitive models which incorporate a concept of internalisation of rules and attitudes (Hargreaves, 1986). This is a central concept in psychoanalytical theories, but the process is less clearly specified in the more cognitive models.

Psychobiological explanations

Psychobiological explanations of sex differences have referred to genetic mechanisms, brain organisation, and hormonal factors. With respect to the affective or temperamental differences which are perhaps most relevant to an understanding of sex and gender differences in psychopathology, research has generally concentrated on hormonal factors. Psychobiologists have concentrated on explanations of 'masculine' behaviour in terms of testosterone levels, and 'feminine' behaviour in terms of oestrogen levels.

Research into masculine behaviour and testosterone has concentrated on aggression. Much work has been carried out on animals, with consequent difficulties in applying the findings to humans. There appears to be a relationship between testosterone levels and aggression as measured by place in a dominance hierarchy in baboons, for example (Claiborne, 1974). Whether this is a causative or correlational relationship is not known; the clear effect of learning factors militates against a straightforward biological explanation (Sayers, 1982).

The relevance of such studies to psychopathology depends partly on whether extremes of aggression are classified as examples of criminal behaviour and, furthermore, whether criminal behaviour is classified as psychopathological, which is itself a matter of debate.

With respect to explanations of 'feminine' behaviour, studies have concentrated on the effects of variations in oestrogen levels or on the effects of anomalous hormones. Two major research areas in this field are the study of behavioural changes in the premenstrual phase of the menstrual cycle (Dalton, 1964; Asso, 1983), and the study of behavioural characteristics of people with hormonal abnormalities (Money & Ehrhardt, 1972). Both contain examples of the theoretical and methodological flaws which can be characteristic of such research (Archer & Lloyd, 1982).

Studies of the menstrual cycle have generally concentrated on negative changes, such as decline in performance, accidents, and problems such as anxiety and irritability; these are claimed to be concentrated just before the onset of menstruation. This collection of symptoms is known as premenstrual tension (PMT) or the premenstrual syndrome (PMS). The existence of this biologically caused behavioural problem is supported by evidence of self-report on scales such as the Premenstrual Distress Questionnaire; by data on accidents and poor examination performance, and by observations of affective variations as a function of cycle phase.

One consequence of the reification of this 'biological' syndrome is that it can often be used to explain or to be blamed for events which may have a different context. Koeske & Koeske (1975) demonstrated the primacy of premenstrual tension as an explanation for negative mood changes, even when external events could equally well be seen to be the cause. Women themselves will often explain negative events by the 'time of the month', even though alternative explanations in terms of social circumstances or life events would be appropriate (Weideger, 1977). These and other aspects of the methodological and interpretive aspects of such research have been the subject of several critical reviews (e.g. Parlee, 1973; Sommer, 1973).

An example of the studies of hormonal abnormalities can be found in Money & Ehrhardt's (1972) work on the adrenogenital syndrome, in which genotypic females were exposed prenatally to high levels of androgen. As well as having a masculinising effect on the external genitalia, it is claimed that behavioural characteristics were affected. Reports and follow-up studies on girls with this syndrome reported their higher levels of 'masculine behaviour'. Masculine behaviour was defined in terms of 'tomboyishness', lack of interest in dolls, and lack of interest in marriage. This in itself indicates the operation of stereotypes. Also, much of the data were based on observer rating, often by the parents, who were aware of their daughter's condition, and who frequently evidenced similar stereotype bias, such as describing a girl's behaviour as rough 'for a girl' (Archer & Lloyd, 1982).

Overall, much criticism has been levelled at the use of biological theories to explain sex differences. Firstly, there is the operation of rather naive logic, such as: men and women behave differently; men and women are biologically different; therefore (1) behaviour is biologically determined and (2) male–female differences in behaviour are biologically determined. As we have seen, the behaviour of men and women is not actually very different, but this observation is usually not raised as an issue in psychobiological research.

The mistaking of cause for correlation is another problem in psychobiology: the assumption that if a biological difference and a psychological difference are found together, then one has caused the other, rather than the two being associated in a rather more complex relationship. It is generally not possible to manipulate human biology directly, in order to watch changes in behaviour; research into natural 'accidents', such as the adrenogenital syndrome, would appear to be a way round this, but difficulties are still evident. Furthermore, the interpretation of correlations is almost always unidirectional, with differences in biology claimed to be causing differences in behaviour, even though the converse can be shown. Research into the premenstrual syndrome provides many examples of this sort of problem (Ruble *et al*, 1980).

In a wider context, the social construction of biology cannot be ignored. A biological argument is a powerful argument – "if it's natural it can't be changed", attempts at change are "going against nature" – even if these tenets are in fact erroneous. Biological arguments are often used to support attempts to maintain a status quo even if that status quo is maladaptive to some people (Sayers, 1982). In the context of human behaviour, the notion of a close relationship between biology and behaviour is generally used pejoratively: the raging hormones theory (Weideger, 1977). The findings of such research can contribute to the establishment of 'biological' stereotypes as powerful as their social and psychological counterparts.

Psychosocial explanations

An important aspect of society is the maintenance of the status quo. An aspect of this will be to ensure continuity in the roles people have to play in that society, and the demands that the society will make upon them.

Weitz (1977) observes that much of the stereotyping socialisation of an individual is a preparation for that individual to take a given place within society. Everyone must therefore learn what is appropriate to that place.

Information about appropriate behaviour is conveyed to members of society initially within the family. Lewis (1986) has reviewed the work on early sex-role socialisation. He reports significant differences in the ways in which parents interact with their children. This was particularly true of fathers; they were likely to be more critical of play for being sex-inappropriate (such as boys playing with dolls) or to initiate 'sex-appropriate activities'.

Subsequent sources of information about 'sex-appropriate' behaviour and roles can be conveyed within education (Spender, 1982; Rogers, 1986), and through literature (Walkerdine, 1990) and other sources of information, such as the mass media (Durkin, 1986).

Labour in society is divided according to particular sex roles; thus, females and males will learn that they are expected to fulfil different roles (Hollin, 1986). There are also differences in status between these roles. Ussher (1991) draws attention to the fact that women are economically poorer, are over-represented in low-status jobs or in the lower echelons of high-status jobs (e.g. medicine, the judiciary), and are almost solely responsible for household duties, frequently in conjunction with employment outside the home. This labour and status differential is an additional characteristic that will be associated with being female or male.

Sex differences in psychopathology

Having considered psychological research into sex differences, both real and stereotyped, and various explanations for these differences, we now consider the apparently discrepant consequences of these differences for the mental health of males and females.

The association between being female and suffering from emotional disorders may be due to variables other than genuine differences in mental health problems. The operation of stereotypes may mean that women are more likely to attract a diagnosis of mental illness than men.

The possibility that there is some kind of conflation of female and psychopathological behaviour has a long history (Showalter, 1987) and is well illustrated in a classic study by Broverman *et al* (1970). They asked 79 psychologists, psychiatrists, or social workers (46 men and 33 women) to complete a version of the Rosenkrantz questionnaire (Rosenkrantz *et al*, 1968). A third of the subjects were told to "think of normal adult men and then indicate on each item the pole to which a mature healthy socially competent adult man would be closer"; for example, would he be nearer the "very competitive" or the "not at all competitive" end of a scale? Another third of the subjects completed the ratings for a mature, healthy, socially competent, adult woman, and the remaining subjects were asked to complete the ratings for a mature, healthy, socially competent, adult (sex unspecified). It was assumed that the latter instructions would elicit a picture of the 'ideal' health patterns, irrespective of sex.

There was good agreement between the clinicians as to what constituted the typical male or female and the ideal adult. The clinicians concurred with the masculine and feminine stereotypes held by the general population, that women are, for example, more dependent and submissive, exhibiting traits that are less socially desirable than those of men, who are more adventurous and independent. Furthermore, there was a close similarity between the picture of a typical healthy male and that of the ideal adult, whereas there was a marked discrepancy between the picture of a female and that of the healthy ideal.

Therefore, what is rated as healthy for a woman is neither socially acceptable nor ideal. It should also be pointed out that there was no difference between the female and the male clinicians in the application of these stereotypes. Broverman *et al* (1970) point out the implications of the double standard that the clinicians are operating:

> "Thus for a woman to be healthy from an adjustment viewpoint, she must adjust to and accept the behavioural norms for her sex, even though these behaviours are generally less socially desirable and considered to be less healthy for the generalised competent, mature adult."

The study by Broverman *et al* indicates that there are expectations as to the parallels between female and pathological behaviour. It has also been suggested that when women and men present with the same symptoms, such as anxiety and restlessness, women are more likely to be treated as though they have a psychological problem, whereas the men will receive more physical therapies (Cooperstock, 1981).

This may apply to women who actually seek help and enter the statistics with a diagnosis of mental illness, but community surveys also indicate higher levels of psychopathological problems among women (Clancy & Gove, 1974). Taking the preponderance of women in the mental health statistics as reflecting a real differential, we will now consider possible explanations for this.

Psychological explanations

The depressive personality

One aspect of a woman's psychology that has been identified as relevant to an understanding of her vulnerability to mental health problems is her personality. Rothblum (1987) notes the similarity between the 'depressive' personality and the 'typical female' personality. The passivity and dependence and lack of self-confidence characteristic of the depressive can be viewed as intensifications of normal female characteristics. Hammen & Peters (1977) found that both depressed men and women were rated high on femininity; that is, femininity was equated with the symptoms displayed by the patients.

The phobic personality

Similar observations have been made about the preponderance of women in the statistics for phobias (Brehony, 1983). This is particularly true of agoraphobia, where up to 85% of sufferers are female. In fact, it is often referred to as the 'housewife's disorder', as there is a high incidence of young, married women reporting the problem. In the clinical literature, agoraphobic people are described as having the personality traits of passivity, dependency, avoidance, and non-assertiveness (Brehony, 1983). These are also characteristics which females are expected to exhibit, and for which girls are reinforced. There is a clear relationship between the extreme helplessness and dependency of the agoraphobic, and the social expectations for women (Fodor, 1974).

Learned helplessness

As well as investigating the personality characteristics acquired by women, psychologists have investigated their learning experiences. One particular concept that has been applied to the understanding of depression is learned helplessness. This was developed by Seligman (1975), and is based on studies originally carried out on dogs, but then on college students. He showed that if subjects are faced with repeated failures to control the environment, escaping from an electric shock for the dogs and attempting to solve insoluble puzzles for the students, they will develop a pattern of behaviour known as 'learned helplessness'. When the environmental contingencies change such that control is possible and escape from an unpleasant situation an option, subjects will not attempt to take this option, but passively suffer the unpleasant alternatives. They appear to have learned that their actions will have no consequences on their environment; therefore, they cease to be active agents. Abramson *et al* (1978) suggest that depression arises from internal attribution of this lack of control, from people blaming themselves for their current situation. Hammen (1982) reports on studies showing the tendency of women to attribute success to external causes but failure to internal sources.

A social application of this helplessness concept to the understanding of higher rates of depression in women implies that their learning experiences are such that they believe themselves to be powerless, to be unable to manipulate their environment to alter their circumstances, and that this should be more true of their life experiences than those of men. Beck & Greenberg (1974) suggest that the actual reality of women's social powerlessness may well be associated with the subjective helplessness and hopelessness characteristic of depression.

'Helplessness' and 'hopelessness' are also terms applied to the negative cognitions of depressive people, reflecting a negative view of the self, a negative view of the world, and a negative view of the future (Beck, 1976). The emphasis of this approach is mainly on therapy, on correcting the depressive person's distorted view of the situation, rather than an understanding of how the patient came to have such a view in the first place. It is possible that the operation of sex stereotypes may be of significance in a woman's acquisition of her negative view of herself and her sex (Rothblum, 1983) (see below).

Al-Issa (1980) points out the importance of 'mastery exploration' for alleviating fear, and that girls are not reinforced for this type of mastery. Girls are expected to be helpless, yielding to their fears and needing rescue and protection. There is a parallel between the anxiety management and exposure to fears used to treat phobias in adults, and the 'bravery training' encouraged in most boys.

Eating disorders and the physical stereotype

Stereotypes of physical appearance appear to be particularly powerful for women. Not only can they convey the impression of woman as an object to be used – for example, to sell products (Gallagher, 1979) – or possibly abused (pornography), but they also convey an image of a physical ideal to which women should aspire (Wolf, 1990). In writing on women and eating disorders, Lawrence (1984) stresses two problems which emerge from the emphasis on physical characteristics in women:

(1) the availability of women's bodies to the public gaze (and therefore the importance of ensuring that their bodies live up to any ideal)
(2) the sense of powerlessness and need for approval which women experience in our society (i.e. approval can come only from others, and it comprises living up to some externally determined ideal).

Current images of women stress the relationship between thinness and success and desirability (Lawrence, 1984). The operation of this particular stereotype has been partly blamed for the much higher incidence of eating disorders in females than males, with women starving themselves to achieve this particular image or, at a deeper level, rejecting a physical image of femininity and the associated role (Orbach, 1978).

Expressions of distress

It may also be that gender-appropriate behaviour affects the way women express distress, and hence the particular form of pathological behaviour they display. For example, it has been suggested that depression is for women what alcoholism is for men (Weissman & Klerman, 1977), and that the difference is related to culturally acceptable ways of behaving.

According to psychoanalytical theory, depression arises when someone directs anger inwards against themselves. Friedman (1970) reports lower levels of aggression and hostility in depressive women, and suggests this is associated with their fear at expressing anger outwards to the 'significant others' causing the anger. The expression of anger is less acceptable for women than for men, and so women who feel anger at their situation or at those around them turn this anger against themselves.

A woman's socialisation may make help-seeking behaviour more acceptable for her than for a man, and this may account for greater numbers of women than men in the mental health statistics. This may be related to factors such as women perceiving psychiatric symptoms as less undesirable than do men, or to women more readily seeking help in general. However, Clancy & Gove (1974) and Kessler *et al* (1981) have reviewed the available evidence and conclude that there is no support for such a difference.

One message which emerges from such research is that women's personality characteristics and the way in which they deal with difficulties may well be a major determining factor in the development of psychological problems. Dependence and passivity appear to be common characteristics of women's personalities; the dangers of dependence and passivity are recurrent themes in explanations of mental ill-health. Given this, the concept of psychological androgyny would appear to be helpful.

Androgyny

Androgyny refers to a rejection of the concept of 'appropriate' female or male characteristics, and suggests that for people to be psychologically healthy they should be able to display either characteristics in appropriate situations (Bem, 1974). The consequence should be greater adaptability and development of potential in both sexes (Bem, 1975).

Williams (1979) measured levels of androgyny in women with the Bem Sex Role Inventory (Bem, 1974). Women who described themselves as having high levels of both female and male characteristics formed the 'high androgyny' group. This group reported fewer psychiatric symptoms. Williams related this to the fact that they found their lives less stressful; she suggests that the operation of more masculine characteristics gave the women an experience of greater subjective control over what was happening to them.

Taylor & Hall (1982) have elaborated on the concept by suggesting that the masculine aspect of androgyny appears to offer the most adaptable coping styles. Hargreaves (1986) has reviewed both the theoretical assertions that androgyny is psychologically more healthy, and ways of measuring this androgyny. To some extent, problems with the latter have confounded research into the former, but given the problems which appear to be associated with rigid dichotomising, it would appear to be an appropriate avenue to explore.

A recurrent theme in the literature on women's psychopathology is the lack of control women have in their life and the consequences of this for their psychological well-being (Dohrenwend, 1973; Skevington, 1986). A woman's lack of control may be due to her behavioural style, so that passive, dependent people (who are more likely to be female than male) are less able to have any consequential effect on their situation. This may be changed by encouraging the development of a more androgynous personality or by incorporating skills such as 'assertiveness' into a women's behavioural repertoire. Williams (1979) suggests that effectiveness in interacting with the environment is one of the apparently protective aspects of psychological androgyny.

It is clear that rigidly dichotomised feminine and masculine personalities are maladaptive; breaking down the boundaries and allowing the development of both masculine and feminine traits in everyone would appear to be of a great advantage in the avoidance of mental health problems.

Psychobiological explanations

Given the predominance of the biomedical model in psychopathology, it is perhaps not surprising that the high incidence of psychopathological problems in women has been attributed to their biology. An example of this can be found in the concentration on hormones as the cause of women's ills.

The role of hormones

One of the sources of evidence is PMT studies, which have already been found to be problematic. Similarly, another source of evidence is the mild to severe psychiatric symptoms which can occur postnatally in women. After a woman has given birth, the previously high levels of progesterone and oestrogen drop dramatically; it is also a time at which many women may display mild depressive symptoms and when most puerperal psychoses have their onset. Less severe postnatal depression may occur many months after the birth and is therefore difficult to link closely to hormonal changes. From one to two women in 1000 may suffer such severe psychotic disturbances (Elliot, 1984). Critics of the conclusion that the more common postnatal depression proves the relationship between hormones and behaviour point out that the social impact of motherhood, attitudes towards motherhood, and its social and economic implications are frequently ignored in reaching this conclusion (Magnus, 1980; Nicolson, 1990). Similar criticisms are levelled at the interpretation of depressive symptoms which may be associated with the menopause (Weissman & Klerman, 1977).

Depression

It is interesting to note that in depression, which is characterised by a high rate of female sufferers, and for which there is strong evidence for a biological component, there is little direct research into sex differences in this component.

Klaiber *et al* (1982) have reviewed evidence that oestrogen may act as a form of antidepressant, but there is no evidence for this as a primary factor in depression in women. As Willner (1985) has pointed out, the sex differences interact with a social-class factor, as working-class women, in particular, are more prone to depression. It is difficult to explain this in hormonal terms.

Shortcomings of the biological approach

Biological arguments are potentially powerful in the area of sex and gender differences. Biological stereotyping and the concept that women's mental health problems are 'inevitable' because of their biological processes has been a consistent theme in psychopathology (Showalter, 1987). Because of the power of the arguments and the persistence of the stereotyping in spite of contrary evidence, it is an area where greater awareness is needed (Sayers, 1982).

Psychosocial explanations

In considering the effect of social roles on mental health, it will be seen that, for women, the roles themselves, attempts to reject them, and conflict between them can all have pathological consequences.

Women's work

Women's work is low in "recognition and reward" (Nairne & Smith, 1984). In a society in which earning power equates with status, women are low earners (Ussher, 1991). The jobs they do, such as housework and caring, are invisible (Oakley, 1976). Status and reward are also factors in determining the extent of control one has in society, a factor already discussed as important in understanding psychological problems. A woman's feeling of lack of control in her life may reflect the reality of her social situation.

The family

Marriage and parenthood are two of the major roles in society for which people are prepared. They are also roles which appear to have different significance for men and women. Studies of social factors in depression have noted the differential effects of marriage: in a direct comparison of the incidence of depression in married and unmarried men and women, the highest incidence was in married women, whereas married men showed fewer incidences of depression than unmarried men (Gove & Tudor, 1973; Radloff, 1975).

There is some interrelation with employment, in that married women with employment outside the home showed lower rates of depression than married women without such employment (Gove, 1972). Hammen (1982) suggests that this is because, for women, marriage means loss of status, possible social isolation, and economic dependence.

Motherhood can have many meanings for women, not all of them positive. Married women in the UK with children are more likely to suffer from depression than those without children (McBride, 1990). However, the opposite is the case in New Zealand. Motherhood can have major consequences for a woman's identity, and can also affect her access to supportive family or social networks (Fransella & Frost, 1977; Ussher, 1989; Nicolson, 1991), thus increasing her risk of emotional disorders (see Chapter 12). The life changes consequent on fatherhood are usually less extreme.

Rejecting roles: eating disorders and agoraphobia

It is clear that acceptance of these roles for women can cause difficulties. However, rejection can also cause problems. For example, feminist theories have suggested that eating disorders in women (who comprise up to 95% of the eating-disordered population) may arise from specific rejection of the female role as characterised by the special relationship of women and food (Lawrence, 1984; Dana & Lawrence, 1988). Women are the prime targets of all propaganda about food, both medical and commercial. Feeding the family well (thoroughly and/or healthily) is a central part of many women's lives. It is a way of pleasing the people they care about. Responsibility for feeding (deciding what to eat, shopping for it, cooking it, etc.) is the main responsibility of many women's lives. Denial of food may be a way of denying such responsibility, and an indication of the problems a girl has with this role.

Similar suggestions have been made about the high incidence of agoraphobia in young married women. This may be related to their wish to avoid a situation for which they are ill-prepared, to emphasise their dependency, and to elicit protection from their family. The role of housewife may be one with which they are discontented, yet they do not have the resources to reject it directly. Their distress is expressed through their phobic symptoms (Fodor, 1982).

An additional aspect of role rejection is that this in itself may be seen as evidence of abnormality (Chesler, 1972) and attempts at therapy and treatment will concentrate on inducing a woman to accept her 'appropriate' role, however pathological it has apparently been for her (Chesler, 1972; Penfold & Walker, 1984).

Similarly, conflict between different roles can cause difficulties. This is an aspect of Lawrence's (1984) approach to anorexia in girls. She reports the results of a survey among her own patients; a large proportion of the anorexic girls were high achievers, frequently in an academic sphere. She suggests such achievement is in conflict with the feminine role signalled by the onset of menstruation and the acquisition of a feminine body. Denial of this feminine body by starving it is a way of resolving the conflict. It is suggested that contemporary society is increasingly difficult for women because of possible role conflicts:

> "The pervasive shift away from traditional feminine roles into more ambiguous territory has created a situation where women's former values are questioned, but the propriety of newer behaviours and multiple roles has not been established or accepted without guilt. The encouragement for women to become more assertive and demonstrative has resulted in an increasing incidence of female roles and behaviour that bring about internal dissension and uncertainty. When combined in some cases with the greater practical stresses of carrying out multiple roles in the family and society at large, and inexperience in dealing with the greater amount of personal economic freedom, it is little wonder that women's behaviour and attitudes regarding drink and drinking behaviour should have begun to move in a manner consistent with all these trends and pressures."
> (Shaw, 1980)

Although this refers to the increasing number of female alcoholics, it could well be a general description of contemporary problems of women.

The central significance of gender roles as factors in determining vulnerability to mental disorder will be a difficult issue to address. It may partly rely on the success of organisations such as the Equal Opportunities Commission. However, 'agents of socialisation' can play a part, by being aware of the difficulties associated with overly rigid adherence to the traditional stereotypes. This can apply to sources of socialisation as diverse as the mass media (Durkin, 1986) and the psychiatric profession (Penfold & Walker, 1984).

Conclusions

This chapter has examined the evidence for psychological and social sex differences, both real and stereotyped, as a way of understanding sex differences in psychopathology. It will be noted that, in the context of problems that are often approached from a biological perspective, explanations of gender differences in mental health problems are frequently couched in terms of the more psychological and psychosocial concepts of gender roles and behaviour. Psychological problems are seen as a direct result of gender role 'training' – for example, the dependence and passivity characteristic of women make them specifically vulnerable to depression (Nairne & Smith, 1984) – or, conversely, as deviations from gender role training, in which attempts to 'break the mould' result either in stress, which itself is associated with mental disorder, or in patterns of behaviour which, by definition, are abnormal and liable to attract the label of 'mad' (Chesler, 1972).

An additional aspect is that gender roles may allow people to express psychological distress in different ways, with women more prone to suffer from disorders characterised by passivity and dependence, such as depression, as opposed to the more aggressive and antisocial disorders such as alcoholism or criminality.

This chapter has examined only female psychopathology, mainly because of the preponderance of women in the mental health statistics, but also because of the epidemiological information that such research has provided. An understanding of what makes a particular group of people vulnerable will bring an understanding of vulnerability as a whole. Although it might be felt that only part of the story has been discussed, it is an important part of the story, obviously important for women themselves but also for those who hope to help.

References

Abramson, L. Y., Seligman, M. E. P. & Teasdale, J. D. (1978) Learned helplessness in humans: critique and reformulation. *Journal of Abnormal Psychology*, **87**, 49–74.

Al-Issa, I. (1980) *The Psychopathology of Women*. Englewood Cliffs, NJ: Prentice-Hall.

—— (1982) *Gender and Psychopathology*. New York: Academic Press.

Archer, J. & Lloyd, B. (1982) *Sex and Gender*. London: Penguin.

Asso, D. (1983) *The Real Menstrual Cycle*. London: Wiley.

Bandura, A. (1968) Social learning theory of identificatory processes. In *Handbook of Socialisation Theory and Research* (ed. D. Goslin). Chicago: Rand McNally.

Beck, A. (1976) *Cognitive Therapy and Emotional Disorders*. New York: International Universities Press.

—— & Greenberg, R. L. (1974) Cognitive therapy with depressed women. In *Women in Therapy: Psychotherapies for a Changing Society*. New York: Brunner/Mazell.

Bem, S. L. (1974) Measurement of psychological androgyny. *Journal of Consulting and Clinical Psychology*, **42**, 155–162.

—— (1975) Sex-role adaptability: one consequence of psychological androgyny. *Journal of Personality and Social Psychology*, **31**, 634–643.

Brehony, A. (1983) Women and agoraphobia. In *Sex Role Stereotypes and Women's Mental Health* (eds V. Franks & E. Rothblum). New York: Springer.

Briscoe, M. (1982). Sex differences in psychological well-being. *Psychological Medicine* (monograph suppl. 1).

Broverman, I. K., *et al* (1970). Sex role stereotypes and clinical judgement of mental health. *Journal of Consulting and Clinical Psychology*, **34**, 1–7.

Chesler, P. (1972) *Women and Madness*. London: Allen Lane.

Claiborne, R. (1974) *God or Beast: Evolution and Human Nature*. New York: Norton.

Clancy, K. & Gove, W. (1974) Sex differences in mental illness: an analysis of response bias in self-reports. *American Journal of Sociology*, **80**, 205–216.

Clare, A. (1980) *Psychiatry in Dissent* (2nd edn). London: Tavistock.

—— (1985) Sex and mood. *Health and Hygiene*, **6**, 43–60.

Cooperstock, R. (1981) A review of women's psychotropic drug use. In *Women and Mental Health* (eds E. Howell & M. Bayes). New York: Basic Books.

Dalton, K. (1964) *The Premenstrual Syndrome*. Springfield, IL: Charles Thomas.

Dana, M. & Lawrence, M. (1988) *Women's Secret Disorder*. London: Grafton.

Department of Health and Social Security (1987) *Mental Health Statistics for England 1986. Booklet 1: Mental Illness Hospitals and Units in England: Trends in Admissions Discharges and Residents*. London: DHSS.

Dohrenwend, B. P. (1973) Social status and stressful life events. *Journal of Personality and Social Psychology*, **28**, 225–235.

Durkin, K. (1986) Sex roles and the mass media. In *The Psychology of Sex Roles* (eds D. Hargreaves & A. Colley). London: Harper and Row.

Elliot, S. (1984) Pregnancy and after. In *Contributions to Medical Psychology*, vol. 3 (ed. S. Rachman). Oxford: Pergamon Press.

Equal Opportunities Commission (1990) *Occupation Group Earnings, 1988*. London: EOC.

Fodor, I. G. (1974) The phobic syndrome in women: implications for treatment. In *Women in Therapy* (eds V. Franks & V. Burtle). New York: Bruner/Mazell.

—— (1982) Gender and phobia. In *Gender and Psychopathology* (ed. I. Al-Issa). New York: Academic Press.

Fransella, F. & Frost, K. (1977) *On Being a Woman*. London: Tavistock.

Freud, S. (1925) Some psychical consequences of the anatomical distinction between the sexes. *Standard Edition of the Psychological Works of Sigmund Freud*, vol. 19 (ed. J. Strachey). London: Hogarth Press.

Friedman, A. L. (1970) Hostility factors and clinical improvement in depressed patients. *Archives of General Psychiatry*, **23**, 524–537.

Frodi, A., Macaulay, J. & Thome, P. R. (1977) Are women always less aggressive than men? A review of the experimental literature. *Psychological Bulletin*, **84**, 634–660.

Gallagher, M. (1979) *The Portrayal and Participation of Women in the Media*. Paris: UNESCO.

Gove, W. (1972) The relationship between sex roles, marital status, and mental illness. *Social Forces*, **51**, 34–44.

—— (1979) Sex differences in the epidemiology of mental illness: evidence and explanations. In *Gender and Disordered Behaviour* (eds E. Gomberg & V. Franks). New York: Brunner/Mazel.

—— & Tudor, J. (1973) Adult sex roles and mental health. *American Journal of Sociology*, **78**, 812–835.

Halpern, D. F. (1986) *Sex Differences in Cognitive Abilities*. Hillsdale, NJ: Lawrence Erlbaum.

Hammen, C. L. (1982) Gender and depression. In *Gender and Psychopathology* (ed. I. Al-Issa). New York: Academic Press.

—— & Peters, S. D. (1977) Differential responses to male and female depressive reactions. *Journal of Consulting and Clinical Psychology*, **45**, 994–1001.

Hargreaves, D. (1986). Psychological theories of sex role stereotyping. In *The Psychology of Sex Roles* (eds D. Hargreaves & A. Colley). London: Harper and Row.

Hartnett, O. & Bradley, J. (1986) Sex roles and work. In *The Psychology of Sex Roles* (eds D. Hargreaves & A. Colley). London: Harper and Row.

Hollin, C. (1986) Sex roles in adolescence. In *The Psychology of Sex Roles* (eds D. Hargreaves & A. Colley). London: Harper and Row.

Horner, M. S. (1972) Motive to avoid success and changing aspirations of women. In *Readings on the Psychology of Women* (ed. J. Bardwick). New York: Harper and Row.

Hothersall, D. (1985) *Psychology*. Columbus: Merrill Publishing.

Hyde, J. S. (1984) How large are gender differences in aggression? A development meta-analysis. *Developmental Psychology*, **20**, 722–736.

Kagan, J. (1964) Acquisition and significance of sex-typing and sex-role identity. In *Review of Child Development Research*, vol. 1 (eds M. Hoffman & L. Hoffman). New York: Russell Sage.

Kessler, R. C., Brown, R. L. & Broman, C. L. (1981) Sex differences in psychiatric help-seeking: Evidence from four large-scale surveys. *Journal of Health and Social Behaviour*, **22**, 49–64.

Klaiber, E. L., Broverman, D. M., Vogel, W., *et al* (1972) Effects of oestrogen therapy on plasma MAO activity and EEG driving response of depressed women. *American Journal of Psychiatry*, **128**, 1492–1498.

Koeske, R. K. & Koeske, G. F. (1975) An attributional approach to moods and the menstrual cycle. *Journal of Personality and Social Psychology*, **3**, 473–478.

Kohlberg, L. (1966) A cognitive-developmental analysis of children's sex-role concepts and attitudes. In *The Development of Sex Differences* (ed. E. Maccoby). Stanford, CA: Stanford University Press.

Lawrence, M. (1984) *The Anorexic Experience*. London: Women's Press Handbook.

Lewis, C. (1986) Early sex-role socialisation. In *The Psychology of Sex Roles* (eds D. Hargreaves & A. Colley). London: Harper and Row.

Maccoby, E. & Jacklin, C. (1975) *The Psychology of Sex Differences*. Stanford, CA: Stanford University Press.

MacLeod, S. (1981) *The Art of Starvation*. London: Virago.

Magnus, E.M. (1980) Source of maternal stress in the postpartum period: a review of the literature and an alternative view. In *The Psychobiology of Sex Differences and Sex Roles* (ed. J. E. Parsons). New York: Hemisphere.

McBride, A. (1990) Mental health effects of women's multiple roles. *American Psychologist*, **45**, 381–384.

Miles, A. (1988) *Women and Mental Illness: The Social Context of Female Neurosis*. Brighton: Wheatsheaf.

Money, J. & Ehrhardt, A. A. (1972) *Man and Woman: Boy and Girl*. Baltimore, MD: Johns Hopkins University Press.

Nairne, K. & Smith, G. (1984) *Dealing with Depression*. London: Women's Press.

Nicolson, P. (1990) Understanding post-natal depression: a mother-centred approach. *Journal of Advanced Nursing*, **15**, 689–695.

—— (1991) Menstrual cycle research and the construction of female psychology. In *Cognition and the Menstrual Cycle* (ed. J. Richardson). London: Lawrence Erlbaum.

Oakley, A. (1976) *Housewife*. London: Penguin.

Orbach, S. (1978) *Fat is a Feminist Issue.* London: Hamlyn.

Parlee, M. B. (1973) The premenstrual syndrome. *Psychological Bulletin*, **80**, 454–465.

Penfold, P. S. & Walker, G. A. (1984) *Women and the Psychiatric Paradox.* Milton Keynes: Open University Press.

Radloff, L. (1975) Sex differences in depression: the effects of occupation and marital status. *Sex Roles*, 249–265.

Rogers, C. (1986) Sex roles in education. In *The Psychology of Sex Roles* (eds D. Hargreaves & A. Colley). London: Harper & Row.

Rosenhan, D. L. & Seligman, M. E. P. (1989) *Abnormal Psychology* (2nd edn). New York: Norton.

Rosenkrantz., P., Vogel, S., Bee, H., *et al* (1968) Sex-role stereotypes and self-concepts in college students. *Journal of Consulting and Clinical Psychology*, **32**, 287–295.

Rothblum, E. D. (1973) Sex-role stereotypes and depression in women. In *The Stereotyping of Women: Its Effects on Mental Health* (eds V. Franks & E. D. Rothblum). New York: Springer.

Ruble, D. N., Brooks-Gunn, J. & Clarke, A. (1980) Research on menstrual related psychological changes: alternative perspectives. In *The Psychobiology of Sex Differences and Sex Roles* (ed. J. E. Parsons). New York: Hemisphere.

Sayers, J. (1982) *Biological Politics.* London: Tavistock.

Seligman, M. E. P. (1975) *Helplessness: On Depression, Development and Death.* San Franciso, CA: Freeman.

Shaw, S. (1980) The causes of increasing drinking problems amongst women. In *Women and Alcohol. Camberwell Council on Alcoholism.* London: Tavistock.

Showalter, E. (1987) *The Female Malady.* London: Virago.

Skevington, S. (1986) Sex roles and mental health. In *The Psychology of Sex Roles* (eds D. Hargreaves & A. Colley). London: Harper and Row.

Sommer, B. (1973) The effect of menstruation on cognitive and perceptual-motor behaviour: a review. *Psychosomatic Medicine*, **35**, 515–534.

Spender, D. (1982) *Invisible Women: The Schooling Scandal.* London: Writers and Readers Publishing Co-operative.

Taylor, M. & Hall, J.A. (1982) Psychological androgyny: theories, methods and conclusions. *Psychological Bulletin*, **92**, 347–366.

Ullian, D. Z. (1976) The development of concepts of masculinity and femininity. In *Exploring Sex Differences* (eds B. Lloyd & J. Archer). London: Academic Press.

Ussher, J. (1989) *The Psychology of the Female Body.* London: Routledge.

—— (1991) *Women's Madness: Misogyny or Mental Illness?* London: Harvester Wheatsheaf.

Walkerdine, V. (1990) *School Girl Fictions.* London: Virago.

Weideger, P. (1977) *Female Cycles.* London: Women's Press.

Weissman, M. & Klerman, G. (1977) Sex differences in the epidemiology of depression. *Archives of General Psychiatry*, **34**, 98–111.

Weitz, S. (1977) *Sex Roles: Biological, Psychological and Social Foundations.* New York: Oxford University Press.

Williams, J. (1979) Psychological androgyny and mental health. In *Sex-Role Stereotyping* (eds O. Hartnett, G. Boden & M. Fuller). London: Tavistock.

Willner, P. (1985) *Depression: A Psychobiological Synthesis.* Chichester: Wiley.

Wolf, N. (1990) *The Beauty Myth.* London: Vintage.

12   Adversity and resilience

Martin J. Eales

Methodological issues • Recent adversity as a cause of psychiatric illness • Factors modifying the effects of recent adversity • Long-term effects of adverse experience • Conclusions

---

Links between disturbing experiences and psychiatric disorder have been recognised for centuries, are prominent in lay conceptions of mental disorder in industrialised societies, and are encountered daily by practising psychiatrists. Nonetheless, there are several possible reasons why these phenomena may be associated, and life experiences that appear to cause some people to succumb are taken by many others in their stride.

Until relatively recently it was still possible to argue that links between adversity and disorder are largely artefactual, and of negligible causal importance relative to 'endogenous' factors. Research in the last 25 years has changed this. The causal significance of adversity has been documented in a number of conditions, and attention has shifted increasingly to an exploration of the mechanisms involved.

The early history of research into the effects of life experience on mental health was bound up with the term 'stress'. This was (and still is) used to refer to any threatening or unpleasant experience, on whatever time-scale, or more broadly still to any situation involving a demand to adapt to changing conditions, extending from experiences such as parachute jumping or brief intense pain, which can be studied experimentally, to events or circumstances with longer-term implications, such as bereavement or losing one's job. Grouping these diverse experiences under a single term was originally justified by the belief that they all served to activate a *single non-specific mediating process*, which produced a wide range of effects, a view formulated by Hans Selye on the basis of experimental research into pituitary–adrenocortical function.

Selye believed that his findings provided a general model for psychosomatic disease in man. His ideas were reflected in much early medical research into adverse life experience; for example, in definitions of 'stress' in terms of life changes requiring adaptation of functioning, regardless of their implications for the individual's plans or motivations, and in attempts to 'quantify stress' on a single continuous dimension, and to use this to predict the risks of a wide range of diseases.

The unitary notion of 'stress' has now been abandoned. Adverse experience is multidimensional. More precise and focused measurement based on this recognition has enabled research to progress from simply testing the proposal that adverse life experiences, or environmental factors more generally, play some part in mental health, to identifying particular components or dimensions of adverse experience relevant to different disorders, and exploring the conditions under which their effects are observed (including the ways in which they interact with the person's pre-existing characteristics).

The present chapter is concerned only with stressful events and difficulties occurring in the course of people's everyday lives, usually referred to by the terms 'adversity' or 'life stress'; laboratory studies are not covered. It focuses on adversity as commonly recognised, and therefore on those life stresses, and emotional responses to them, that depend least on idiosyncratic sensitivities. For this reason, much of the discussion centres on depression (here taken to include mixed states of depression and anxiety), which is the commonest and in a sense the most typical product of adversity. The chapter begins by discussing research into consequences of recent adverse life experience, with particular attention to methodological issues and to the links between life events and difficulties and depressive disorders. Attempts to explain variation in responses to adversity are covered in the following section on resilience and vulnerability. Some very long-term consequences of adverse life experience are discussed briefly in the final section.

Methodological issues

Measurement of adversity

In most studies relating recent adversity to psychiatric disorder, exposure to adversity is assessed *retrospectively* in subjects selected from the general population or in the context of a case-control design. Prospective studies are possible, where those experiencing a particular type of event can be identified (as in studies of outcome after bereavement, divorce, or unemployment), but here also retrospective information about experiences during the follow-up period will be needed if exposure to adversity is to be assessed adequately.

Retrospective assessment carries the danger of fall-off in recall over time and, more seriously, *bias* in recall. People who are suffering from or predisposed to illness may report adverse experiences more readily or recall them as more severe or threatening than would others. This is especially likely in some psychiatric conditions; for example, as a result of mood-related cognitive sets.

Bias may also arise through the more general human tendency to seek meaningful patterns in experience, and so to remember more readily (or place a particular construction upon) items which might explain a personal misfortune. An often-quoted example of this 'effort after meaning' is Stott's (1958) finding, shortly before the chromosomal basis of the condition became clear, that mothers of children with Down's syndrome reported more 'shocks' during their pregnancies than mothers of normal children. Effort after meaning is also one possible basis for rating bias on the part of the investigator, where knowledge of outcome (e.g. knowledge that a depressive episode ensued) may influence judgements about the presence or severity of adversity in the subject's history.

Viable measures of adversity must contain procedures to avoid bias but must also aim at completeness and sensitivity. If only a small proportion of relevant instances of adversity are detected by the method, or if the measurement of their attributes is insensitive, this will weaken or even preclude finding any relationship with subsequent illness.

Identifying instances of adversity

The first stage of measurement involves cataloguing instances of adversity (life events, life changes, difficulties) that have occurred during the time covered. This is inevitably selective, as anyone's history contains stresses of varying severity, which at their lower bound merge into the trivial events of everyday life. The 'units' of adversity covered must be predefined, using a list of some kind, as informal selection by the subject (or investigator) will be highly susceptible to bias.

The earliest reasonably comprehensive list of stressful life events to be developed was the Schedule of Recent Experiences (SRE), introduced by Holmes & Rahe in 1967. This is a self-report questionnaire requiring respondents to tick items on a list of 43 classes of event, such as 'divorce', 'death of a close family member', 'vacation', or 'minor violation of the law', which they have experienced during the period covered. No dating of individual events is attempted, and ongoing life difficulties are not covered. Although it is widely used, the reliability of data collected by the instrument is poor, with substantial discrepancies when subjects are retested or the responses of other informants are examined (Paykel, 1983; Katschnig, 1986, pp. 74ff.). This probably arises from the lack of a probing interview structure to encourage the accurate recall of relevant material, and from reliance on brief event descriptions which respondents may interpret in different ways; for example, whether 'illness' includes brief minor ailments, or whether 'close family member' includes certain categories of relative.

Other methods using check-lists or highly structured interviews suffer from similar difficulties and they have now been largely superseded by semistructured interviews. The most widely used are the Life Events and

Difficulties Schedule (LEDS; Brown & Harris, 1978, 1989), and the interview developed by Paykel *et al* (1969).

The LEDS systematically probes for instances of adversity in 38 different areas, the interviewer applying detailed criteria that specify the characteristics of those life events, and persistent life difficulties, to be included. Detailed narrative information is collected about the nature and timing of any event or difficulty identified, the circumstances in which it occurred, and its implications for the person concerned. This method has a demonstrated high reliability and validity.

Measuring dimensions of adversity

Having identified the life events or other units of adversity that have occurred, most methods use a second stage, in which dimensions or attributes of those units, such as their degree of threat or unpleasantness, are measured.

One approach is to allocate a predefined weight to each class of event. The Social Readjustment Rating Scale, for example, allocates each item in the SRE a weight derived from surveys in which large numbers of people were asked to judge the amount of disruption caused by each class of event: 'death of spouse' is scored 100, 'divorce' 73, and 'vacation' 12. The sum of the relevant weights forms the individual's 'total life change' score for the period considered.

Scaling methods of this type avoid bias, but often at the cost of insensitivity, as events with widely differing implications are treated as equivalent. For example, a 'change in residence' may be a hoped-for event or an eviction into substandard accommodation; 'pregnancy' may involve the planned completion of a family, or an unplanned event requiring a woman to give up a college course and with it cherished ambitions for a future career.

These variations in the meaning of events in the light of the subject's circumstances are examined by an alternative method devised by Brown and colleagues, which is used in conjunction with the LEDS. This involves *investigator-based* measurement drawing on detailed interview material. Information on the context of the event is used to rate qualities it would have (e.g. its long-term threat) for an average person in similar circumstances. To avoid bias, the research subject's own appraisal of the event is excluded from consideration, and the ratings are made by (one or more) investigators unaware of the subject's actual response. These *contextual ratings* are highly reliable, and their validity is supported by the fact that the method has been more successful than any other in identifying links between adversity and illness. A similar contextual approach has been adopted by other investigators; for example, in Paykel's concept of the 'objective negative impact' of an event.

Many different dimensions of adverse experience can be measured contextually. Brown & Harris' (1978) original study considered 28 dimensions of events, such as the degree of short-term and long-term threat, and the amount of change in routine involved. More recently, attention has been focused on event dimensions which might be related to particular types of psychiatric or psychosomatic disorder, such as ratings of loss and disappointment (depression), danger (anxiety), and goal-frustration (gastrointestinal disease).

Causal interpretation

Some life events – for example, those involving loss of employment or conflict in close relationships – may be associated with psychiatric disorder because they are consequences rather than causes of disorder. Most of these can be excluded if attention is confined to events before the onset of the disorder. But even where the dating of symptom onset is valid, it can be argued that the insidious development of a condition may have led to subtle changes in the person's behaviour before symptoms became overt. For this reason, Brown & Birley (1968) introduced a rating of the *independence* of each event of the subject's own behaviour: for example, a spouse's death from cancer would be independent of the subject's behaviour, whereas divorce would be only possibly independent. This can be used to rule out the possibility that increased rates of life events preceding the onset of illness merely reflect events resulting from the illness or its prodrome.

A second issue of causal interpretation is whether exposure to adversity is confounded with other variables that might independently influence the risk of disorder, leading to a spurious association between adversity and disorder. It has been suggested that aspects of personality might play such a role. In practice, information about the relationship in time between the occurrence of life events and the onset of disorder can be used to rule out this possibility (see below).

Recent adversity as a cause of psychiatric illness

Depression

Over the last 25 years, there has been a steady accumulation of research showing that people suffering from depression are about three to five times more likely to have experienced a life event with major unpleasant long-term implications in the 6–12 months preceding onset of the disorder than normal subjects over a similar period.

In a study of women in London, Brown & Harris (1978) showed that the events linked with depression were specifically those with high long-term threat (*severe events*); most of these involved loss, in a broad sense which includes not only exits from the social field but also damage to cherished ideas or ambitions. Brown & Harris also found that depressed women were more likely to have had a *major difficulty* at the time of onset (a difficulty with high contextual severity and lasting at least 18 months). Severe events and major difficulties were referred to as 'provoking agents'.

These findings have been well replicated in other studies using the LEDS in samples from the female general population, although findings for difficulties have been slightly less consistent than those for life events. Evidence in men is comparable but much less extensive.

Studies of psychiatric patients have produced generally similar results, although a higher proportion of depressed patients have an unprovoked onset (30–60% in different studies, compared with 10–30% of depressed subjects in general population samples). This is probably due to an increased proportion of genuinely 'endogenous' illness among patients, but it may also reflect the processes whereby depressed people are selected for psychiatric care. Indeed, disorders with the symptom patterns traditionally regarded as markers of endogenous conditions ('melancholic' symptoms) differ little, if at all, from other types of depression in their association with recent adversity (Katschnig, 1986, pp. 201ff.).

Severe events are concentrated in the month or two preceding onset of illness, but increased rates are found throughout the preceding 6–9 months, which is usually taken as the *causal period* for life events in depression. Most current evidence indicates that someone experiencing two (or more) severe events is at little or no greater risk than someone who experiences a single severe event, suggesting a threshold phenomenon rather than additivity.

In assessing the overall importance of the link between adversity and depression, the fact that they sometimes occur together by chance must be taken into account. Using a measure which allows for this, attributable risk per cent, most studies show that 70–80% of women with onset of depression in the general population have experienced a provoking agent unattributable to chance co-occurrence (the comparable figure in Doll & Hill's (1952) study of smoking and male lung cancer is 79%).

Nonetheless, only about 20% of women experiencing major adversity actually go on to develop a disorder. Some improvement in the predictive value of adversity may be achieved by taking into account factors that render particular types of event prepotent stressors for particular people, such as high commitment or role conflict in specific areas of life (Brown & Harris, 1989). However, much of the variation in outcome reflects differences in individual predisposition (see below).

Are people liable to depression 'event-prone'?

Although exposure to adversity depends largely on factors in the social environment, personal characteristics play some part: many life events emerge from situations which that person's past behaviour played some part in creating, even where they are independent of more recent behaviour.

This has led to suggestions that the association between adversity and depression might be due to personal factors that are confounded with exposure to adversity. However, any confounding factor capable of explaining the marked peak in life event rates in the one to two months preceding onset of depression would not only have to be associated with exposure to adversity, but would have to vary over time in synchrony (or at least in a strictly temporal relationship) with its occurrence: the relationship in time between adversity and onset of depression is difficult to explain by confounding with any stable attribute. It is more likely that any link between 'event-proneness' and depression depends on the actual occurrence of events and the increased risk of depression as a consequence of these.

Chronicity and recovery from depression

Although chronic depression is common – about half the cases of depression in the community at any one time will have lasted for at least a year – much less research has been devoted to the social factors maintaining these disorders.

Studies using the LEDS have shown that depression is more likely to become persistent where there is an ongoing life difficulty. Recovery is more likely after events which terminate or neutralise such a difficulty, or other events with positive implications which may inspire renewed hope.

Other disorders

Information on disorders other than depression is more limited, and a brief summary can be given here (detailed reviews are available in Brown & Harris (1989)).

Psychosis

One of the earliest rigorous studies of recent life experience in schizophrenia was reported in 1968 by Brown & Birley, who found a raised frequency of independent life events in the period immediately preceding relapse of florid symptoms. This has been broadly supported by subsequent research, although there have also been some conflicting results.

Most of the positive findings in schizophrenia differ from those in depression in showing elevated rates of both minor and major events, and in the much shorter causal period (about three weeks). This suggests that recent adversity plays at most a non-specific precipitating role in those already at high risk of relapse. This may also apply to some cases of mania, where the evidence of any link with life stress is less consistent. It is important to recognise that bipolar (and schizophrenic) disorders may be heterogeneous in their responsiveness to environmental factors.

Anxiety

To date, there have been relatively few systematic studies of the role of adversity in non-psychotic disorders other than depression. Anxiety disorders of recent onset are associated with events involving long-term threat about as strongly as are depressive disorders, but the events tend to involve the more specific dimension of danger, rather than loss; this relationship is not confined to post-traumatic stress disorders, although these provide particularly clear examples.

Physical illness

The improved methods of assessing life stress described above are being applied increasingly to physical disorders where there may be a psychosomatic contribution to the onset or the course of illness. Recent studies have found increased rates of adversity in patients who have physical complaints without a detectable organic cause (e.g. abdominal pain, low back pain), and in patients with certain types of organic disease (e.g. peptic ulcer disease).

Factors modifying the effects of recent adversity

Factors that protect against, or predispose to, the onset of disorder in the face of life stress are often referred to by the terms 'resilience' or (its converse) 'vulnerability', which cover a potentially wide range of different factors, physiological, psychological, and social. 'Vulnerability' is also sometimes used simply to mean a predisposition to a particular disorder (e.g. a genetic 'vulnerability' to schizophrenia), but the present discussion is confined to factors thought to operate by moderating or exacerbating adversity. Some of these may exert a non-specific influence on the risk of a range of disorders (e.g. both depressive and anxiety disorders), while others may be more specific in their effects. The question of specificity is largely unexplored, and most of the available evidence concerns vulnerability to depression.

Biological factors

Individual differences in brain anatomy or physiology are undoubtedly involved in the predisposition to psychiatric disorders, but at present they remain largely undefined. Even less is known about any specifically stress-modulating effects they may have.

There may be variation in the sensitivity of certain physiological processes to environmental influence; for example, in animal research, altered autonomic responsiveness to short-term physical stress has been related to specific changes in neurochemical functioning. Phenomena such as these may underlie individual differences in temperament in man (which are partly determined by genetic factors), which may contribute to psychological vulnerability (see below).

Factors in the current social environment

In their study of women in Camberwell, Brown & Harris (1978) found that the lack of a supportive close relationship, the presence of three or more young children in the home, and lack of employment were each associated with an increased risk of depression among women exposed to a provoking agent. It was suggested that these factors were causes of, and for this reason indicators of, psychological vulnerability to depression.

In fact, the findings for the latter two of these three factors have not been widely replicated (see Goldberg & Huxley, 1992), perhaps because they predict psychological vulnerability only under certain social conditions. For example, an association between having several young children in the home and low self-esteem is likely to depend on local conditions concerning housing, marital roles, and reproductive expectations, and whether assistance with child care from nurseries or relatives is available. Where social factors are indirectly and conditionally related to vulnerability, consistent findings will emerge only when the pathways mediating their effects are defined in more detail.

In contrast, close relationships involving trust and intimacy have been found to confer protection against depression in many different sociocultural settings (Brown & Harris, 1986), suggesting a more fundamental or direct effect. Much of the evidence is retrospective, and comes from studies of women; there have been few relevant studies of men, but most of these have produced similar results.

Some negative findings have come from prospective studies that did not examine crisis support during adversity in the follow-up period (e.g. Henderson *et al*, 1981); this is important, as prospective information about close relationships does not predict later support perfectly, and the failure of expected support to materialise during adversity carries a substantially increased risk of depression. Close relationships do not appear to protect against the onset of anxiety disorders, and their effect may be relatively specific to depression, perhaps because they assist in repairing or neutralising experiences of loss.

There is very little evidence that distant social contacts moderate the emotional response to adversity, but a person's wider network of relationships may, as a source of information or practical help, influence whether adversity actually occurs or persists.

Psychological vulnerability

Much of the life events research described earlier supports the view that the effects of recent experiences depend critically on their meaning for the person concerned, and therefore on how they are interpreted and evaluated. This exemplifies the more general role of cognitive appraisal in mediating emotional responses (Lazarus & Folkman, 1984; see Chapter 5). Accordingly, hypotheses about psychological vulnerability have focused on cognitive factors that might bias the appraisal of adversity, whether these are inferential habits, or more complex cognitive schemata in which affective and motivational elements are also implicated, overlapping with the schemata considered in psychodynamic theory.

These factors have mainly been discussed in relation to depression, but a broader range of disorders has been considered by authors such as Beck (1976). They include:

(1) inferential traits exacerbating adverse experiences, such as catastrophisation, dichotomous thinking, and overgeneralisation

(2) low self-esteem: affect-laden schemata or self-representations associated with a wide range of negative self-evaluations and self-attributions

(3) assumptions of personal inefficacy or helplessness in the face of difficulty

(4) dysfunctional attributional styles in which negative outcomes tend to be attributed to the self, and positive outcomes to outside influences.

Research aiming to test proposed links between these factors (which clearly overlap with each other) and vulnerability to psychiatric disorder has had to contend with two connected difficulties. First, as mood itself affects cognitive activity, prospective research is needed if the causal relationship between the two is to be examined. But attempts to assess these factors prospectively may fail to detect schemata which are partially latent, and expressed fully only when primed by the presence of adversity (or indeed by interaction with a particular mood state). The results of prospective studies are likely to depend strongly on the sensitivity of the assessment methods used, and this is probably the major reason for divergent research findings. Some studies have found no premorbid difference between those who later develop depressive disorders and those who do not, while other well-designed studies, using different measures, have shown that negative self-schemata do predict onset of depression in the face of subsequent adversity (see Brown *et al*, 1990).

Coping skills

A number of authors have catalogued and classified the strategies or mechanisms that people use when attempting actively to manage stressful life circumstances; an influential account by Lazarus & Folkman (1984) lists 64 separate mechanisms.

A broad distinction is often made between action-orientated, problem-solving coping mechanisms, aimed at altering the life situation giving rise to stress, and mechanisms which involve cognitive or other 'intrapsychic' activity and have an emotion-regulating function. Those in the second group overlap conceptually with defence mechanisms as described in psychoanalysis.

Methods have been developed to assess people's coping styles or strategies, either as dispositions or as actually displayed in managing a particular stressful experience. Coping activity during a crisis will be influenced by psychiatric state, and dispositional measures must be used if a role in determining psychiatric outcome is to be demonstrated.

Attempts to evaluate the global effectiveness of different coping strategies have as yet produced few replicated findings. This probably reflects the fact that much coping behaviour is specific to a given situation. Dispositional measures may be weak predictors of how the subject actually responds. Even where the strategies adopted are predicted adequately, whether they are effective probably varies according to the types of situation they are used to deal with, or according to different outcome criteria: for example, a strategy that limits distress in the short term might lead to greater disability in the longer term.

More consistent findings might emerge if research in this area addressed more specific questions. However, it has been argued that the most important factors may not be the characteristics of specific coping strategies themselves, but the availability of a varied repertoire of such strategies, their flexible use guided by situational requirements, and an over-riding attitude of confidence that active mastery of the difficulties encountered is possible (Rutter, 1985). This last point suggests that resourceful coping may depend as much on the cognitive and attitudinal sets discussed in the previous section as on any specific coping skills.

Long-term effects of adverse experience

Adverse experience may be linked with psychiatric disorder many years later in three main ways:

(1) it may provoke a persistent disorder
(2) it may be associated with adversity and other social risk factors later in life, through continuities or predictable sequences in the environment
(3) it may have a formative influence on personal attributes related to psychological vulnerability.

Over the course of time, the second and third of these may interact with each other to produce complex transactional processes between personal attributes and the nature and qualities of the social environment encountered.

It has often been suggested that adverse experience might reduce vulnerability to subsequent stress through a 'toughening' effect, although little evidence is available showing this. Much more research has been devoted to the (not incompatible) possibility that certain adverse experiences cause a lasting increase in vulnerability to later stresses. (See Chapter 10 for an alternative view.)

Childhood adversity

There is some evidence that major adversity during adult life has a cumulative effect on vulnerability to depression, but most research, stimulated by the important work of John Bowlby (see Chapter 8), has dealt with long-term effects of experiences in childhood. Here, some long-term effects have been found quite consistently (e.g. major family disharmony linked with later antisocial behaviour; childhood physical or sexual abuse with adult emotional disorders), while others, such as a link between early loss of mother and adult depression, have been more controversial. It is important to recognise two difficulties in tracing links between childhood experience and later psychiatric disorder.

First, major adversity amenable to study many years later often involves multiple risk factors. For example, children who have lost their mothers (by death or by separation) are also more likely to have experienced prolonged maternal illness or disability, disharmony or violence between the parents, unsatisfactory subsequent care by the surviving parent, step-parent or an institution, and indeed a variety of other potential stressors. Although the disruption of the bond with the mother has often been emphasised as crucial, any of the other factors may be more specifically linked with the later risk of a particular type of psychiatric disorder (Rutter, 1972). Strong and reliable links with adult illness are unlikely to be found unless the relevant factors are identified with precision.

The second difficulty concerns the complexity of the pathways involved. Lasting effects of early experience on psychological make-up, in the form of maladaptive assumptions, affect-laden memories, or more complex dysfunctional mental models, may influence vulnerability to disorder in adult life quite directly. But the environmental and transactional pathways mentioned earlier produce causal sequences that are complex and often indirect. As a result, links between early experience and later disorder may be progressively diluted or obscured unless the intervening stages are taken into account.

Research into the long-term consequences of early loss of a mother provides examples of both phenomena. Recent evidence (Harris *et al*, 1990) suggests that the link with adult depression depends on the association of early loss with unsatisfactory subsequent care in childhood: where care by the father or substitute parent is adequate, there is little or no excess risk of depression in adult life. Moreover, inadequate care in childhood predicts later depression in women partly because it is associated with premarital pregnancy and thence marriage to an unsupportive husband, an excess risk of depression arising from the higher rate of marital adversity and lack of support later in life.

The components making up sequential processes such as this (e.g. the link between early loss and lack of care) may vary in importance in different populations, and this may explain some inconsistencies of research into long-term consequences of early experience.

Conclusions

Much progress has been made in life events research over the last 25 years. Improved methods have enabled pitfalls to be avoided while retaining sensitivity of measurement, and more specific relationships have been explored than those considered in the older research into 'stress'. As a consequence, research has moved on from establishing that important environmental effects do occur, to examining in more detail how they are mediated, in particular how life stresses interact with predisposing or vulnerability factors. Future research into the nature and origins of vulnerability to life stress is likely to have important practical implications in psychiatry and clinical psychology.

References

Beck, A. T. (1976) *Cognitive Therapy and the Emotional Disorders.* New York: International Universities Press.

Bowlby, J. (1969–80) *Attachment and Loss.* London: Hogarth Press.

Brown, G. W. & Birley, J. L. T. (1968) Crises and life changes in the onset of schizophrenia. *Journal of Health and Social Behaviour,* 9, 203–214.

—— & Harris, T. O. (1978) *Social Origins of Depression.* London: Tavistock.

—— & —— (1986) Stressor, vulnerability and depression: a question of replication. *Psychological Medicine,* 16, 739–744.

—— & —— (eds) (1989) *Life Events and Illness.* London: Unwin Hyman.

——, Andrews, B., Bifulco, A., *et al* (1990) Self-esteem and depression. *Social Psychiatry and Psychiatric Epidemiology,* 25, 200–209, 225–249.

Doll, R. & Hill, A. B. (1952) Study of the aetiology of carcinoma of the lung. *British Medical Journal,* ii, 1271–1286.

Goldberg, D. P. & Huxley, P. (1992) *Common Mental Disorders: A Bio-social Model.* London: Routledge.

Harris, T. O., Brown, G. W. & Bifulco, A. (1990) Loss of parent in childhood and adult psychiatric disorder: a tentative overall model. *Development and Psychopathology,* 2, 311–328.

Henderson, S., Byrne, D. G. & Duncan-Jones, P. (1981) *Neurosis and the Social Environment.* London: Academic Press.

Holmes, T. H. & Rahe, R. H. (1967) The Social Readjustment Rating Scale. *Journal of Psychosomatic Research,* 11, 213–218.

Katschnig, H. (ed.) (1986) *Life Events and Psychiatric Disorders: Controversial Issues.* Cambridge: Cambridge University Press.

Lazarus, R. & Folkman, S. (1984) *Stress, Appraisal and Coping.* New York: Springer.

Paykel, E. S. (1983) Methodological aspects of life events research. *Journal of Psychosomatic Research,* 27, 341–352.

——, Myers, J. K., Dienelt, M. N., *et al* (1969) Life events and depression: a controlled study. *Archives of General Psychiatry,* 21, 753–760.

Rutter, M. (1972) *Maternal Deprivation Reassessed.* Harmondsworth: Penguin.

—— (1985) Resilience in the face of adversity. *British Journal of Psychiatry,* 147, 598–611.

Stott, D. (1958) Some psychosomatic aspects of causality in reproduction. *Journal of Psychosomatic Research,* 3, 42–55.

13 Social support and mental health: positive and negative aspects

Lorna A. Champion & Gillian M. Goodall

The definition and conceptual development of social support • Where does support come from? • The perceived adequacy of support • The measurement of social support • Process issues: how does social support exert its effect on mental health? • The confounding of stress and social support • Expressed emotion • Schizophrenia: a special case • What may contribute to the presence or absence of effective social support? • Social support from a life-span perspective

---

This chapter embraces the broad concept of social support, to define what it is, and to make some sense of how it influences on mental health.

There is nothing new or innovative about social support; it is a natural feature of all social life. However, as an area of academic study, social support has only really come into its own since the early 1970s. At this time there were just a few papers directly about social support. Now, hundreds of papers are being published every year on the subject. There has been an explosion of interest in the links between social support and health. Most explosions create confusion. Our task is to bring some order to the confusion so the interested reader can make an informed search through the outpouring of research available on this topic.

Various disciplines in social science have made a contribution to our understanding of the effect of social relationships on mental health (Henderson *et al*, 1981). One major example is the work on attachment theory (Bowlby, 1988). In contrast to the intensive study of attachment, other research published in the 1970s showed that quite crude indicators of social support were associated with decreased mortality (Berkman & Syme, 1979) and psychiatric morbidity (Silberfield, 1978).

At around the same time, the publication of research on stress, particularly the study of life events and their association with psychiatric disorder (Chapter 12), was also beginning to suggest that social support could protect against such stressors (e.g. Brown & Harris, 1978). The appealing proposal was made that social support may be more amenable to intervention than stress (Cassel, 1974). By the early 1980s the relationship between social support and health was attracting a great deal of research interest; the concept of social support clearly needed careful definition.

The definition and conceptual development of social support

Social support can be usefully regarded as having two main components which interact with a third (Leavy, 1983):

(1) *structure* – relationships either exist or do not exist, and any adequate assessment of social support must consider the availability of relationships in the person's environment
(2) *function* – what functions do relationships provide?
(3) *process* – how people make use of potentially supportive relationships in their environment.

Both structure and function are considered in detail below; the more complex issue of process later.

The structure of social support

At the most basic level, the analysis of the structure of social support needs to describe how many people are available to someone to provide support, and what role they play in relation to that person, for example, mother, sister, doctor (Power *et al*, 1988).

Social network analysis provides the most comprehensive approach to measurement and analysis of the structure of social support (see Greenblatt *et al*, 1982; Hall & Wellman, 1985; House & Kahn, 1985). A genuine network analysis would consider all of a person's social contacts and the relationships between those social contacts (Box 13.1). Some researchers have also examined the range of activities each relationship involves (Hirsch, 1981).

Functions of social support

The work of Robert Weiss (e.g. Weiss, 1974) provided a rich conceptual basis for identifying the functions of social support; he outlined six

---

Box 13.1   A comprehensive network analysis

The size of the network
The frequency of contact among members (density)
The strength of ties between network members
Similarity of people in the network (homogeneity)
The degree of initiative versus receptivity among members
   (reciprocity)
The relationship between the network and outside influences

relational provisions that an adequate social life should make available. Following on from this work, a host of widely cited definitions of the functions of social support have been devised (e.g. Cobb, 1976; House, 1981). The main functions are defined below (Wills, 1985).

Esteem support or emotional support

This support function provides reassurance about a person's worth and can be linked with the concept of unconditional positive regard (Rogers, 1961). Such support is often sought when doubts about one's ability or worth are experienced and there are inevitable shortfalls in self-esteem. This function will usually involve confiding about problems or concerns. It is usually provided by relationships that are felt to be very close and are reasonably long-standing. Most commonly, the relationships that provide this function would be with a spouse or partner, a close relative, or a close friend. Absence of the support that serves this function may result in emotional isolation.

Instrumental support

This is also termed aid, practical support, tangible support, or material support. It describes the provision of direct assistance such as help with the housework, child care, and shopping, or facilities such as the provision of money, transport, and tools or practical skills such as plumbing or cooking.

Social companionship

This support function involves the experience of being in the company of known others while engaging in activities which are partly or solely for the purpose of pleasure, leisure, or relaxation. Examples of these activities would include visiting, parties, outings and excursions, sporting activities of all kinds, hobbies or non-work interests, meals, and so on.

Emotional support, instrumental support, and social companionship can be regarded as the three core support functions that have been addressed in research on the link between mental health, social support, and stress. In addition to these three functions, Wills (1985) also discusses two other support functions. These are informational and motivational support.

Informational support

This function involves the provision of information, advice, and guidance. Such information may involve providing a more objective view of the person's own situation or problem, including, for example, advice on how common-place an experience is and what can be done to help. Wills (1985) points out that informational support often comes from the same source as emotional support, and the two functions are often highly correlated. It is of interest to those concerned with psychiatric patients to consider in what circumstances informational support may not be available, and how it may be provided even if emotional support appears to be absent or inadequate.

Motivational support

This function is essentially theoretical, and there is no direct research evidence to support its effect on mental health. However, Wills (1985) argues that much stress associated with psychiatric disorder is chronic in nature. Support that consistently helps to maintain hope in chronically difficult circumstances and helps someone to sustain a belief in a chosen course of action, especially if this is demanding, may be important in preventing psychiatric disorder. As with informational support, motivational support may be appropriately supplied by professionals.

Support for patients

It is of interest for those in the caring professions to consider which, if any, of the support functions they may be providing for their patients. Such consideration should influence the professional's behaviour towards the patient regarding, for example:

(1) how consistent the relationship with the patient can be
(2) how significant changes in the frequency of meeting or accessibility should be handled
(3) how separations or ending of the professional relationship may adversely affect the patient.

Such an assessment would be carried out in the context of the patient's existing social resources, taking into account to what extent the necessary provisions are available and to what extent they have been disrupted by the disorder, and so on.

Where does support come from?

Different domains as a source of support

The question of where relationships are placed in the broad domains of a person's life needs to be considered. Examples of which domains are important will depend on life stage, but examples that apply across the life span may include family, friends, and social activities. For many, especially men, work is an important domain; for some, such as adolescents and some adults, education, school, or college may be another.

The protective effect of diffuse domains

Research has suggested that if people participate in a broad range of domains, they have better mental health than those who confine their participation to one or two domains (Thoits, 1986). This ties in with the evidence indicating that the density of the social network is important in aiding recovery from certain psychiatric disorders (Greenblatt *et al*, 1982). Additionally, patients with a wider social network have been found to be less of a burden to their families (Maurin & Boyd, 1990). Also, the density of the network is related to effective adjustment to major life transitions, such as teenage pregnancy (Barrera, 1981), divorce (Wilcox, 1981), bereavement, or returning to education (Hirsch, 1981). In most of these circumstances, a more diffuse network, where, for example, there is little or no interconnection between family and friends, is associated with a more positive outcome. Thus, having support which derives from a range of domains is more likely to meet the demands for a more diffuse network than a situation where all support is derived from the same domain.

The finding that work outside the home can offer protection against depression for women under stress (Brown & Harris, 1978; Warr & Parry, 1982) may, in part, be due to the positive effect of work on social support. The workplace and the social relationships that may exist there have the potential to provide many of the key support functions outlined above.

Gender differences in social support

The question of support arising from different domains leads to speculation about whether men and women derive their support from different sources. Schuster *et al* (1990) found this to be the case in that, in general, men derive more support from their spouses than from other sources outside the family, whereas women often look to family and friends for support, mostly other women.

Cohen & Wills (1985), in their review of the literature, also concluded that women have different styles of relating. Women derive satisfaction from intimate, confiding relationships, whereas men find satisfaction from relationships that involve taking part in social activities and accomplishing tasks. These findings suggest there may be a sex difference both in the type of support that is found most benefical, and the source or type of the supportive relationships themselves. To what degree these differences have arisen as a result of varying needs or cultural norms which influence the availability and acceptability of different types of relationship is open to question.

Variations in the type of social stresses experienced by men and women are discussed later.

Availability

Having considered the domains from which support may come, the availability of the people who are identified as potential providers of support must be assessed (Henderson *et al*, 1981). Availability needs to be assessed for each key relationship. It is self-evident that a relationship that is positively supportive will be less effective in providing support if the person who provides it is not readily available in the way required by the particular individual in question.

Acceptability

The availability of potential support is of no use unless the person concerned feels it is acceptable to have and make use of it. There is a danger in assuming that because people in a person's network seem to be able to provide support of a certain kind they necessarily will be able to do so.

People often have strong beliefs about the kind of person who should provide support; for example, a relative may be regarded as an acceptable provider, whereas a friend or professional would not be. Some depressed women, for example, may regard only their mothers or their partners as acceptable sources of emotional support. Beliefs such as these may not be articulated by a patient, but they can nevertheless be substantial barriers to the effective use of support in a patient's network.

The perceived adequacy of support

Both availability and acceptability relate to the perceived adequacy of the support a people receive from their social relationships. The assessment of the perceived adequacy of social support has proved to be a major predictor of mental health (Henderson *et al*, 1981). It is very important to recognise that, apart from the most basic structural measures of support, most assessments conducted by questionnaire or interview assess the respondents' *perception* of the support available to them. Perception of the adequacy of the support received should be directly examined. Assessing how the support received, especially in a crisis, matches ideals or expectations should form a part of any research on the protective effects of support (Brown *et al*, 1986).

The main aspects of the definition of social support presented so far are shown in Box 13.2.

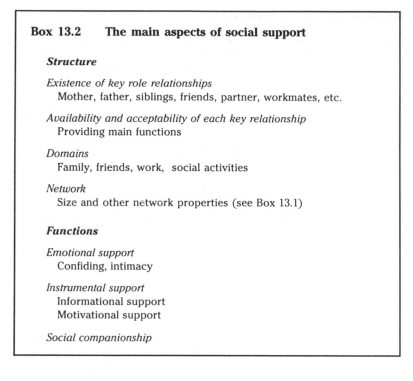

Box 13.2   The main aspects of social support

Structure

Existence of key role relationships
   Mother, father, siblings, friends, partner, workmates, etc.

Availability and acceptability of each key relationship
   Providing main functions

Domains
   Family, friends, work, social activities

Network
   Size and other network properties (see Box 13.1)

Functions

Emotional support
   Confiding, intimacy

Instrumental support
   Informational support
   Motivational support

Social companionship

The measurement of social support

Research on social support proliferated so quickly that precise definitions and, consequently, reliable measurement instruments have not been established and used across a range of different studies. There are now instruments available which have published evidence of their validity, reliability, and other psychometric properties, and these are briefly summarised in Table 13.1.

A review by House & Kahn (1985) sets out to clarify issues of measurement; they conclude that it is not possible to recommend one or a few standard measures for widespread use. We have repeated the key points of this summary below, updating it in the light of more recent developments and with psychiatric patients particularly in mind.

(1) Some attempt should be made to measure each of the main aspects of social support outlined in Box 13.2; that is, structure, function, perceived adequacy, and crisis support.
(2) The quality of individual relationships needs to be assessed in relation to specific functions; it should not be assumed that support from different relationships can be added together to produce a score. The question of who provides the support is likely to be crucial.

Table 13.1 Factors in measurement

Instrument	Type	Comments	Reference
Interview Schedule for Social Interaction (ISSI)	Interview: lengthy.	Some distinction of function in two broad categories of attachment and social integration. Repetitive to administer. Distinguishes between availability and adequacy. Summates relationships.	Henderson *et al*, 1981
Self-Evaluation and Social Support Schedule (SESS)	Interview: very complex lengthy, extensive training required.	Focuses on emotional support, including crisis support. Some distinction of function. Each relationship assessed individually for function.	Brown *et al*, 1986, 1990
Interview Measures of Social Relationships (IMSR)	Interview: shorter than ISSI or SESS.	Based on ISSI. Measures of network density, including negative interactions.	Brugha *et al*, 1987
Mannheim Interview (MISS)	Interview: structured.	Distinction of all key functions and perceived adequacy. Assesses individual relationships. Can be adapted to assess network characteristics of importance to specific investigations. Covers crisis support.	Veiel, 1990
Significant Other Scale (SOS)	Question-naire or structured interview: various versions including simple short form.	Distinction of instrumental and emotional support and assessment of perceived adequacy of a range of specified key role relation-ships.	Power *et al*, 1988

A number of relationships providing a low level of support may operate quite differently from one relationship providing a high level of support.

(3) The collection of detailed information should generally be limited to between five and ten people. Network analysis should be used selectively, with density, reciprocity, and gender being the most useful measures. Limiting demands on respondents is likely to be especially important for many psychiatric populations.

(4) If time is limited, priority should be given to the assessment of emotional support, because this function has shown the clearest links with health. However, this point should be modified for special groups such as chronic and schizophrenic patients (see below), who may show atypical patterns of what is regarded as useful support.

Process issues: how does social support exert its effect on mental health?

Two main hypotheses have been formulated and have become the focus of intensive debate and study (Fig. 13.1):

(1) social support has a *direct* effect on mental health: low levels of social support (i.e. absent or impoverished social relationships) are associated with poor mental health and may have a causal role in the onset of the illness itself

(2) social support is only *indirectly* related to health, via its protective or buffering effect in the face of stress; this hypothesis, known as the 'buffering hypothesis', states that in the absence of a high level of stress, social support will show no relationship with mental health.

There is no space in a chapter of this length to attempt a general review of the evidence for the role of social support in promoting mental health.

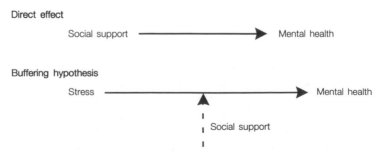

Fig. 13.1 How social support exerts its effects on mental health

Some excellent reviews of studies exist; these reviews provide details of the measures used and the samples studied (e.g. Cohen & Wills, 1985; Alloway & Bebbington, 1987).

A great deal of attention has also been given to how the buffering hypothesis should be examined statistically; in this area of controversy, the issues have been clearly discussed by Parry & Shapiro (1986) and Landerman *et al* (1989).

The work of two distinct research groups also deserves attention because of their pioneering work on the measurement of social support and their detailed attention to the buffering hypothesis and the possible mechanisms involved. These two research groups are George Brown and his co-workers in London, who have researched exclusively on women (e.g. Brown, 1989), and Scott Henderson and his co-workers in Canberra, Australia (e.g. Henderson *et al*, 1981). A very useful comparison of the two approaches is presented by Henderson & Brown (1988). A brief summary of the main finding of the reviews cited above is outlined below.

Evidence for buffering

There is consistent evidence for a buffering effect of social support in the face of severe stress. Most of the research in this area has focused on general measures of mental health, particularly the symptoms of depression and anxiety in community samples. Buffering effects are most consistently found when broadly defined measures of emotional support are used, usually in the form of some assessment of confiding.

Of the 13 studies measuring confiding reviewed by Cohen & Wills (1985), 11 showed a buffering effect. It is of interest that 11 of these 13 studies also showed a direct effect for social support (i.e. low social support itself was associated with mental illness). While the evidence for the importance of emotional support as a buffer against stress is impressive, it is important to bear in mind that the assessment of confiding is not the same as a careful assessment of each support function as defined in this chapter. While confiding almost certainly indicates the presence of emotional support, it is likely that other key functions are also provided by the confidant.

Type of support

Cohen & Wills (1985) conclude that evidence for a buffering model is found when the social support measure assesses interpersonal resources that are responsive to the needs elicited by stressful events. In general, emotional support would seem to be the most important function in providing a buffering effect; however, the quality of the measurement in most studies does not rule out a potentially major contribution of instrumental support.

Buffering effects are not usually found when more general measures of social integration are used. However, studies using these measures generally find evidence for 'main effects' on mental health. Similarly, most studies that have assessed social companionship have not found this support function to be important in protecting against stress (Henderson *et al*, 1981; Cohen & Wills, 1985). However, social companionship may be associated with well-being and good mental health more generally.

Evidence for a direct effect

Mental health seems to be directly associated with the person's degree of integration in a community social network; integration in a reasonably large social network which indicates the presence of a wide range of stable community connections is generally associated with good mental health.

The confounding of stress and social support

In the spirit of attempting to understand the processes by which social support exerts its effects on mental health, a number of issues need to be considered in the light of the basic findings presented so far. In particular, inadequate attention has been paid to the overlap of measurement in assessing stress and social support. It is important to recognise the likelihood of confounding for the following reasons (Eckenrode & Gore, 1981):

(1) Sources of support are often the same as sources of stress; any given relationship is likely to involve both stress and support.
(2) The perception of stress does not occur independently of the perception of support, nor vice versa.
(3) Stress can directly change available support because it may involve the actual loss of relationships or impair the ability to make use of support. Conversely, the presence of support may prevent stressors from occurring in the first place (Champion, 1990) and may ameliorate their effect in various ways, particularly by influencing coping strategies.

As Gore (1985) points out, little attention has been paid to how social support fits into the broader picture of personal coping styles or characteristics. Future research on how support 'buffers' against stress must take into account what is known about differences in coping style.

The social network as a source of stress

Most of the research linking social support and mental health has focused on the positive effects of social support. However, most relationships involve both positive and negative aspects, although not necessarily at the same time. In fact, it is the people who are the closest to the individual, particularly spouses, who are likely to be the major source of stress (Schuster *et al*, 1990).

A related finding is presented by Wortman & Conway (1985); they found, in their work on the physically ill, that although a patient may want and be very reliant on the support from a medical professional, the treatment offered may be far from pleasant and cause a great deal of stress.

Those who are vulnerable to depression seem to be particularly susceptible to interpersonal stress; Paykel (1979) found that interpersonal events and difficulties of an upsetting or threatening nature were especially common among depressed patients before the onset of disorder, as compared with controls (see Chapter 12). Bebbington *et al* (1988) also suggested that the rate of interpersonal events and difficulties may be chronically raised in those who develop depression, particularly neurotic depression.

The processes by which both the positive and negative aspects of social support exert their effects on mental health are likely to be equally complex; negative aspects are likely to exert both direct and indirect effects. Although there is not space here to go into detail about the processes involved in negative effects, it is important to recognise that this area has been given insufficient attention and should be researched in the future. Indeed, those researchers who have looked at both positive and negative aspects of social relationships have found that the negative aspects seem to be more potent in influencing mental health, despite their less frequent occurrence (Fiore *et al*, 1983; Rook, 1984; Schuster *et al*, 1990).

The care of social ties

Members of a social network may require much support themselves. This is well exemplified by the research on those who are the main carers of the chronically ill. In their review, Maurin & Boyd (1990) found that studies consistently showed that mental illness places a significant burden on carers because their own needs are superseded by those of the patient. This burden may not only be seen objectively, as, for example, in increased financial and practical demands, but it also has a subjective component that relates to how the carer feels about the situation. For example, the carer may have feelings of frustration and impatience at the slow pace of change (Pearlin, 1985). Both of these factors are important when assessing the burden a carer is experiencing and will have implications for any intervention recommended. There would be little point in suggesting that a family provide more support for a patient if that family is already stretched to the limit of its resources.

The stress associated with caring has also been put forward to explain the higher rates of depression found in women than in men (e.g. Weissman & Klerman, 1985). Belle (1982), in her work on women under stress, found that women often protect men from bad news. Cochrane & Stopes-Roe (1981) present the interesting finding that marriage is less protective against hospital admission for depression for women than for men. They suggest that this sex difference is due, at least in part, to women more often providing care for men and so keeping them out of hospital, whereas such care of depressed women is rarely provided by men. Women are therefore forced to rely on hospital care more often than men in the same situation.

Being let down

Social ties can fail to provide the support which is needed or expected, and hence create a feeling of being 'let down' (Brown *et al*, 1986). Brown and his co-workers have emphasised the importance of being 'let down' for the onset of depression in women. They found, in a prospective study, that a positive perception of available support from a husband followed by inadequate support from the husband in a crisis, was associated with the onset of depression, regardless of other support available to the women. Support from close ties outside the home was protective for married women only if their husbands had been unsupportive at initial assessment, or, in other words, they were not let down by their husbands.

However, it could be that certain people are prone to being 'let down' because of their distorted perceptions. Fiore *et al* (1983) postulated that depressed patients may have particularly unrealistic expectations of those in their social network (Power *et al*, 1988), which may lead to more occasions where they feel let down. Unrealistic expectations of support, and other problems depressed patients have in effectively mobilising support, can be tackled as part of treatment. Details of various ways of doing this are outlined by Parry (1988).

Caring debts

Generally, social relationships operate in a reciprocal fashion, where one is expected to return support given. As illustrated above, this ideal does not always exist or may break down in a crisis. Circumstances such as these, where there is a failure of reciprocity, can lead to 'caring debts', where the recipient of aid is likely to be called upon to pay dues as a donor at some future time (Pearlin, 1985). The accumulation of these 'debts' can be an additional source of stress.

Schuster *et al* (1990) attributed the more frequently negative interactions found with relatives than with friends to their permanence, and the obligations to reciprocate which "expose people to disappointments, conflicts, tensions, and unpleasantness" (p. 424). Social ties that are characterised in this way are more likely to be a feature in cultures where the family is tightly enmeshed and the extended family is seen as the primary source of support (Pearlin, 1985).

Caring debts are also likely to appear whenever people are not in a very good position to reciprocate, as among low-income groups and the psychiatrically ill. The latter could equally feel in debt to professionals involved in their care over extended periods of time.

Parry (1988) points out that the low self-esteem of depressed patients may lead them to focus excessively on the negative aspects of receiving support. These negative aspects are likely to include an assumption that they will be unable to repay any caring debts which accumulate. If depressed patients assume this, it is likely to interfere with their ability to mobilise support or accept the support that is offered.

Low income

It is well known that low socio-economic status is associated with an increased risk of psychiatric disorder (Brown & Harris, 1978; Cochrane, 1983). The greater incidence of stressful social relationships among those on a low income may partly explain this finding. Research shows that those in this group have less opportunity to choose the composition of their network and to determine the type of interaction that can be engaged in with network members (Rook, 1984). The difficulties for those on low incomes are further exacerbated by the likelihood that they will only have access to a support network which is also needy and stressed (Belle, 1982).

Expressed emotion

People can be interfering, intrusive, or excessively critical; the effects of this has been researched in the link between relapse of schizophrenic patients and the level of 'expressed emotion' (EE) in the relatives with whom they live (Vaughan & Leff, 1976).

The importance of the concept of EE in the close relatives of the mentally ill has been shown in many studies (see Kuipers & Bebbington, 1988, for a review). Three factors have been found to be important in predicting relapse in patients diagnosed as schizophrenic:

(1) critical comments
(2) hostility
(3) emotional overinvolvement.

Vaughan & Leff (1976) showed that a patient's coming from a home where the relatives showed a high level of EE, with more than 35 hours a week of contact between patient and relatives, was a better predictor of relapse of schizophrenia than non-compliance with medication. More recent studies have confirmed the robustness of EE as a predictor of relapse in schizophrenia across a range of cultures (Kuipers & Bebbington, 1988).

Vaughan & Leff (1976) found that depressed patients were also more likely to relapse if they came from high-EE homes, although in this case the level of critical comments was the crucial factor. For depressed patients, a low level of face-to-face contact and communication was associated with poor outcome; this is in direct contrast to schizophrenia, where a low level of contact of this type was protective.

The research on EE provides a clear example of how a source of support can be confounded with a source of stress.

Schizophrenia: a special case

The work on EE indicates that those patients diagnosed as schizophrenic may be especially vulnerable when certain aspects of social support are considered, and because of this they present a special case in relation to the general statements made so far in this chapter on the effects of social support on mental health.

Those diagnosed as schizophrenic tend to have very small social networks, largely comprised of relatives, and the density of these networks therefore tends to be high. There does seem to be an association between small network size and readmission for some subgroups of schizophrenic patients.

Cohen & Kochanowicz (1989) present the interesting finding that the smaller networks of older schizophrenic patients, often because kin are no longer available, were associated with increased satisfaction with their social ties. In a sample of older black schizophrenic patients, they found that increased contacts were made with the church and other 'outside' agencies, emphasising the importance of low-level contacts for this group. The work of Leff *et al* (1990) is of relevance here; detailed investigation of social support in a large group of chronic psychiatric patients revealed how the support was in many ways atypical. Apparently superficial contact and conversation were highly valued.

Overall, emotional support involving intimate confiding may be much less important for this group. Professionals are likely to be especially important in the network of schizophrenic people; they are in an ideal position to provide low-level emotional and instrumental support of the kind that is needed, without the negative pressures often present in the patient's family network (Birley & Hudson, 1983). However, the consistency of the support offered by professionals is likely to be especially important for this vulnerable group and for the relatives who care for them (Hogarty *et al*, 1991).

Interventions

There is now an impressive group of studies examining the effectiveness of a wide range of psychosocial treatments to help those diagnosed as schizophrenic and their families. These interventions directly involve EE, coping, and relationship issues; an excellent review of these studies is provided by Lam (1991). There is some suggestion by this work that professionals provide a range of support functions for patients (Hogarty *et al*, 1991) and their relatives (e.g. MacCarthy *et al*, 1989), and that the interventions may have a benefical effect on the wider support available to patients and relatives. However, the topic of social support as presented in this chapter has not been directly investigated, and this may be a useful direction for future research. It seems clear from the work that has been done so far that any assessment of social support in this area needs to be considered in the broader context of coping with specific stresses faced by patients and their families.

What may contribute to the presence or absence of effective social support?

To conclude this chapter, we return to the complex issue of the processes by which social support is created and used. Social support can be treated, for research purposes, as if it were a relatively stable attribute of an individual. However, this conceptualisation can be misleading because it distracts attention from the important interactional nature of the concept (Pearlin, 1989). People actively create and maintain most of their social relationships.

Issues that relate to someone's ability to form and maintain relationships are crucial for clinical interventions that aim to provide more adequate social support (Gottlieb, 1985). Creating the opportunity for support to develop is very different from creating support itself; the individual's contribution to the relationship is usually essential for its survival and effectiveness.

Personality and social support

This discussion raises the question of whether the measurement of social support is just a proxy measure for more stable features of personality (Cohen & Syme, 1985). As Henderson & Brown (1988) point out, even though personality almost certainly does play a role in the development and effectiveness of most supportive relationships, this does not necessarily detract from the importance of support. For example, in a prospective study of the development of depression in a largely working-class sample of women in inner London, it was clear that the negative effect of low self-esteem (a personality characteristic measured before the onset of depression) was greatly reduced when there was good emotional support in a crisis (Brown *et al*, 1986).

A study conducted in Canberra, Australia (Henderson *et al*, 1981) examined the relationship between neuroticism and a comprehensive assessment of social support in a large community sample. Trait neuroticism was correlated with measures of emotional support (in this case attachment) and with more general measures of social integration. As predicted, high trait neuroticism was associated with low levels of support for all measures. Further analysis of the data suggested that neuroticism showed the clearest relationship with inadequate support only under conditions of high stress. However, it is important to note that neuroticism was also associated with high stress and may therefore have contributed to the level of stress in the first place.

In addition to these considerations, Monroe & Steiner (1986) point out that some of the items on the neuroticism scale are actually assessments of the perception of support. Therefore, confounding of measurement among the three variables of support, stress, and personality remains a real possibility (Monroe & Steiner, 1986).

Social support from a life-span perspective

To take the argument presented above still further, we think that, from a theoretical perspective, social support needs to be understood in a developmental context. The ability to form positive, supportive ties with others is likely to be established early in life.

A fascinating study by Skolnick (1986) examines the links between earliest mother–infant attachment and the quality of social relationships through each stage of the life course, up to middle age, in a sample of men and women born in America. The results, which chart each individual on a series of paths, are not as consistent as attachment theory (see Chapter 8) would predict. Poor mother–child relations in the first two years of life do not inevitably lead to poor social relationships in childhood and adolescence. One of the most interesting findings from this research was the apparent importance of peer relationships in childhood; the quality of these childhood relationships was associated with the development of satisfactory relationships in adolescence and adulthood.

The results of this study suggest that changes in the social environment and their effect on the individual are likely to be crucial, but throughout it is also important to consider the reverse effects of the individual on the environment. Temperament and style of relating, which are likely to be passed on from one generation to another, are likely to be important here (Elder *et al*, 1986; Caspi *et al*, 1987).

There have been few studies which examine similarities in the pattern of social networks and the perceived adequacy of support across generations (Tietjen, 1985). The processes underlying such hypothetical continuity may be linked to the finding reported by McGuffin *et al* (1988) that the rates of threatening life events were higher in the relatives of depressed patients, suggesting that patterns of stress run in families.

This last point forces us back to the inter-relationship between stress and support. When the relationship between stress and social support is examined in a developmental context, and not confined to the immediate circumstances surrounding the onset of psychiatric disorder, there is the likelihood that good social support may operate by protecting against the occurrence of threatening life events in the first place. A reanalysis of data from studies of life events and depression suggested that a lack of emotional support was associated with an increased rate of negative events (Champion, 1990). It is of interest to note in the context of a life-span approach that there seems to be an increase in satisfaction with social support in old age (Lam & Power, 1991), as well as a decrease in the rate of life events (Henderson *et al*, 1981).

There is not the space here to consider how social support may be usefully studied in the context of a life-span approach; the interested reader is referred to the following references (Schulz & Rau, 1985; Maughan & Champion, 1990). The main point of the brief discussion presented above is that for useful study of the processes by which social support exerts its effect on mental health, a developmental approach is likely to be informative.

Such an approach needs to consider, firstly, the contribution of the internal characteristics of the person, which could include personality, coping style, temperament, self-esteem, self-confidence, and social skills, and, secondly, experiences in the external world or social environment, which could include, for example, the presence or absence of significant others to provide adequate role models, the quality of care received from those others, the experience of adversity, including significant losses or significant gains in the social and material world, cultural values, and the type of community experienced. In addition, the experience and timing of normative transitional events, for example leaving the parental home, starting work, marriage, and retirement may be important markers of changes in external experience.

Further reading

Cohen, S. & Syme, S. L. (eds) (1985) *Social Support and Health*. London: Academic Press.

Henderson, S., Byrne, D. G. & Duncan-Jones, P. (1981) *Neurosis and the Social Environment.* Sydney: Academic Press.
—— & Brown, G. W. (1988) Social support: the hypothesis and the evidence. In *Handbook of Social Psychiatry* (eds A. S. Henderson & G. D. Burrows). Amsterdam: Elsevier.

References

Alloway, R. & Bebbington P. (1987) The buffer theory of social support – a review of the literature. *Psychological Medicine*, **17**, 91–108.
Barrera, M. (1981) Social support in the adjustment of pregnant adolescents. In *Social Networks and Social Support* (ed. B. Gottlieb), pp. 69–96. Beverly Hills, CA: Sage.
Bebbington, P. E., Brugha, T., MacCarthy, B., *et al* (1988) The Camberwell Collaborative Depression Study. I: Depressed probands: adversity and the form of depression. *British Journal of Psychiatry*, **152**, 754–765.
Belle, D. (1982) Social ties and social support. In *Lives in Stress: Women and Depression* (ed. D. Belle), pp. 133–144. Beverly Hills, CA: Sage.
Berkman, L. & Syme, S. L. (1979) Social networks, host resistance and mortality: a nine-year follow-up study of Alameda county residents. *American Journal of Epidemiology*, **109**, 186–204.
Birley, J. & Hudson, B. (1983) The family, the social network and rehabilitation. In *Theory and Practice of Psychiatric Rehabilitation* (eds F. N. Watts & D. H. Bennet), pp. 171–188. Chicester: Wiley.
Bowlby, J. (1988) *A Secure Base: Clinical Applications of Attachment Theory.* London: Routledge.
Brown, G. W. (1989) Depression: a radical social perspective. In *Depression: An Integrative Approach* (eds K. Herbst & E. Paykel), pp. 21–43. Oxford: Heinemann.
—— & Harris, T. (1978) *The Social Origins of Depression: A Study of Psychiatric Disorder in Women.* London: Tavistock.
——, Andrews, B., Harris, T., *et al* (1986) Social support, self-esteem and depression. *Psychological Medicine*, **16**, 813–831.
——, Bifulco, A., Veiel, H. O. F., *et al* (1990) Self-esteem and depression. II: Social correlates of self-esteem. *Social Psychiatry and Psychiatric Epidemiology*, **25**, 225–234.
Brugha, T. S., Stuart, E., MacCarthy, B., *et al* (1987) The interview measure of social relationships: the description and evaluation of a survey instrument for assessing personal social resources. *Social Psychiatry*, **22**, 123–128.
Caspi, A., Elder, G. H. & Bem, D. J. (1987) Moving against the world: life-course patterns of explosive children. *Developmental Psychology*, **23**, 308–313.
Cassel, J. (1974) Psychosocial processes and "stress": theoretical formulation. *International Journal of Health Services*, **4**, 471–481.
Champion, L. (1990) The relationship between social vulnerability and the occurrence of severely threatening life events. *Psychological Medicine*, **20** (suppl. 1), 157–161.
Cobb, S. (1976) Social support as a moderator of life stress. *Psychosomatic Medicine*, **38**, 300–312.

Cochrane, R. (1983) *The Social Creation of Mental Illness.* London: Longman.
—— & Stopes-Roe, M. (1981) Women, marriage, employment and mental health. *British Journal of Psychiatry*, **139**, 373–381.
Cohen, C. I. & Kochanowicz, N. (1989) Schizophrenia and social network patterns: a survey of black inner-city outpatients. *Community Mental Health Journal*, **25** (suppl. 3), 197–207.
Cohen, S. & Syme, S.L. (1985) Issues in the study and application of social support. In *Social Support and Health* (eds S. Cohen & S.L. Syme), pp. 3–22. London: Academic Press.
—— & Wills, T. A. (1985) Stress, social support and the buffering hypothesis. *Psychological Bulletin*, **98**, 310–357.
Eckenrode, J. & Gore, S. (1981) Stressful events and social supports: the significance of context. In *Social Networks and Social Support* (ed. B. Gottlieb), pp. 43–68. Beverly Hills, CA: Sage.
Elder, G. H., Jr, Caspi, A. & Downey, G. (1986) Problem behaviour and family relationships. In *Human Development and the Life Course: Multidisciplinary Perspectives* (eds A. B. Sorensen, F. E. Weinert & L. R. Sherrod), pp. 293–340. Lawrence Erlbaum: London.
Fiore, J., Becker, J. & Coppel, D.B. (1983) Social network interactions: a buffer or a stress. *American Journal of Community Psychology*, **11**, 423–439.
Gore, S. (1985) Social support and styles of coping with stress. In *Social Support and Health* (eds S. Cohen & S.L. Syme), pp. 263–278. London: Academic Press.
Gottlieb, B. H. (1985) Social support and community mental health. In *Social Support and Health* (eds S. Cohen & S.L. Syme), pp. 303–326. London: Academic Press.
Greenblatt, M., Becerra, R. M. & Seafetinides, E. A. (1982) Social networks and mental health: an overview. *American Journal of Psychiatry*, **139**, 977–984.
Hall, A. & Wellman, B. (1985) Social networks and social support. In *Social Support and Health* (eds S. Cohen & S. L. Syme), pp. 23–41. London: Academic Press.
Henderson, A. S., Byrne, D. G. & Duncan-Jones, P. (1981) *Neurosis and the Social Environment.* Sydney: Academic Press.
—— & Brown, G. W. (1988) Social support: the hypothesis and the evidence. In *Handbook of Social Psychiatry* (eds A. S. Henderson & G. D. Burrows). Amsterdam: Elsevier Science.
Hirsch, B. J. (1981) Social networks and the coping process: creating personal communities. In *Social Networks and Social Support* (ed B. Gottlieb). Beverly Hills, CA: Sage.
Hogarty, G. E., Anderson, C. M., Reiss, D. J., *et al* (1991). Family psychoeducation, social skills training and maintenance chemotherapy in the aftercare treatment of schizophrenia. II: Two year effects of a controlled study on relapse and adjustment. *Archives of General Psychiatry*, **48**, 340–347.
House, J. S. (1981) *Work Stress and Social Support.* Reading, MA: Addison-Wesley.
—— & Kahn, R.L. (1985) Measures and concepts of social support. In *Social Support and Health* (eds S. Cohen & S. L. Syme), pp. 83–108. London: Academic Press.
Kuipers, L. & Bebbington, P. E. (1988) Expressed emotion research in schizophrenia: theoretical and clinical implications. *Psychological Medicine*, **18**, 893–909.
Lam, D. H. (1991) Psychosocial family intervention in schizophrenia: a review of empirical studies. *Psychological Medicine*, **21**, 423–441.
—— & Power, M. J. (1991) Social support in a general practice elderly sample. *International Journal of Geriatric Psychiatry*, **6**, 89–93.

Landerman, R., George, L. K., Campbell, R. T., *et al* (1989) Alternative models of the stress buffering hypothesis. *American Journal of Community Psychology*, **17** (suppl. 5), 625–642.

Leavy, R. L. (1983) Social support and psychological disorder: a review. *Journal of Community Psychology*, **11**, 3–21.

Leff, J. P., O'Driscoll, C., Dayson, D., *et al* (1990) The TAPS Project 5. The structure of social network data obtained from long-stay patients. *British Journal of Psychiatry*, **157**, 848–852.

MacCarthy, B., Kuipers, L., Hurry, J., *et al* (1989) Counselling the relatives of the long-term adult mentally ill. I: Evaluation of the impact on relatives and patients. *British Journal of Psychiatry*, **154**, 768–775.

McGuffin, P., Katz, P. & Bebbington, P. (1988) The Camberwell collaborative depression study. III: Depression and adversity in the relatives of depressed probands. *British Journal of Psychiatry*, **152**, 775–782.

Maughan, B. & Champion, L. (1990) Risk and protective factors in the transition to young adulthood. In *Successful Aging: Perspectives from the Behavioural Sciences* (eds P. B. Baltes & M. M. Baltes), pp. 296–331. Cambridge: Cambridge University Press.

Maurin, J. T. & Boyd, C. B. (1990) Burden of mental illness on the family: a critical review. *Archives of Psychiatric Nursing*, **4** (suppl. 2), 99–107.

Monroe, S. M. & Steiner, S. C. (1986) Social support and psychopathology: interrelations with preexisting disorder, stress and personality. *Journal of Abnormal Psychology*, **95**, 29–39.

Parry, G. (1988) Mobilizing social support. In *New Developments in Clinical Psychology*, vol. 2 (ed. F. N. Watts), pp. 83–104. Chichester: Wiley.

—— & Shapiro, D. A. (1986) Social support and life events in working class women: stress buffering or independent effects. *Archives of General Psychiatry*, **43**, 315–326.

Paykel, E. S. (1979) Recent life events in the development of the depressive disorders. In *The Psychology of the Depressive Disorder* (ed. R. A. Depue). New York: Academic Press.

Pearlin, L. I. (1985) Social structure and process of social support. In *Social Support and Health* (eds S. Cohen & S. L. Syme), pp. 43–60. London: Academic Press.

—— (1989) The sociological study of stress. *Journal of Health and Social Behaviour*, **30** (suppl. 3), 241–256.

Power, M. J., Champion, L. A., Aris, S. J. (1988) The development of a measure of social support: the significant others (SOS) scale. *British Journal of Clinical Psychology*, **27**, 349–358.

Rogers, C. R. (1961) *On Becoming a Person: A Therapist's View of Psychotherapy*. London: Constable.

Rook, K. S. (1984) The negative side of social interaction: impact on psychological well-being. *Journal of Personality and Social Psychology*, **46** (suppl. 5), 1097–1108.

Schulz, R. & Rau, M. T. (1985) Social support through the life course. In *Social Support and Health* (eds S. Cohen & S. L. Syme), pp. 129–149. London: Academic Press.

Schuster, T. L., Kessler, R. C. & Aseltine, R. H. (1990) Supportive interactions, negative interactions and depressed mood. *American Journal of Community Psychology*, **18** (suppl. 3), 423–438.

Silberfield, M. (1978) Psychological symptoms and social supports. *Social Psychiatry*, **13**, 11–17.

Skolnick, A. (1986) Early attachment and personal relationships across the life course. In *Life-Span Development and Behaviour*, vol. 7 (eds P. B. Baltes, D. L. Featherman & R. M. Lerner). London: Lawrence Erlbaum.

Thoits, P. A. (1986) Multiple identities: examining gender and marital status differences in distress. *American Sociological Review*, **51**, 259–272.

Tietjen, A. M. (1985) Relationships between the social networks of Swedish mothers and their children. *International Journal of Behavioural Development*, **8**, 195–216.

Vaughan, C. E. & Leff, J. P. (1976) The influence of family and social factors on the course of psychiatric illness: a comparison of schizophrenia and depressed neurotic patients. *British Journal of Psychiatry*, **129**, 125–137.

Veiel, H. O. (1990) The Mannheim interview on social support. Reliability and validity data from three samples. *Social Psychiatry and Psychiatric Epidemiology*, **25** (suppl. 5), 250–259.

Warr, P. & Parry, G. (1982) Paid employment and women's psychological well-being. *Psychological Bulletin*, **91** (suppl. 3), 498–516.

Weiss, R. (1974) The provisions of social relationships. In *Doing Unto Others* (ed. Z. Rubin). Englewood Cliffs, NY: Prentice-Hall.

Weissman, M. M. & Klerman, G. L. (1985) Gender and depression. *Trends in Neuroscience*, September, 416–420.

Wilcox, B. (1981) Social support in adjusting to marital disruption: a network analysis. In *Social Networks and Social Support* (ed. B. Gottlieb), pp. 97–115. Beverly Hills, CA: Sage.

Wills, T. A. (1985) Supportive functions of interpersonal relationships. In *Social Support and Health* (eds S. Cohen & S. L. Syme), pp. 61–82. London: Academic Press.

Wortman, C. B. & Conway, T. L. (1985) The role of social support in adaptation and recovery from physical illness. In *Social Support and Health* (eds S. Cohen & S. L. Syme), pp. 281–302. London: Academic Press.

14 The family

Neil Frude

The effect of the family on the individual • Explanations for the link between health and family • The family unit • Differences between families • Optimal families • Dysfunctional families • Families and stress

---

We often understand someone better when we know about their social background. We gain insight into their beliefs and attitudes, and we can interpret their behaviour more satisfactorily, if we know about their culture, neighbourhood, and family.

Adults remain affected by many aspects of their early social environment, and their day-to-day behaviour is influenced in many direct and indirect ways by their relationships with 'significant others'. An understanding of families can provide us with many insights into individual psychology, but families are more than simply a backcloth against which people act. Family groups are significant in their own right, and our understanding of social interaction and social identity can be substantially advanced by studying family units as 'foreground' rather than background.

This chapter begins by examining the family as the background or context for the individual. In particular, it is shown that close relationships are significant determinants and mediators of a person's health and psychological well-being. The family unit is considered next, and ideas about healthy and dysfunctional families are examined, along with how families respond to stress.

Within a single chapter it would not be possible to present even a synopsis of the voluminous literature on such important topics as family conflict, violence, sexual dysfunction, sexual abuse, separation and divorce, family bereavement, and so on. An integrated review covering many of these topics is provided by Frude (1991), and many specific reviews of particular topics and issues are available elsewhere. The aim of this chapter is to present a general overview of family psychology.

The effect of the family on the individual

Society derives a number of benefits from the organisation of people into family groups. When sociologists evaluate the societal 'functions' of the family, they include:

(1) the regulation of sexual behaviour and reproduction
(2) the provision of basic needs such as food and shelter
(3) the protection and socialisation of children
(4) the implementation of social prescriptions and proscriptions
(5) the provision of emotional support.

The family unit is also recognised as a basic economic and 'consumer' unit. There may be certain costs to society in having people organised into family groups but, overall, the benefits far outweigh any costs.

Social exchange

For the individual, too, being part of a family brings benefits and costs. One wide-ranging psychological theory, the social-exchange theory (see also Chapter 9), maintains that the decisions people make about their lives, including their family life, reflect their own cost–benefit analyses (Nye, 1982). Whether or not they are accurate in their prediction, people choose to enter a partnership because they anticipate certain benefits, and they judge that the benefits will outweigh the costs.

The same kind of analysis can be used to explain why people choose to have children, why they choose to separate, and why they choose to have extramarital affairs. In a study aimed at establishing the benefits adults anticipated from a partnership, Weiss (1974) interviewed people whose relationship had recently ended, and asked them what they felt was now missing from their life as a single person. Six basic 'provisions of relationships' were identified:

(1) attachment
(2) social integration
(3) reassurance of worth
(4) a sense of reliable alliance
(5) the opportunity for nurturance
(6) guidance.

Each of these actually relates to a whole cluster of benefits. 'Reassurance of worth', for example, covers the various effects that interactions with an intimate have in making the person feel 'valued' and 'respected'.

When people are asked what makes them happy, what provides them with satisfaction, and what gives meaning to their lives, they emphasise their family relationships much more than any other aspect of their life, including their occupation, hobbies, health, or money (Freedman, 1978). But although people prize family relationships and regard them as a prime source of happiness and personal satisfaction, they also understand that family relationships are frequently sources of distress and dissatisfaction. Irritations and conflicts within the family frequently rouse people to extreme anger, and in many cases family relationships lead to profound distress. Marital difficulties often lead to depression, and marital conflicts can escalate to extreme violence (a high proportion of murders, for example, involve partners as murderer and victim).

Thus, having an intimate relationship is certainly no guarantee of happiness, although, in general, family relationships appear to have more positive than negative effects. Most people evaluate their close alliances as having a favourable effect on their lives, and the objective evidence tends to confirm the beneficial effect of close alliances on health and well-being.

Life-event studies

Research over the past 30 years has established that people's psychological and physical health is profoundly affected by their life events (see Chapter 12). The research instrument most commonly used to measure the life events experienced by someone in the recent past is the Life Event Inventory. Such inventories, which are based on extensive interviews with many subjects, list the most common of important life events. Even a cursory examination of such lists (e.g. those compiled by Holmes & Rahe, 1967, and by Paykel *et al*, 1976) reveals that a high proportion of the events listed directly reflect aspects of family life (e.g. the illness of a relative, a bereavement, a child leaving home, marital separation, sexual problems).

Similarly, when lists are drawn up of only positive life events (Argyle & Henderson, 1985) or of relatively minor positive and negative events and changes of circumstance (sometimes referred to as 'uplifts' and 'hassles', respectively), high proportions of family events are again evident. (Incidentally, the effects of uplifts and hassles are by no means negligible and can have important effects on people's well-being (Kanner *et al*, 1984).)

The lives of those who are surrounded by other family members tend to be filled with incident. They will experience more 'entrances' (such as the birth of a child) and more 'exits' (the death of a relative, marital separation, or a young adult leaving home), more 'uplifts' (such as birthdays, anniversaries, and school successes), and more 'hassles' (such as minor illnesses of relatives, or occasions of family discord).

The effects of living alone

Not only are those who live in isolation likely to be lonely, but their lives may lack interest, excitement, and involvement. Early studies of the effect of life events focused on the damaging effects of too much change, but it is now appreciated that it is healthy for people to experience at least a modest degree of incident and transition in their life.

Box 14.1 The advantages and disadvantages of an intimate relationship

Disadvantages
    disordered and unhappy relationships, or losses of key relationships, may precipitate psychological distress and even physical illness

Advantages
    a greater sense of well-being
    protection from stressors
    more positive events
    greater ability to muster more practical resources and aid in times of crisis
    availability of a 'resident therapist'

Close relationships, health, and well-being

Comparisons of the self-reports of married people, single people, the widowed, and the divorced, concerning their happiness, loneliness, and stress, indicate that those who are currently married have fewer problems and have a greater sense of positive well-being than those in any of the other groups (see Box 14.1, and Frude, 1991). The same pattern emerges from studies that have used more objective indices.

Overall, married people have better physical health than those who have never married or are divorced or widowed, and are less likely to suffer from a wide range of ailments, including asthma, diabetes, ulcers, tuberculosis, cancer of the mouth and throat, hypertension, and strokes and coronaries (Lynch, 1977; Reed *et al*, 1983; Cohen & Syme, 1985).

The association between health and being married is even apparent in mortality data. Compared with those who are single, widowed, or divorced, few married people die young (Berkman & Syme, 1979; Verbrugge, 1979; Perlman & Rook, 1987).

Mental health statistics reveal a broadly similar pattern. Comparing groups of people matched for age, sex, and social class, psychiatric admission rates are lower for the married. Similarly, general community surveys reveal that married people experience the fewest psychological symptoms. Such symptoms occur at an intermediate rate among widowed and never-married adults, and at the highest rates among the divorced and separated (Gove, 1972; Bloom *et al*, 1978; Argyle & Henderson, 1985).

The overall advantage established for the married with regard to health and well-being is clearly an 'average' effect, and hides the fact that many people suffer substantially as a result of joyless, conflictual, oppressive, and violent relationships. The health and well-being of many people is placed in jeopardy by those who are close to them, and might well improve if the relationship were to end.

For example, although divorced people fare badly, as compared with the married group as a whole, those who have been divorced for a number of years may be healthier and better adjusted than those who remain in a chronically confrontational or violent marital relationship (Frude, 1991).

Certain styles of family interaction have also been identified as increasing the risk of particular 'psychosomatic' disorders in both adults and children (Lask & Fosson, 1989). Thus, a man who frequently becomes extremely angry with members of his family, but who does not openly express this anger, may be at increased risk of hypertension (McClelland, 1979). Other work in this field has linked patterns of family interaction to such disorders as asthma, diabetes, and anorexia nervosa (Minuchin *et al*, 1980).

The results reported above might be criticised for ignoring possible sex differences in the association between health and marital status. However, an early claim that marriage is good for men but bad for women (Bernard, 1973), although it provoked a lively debate, has not been substantiated by later research. It now appears that although the advantages of being married, as gauged by health indices, may be somewhat greater for men than for women, the married of both sexes are happier and more healthy. In a recent 'meta-analysis' of 93 studies comparing the self-reported happiness (morale, well-being, etc.) of men and women, Wood *et al* (1989) found that, overall, women reported greater happiness and life satisfaction than did men, and that marriage was associated with greater well-being for both sexes (see also Chapter 11).

Explanations for the link between health and family

Thus, the evidence strongly suggests that, on average, family relationships (particularly close partnerships) are associated with relatively good physical and psychological health. There are several explanations for this association, only three of which are examined here (for a fuller discussion see Frude, 1991).

(1) The finding is artefactual

The strength and the quality of evidence linking personal relationship factors and health variables makes it highly implausible that the association is entirely artefactual. In some cases health factors undoubtedly play a part in changing the nature of relationships (thus a person might choose to leave a partner who is constantly depressed), but such links are much less significant than the influence of relationship factors on health. The evidence points to a complex network of causal influences. Ideally, it would need prospective studies of fairly large populations to disentangle the various causal pathways.

(2) Lesser vulnerability to stress

One explanation for this connection is that those with stable relationships have an increased sense of well-being, as a result of which they are less vulnerable to stress. Another suggestion is that a partner may reduce stress at critical periods; for example, by providing informal therapy.

Several studies testify to the fact that people often 'consult' their partners during times of personal difficulty and feel that they benefit from their partner's counsel. When people are asked whom they 'really depend on' when personal problems arise, they are more likely to cite their partner than anyone else (Griffith, 1985).

Nye & McLaughlin (1982) found that informal psychotherapy takes place in most marriages and, furthermore, they discovered that people's satisfaction with their partners as a 'therapist' was highly correlated with their overall satisfaction with their marriage. In their study of the social origins of depression among women, Brown & Harris (1978) found that the presence of an intimate and confidant was associated with low vulnerability to stressful events.

(3) The role of regulation

Another reason why family relationships may promote physical and mental health relates to the regulatory effect of those who take a caring and protective role. Regulation, indeed, may be regarded as one of the basic functions of intimacy (Rook, 1985).

A partner, relative, or close friend is often in a position to advise or even scold a person, thus coercing them to comply with certain 'rules' or 'norms', and helping them to refrain from activities that are deviant or dangerous (Hughes & Gove, 1981). Those who are socially isolated are more likely to expose themselves to danger. Thus some newly divorced people lead disordered lives, eating and sleeping irregularly and smoking and drinking more.

The family unit

The family unit has been defined as "an arena of interacting personalities" (Nye & Berardo, 1966) and as "a set of mutually contingent careers" (Farber, 1964). Such social, or psychological, definitions do not refer to biological, legal, or residential criteria, as some other definitions might, but focus instead on qualities of interaction and relationship between certain people.

The disparity between psychological definitions of the family and other definitions highlights some important issues. For example, an adopted child becomes a full family member in law as soon as the relevant papers are signed, but the psychological reality is more complex. Psychologically, some adopted children become part of 'the family' soon after moving into the home, whereas others take much more time (and in some cases it may never happen).

A divorced person's cohabitee, or even a lodger, may become, in terms of mutual emotional involvement, a 'family member', even though there are no biological or legal ties. A psychological definition will typically admit as 'families' certain non-traditional groups such as gay couples and heterosexual cohabiting couples.

Psychological definitions of 'the family' emphasise the fact that a family is not just a collection of people. A family involves a network of close relationships between the individual members. Like other social groups, the family is also an organisation that is more than the sum of its parts. Thus the family may be thought of as an 'organic' entity.

The life cycle of the family

Like organisms, families pass through a developmental sequence or 'career'. They are 'formed', they undergo changes, and in the end they 'die'.

Some analysts divide the 'family life cycle' into a number of stages. Duvall (1977), for example, formulated eight stages, starting with the married couple who have no children and ending with the ageing family – a stage that lasts from retirement until death. Such models are clearly oversimplified, but they can be useful in mapping broad patterns of change and identifying common problems at particular stages of development. Thus the pressures typically experienced by 'young families' are somewhat different from those faced by families with adolescent children.

Families must adapt in response to both internal and external changes. The birth of a first child, for example, presents the couple (assuming that two parents are present) with many new tasks, and gives them new roles as parents. The family boundary extends to include the infant, and the nature of the couple's interaction will change. Instead of just the one two-person ('dyadic') relationship, there are now three dyadic relationships within that family group.

Any major change, such as an 'entrance' (a child being born; an elderly relative coming to live in the home) or an 'exit' (the death of a family member; an adolescent leaving), affects not only the individual family members but also the relationships between them. Such changes alter many aspects of the structure of the family and alter the nature of many interactions within the family system.

Any family is likely to experience several 'entrances' and 'exits' throughout its lifetime, and many other changes will also alter the pattern of family relationships. Over a 30-year or 40-year span, there may be a complete reversal in roles, as the once helpless infants grow towards middle age and take care of their now aged parents.

Thus, family structure may change radically and repeatedly over the course of normal development, while additional major adaptations may be required in response to 'non-normative' family events (the birth of a handicapped child, for example, or a disclosure of intrafamilial sexual abuse). In addition, the family will have to cope with pressures that originate outside the family (from unemployment, for example, or imprisonment).

Differences between families

Families differ in many ways. They differ in terms of their structure (there are single-parent families, childless couples, etc.), in their stage of development, and in their cultural setting. There are also marked differences in the 'interactive styles' or 'socio-emotional structures' of families.

Numerous dimensions can be used to differentiate between the interactive styles of families, but experienced therapists and research teams have consistently identified two dimensions as being of key importance – 'adaptability' and 'cohesion'.

Adaptability and cohesion

'Adaptability' refers to the family's ability to change its structure, roles, and rules in response to both situational and developmental pressures. 'Cohesion' relates both to the emotional attachment between family members and to their autonomy as individuals.

A model that incorporates these dimensions is the 'circumplex model' devised by David Olson and his colleagues (Olson *et al*, 1979). Their Family Adaptability and Cohesion Evaluation Scales (FACES III is the current version) measure family members' perceptions of family functioning and enable a particular family to be located along each of the two key dimensions. Families are classified into one of four 'types' on each dimension:

adaptability

(1) rigid
(2) structured
(3) flexible
(4) chaotic.

cohesion

(1)   enmeshed
(2)   connected
(3)   separated
(4)   disengaged.

The labels used for the extremes of each dimension suggest that all extreme positions are regarded as 'unhealthy'. Thus both rigid and chaotic families are seen as likely to experience special problems, particularly when they face a need to change.

In rigid families, roles are strictly defined, the power structure is inflexible, leadership is authoritarian, and discipline is managed in an autocratic way. Rules are regarded as non-negotiable and compromise is rare.

Chaotic families, on the other hand, have few clear rules. In the absence of clear guidelines, many things have to be negotiated 'from scratch'. The power structure is unsettled, and sanctions are imposed in an irregular and somewhat arbitrary way. Lacking explicit guidelines, children often become confused and uncontrollable, especially if their discipline is erratic and inconsistent.

Families with extremely low scores on the cohesion dimension are said to be 'disengaged'. The bonds between members are extremely weak, and each member operates more or less independently. There is little family unity and little sense of family identity.

Members of 'enmeshed' families, at the other extreme, identify with the family very closely. The bonds between them are so tight that each retains little sense of personal identity. Enmeshed families also tend to be 'closed' to the outside world, keeping themselves to themselves and regarding other families and agencies with contempt or suspicion.

Optimal families

It is evident that many families function very well. Individual members are psychologically healthy and are happy with their family relationships, and there is relatively little intrafamilial conflict. Such a family is likely to adapt well to normal developmental changes and to cope effectively with most stressful events. Such families are variously labelled 'healthy', 'well functioning', 'energised', or 'optimal'. Of course, faced with disaster even an optimal family would become distressed. No family is immune from outside pressures, but in a healthy family few problems arise from defects or dysfunctions in the internal dynamics (we might say that there are few 'endogenous' problems), and the family is able to cope relatively well with external stressor events.

Such a description, however, amounts to little more than a definition of the 'optimal family'. What qualities characterise such families; what makes a family 'healthy'? Many theorists, clinicians, and researchers have suggested attributes that characterise such families. The following compilation, or 'portrait of the optimal family', includes the characteristics most frequently mentioned in the clinical and research literature (for a fuller review and a list of sources, see Frude, 1991).

Internal and external relationships

In healthy families, members have warm and close relationships with one another. Each identifies with the family as a whole and has a sense of 'family pride'. The unit has fusion and solidarity, while allowing each person to retain a certain degree of autonomy. Healthy families act as 'open' systems and are willing to accept help and advice from external sources. They interact frequently with neighbours and the community, and their interactions with other groups are generally positive. Any attempt by an outside agency to challenge the family, however, or any intrusive, deviant, or disruptive environmental influence, meets with a collective rejection.

Power

Power is distributed relatively equally within generations, but not between generations. Both parents share power, but they are united as parents and together they keep control of their children. Thus the children do not 'take over', and no child enters into a strong alliance with one parent against the other. Roles within healthy families are clearly differentiated and are complementary. Individuals are assigned to particular tasks and acknowledged to have specific rights and duties. But although roles are clearly defined, substantial flexibility is maintained so that when one person is temporarily unable to play a particular role another person takes over.

Rules

There are 'rules', many of which are explicit. Whether explicitly expressed or not, the rules are understood and supported by all family members. Behaviour that infringes rules is confronted openly, appropriate sanctions being applied firmly but without hostility or vindictiveness.

Rules are flexibly applied and change as circumstances change (as children get older, for example, or as members gain or lose employment). Such rule changes are explicit and often follow a process of negotiation, for healthy families engage in open and effective communication.

Communication

The meaning of messages is clear and it is always apparent to whom a message is addressed. Questions are clearly asked and plainly answered, and all transactions have a clear ending (Satir, 1972).

Members are able to communicate their opinions, hopes, and fears freely and without anxiety. They are encouraged to express their sentiments openly, although there is also a respect for privacy.

Dealing with conflict

Healthy families recognise issues of conflict and are able to resolve many of them by negotiation and compromise. After a conflict has subsided, measures are taken to repair any damage to relationships and to strengthen bonds between the erstwhile adversaries. Healthy families are thus able to deal with conflict effectively, just as they deal with a wide range of other challenges. They have at their disposal a wide repertoire of effective strategies for dealing with difficulties, and they are able to respond flexibly and to generate new tactics.

A view of the world

All families are involved in a continual process of 'reality construction' (Reiss, 1981). Family members develop a collective impression of the world, including the family itself, neighbours, relatives, the community, national and international politics, and the physical environment.

Within healthy families there is consensus, although differences and idiosyncrasies are permitted and are not regarded as threatening. The family's vision is unique but not preposterous; it is not static, but does not change frenetically in response to every new proposal. Judgements regarding the family's ability to control events are realistic, the outlook being neither overoptimistic nor unreasonably pessimistic.

Even healthy families create their own 'myths', but these are innocuous and used mainly to foster solidarity and to reinforce the family's positive view of itself.

Dysfunctional families

A family may be dysfunctional in many different ways, and so the term 'the dysfunctional family' does not refer to a single family type. Various indicators may signal family dysfunction, including an inability to deal successfully with routine practical matters, a highly conflictual or chaotic climate within the home, or symptoms in one or more members (see below).

Dysfunction may arise when family members are emotionally very distant from one another or, on the other hand, when they are excessively closely bound together (i.e. when the family is 'enmeshed').

Enmeshed families

In an enmeshed family, the individual members may be so engulfed by their family roles and relationships that they lack autonomy and lose their own identity. Because individual members vary so little in their experience and their opinions, the family is unable to benefit from diverse input in discussions about family plans or activities, or in the solving of problems. Many enmeshed families attempt to preserve their outer boundary very forcefully, so that a variety of pathological strategies develop, as for example, in an attempt to prevent an adolescent from leaving home.

Disengaged families

Families at the other extreme, where there is a total lack of closeness, are said to be 'disengaged'. In these families, there is little sense of family identity and it is difficult for the group to function together as an effective unit. Members have only a weak attachment to the family group and provide each other with little support or guidance. Those who lack the direction and control usually provided by the family may feel deserted and alone, or they may seek to form strong alliances with people outside the family.

Triangulation

Some families show a mixture of close and distant relationships. Thus one of the parents may withdraw from the other and form an enmeshed relationship with one of the children. The father may develop an exclusive alliance with one of his daughters, for example, and the 'couple' that is formed by their partnership may draw away from the mother and any other children. Such 'triangulation', as it is termed, is likely to generate problems. The mother's parental power is undermined, for example, and she is unable to exercise any control over the daughter.

However, like other dysfunctional structural patterns, triangulation may represent an attempt to solve a serious problem. A strong and 'inappropriate' father–daughter alliance, for example, may be all that is keeping the father from leaving the family. In such a situation all family members might have a vested interest in maintaining the triangulation, since the survival of the family would depend on it.

Communication

Communication in dysfunctional families may be ambiguous, and there is often some degree of incongruity between the literal meaning of a statement and the way in which it is expressed. A compliment, for example, may be delivered in a tone that conveys suspicion or disapproval. For many dysfunctional families, conflictual issues produce destructive patterns of response. Conflicts of interest or opinion may be quashed by the exercise of unilateral power rather than being resolved by discussion and negotiation. Strategies that would be useful in de-escalating a conflict are rarely used, and humour, compromise, or apology may be totally alien.

The role of myth

Many dysfunctional families create myths that amount to dangerous delusions. Thus some families with a history of violence create the myth that 'real violence' has never occurred within the family. 'Myths of harmony' paint a glowing picture of family life, while 'rescue myths' offer the promise that 'help is on the way' – that some helper will provide a perfect solution to current problems. Such a myth is counterproductive, because it carries the implication that there is no need for the family to strive actively to solve its own problems (Stierlin, 1973).

Individual abnormality in the dysfunctional family

The idea that members of dysfunctional families may suffer as a result of their family life, and that they are more likely to exhibit various physical and psychological symptoms than members of well-functioning families, is supported by clinical and research evidence (Sprenkle & Olson, 1978; Olson & McCubbin, 1983; Lask & Fosson, 1989).

In a bid to contain conflict, or to divert attention from long-standing problematic issues, the family may attempt a number of ineffectual strategies, some of which will have unfavourable consequences for one or more family members. Thus a particular child may become the focus of concern (this may take the form of anxiety, anger, or blame), thereby deflecting attention from severe parental discord. The continued presence of the child's symptom or problem behaviour would have survival value for the system as a whole, and the family might therefore act in concert to maintain the problem.

Thus, in some cases, someone's recovery from a physical or psychiatric illness may disturb a precarious and useful equilibrium within the family, thus posing a threat or causing the system to react in an erratic and volatile fashion. One suitable way of dealing with such a situation would be to intervene in the family system as a whole, rather than treating one member in isolation; this is the rationale behind 'family therapy' (see below).

Psychosomatic illness

Living in a dysfunctional family is often a stressful experience, and stress is a major precursor of psychological illness (Chapter 12). It is also a precursor of various types of physical disorder, including those that are labelled 'psychosomatic'. Among the childhood disorders categorised in this way, for example, are non-organic recurrent abdominal pain, certain bladder and bowel disorders, some cases of asthma, and some skin disorders such as eczema and urticaria.

The most significant research linking family factors to psychosomatic illness in children is probably that concerning asthma. In many cases, psychological factors seem to be of little importance, the intermittent asthma attacks being triggered either by environmental conditions (e.g. a high pollen count or a smoky atmosphere) or by infection. But in other cases the illness is clearly exacerbated by psychological factors. Studies on the parent–child relationship suggest that a number of parental characteristics, including overprotectiveness and perfectionism, play a causal role in asthmatic attacks (Cheren & Knapp, 1980).

Clinical evidence and systemic studies have indicated that the symptoms of some asthmatic children are relieved as a result of separation from the parents. Thus Purcell *et al* (1969) measured the amount of wheezing and the number of asthma attacks in a group of children diagnosed as having 'primary psychological cause' asthma. Measurements were first taken during a period of normal family life, then during a two-week period when the parents lived away from home (the children were cared for by a substitute mother), and again after the family have been reunited. It was found that the children experienced significantly less wheezing, and suffered significantly fewer asthma attacks, during the separation phase than during either of the other phases. They also required less medication when their parents were absent.

In a study of asthma, diabetes, and other complaints, Minuchin *et al* (1980) found additional support for the hypothesis that family interactions play an important role in determining the course of chronic conditions. They suggested that certain characteristics of families are related to both the pathogenesis and symptom exacerbation of chronic psychosomatic illnesses in children.

The maladaptive family characteristics identified by the group include enmeshment, overprotectiveness, and rigidity. Minuchin *et al* also suggested that many families of children with psychosomatic symptoms strive to avoid open conflict. They fear change, and because conflict might challenge the established order within the family, many contentious issues are never addressed or brought into the open. The parents may inhibit expression of conflict because they are concerned that this will adversely affect the child. Another dysfunctional pattern reported by Minuchin *et al* involves conflict between the husband and wife, with the child entering into a coalition with one or other parent.

Minuchin *et al* do not claim that dysfunctional family patterns are sufficient by themselves to cause the psychosomatic symptoms, and are careful to acknowledge that the child's physical vulnerability is another important factor.

Family therapy

The fact that the quality of family relationships affects the development and maintenance of physical and psychological symptoms suggests that treatment might focus on such relationships. Family therapy focuses on changing inappropriate family relationships or communication patterns (Burnham, 1986; Jones, 1993). If a person's problem has arisen from or is maintained by dynamic processes within the family, the therapeutic team will attempt to change the family structure, or the family process, so that the fundamental problem is ameliorated and the symptom therefore rendered 'unnecessary'.

Thus an attempt is made to bring about changes in dysfunctional features of family interaction. The expression of latent conflicts may be encouraged, for example, or overprotectiveness may be challenged and changed. The popularity of this approach to intervention has grown considerably in the past decade in many countries, including Britain.

There are considerable difficulties in assessing the effectiveness of this means of intervention (Frude, 1980), but the best available evidence suggests that it is often effective in modifying family patterns and in relieving the symptoms of individual family members (Gurman *et al*, 1986).

Families and stress

Family life is the source of many stressful events. When we bring the family into the foreground, and consider it as a unit or system, it becomes clear that the family is not only a source of stressor events (a 'stressor' event is an event requiring substantial adjustment of an organism or a system) but also that it responds in an 'organic' or 'systemic' way to various stressor events that originate both inside and outside the system.

How a family responds to stressor events reflects the adaptability and resourcefulness of the system, previous experience in dealing with stressful situations, and many other strengths and weaknesses. It also depends on whether effective help from external sources is available and is acceptable to the family.

Not surprisingly, healthy families are more resilient in the face of stressor events than are dysfunctional families. Cohesive families are likely to provide more comfort and reassurance than disengaged families, for example, and flexible families are able to take pressure off a member by reallocating roles and tasks during periods of acute stress, whereas rigid families are less able to do this.

High levels of stress may increase family conflict, or one or more members may experience physical or psychological symptoms. Such conflicts or symptoms are likely to act as additional stressors, so that a vicious circle may develop. When stress mounts to such a degree that the family unit is unable to perform its normal functions, it is said to be in a state of 'crisis'. Essential tasks may be neglected, people may abandon their customary roles, and the normal family rules may be ignored. In order to attenuate stress and to prevent crisis, families engage in many cognitive and behavioural activities that are collectively labelled 'coping strategies'.

Family coping

Families are very active in trying to protect themselves from a threatened crisis. In certain cases, where the stressor is potentially controllable, they may find a way of avoiding the unwanted change altogether (e.g. they may find a way of solving a short-term financial crisis in order to avoid moving house).

When such avoidance is not possible, knowing in advance that the stressor is imminent can allow the family to brace itself against the impact of the change. This may be achieved by engaging in effective cognitive and social processes that are sometimes labelled 'anticipatory coping'. The value of such coping has been shown for bereavement, marital separation, serious illness, and other major stressors (for more detailed information, see Frude, 1991).

When a substantial change of circumstance occurs, whether it was anticipated or not, initial efforts are directed towards minimising or reducing the impact of the stressor ('resistance coping'), but later strategies are directed towards reorganising and stabilising the system ('adaptive coping').

Coping, at both the individual and the family level, involves many different strategies. Common to many of them is the goal of forming an adaptive view of the nature of the stressor event. Thus a family may explore various comforting hypotheses about the origin of the stressor, its 'meaning', and its long-term significance. They may seek to minimise the likely impact of the stress ('We'll be able to carry on in our own sweet way') or may console themselves with the thought that 'it could have been a lot worse'. Families redefine, relabel, and 're-frame' events, so that something which might well be considered 'a disaster' may be reframed so that it is seen as 'a challenge'.

Some forms of coping involve psychological denial. A family may conspire together, subtly and covertly, to act as if the terrible event has not happened or will not happen. They may refuse to anticipate the loss of a loved one, for example, even if the fact that the person is dying would be plain to any reasonable person.

Although the usual view of such denial is that it is a pathological and unhealthy distortion, it may sometimes be adaptive for the family to deny the reality of the stressor, to ignore the most unpalatable aspects, and to disbelieve a pessimistic prognosis (Pearlin & Schooler, 1978). Hope, even

---

Box 14.2   Methods of coping

Anticipatory coping – cognitive and social processes engaged in advance of a crisis

Resistance coping – initial efforts to minimise or reduce the impact of a stressor

Adaptive coping – reorganisation and stabilisation of the family system

Psychological denial

---

if it is unrealistic, may help to maintain the system through an emergency. Fantasy and myth may foster a positive atmosphere when a more realistic view would lead to dejection and paralysis.

Some coping strategies involve structural changes in the family. Stress may bring a family together or drive members apart. In many cases, family members feel united and bound together when facing a threatening situation, so that the level of cohesion within the family unit increases. When faced with a sudden change, family tasks may be redistributed and family roles reallocated. Power may be redistributed, so that, for example, a family in which decision-making is normally shared between several members may delegate executive power to one particular person in an emergency.

Family rules may also be modified in the face of a special challenge. Some families attempt to cope by becoming more tolerant, while others become more authoritarian.

The urgency of the situation may also encourage straight talking and frank disclosure, so that communication becomes more explicit and revealing than ever before. Sudden adversity may lead a family to shelve conflict, and a temporary cessation of hostilities may be achieved in families which are normally embattled. Thus some families function more effectively and more harmoniously in situations of near crisis than they do under normal circumstances.

Support

When they are under stress, some families change by becoming more open to advice, emotional support, and practical help from friends and relatives (Olson & McCubbin, 1983). Other potential sources of help include church organisations and self-help groups, including those that focus on a specific problem such as alcoholism, bereavement, or family violence.

Such groups can help the family by providing information about the problem and the available resources, by encouraging communication within the family and between families, and by describing strategies and remedies that are 'tried and tested'.

In addition to informal community services, many social agencies and professional services offer help in terms of advice, counselling, and practical aid, although some families are much more ready than others to seek help from welfare agencies and professional therapists.

Resilience

The resilience a family is able to show when facing stress depends not only on its coping strategies but also on the kinds of resources that have been labelled 'family strengths' (Olson & McCubbin, 1983). Such strengths include many of the qualities described previously as the attributes of optimal families, including moderate levels of cohesiveness and adaptability, explicit rules, the flexible operation of these rules, shared power, good communication, effective means of dealing with conflict, and pride in the family.

Olson & McCubbin (1983) found that resilient families also had highly effective patterns of communication, that they shared many leisure activities, and that they had a high level of satisfaction with themselves and their overall quality of life.

Although families can be decimated and destroyed by serious troubles, in many cases both family members and family units manage to endure the most formidable upsets and tragedies. The extent to which people and families are able to adjust to severe misfortune is often remarkable. Thus despite the high number of people whose family circumstances cause them to experience serious psychological symptoms, and despite the very high (and increasing) number of family relationships that end in breakdown, research on family problems provides much evidence of the persistence, resourcefulness, and resilience of families.

Recovery

Although the immediate effects of major stressors often appear to be devastating, in the vast majority of cases there is clear evidence of recovery over time. Thus both members and family units usually make substantial readjustments after such major events as divorce or the death of a child.

The adage 'Time will heal' suggests that time alone is necessary for the reduction of psychological pain and the restoration of order. However, the alleviation of distress and the return to stable functioning results from active processes rather than the mere lapse of months or years. Crucial activities engaged in by individual members and family systems in anticipation of a major change, and in response to such a change, do much to becalm the stressor, to soften the impact, and to aid recuperation. A good deal is now known about individual coping strategies, and clinicians and family researchers are now learning more of the many dynamic changes that occur within family systems in response to threat and change.

Further reading

Brown, G. & Harris, T. (eds) (1989) *Life Events and Illness*. New York: Guilford Press.

Burnham, J. (1986) *Family Therapy: First Steps Towards a Systemic Approach*. London: Tavistock.

Frude, N. (1991) *Understanding Family Problems: A Psychological Approach*. Chichester: Wiley.

Jones, E. (1993) *Family Systems Therapy: Developments in the Milan Systemic Therapies*. Chichester: Wiley.

Lask, B. & Fosson, A. (1989) *Childhood Illness – The Psychosomatic Approach: Children Talking with their Bodies*. Chichester: Wiley.

References

Argyle, M. & Henderson, M. (1985) *The Anatomy of Relationships*. Harmondsworth: Penguin.

Berkman, L. F. & Syme, S. L. (1979) Social networks, host resistance and mortality: a nine-year follow-up study of Almeda residents. *American Journal of Epidemiology*, **109**, 186–204.

Bernard, J. (1973) *The Future of Marriage*. New York: Bantam.

Bloom, B. L., Asher, S. R. & White, S. W. (1978) Marital disruption as a stressor. *Psychological Bulletin*, **85**, 867–894.

Brown, G. W. & Harris, T. (1978) *The Social Origins of Depression*. London: Tavistock.

Burnham, J. B. (1986) *Family Therapy: First Steps Towards a Systemic Approach*. London: Tavistock.

Cheren, S. & Knapp, P. (1980) Gastrointestinal disorders. In *Comprehensive Textbook of Psychiatry*, vol. 3 (eds H. Kaplan, A. Freedman & B. Sadock). Baltimore, MD: Williams and Wilkins.

Cohen, S. & Syme, S. L. (eds) (1985) *Social Support and Health*. New York: Academic Press.

Duvall, E. (1977) *Marriage and Family Development*. Philadelphia: J. B. Lippincott.

Farber, B. (1964) *Family: Organization and Interaction*. San Francisco, CA: Chandler.

Freedman, J. L. (1978) *Happy People*. New York: Harcourt Brace Jovanovich.

Frude, N. (1980) Methodological problems in the evaluation of family therapy. *Journal of Family Therapy*, **2**, 29–44.

—— (1991) *Understanding Family Problems: A Psychological Approach*. Chichester: Wiley.

Gove, W. R. (1972) The relationship between sex roles, marital status and mental illness. *Social Forces*, **51**, 34–44.

Griffith, J. (1985) Social support providers: Who are they? Where are they met? And the relationship of network characteristics to psychological distress. *Basic and Applied Social Psychology*, **6**, 41–60.

Gurman, A., Kniskern, D. & Pinsoff, W. (1986) Research on the process and outcome of marital and family therapy. In *Handbook of Psychotherapy and Behavior Change* (3rd edn) (eds S. Garfield & A. Bergin). New York: Wiley.

Holmes, T. H. & Rahe, R. H. (1967) The Social Readjustment Rating Scales. *Journal of Psychosomatic Research*, **11**, 213–218.

Hughes, M. & Gove, W. R. (1981) Living alone, social integration and mental health. *American Journal of Community Psychology*, **87**, 48–74.

Jones, E. (1993) *Family Systems Therapy: Developments in the Milan Systemic Therapies.* Chichester: Wiley.

Kanner, A. D., Coyne, J. C. & Schaefer, C. (1984) Comparison of two modes of stress measurement: daily hassles and uplifts versus major life events. *Journal of Behavioral Medicine*, **4**, 1–39.

Lask, B. & Fosson, A. (1989) *Childhood Illness – The Psychosomatic Approach: Children Talking with their Bodies.* Chichester: Wiley.

Lazarus, R. (1966) *Psychological Stress and the Coping Process.* New York: McGraw-Hill.

Lynch, J. J. (1977) *The Broken Heart.* New York: Basic Books.

McClelland, D. (1979) Inhibited power motivation and high blood pressure in men. *Journal of Abnormal Psychology*, **88**, 182–190.

Minuchin, S., Rosman, B. L. & Baker, L. (1980) *Psychosomatic Families: Anorexia Nervosa in Context.* Cambridge, MA: Harvard University Press.

Nye, F. I. (1982) *Family Relationships: Rewards and Costs.* Beverly Hills, CA: Sage.

—— & Berardo, F. (1966) *Emerging Conceptual Frameworks in Family Analysis.* New York: Macmillan.

—— & McLaughlin, S. (1982) Role competence and marital satisfaction. In *Family Relationships: Rewards and Costs* (ed. F.I. Nye). Beverly Hills, CA: Sage.

Olson, D. H., Russell, C. S. & Sprenkle, D. H. (1979) Circumplex model of marital and family systems. II: Empirical studies and clinical intervention. In *Advances in Family Intervention, Assessment and Theory* (ed. J. Vincent). Greenwich, CT: JAI.

—— & McCubbin, H. I. (1983) *Families: What Makes Them Work?* Beverly Hills, CA: Sage.

Paykel, E. S., McGuinness, B. & Gomez, J. (1976) An Anglo-American comparison of the scaling of life-events. *British Journal of Medical Psychology*, **49**, 237–247.

Pearlin, L. & Schooler, C. (1978) The structure of coping. *Journal of Health and Social Behavior*, **19**, 2–21.

Perlman, D. & Rook, K. S. (1987) Social support, social deficits, and the family: toward the enhancement of well-being. In *Family Processes and Problems: Social Psychological Aspects* (ed. S. Oskamp). Beverly Hills, CA: Sage.

Purcell, K., Brady, K., Chai, H., *et al* (1969) The effect on asthma in children of experimental separation from the family. *Psychosomatic Medicine*, **31**, 144–164.

Reed, D., McGee, D., Yano, K., *et al* (1983) Social networks and coronary heart disease among Japanese men in Hawaii. *American Journal of Epidemiology*, **115**, 384–396.

Reiss, D. (1981) *The Family's Construction of Reality.* Cambridge, MA: Harvard University Press.

Rook, K. S. (1985) The functions of social bonds: perspectives from research on social support, loneliness and social isolation. In *Social Support: Theory, Research and Application* (eds I. G. Sarason & B. R. Sarason). The Hague: Martinus Nijhoff.

Satir, V. (1972) *Peoplemaking*. Palo Alto, CA: Science and Behavior Books.

Sprenkle, D. H. & Olson, D. H. (1978) Circumplex model of marital systems. IV: Empirical studies of clinic and non-clinic couples. *Journal of Marriage and Family Therapy*, **4**, 59–74.

Stierlin, H. (1973) Group fantasies and family myths: some theoretical and practical aspects. *Family Process*, **12**, 111–125.

Verbrugge, L. M. (1979) Marital status and health. *Journal of Marriage and the Family*, **41**, 267–285.

Weiss, R. S. (1974) The provisions of social relationships. In *Doing Unto Others: Joining, Molding, Conforming, Helping, Loving* (ed. Z. Rubin). Englewood Cliffs, NJ: Prentice-Hall.

Wood, W., Rhodes, N. & Whelan, M. (1989) Sex differences in positive well-being: a consideration of emotional style and marital status. *Psychological Bulletin*, **106**, 249–264.

Part III
Social science

15 Class and underclass

Robert Moore

Contemporary ideas on class • The United States • Britain • The underclass in modern history • The new populism • The future of the idea

---

Class seems almost tangible, because it pervades all our lives, but it is not a thing. In using the term 'class', sociologists are usually summarising a complex of relatively permanent social arrangements that take different forms. These arrangements are persistent, although not static, and are typified by inequalities in wealth, income, power, and social esteem.

The different ways used to discuss class reflect different intellectual interests. For certain kinds of analysis, a sharp dichotomy may be drawn between owners and non-owners of the means of production, or between rulers and ruled. However, the term 'class' is commonly used to describe social gradations; the Registrar General's social classes are a hierarchy not only of income and esteem, but also of educational achievement and life expectancy.

Some of the most interesting sociology has been concerned with the relationship between gradations and discontinuities. Most notably, debates about the 'new middle class' have raised questions about the social position of people who appear to be neither proletariate nor rulers, but whose lives have features of both. Are they really a new class, distinct from previous classes, or people located at the intersection of two classes?

The underlying economic interests that constitute class may become the basis for organisation and action. Class may be seen and recognised in the mobilisation of people around these interests, quite obviously in trades unions, and less obtrusively in the organisations and networks of 'the City' and financial institutions. Class interests are not homogeneous: financiers have different interests from industrialists and the employed from the unemployed. Political parties more or less represent the interests of classes while seeking to win the votes of a majority of the electorate. In winning majorities they seek both to exploit the ambiguities of the material interests and to invoke non-material, ideal, interests ranging from 'the family' and 'the nation' and 'race', to appeals for social justice, equality, and the rule of law. They may succeed in persuading people to act, and vote, against their material interests.

The so-called post-war consensus in Britain may be seen as the institutionalisation of a truce between classes, conflicting interests recognising the benefits of compromise and the costs of conflict. From 1979 the truce was called off. Government policy promoted inequalities of income, wealth, and power, while reducing the benefits enjoyed by the least privileged and ensuring that those benefits which remained were given in conditions that emphasised the powerlessness and marginality of the claimants (Oppenheim, 1990; Walker, 1990).

Models of social class themselves change and become more complex with the development of new economic and political forms. With labour migration and the migration of capital to the Third World, we have to recognise the actuality of a world labour market and an international division of labour – how shall we now discuss social class? (Moore, 1977, 1989; Frobel *et al,* 1980).

Contemporary ideas on class

Structural changes in the economies of the industrialised nations have also led to new kinds of analysis. Much contemporary discussion is concerned with the intersection of gender and 'race' with traditional class divisions. Contemporary analysis has also put less stress on a hierarchy of classes and uses the ideas of core and periphery.

The core and the periphery

At the core are full-time employees, ranging from professional and white-collar workers, to unskilled manual workers. These men and women have security in common. They all look forward to long-term employment, and the professionals to 'careers'.

In the periphery are the part-time, temporary, and self-employed workers whose work buffers the lives of those in the core, providing them with the goods and services needed in their work and leisure during boom times, and bearing the burden of unemployment in recession.

Beyond them are the short- and the long-term unemployed; some work in the periphery with spells of unemployment, and others spend most of their time out of employment, with occasional spells of work in the periphery. The proportions of women, black people, disabled, elderly, and young increase as one moves out through these rings or segments of the economy.

Is there anyone beyond the outer ring? Is there anyone below or beyond the class system? There is a growing debate about those excluded from society – those who are in society but not of it. The language used is indicative of their status, suggesting that there is a mainstream society and then some subterranean pool of people dwelling in economic and social twilight. These may be migrants who literally lack citizenship and in principle could be physically removed from society at the state's will.

They may be people who are full citizens in the legal sense, but without the means to maintain or perhaps ever achieve a standard of life regarded as acceptable in the mainstream. They may be seen and may come to see themselves as foreigners in their own country. Furthermore they may be regarded as alien and threatening by others.

This kind of debate has been focused upon the underclass, and it is a debate of particular importance to those concerned with either social pathology or individual pathologies. It is important for the relatively successful both to attribute their success to their own efforts and to believe that they deserve the benefits they enjoy. But it is equally important to attribute failure to individual causes, because to blame society for others' apparent failure is to question to basis of one's own success. Uncoupling one's good fortune from others' deprivation is as important to individuals as the uncoupling of their policies from social distress is for governments. If the problem is seen to be one of individuals and 'cases', then perhaps they can be identified and treated. The implications of this are explored below.

The idea of an underclass has taken many historical forms, but the revival of the term and its contemporary currency derives in large part from work in the USA and the activities of North American commentators in popularising it in Britain. The discussion therefore begins in the USA.

The United States

The earliest post-war reference by a social scientist to the idea of an underclass is in Gunnar Myrdal's *Challenge to Affluence* (Myrdal, 1964). Looking at the booming US economy, he saw unemployment as no longer cyclical or amenable to demand stimulation. New technical developments were eliminating altogether the need for wide categories of labour. This was creating an underclass

> ". . . of unemployed and, gradually, unemployable persons and families, at the bottom of a society in which, for the majority of people above that level, the increasingly democratic structure of the educational system created more and more liberty – real liberty – and equality of opportunity. . . .
>
> Opening up more opportunities to more people has closed some opportunities for some. And now in the end it threatens to split off a true 'underclass' – not really an integrated part of the nation at all but a useless and miserable substratum" (Mydral, 1964, pp. 40–41).

None of the institutions intended to protect the poor and poorest actually helped the underclass: benefits and protection stopped at the stratum above. In addition, the underclass did not vote or participate in politics and there were no movements of protest on their behalf.

Recently, the term 'underclass' has been more systematically developed by William Julius Wilson, notably in his book *The Truly Disadvantaged*

(Wilson, 1987), in which he discusses problems of inner-city social dislocation, joblessness, teenage pregnancy, welfare dependency, and serious crime.

The 1965 Moynihan report (Moynihan, 1965) was said to have blamed the black family for the poverty and exclusion of the black population from US society. This judgement on Moynihan is itself controversial, but the reaction to it created an intolerant climate in which sociologists in the USA and Europe became reluctant to conduct research that might be thought to be unflattering to the black population. One result was that commentators more conservative than Moynihan elaborated analyses that stressed personal responsibility and then, increasingly, identified the level of social welfare benefits as the cause of social dislocation (Auletta, 1981).

Tackling these issues head on made Wilson's book politically controversial in both black and white America. The important feature of Wilson's work is that he offered sociological explanations of marginalisation and exclusion; he did not seek explanations in the character, mind, or culture of individuals.

Wilson was able to deal with the welfare argument quite simply by pointing out that during the period for which conservative analysts were correlating rising poverty and welfare benefits, rising unemployment was creating more poverty while benefits kept even more people above the poverty line. Without welfare there would have been even more in poverty.

Shaping the ghettos

The dislocation of the ghetto areas had to be explained. Wilson argued firstly that young black males were concentrated in the educational categories for whom employment opportunities were declining the fastest. Most new jobs require above-average education, and those new entry-level jobs that were being created for the lower educational categories were largely to be found in the peripheral areas of the city. The ghetto population was therefore unable to respond to economic recovery because young men had the wrong qualifications and were in the wrong place.

Secondly, one effect of the civil rights campaigns of the 1960s was to enable the black professionals who had previously been held in the ghetto areas by discrimination to move out. This not only left a residual inner-city population – the apparently least successful and least skilled and educated – but it also removed from these areas models of black success that could serve to motivate and encourage others to strive. Furthermore it removed those key members of the local community who managed the churches and voluntary associations that sustained the vitality of the community.

An effect of both these changes was that the young (literally) did not see the value of work, nor the connection between education and employment, nor did they see many families not living on welfare.

The areas in which the ghetto poor live are avoided by others and so they become more isolated – and more isolated from what Wilson called "the mainstream patterns of behaviour". Residents, and especially the young, become detached from job-finding networks and fall into patterns of life associated with casual rather than regular work.

This last point is especially important because Wilson was not arguing that the poor live in a 'culture of poverty', but that they suffer the effects of social isolation. The isolation of the poor leads to the concentration of their problems.

Single mothers

How did Wilson account for the rise of single motherhood? Firstly, there is a simple demographic point: the proportion of births to unmarried mothers is rising because the fertility of married women has fallen, and the proportion both of young women in the population and of young women who never marry is rising (Wilson, 1987, p. 72).

Secondly, young black women are finding it increasingly difficult to find a marriage partner who is economically active and fully employed. Unemployment, early death, drugs, and incarceration have reduced the pool of marriageable men. Marriage would entail a greater burden of dependency for a woman supporting a non-working man in addition to a child. The statistics are compelling: in the early 1950s, for every woman aged 16–17 there were 40 'eligible' men; by the late 1980s, 14. For every 100 18–19-year-olds, the pool of men had declined from 55 to 30. For black women aged 20–44 in the northern USA, the pool of eligible men had declined by more than 11 men per 100 women. For white women the pool had stayed the same or slightly increased.

Thus teenage women have fewer serious marriage opportunities. At the same time, women are expected to be economically more independent, and single parenthood is losing its stigma.

The importance of male employment for marriage has been underlined by more recent research in the USA which suggests that after the conception of their first child, employed men are more likely to marry the mother than unemployed men.

It was the young single mothers, who were making demands on Aid to Families with Dependent Children (originally intended for widows with children), who became a public issue in the late 1960s; they were also the group who, in the 1970s, experienced the sharpest decline in their real income. Wilson pointed out that poverty and dependency had increased as the real value of welfare benefits had declined.

The economics of the underclass

The ghetto underclass is, according to Wilson, very much the product of the organisation of the US economy, in conditions where the history of discrimination and deprivation has disadvantaged the black population. We are seeing not pathologically disorganised people, but the effects of the decline of smokestack industries and the flight of blue-collar jobs from the centre of large cities, in conditions where most of the black working class was historically confined to those jobs.

Britain

If we were to try simply to import Wilson's idea of underclass and apply it to British society, we would encounter problems. The extensive ghettos of the northern American cities in which large black populations have lived for generations are not a feature of British society.

When Wilson refers to "the mainstream patterns of behaviour", he refers to conventional behaviour as worker, consumer, and parent. Working and spending in the markets for labour and goods are central values in the dominant North American culture. The open and competitive society, with values of openness and competition implied by Myrdal, is not found in Britain.

In the 20th century, however, British society has seen the rise of a welfare state based upon an implied contract between capital and important sections of organised labour. This contract was constructed along lines of gender and race from its beginning (Williams, 1988; Lister, 1990). With this serious proviso we can say that belonging to the mainstream of British society entailed fully participating in the rights and benefits of the welfare state, and enjoying the security that citizenship confers.

The working classes enjoyed a measure of industrial power, the benefits of full-employment policies, support in unemployment, health care, and education. The first they secured by industrial organisation in trades unions, and the other benefits as part of the near-universal provision for the whole population. Minorities would become a part of the mainstream when they shared those rights.

The position of ethnic minorities

Rex & Moore (1967) showed how Birmingham City Council systematically excluded immigrants (as they then were) from public housing, and punished and stigmatised them for the alternatives they were forced to adopt. It was suggested that immigrants were being excluded from the full benefit of the welfare state to which they were entitled by virtue of citizenship. We did not then use the term 'underclass'.

John Rex adopted the term in his second Birmingham study (Rex & Tomlinson, 1979). They said that Britain has a working class in a secure contractual relationship with those who run the economy, and an underclass which enjoys no security. They described minorities as

"systematically at a disadvantage compared with working class whites
. . . a separate underprivileged class" (Rex & Tomlinson, 1979, p.
275).

It would be possible to elaborate this analysis by reference to a number
of recent changes: the increasing concentration of the black and Asian
populations in Britain; the loss of rights to family life, and now – effectively
– freedom of movement in Europe; the *de facto* denial of access to many
state welfare services through the extension of surveillance to all non-
white people; and harassment by the police and the relative lack of
protection afforded the non-white community by the police. We might
argue that incremental exclusions and deprivations eventually push British
ethnic minorities over a threshold into a qualitatively different position
from the white population, where they do have separate and at times
conflicting interests.

The deterioration of the situation of ethnic minorities in Britain is both
relative and absolute, because after the breaking of the post-war contract,
the rights and protections afforded by the welfare state have been
substantially reduced for most of the population – but it has been worse
for minorities, because, in addition, their basic citizenship status has been
brought in question and limited by legal restrictions. Their needs have
largely disappeared from the social agenda and their presence has moved
to the law and order agenda.

Nonetheless, is would be hard to sustain the argument that the black
British population is downtrodden into isolation, apathy, and despair. There
is no research which says that this is the case. Work by Connolly and her
colleagues suggests, for example, that young blacks in Liverpool display
a range of attitudes towards their employment chances, from despair to
high aspirations (Connolly *et al*, 1992). Minorities are actively involved in
trade union and political life.

Furthermore, in an area like Brixton, young black people can see others
going to work every day, many in suits and carrying briefcases. In the
evenings they can see black people dressed up and leaving home for an
evening out. In minority communities we also find the thriving political,
cultural and religious life that used to typify white working-class
communities in adversity. We also find successful entrepreneurship, even
though this may be precarious when it is situated in a niche created by
the flight of capital and the abandonment of the inner city.

The British underclass

So far we have equated the underclass with ethnic minorities. Rather than
starting with a consideration of ethnic minorities we might, like Halsey
and Dahrendorf, observe how people in general are now becoming surplus
to the requirements of the European labour market. This approach to the

underclass, like Myrdal's, stresses exclusion deriving from changes in the industrial structure and the consequences for inner-city populations, rather than ethnic or 'racial' recruitment to its ranks.

The term 'underclass' also appeared in the subtitle of Frank Field's book *Losing Out: The Emergence of Britain's Underclass* (Field, 1989). Field is less concerned with the position of ethnic minorities than with the condition of the very poorest, who, he suggests, have been separated from other low-income groups and from the working class in general. His underclass comprise the long-term unemployed, single-parent families, and the poor elderly. We might reasonably add to his underclass the impoverished and homeless young people who are now forced to live on our city streets by changes in the social security rules.

We can see in these contrasting but complementary views of the underclass that there are important issues concerning, for example, how significant the difference between the employed and unemployed is in defining an underclass, and the relative importance of ethnicity and poverty in creating and perpetuating conditions of exclusion and isolation. These are key research topics.

Recent discussion of the underclass in Britain has moved from academic publications into colour supplements and tabloid newspapers. The term has been applied to 'meths drinkers' and homosexuals; to people sleeping rough, beggars, football hooligans, and 'ram-raiders'. In this public discourse, the idea of the underclass has taken on an older meaning, conjuring up the drunks, idlers, and degenerates who were thought to threaten society in the late 19th century.

The underclass in modern history

In the late 19th and early 20th centuries, concern was expressed at the degeneration of the national or 'racial' stock. It was a concern with social inefficiency and national decline, not structural inequality. What we would today call a 'moral panic' sprang in large part from the apprehension felt by middle-class people on encountering teeming inner-city populations – slum-dwellers and the beggars who reached out to touch them on the pavements.

With the extension of the franchise, there was also a feeling of alarm that those seeking election would increasingly appeal to the 'pauper vote', with promises to be redeemed by taxes on a working population who would be impoverished thereby (Armstrong, 1929).

The panic was amplified by the decline of what were thought to be the better classes. Mary Drew commented to her father William Gladstone in 1886 on the small families of aristocrats married in the past 15 years, and wrote to her sister 25 years later, in 1911,

> "really it is a tremendous and awe inspiring fact that since 1875, the
> educated and aristocratic classes have more than halved their

families, so that the fittest are rapidly declining while the less fit, the feeble minded, the unhealthy alone increase (except in the case of Jews, R.C.s and the clergy, blessings be on them)" (Jalland & Hooper, 1986).

Here we see an alarm, which has not abated in two and a half decades, at the fecundity of what Karl Pearson thought of as the least useful members of society. The physical condition of men volunteering for the Anglo-Boer wars heightened the panic.

Feeble-mindedness was a major concern; therefore, one direction in which these panics and the possible inheritance of underclass characteristics led was to inquiries into mental deficiency. Thus the inter-war years saw the establishment of the Wood Committee on Mental Deficiency (of which Cyril Burt was a member). The Eugenics Society also sponsored research into the "social qualities and health of a sample of our population". Professor Carr-Saunders (Professor of Social Studies in Liverpool University) was an active participant, although a planned Liverpool study never appeared. Carr-Saunders was joined by Caradog Jones in 1924, who believed

> "that in any large centre there exists a social problem group, the source from which the majority of criminals and paupers, unemployables and defectives of all kinds are recruited" (Macnicol, 1987, p. 311).

According to Macnicol (p. 312), Jones made constant reference to the Wood and Brock reports (see below) but was never able either to identify the problem group or separate hereditary from environmental factors. In general, all research on the question of heritability was (and remains) methodologically weak and the results inconclusive.

Sterilisation

Because the "social problem group" was believed to be more prolific than the more valuable members of society, prominent members of the Eugenics Society advocated voluntary sterilisation. Proponents of voluntary sterilisation saw it as a step towards compulsory provision. Compulsion was adopted in some states of the USA, where, on evidence which included truanting and unmarried motherhood, about 43 000 young women are believed to have been sterilised in state institutions between Buck *v.* Bell (1927) and 1944 (Kevles, 1986, p. 116; Trombley, 1988, p. 114).

According to Kelves, Buck *v.* Bell was decided on the basis of an IQ test – concern with feeble-mindedness was a central issue in US sterilisation policies. We cannot know the total number of sterilisations, because many were carried out after pressure had been exerted to obtain the consent of the subjects or their kin. It was to the USA that Hitler's government sent observers to see how such a policy was implemented.

When in 1933 the German Law for the Prevention of Progeny with Hereditary Defects was passed, congenital mental defect, schizophrenia, epilepsy, hereditary blindness and deafness, and alcoholism were included in the list of conditions for qualification for sterilisation. This was part of a scheme to prevent national decline, improve the 'stock', and rid the country of the psychopaths who had contributed to the loss of World War I (Muller-Hill, 1988, p. 43).

The first victims of Nazi gassing were people suffering from mental illness or handicap, who were taken from asylums, shut in vans, and gassed with carbon monoxide from the exhausts. Later such people were killed with gas supplied by I. G. Farben, shot in concentration camps, or simply starved to death in hospitals. In total, about 175 000 mental patients died in these ways (Muller-Hill, 1988, pp. 39–65). For those who escaped death, there was forced labour or electrodes – a crude form of 'short sharp shock' for sociopaths and shirkers.

In Britain, the Interdepartmental Committee on Sterilisation (the Brock Committee) was established after the failure of the eugenics lobby to get a sterilisation bill through Parliament. It reported in 1934, and recommended extending what it called 'the right to sterilisation' to, in effect, 3.5 million people, and some of its members approved the wide-ranging powers of Nazi laws.

There was a wide range of eugenic views, many quite benign by the standards of the Brock Report. Eugenic assumptions were part of the common currency of debates on social issues, and they were accepted right across the political spectrum. Eleanor Rathbone, for example, wanted an income-tax regime that would facilitate larger middle-class families. The arguments were entirely congruent with more populist notions dividing the rough from the respectable, and the deserving from the undeserving poor.

Only with the quite recent establishment of the science of genetics and the discrediting of Burtian ideas of IQ did such arguments cease to be common currency in reformist debate. But they did not entirely die. Eugenic ideas and concern with national deterioration were closely entwined in both the US and the UK with arguments for immigration control which did much to fuel beliefs about the inferiority of non-white immigrants. Debates about the underclass have therefore been racialised from the beginning.

The new populism

In popular thought today there is one new villain, and it is her fertility too that is cause for concern. As *Today* put it, "Single Mums Wreck Society".

Today was responding to a lecture by Charles Murray, an American social scientist, who was brought to Britain to speak and to write an article for *The Sunday Times*. The latter has now been republished by the Institute of Economic Affairs as *The Emerging British Underclass.*

Contemporary sociologists discuss the underclass as people who have been excluded from mainstream society or the welfare state. They are concerned with the process of exclusion and the explanation of why certain people are more likely to be excluded than others. Murray, by contrast, is concerned with behaviour, and wishes to distinguish between the worthy and the unworthy poor, the deserving and the undeserving poor; for him, 'underclass' does not refer to a degree of poverty, but to a type of poverty (Murray, 1990, p. 1).

The vocabulary of the social sciences is replaced by the language of disease. Murray describes himself as "a visitor from a plague area come to see whether the disease is spreading", and later asks "how contagious is this disease?" He suggests that the underclass have values which "are now contaminating the life of entire neighbourhoods".

Murray admits his ignorance of British society, but he has no hesitation transferring ideas based on US experience directly to Britain. His evidence is anecdotal, fragmentary, and speculative; at crucial junctures in his argument he has no evidence at all. Nonetheless, he is able to conclude that:

> "Britain does have an underclass ... out of sight. But it is growing rapidly" (Murray, 1990, p. 3).

Murray suggests that the underclass may be identified in various ways, but he chooses illegitimacy, violent crime, and dropping out of the labour force, which are the main issues focused on by Wilson in the USA. Murray's work may be seen in part as a critique of Wilson.

According to Murray, the 1980s saw a rise of illegitimacy. This category was abolished in 1987, but by using it Murray is able to omit the circumstances of children born in stable unions, or registered by both parents, from his argument. Births out of wedlock certainly increased significantly in the 1980s. Murray suggests that lower class and economically inactive status correlate with illegitimacy, and indeed account for 51% of the variance when a range of factors is considered. In a small enough zone, he says, illegitimate births represent 40% of all births. He does not indicate how small the zone is; a small enough zone would give 100%, no doubt.

Murray seems unaware that in Britain people seen as a problem tend to be housed or rehoused in close proximity to one another. Thus single mothers and economically inactive, lower-class, and other 'problem' people tend to be located near one another as a matter of housing policy. It is therefore rash to assume direct causal connections between statistical coincidences.

Fifteen years ago, Murray argues, poor neighbourhoods had plentiful examples of good fathers, but

> "today the balance has already shifted ... in a few years the situation will be much worse, for this is a problem that nurtures itself" (Murray, 1990, p. 11).

Most importantly, little boys lack role models; they do not know about getting up and going to work every morning, and do not

> "become adolescents naturally wanting to refrain from sex, just as little girls don't become adolescents naturally wanting to refrain from having babies" (p. 11).

Murray has no idea what proportion of lower-class people are indifferent to work – perhaps not even 20% is his arbitrary suggestion. They acquire this indifference by growing up without a clear picture of the meaning and necessity of work; young men cannot picture themselves in their fathers' jobs. Murray collected his evidence on Clydeside and in Birkenhead, and it is surprising that he did not notice the extent to which fathers' jobs no longer exist in these areas.

Indifference to work leads to the community around the work-shy breaking down:

> "Men who do not have to support families find other ways to prove that they are men, which tend to take various destructive forms .... Marriage is an indispensable civilising force ... young men who don't work don't make good marriage material. Often they don't get married at all ... too many of them remain barbarians" (pp. 22, 23).

The reasons for these developments are, according to Murray, that illegitimacy and single parenthood are no longer stigmatised. Furthermore, the level of benefit available to a poor woman and the provisions of the Homeless Persons Act 1977 makes being a single mother "not so bad" rather than "extremely punishing". Thus, having and keeping a baby becomes economically feasible, and if a woman does not need a man, then there is less incentive for a man to plug away at a menial job to support her. It is important to note that in making this kind of point Murray offers no evidence.

Murray has perverted what could have been an important debate about poverty and people excluded from the mainstream, or the underclass as understood by sociologists. Murray's underclass are the undeserving poor. He has little to say about the deserving poor who, for example, have to suffer the declining value of child benefit.

Charles Murray also spoke at a conference organised by the Centre for Policy Studies (CPS). He fully associated himself with the views of a speaker who argued for genetic causes of crime among the lower classes and especially the 'underclass'.

Murray seems to be suggesting that the social problems of the underclass nurture themselves genetically, even if not exclusively so. He is confused and unclear about heredity and environment. Nonetheless, his arguments echo the thesis that Sir Keith Joseph spent nearly £1 million to prove. Thirty-seven studies and 20 books failed to show that social problems were transmitted from generation to generation – an outcome that nearly led to the abolition of the Social Science Research Council.

But Murray echoes the eugenic arguments, also revived by Sir Keith Joseph at the time he discovered the culture of poverty, and culminating in his Birmingham speech of October 1974 when he asserted that

"the balance of our population, our human stock is threatened"

by the birth rate of young mothers in social classes IV and V who were

"producing problem children, the future unmarried mothers, delinquents, denizens of our Borstals, subnormal educational establishments, prisons, hostels for drifters" (Trombley, 1988, p. 203).

At the CPS conference, Kenneth Baker (then Minister of Education) announced himself an admirer of Murray's "brilliant" work; the Home Secretary sent his apologies for not attending through a Deputy Under-Secretary; Lord Joseph was in attendance, as were invited prison governors, senior police officers, lawyers, and academics. Murray and his colleagues were given a tour of the Home Office, Scotland Yard, and the Downing Street Policy Unit (Baxter, 1990).

This contrasts very strikingly with the experience of William Julius Wilson, who, on his way to address the British Sociological Association as President of the American Sociological Association (ASA), was held by the immigration authorities and was released only when he said he would raise the question of his detention at a press conference.

All significant arguments in the social sciences are grounded in social and political experience. Murray's work is politically grounded also. Most importantly, it dissociates the plight of the poor from the effects of social policy and makes them responsible for their own poverty. The plight of the most disadvantaged is individualised and pathologised; they become 'cases' needing treatment or punishment.

The future of the idea

In his presidential address to the ASA, Wilson used the term 'ghetto poor' in order to avoid the controversies that have surrounded the term 'underclass'. Since Murray's visit, there has been renewed pressure to stop using the term in Britain.

What, then, shall we do about the term 'underclass'? Shall we defend it as a useful and illuminating concept, or drop it because of the connotations it has accumulated?

There are good sociological reasons for dropping the term, quite apart from its historical accretions. As a blanket term, it does less than justice to the wide variety of conditions, experiences, and responses of the people to whom it is applied, and for whose problems quite different policies might be appropriate.

The work of Engbersen and his colleagues in the Netherlands is in sharp contrast to Murray's generalisations, and is notable for its attempts to tease out the variety of conditions of the poor and the attitudes and strategies they adopt. Poor people do not refer to themselves as a class, and the poor seldom refer to poverty, but only to their difficulty in making ends meet, or finding money for the council tax. Making ends meet is the day-to-day reality, not an abstract idea of poverty. The term 'underclass' refers to members of that class as objects of study, and perhaps gives an impression of homogeneity, passivity, and resignation that does much less than justice to the culture of the poor and excluded.

There is also a danger of reification; newspaper readers and the public at large can begin to believe that there is actually a body of people 'out there' who constitute a threat to society and its values. Then people showing what are believed to be underclass characteristics or having an address in an underclass area are excluded from employment and other opportunities.

Politically, the use of the term may have the effect of amplifying stigma. It may be thought we are researching people less deserving of consideration as fellow human beings. Those included in the underclass, usually on administrative terms which include dependency and violation of middle-class norms of behaviour, become more isolated and exposed to hostile policy and administration in the field of social security. We know also that such political stigmatisation has led to deportation, incarceration, sterilisation, and murder. This process of amplification is especially dangerous when the term 'underclass' is a thinly disguised proxy for "non-white".

We may, as Herbert Gans (1990) suggests, risk actually creating an underclass, first through intensification of zoning policies, and then through exclusion and control – exemplified by the proliferation of Entryphones and the security guards who keep undesirables (i.e. poor people) out of shopping malls. Visitors to the USA will already be familiar with the next step – equipping private housing estates with chain-link fencing and security guards.

The term 'underclass' has its uses. There are people deprived of and excluded from the full benefits of citizenship. We need some way to talk about them; therefore, we do need a collective term. But we also need to be clear about the subjects of our discourse – marginalised migrant workers and refugees and asylum seekers throughout Europe (for whom, I believe, we do need a separate term, so dire is their exclusion), ethnic minority populations of inner cities, and the very poor or particular sections of the very poor. When we wish to underline the common features of their situations, we do need a term. That they do share common elements of their lives suggests that the term 'class' might appropriately be applied. By class, I mean all persons in the same class position, so it is possible to define an underclass as comprising those who typically have little or no control at all over goods and skills, either within or outside a given economic order. To underline the importance of the external and constraining conditions that create this class, I would add that what deprives an underclass of access to or control over goods and skills are the characteristics ascribed to them by others. In other words, their class position is increasingly derived from their social status.

North American research into problems of inner-city dislocation was largely stimulated by *The Truly Disadvantaged* (Wilson, 1987). Empirical research and theoretical debate continues to flourish in the USA and in Europe, around the idea of underclass and the phenomena of isolation and concentration. Books, articles, symposia, collected essays, and research reports have opened up many of the issues that were apparently closed to sociologists after the publication of the Moynihan report (Moynihan, 1964) (for a good example, see Wilson, 1989). Research has included work on teenage sexual culture, the connection between location and employment, and the effect of welfare payments on work. The use of the term 'underclass' has therefore had positive results.

Most usefully, the term invites us to think of the 'overclass', which in Britain has recently engaged in a massive experiment in social engineering, resulting in what Frank Field described in a memorable phrase as "the most significant redistribution of income to the rich since the dissolution of the monasteries". He was making a party political point, but the evidence for his contention is unequivocal.

Although sociologists have been careful enough in defining what they mean by 'underclass' when they are using the term for a particular research purpose, there will always be the problem of saying what we mean in a way that cannot be turned against a section or sections of the public. Perhaps the problem is insoluble so long as it is important to certain interests to marginalise and stigmatise other groups. Insofar as this is the case, we also have a responsibility to study the interests served by the definitions of terms and the social function those definitions have.

Wilson ended his presidential address to the ASA by saying that:

> "Researchers have to recognise that they have the political and social responsibility as social scientists to ensure that their findings and theories are interpreted accurately by those in the public who use

their ideas .... They have to provide intellectual leadership with
arguments based on systematic research and theoretical analyses
that confront ideologically driven and short-sighted public views."

This is a tall order in Britain, precisely because we are a much less open
society than the US. Ruth Lister is more blunt and pragmatic than Wilson:

"Those who invoke the development of an 'underclass' to make the
case for the restoration of full citizenship rights to the poor are playing
with fire" (Lister, 1990, p. 26).

In March 1991, Wilson himself declared that the term 'underclass' should
no longer be used in Europe. He recognised that its European historical
connotations were quite different from the North American, and the term
was, in Europe, dangerous and inappropriate.

Further reading

Murray, C. (1990) *The Emerging British Underclass*. London: IEA.
Wilson, W. J. (1987) *The Truly Disadvantaged*. Chicago: Chicago University Press.

References

Armstrong, C. W. (1929) *The Survival of the Unfittest*. London: Benn.
Auletta, K. (1981) The underclass: Parts I, II and III. *The New Yorker*, 16, 23, 30 November.
Baxter, S. (1990) In cold blood. *Time Out*, 18 May, p. 13.
Connolly, M., Parsell, G. & Roberts, K. (1992) Black youth in the Liverpool labour market. *New Community*, **18**, 209–228.
Field, F. (1989) *Losing Out: The Emergence of Britain's Underclass*. Oxford: Blackwell.
Frobel, F., *et al* (1980) *The New International Division of Labour*. Cambridge: Cambridge University Press.
Gans, H. (1990) Deconstructing the underclass. *Journal of the American Planning Association*, Spring.
Jalland, P. & Hooper, J. (1986) *Women from Birth to Death*. Brighton: Harvester Press.
Kevles, D. J. (1986) *In the Name of Eugenics: Genetics and the Uses of Human Heredity*. London: Pelican.
Lister, R. (1990) *The Exclusive Society: Citizenship and the Poor*. London: CPAG.
Macnicol, J. (1987) In pursuit of the underclass. *Journal of Social Policy*, **16**, 3.
Moore, R. (1977) Migrants and the class structure of Western Europe. In *Industrial Society: Class, Cleavage and Control* (ed. R. Scase). London: Allen and Unwin.
—— (1989) Ethnic divisions and class in Western Europe. In *Industrial Societies: Crisis and Division in Western Capitalism and State Socialism* (ed. R. Scase). London: Unwin Hyman.
Moynihan, D. P. (1965) *The Negro Family: The Case for National Action*. Washington, DC: US Department of Labor.

Muller-Hill, B. (1988) *Murderous Science* (trans. G. R. Fraser). Oxford: Oxford University Press.

Murray, C. (1990) *The Emerging British Underclass*. London: IEA.

Myrdal, G. (1964) *Challenge to Affluence*. London: Victor Gollancz.

Office of Population Census and Surveys (1980) *Classification of Occupations 1980*. London: HMSO.

Oppenheim, C. (1990) *Poverty: The Facts*. London: CPAG.

Ossowski, S. (1963) *Social Structure in the Social Consciousness*. London: Routledge & Kegan Paul.

Rex, J. & Moore, R. (1967) *Race, Community and Conflict*. Oxford: Oxford University Press.

—— & Tomlinson, S. (1979) *Colonial Immigrants in a British City*. London: Routledge & Kegan Paul.

Trombley, S. (1988) *The Right to Reproduce, A History of Coercive Sterilisation*. London: Weidenfeld and Nicolson.

Walker, A. (1990) The strategy of inequality: poverty and income distribution in Britain, 1979–89. In *The Social Effects of Free Market Policies* (ed. I. Taylor). London: Harvester Wheatsheaf.

Williams, F. (1988) *Social Policy*. Cambridge: Polity Press.

Wilson, W. J. (1987) *The Truly Disadvantaged*. Chicago: Chicago University Press.

—— (ed.) (1989) *Annals*, special issue January.

16 Culture, race and discrimination

Mark R. D. Johnson

---

*Introduction: psychiatry and power • Biological basis of race •
Language • The transcultural approach • The prevalence of mental
illness among ethnic minorities • Migration and mental health • Service
provision in a multicultural society • Conclusions*

Introduction: psychiatry and power

As all psychiatrists are aware, the definition of a 'normal state' of mental
health is one which has historically been manipulable by, or on behalf of,
the power establishments of society. In this, it perhaps resembles the
concepts of 'race' and ethnicity which also are contested entities. The
existence of a state of mental illness in a patient is, much more than other
ailments, an entity requiring the assent of an appropriate practitioner:
otherwise, people are liable to be labelled 'bad' rather than 'mad'. The
mentally ill can also be defined as being the clients of the psychiatrist, and
the state of being mentally ill or healthy is perhaps as much socially
determined and externally defined as it is inherent. To put it simply: I am
being reasonable; you are being silly; he or she must be 'out of their mind'
to contradict me.

Where the division of power lies along the lines of culture, religion, or
skin colour, there is particular scope for conflict. The 19th-century
description of two diseases apparently specific to black Americans (or in
the language of the time, 'negroes') is illustrative of this: *drapetomania,*
which made slaves run away; and *dysaesthesia aethiopis*, which reputedly
affected free blacks with "rascality" if they had "not got some white person
to direct and take care of them" (Cartwright, 1851, cited by Ranger, 1989,
p. 358).

The cleavages in society associated with what is variously termed 'race'
or 'ethnicity' are among the most entrenched and bitter divisions in our
society. Consequently, those seeking to practise psychiatric and
psychological therapies across those lines, or in a society where groupings
have formed around these divisions, must be prepared to acknowledge
the salience of a 'race relations' perspective, as well as an awareness of
ethnic sensitivity and cultural difference (Fuller & Toon, 1988).

The status of race

As scientists, too, psychiatrists and psychologists must be aware that there
is no biological reality to 'race'; it is merely a socially constructed category

based upon some relatively easily identified physical or phenotypical marker. The nature and size of the 'in-group' and 'out-group' may vary, but they are commonly defined around skin colour and hair type, earlier sociobiologists having failed to establish the scientific basis of differences in head shape. Nor are the groups always finely and carefully defined, 'black' or 'ethnic minority' being a construct that may cover everyone who is 'not like us'. Around this construct too are associated stereotypes of 'common knowledge' and, all too often, mutual hostilities. These form what is sometimes referred to as 'racialism', and (particularly when a power relationship is involved) may be expressed in the form of 'racism'.

Racism

Racism, like madness, is a problematic attribute. Few people will admit to being racist, even when their actions all point to a clear dislike of those not belonging to their 'in-group' and operate to the disadvantage of that group. One classic definition of 'racism' is that it is the product of 'prejudice plus power'. Recent analysis has found it more satisfactory to talk of 'institutional racism' – an inbuilt bias in the system operating to the disadvantage of ethnic minority groups. It should not, however, be forgotten that a person can be capable of racist emotions, motives, and actions, and that these are likely to express themselves in such a way as to place great emotional stress upon the victims, a stress multiplied by their everyday experience of the institutional variety of racism.

The victims of racism, at least, usually have little difficulty in recognising the phenomenon, even if they may be too polite or too afraid to say as much. There are clear implications here for the analyst considering a diagnosis of paranoia!

Biological basis of race

The practice of medicine has historically been regarded as a science, and therefore its practitioners prefer to deal with scientific concepts and explanations. In general, this is to be applauded, and the process of scientific investigation has brought about many improvements in understanding and treatment of diseases. Not the least of these has been the discovery of genetic traits and susceptibilities to specific conditions.

Along the way, however, there have been those who would seek by 'genetic engineering' or eugenic programmes of 'social biology' to improve the overall quality of the human race (see Chapter 15). This has led to attempts to argue that a ranking exists among those described as 'Caucasian' or 'Europid' (white, of European origin), 'Asiatic' or 'Mongoloid', and 'Negroid' (black, of African origin). Frequently, this has been expressed in terms suggesting that the black 'races' are mentally inferior. Indeed, the condition now referred to as Down's syndrome was for a long time regarded as a 'regression' of Caucasian stock to a 'Mongol' condition.

In fact, the most recent scientific evidence suggests both that genetic variety is essential for the survival of the species, and that the classification of humans by 'race' is entirely mistaken. Thus Jones, in the 1991 Reith Lectures, stated that:

> "The trends in skin colour are not accompanied by those in other genes. The patterns of variation in each system are independent of each other .... Most of the work on inherited differences in intellect between races is contemptible, and much of the rest is wrong .... Much of the story of the genetics of race ... turns out to have been prejudice dressed up as science" (Jones, 1991).

Race and medicine

Clearly, while the notion of 'race' may have some medical validity as a marker of raised probability of susceptibility to certain inherited conditions (such as cystic fibrosis for white people, or sickle-cell anaemia), it has no legitimate biological reality, at least insofar as mental fitness is concerned. Inherited neurological disorders such as Tay–Sachs syndrome may indicate the *possibility* of linking genetic predispositions to a psychiatric syndrome with ethnic origin: in this case, a particular branch of the Jewish diaspora.

However, while the tendency to endogamy (marrying within a group) is a characteristic means of maintaining the solidarity of an ethnic group, it is no more than that; the boundaries of any such group are far from well defined.

Similarly, while there is growing acceptance that schizophrenia may have a genetic component, it is certainly not true that a single gene can be identified as its cause. It may be true that a particular phenotypical response to stress or some other challenge (such as an infection) may once have proved advantageous; the sickling gene gives some protection against malaria. Currently we do not know what are the genetic components

Table 16.1   A model of terms

	Primary character	Origin	Associated perceptions
Race	Physical	Genetic	Permanent
Culture	Behavioural	Upbringing	Changeable
Ethnicity	Sense of identity	Social pressure	Situational/negotiated

or the environmental stresses implicated in susceptibility to, or the pathogenesis of, schizophrenia. Even if the genes could be identified, it would remain true that they would be located not by 'race', but by membership of a descent group, to which ethnic origin or phenotypical appearance could give only some indication of 'belonging'.

Terminology

If we are unable to use the term 'race' as a valid category, it is (if only for the sake of analysis and to combat observed inequalities) necessary to propose another term. The problem is that every term has its own intellectual baggage, and defining characteristics (see Table. 16.1).

Because culture is highly contingent upon the upbringing of the individual, and is a more than usually value-laden concept, it is perhaps less than useful as a category for this purpose. It also may easily be confused with nationality and context, rather than being an inherent characteristic of a group smaller than the nation. Where 'culture' and religion overlap, there is even more scope for confusion in the varieties of practice and belief within any one faith.

The term 'ethnicity', however, has been increasingly adopted as conveying both a sense of cultural and social identity, without implying any derogatory connotations. As an essentially transactional label, it may also commend itself as a category for those seeking to explain mental distress in terms of psychic dysfunction and personal problems in a social context, provided that clinicians are able at the same time to allow for the degree to which such labels are ascribed as well as owned, and avoid making cultural assumptions that include an implicit acceptance of one (perhaps their own) ethnic group's values. As Fernando (1991, p. 11) observes,

> "The over-riding feature of an ethnic group is the sense of belonging
> ... it is basically a psychological matter. If certain persons are seen
> (by society at large) as belonging together ... and are treated as such,
> a sense of being a part of a group may develop. If the bonds ... are
> seen as 'cultural' or 'racial' or both, an ethnic group is identified".

It is therefore preferable to consider using this alternative formulation to describe and discuss such a societal construct. The notion of 'race' is still current, and informs much public debate, despite its scientific weaknesses. Culture may have a part to play, and is certainly important for the practitioner to be informed about. However, ethnicity has the advantage of being explicitly a construct which may develop and change as we go along. Even so, the practitioner would be best advised to use such ideas with caution.

Language

One key aspect of culture – language – must have an effect upon a medical consultation, and therefore upon the treatment and quite possibly the diagnosis.

It has become a commonplace observation that many of those attending a general practitioner are unlikely to present with a complaint of mental illness, but to 'somatise' their symptoms, presenting rather with an apparently physical problem. In particular, this has become a stereotype of the Asian patient. This may therefore disproportionately reduce the numbers of patients of certain ethnic origins being referred for treatment to mental health services.

As Bennett & Rutledge (1989) observe, the whole practice of psychotherapy is intimately bound up with verbal communication: frequently, however, words (and concepts embedded in language) can get in the way.

It may indeed be true that Asian cultures do not draw the same strict distinction between 'body' and 'soul' that is now the practice in Western society: the so-called 'Cartesian duality'. With the rediscovery of 'holistic' medicine in Europe, that difference may be waning – but it will remain true for some time that Western-trained practitioners are likely to seek more 'scientific' explanations and assume that physical interpretations have greater validity than non-physical ones.

It is not, however, just a question of concepts: it is as much the value placed upon the meaning of phrases in everyday use that may form a barrier to understanding. Two commonly cited phrases, *'Mehra dil duk da he'* ('My heart gives me pain') and *'dil girdha hai'* ('sinking heart'), have been instanced as representative of the way in which Asian patients may present with depression (Krause, 1989). Few British doctors would misinterpret 'I am heartbroken' or 'I need to vent my spleen' – or even 'I felt a bit bilious this morning' as requiring surgical intervention.

The transcultural approach

While accuracy in translation is essential, so is a degree of freedom (and awareness or ability) to choose the appropriate metaphor. However, transcultural psychiatry, an increasingly recognised approach, needs to go beyond that understanding.

The premise for a transcultural approach to medical practice is the recognition that most 'scientific' medicine is based upon the assumptions and codes of expression or behaviour with which its practitioners have been most familiar. Inevitably, this has meant that it is geared towards the expectations and experiences of Western European society. The application of techniques devised in anthropology gives an understanding of these as being relativistic, transactional, and subject to change, and enables one to escape from that Eurocentric view. In so doing, most practitioners would agree that their understanding of, and ability to treat, all patients from whatever background is enhanced (Helman, 1984).

It would be impossible in the space of this chapter to cover the spectrum of cultural variety that exists in the increasingly heterogeneous societies of the 20th century, but the conscientious practitioner will find an increasing number of appropriate and specialised texts available. Unfortunately, some give fascinating detail which may prove to be misleading, or at least merely of historical interest, as customs change to fit situations and fashions. What is important is to gain some familiarity with the key features of major groups, and to be aware of one's own cultural relativism, while at the same time understanding that no culture is static and that therefore descriptions of (say) a 'typical Punjabi Sikh family' are liable to become rapidly outdated. With this awareness, reliance on stereotypes and the operation of unconscious racism will be minimised.

The prevalence of mental illness among ethnic minorities

There is clearly a variety of issues, beyond culture, which need to be covered when considering relative rates of psychiatric disease among ethnic groups. Over-reportage is one cause for concern, but under-reportage may be as much a sign of unmet need as one of good mental health. Nevertheless, few clinicians or epidemiologists need to seek additional case load, and there may indeed be some wish to avoid offence by suggesting that groups 'ought' to have higher levels of mental illness.

As Littlewood & Lipsedge (1989, p. 257) observe, there are problems in researching 'non-problems', such as the absence of Afro-Caribbean alcoholism.

Schizophrenia

On one point all epidemiological studies in Britain agree. There is inflation of the reported rates of hospital admission for those of Afro-Caribbean origin diagnosed as mentally ill, and particularly in the diagnostic categories associated with psychotic illnesses, notably schizophrenia.

The precise differences in relative risk rates vary from study to study, and explanations differ even more markedly (Ineichen, 1989). Most fundamentally, it has been cogently argued that the reported rates are inflated by miscalculation of the base data from which rates are calculated, differences in service use, or misdiagnosis.

Miscalculation of the base data

Before the 1991 census, there was no nationally collected reliable data source with an estimator of the population of Afro-Caribbean origin. Even that census may be flawed, in that its categories were not uncontested, and the groups most likely to represent this population (defined as black Caribbean or black African) may have excluded some others of the relevant ethnic group. However, there is now a commonly agreed denominator for research. All studies based upon the 1981 census had to make assumptions about the numbers of British-born black people, and their demography and local migration patterns. There was, therefore, considerable scope for argument about the necessary comparator populations for analysis (Burke, 1989, p. 184).

Differences in service use

Not only are black patients more likely to be admitted to mental institutions under sections of the Mental Health Act (Cope, 1989), and less likely to be offered less intrusive care, such as counselling and psychotherapy, but they are also less likely to present at what might be an earlier stage of illness as voluntary patients.

In part, this may reflect a natural mistrust of services which have traditionally marginalised their concerns, ignored their cultural background, and devised diagnostic labels which have served as a further means of disparaging the group (Ranger, 1989). Succinctly, this may be summarised as the experience of racism.

Misdiagnosis

Racism also indicates that the group is subject to additional stresses, which themselves may be implicated in the pathogenesis of this little understood but much researched disease. It is also part of the argument against the existence of a real inflation. If, as Ranger (1989, p. 366) argues,

> "'Cannabis Psychosis' was associated with Afro-Caribbeans more than any other group in the minds of psychiatrists mainly because they believed that Afro-Caribbeans tended to use cannabis more often and in larger amounts than other groups ... [so that] if a black youth of around 20 with an 'Afro-Caribbean haircut' came in 'out of his mind' one 'naturally' tended to diagnose 'cannabis psychosis'",

it is possible that a substantial proportion of the inflation might be due to diagnostic artefact rather than real prevalence of disease. This can have significant effects: McGovern (1989, p. 191) reported that one-sixth of the Afro-Caribbean admissions he monitored bore this label.

Social factors in the causation of mental illness

The alternative proposition remains: that there is an excess of psychotic illness among this population, and that the causes should be dealt with. Most epidemiological (and hence most prevalence) studies are dedicated to this quest. When facts are in dispute, causation may be a casualty.

If we ignore the contribution, therefore, of the possibly culture-specific pathogenesis described above, there are possible social causes which act upon the minority population. In this, it is important to go beyond the normal practice in epidemiological studies, which is to point at lifestyle (or, in the terms of this chapter, 'culture'), and consider contextual matters.

The fact remains that ethnic minorities are concentrated in particular social settings, typically 'inner city', and are characterised by deprivation, unemployment, relatively poor housing, high densities of accommodation, and lack of key facilities such as nursery or day care for children and other dependants (cf. Harrison, 1989, p. 199). This can lead to an unexpected level of social isolation, particularly in high-rise flats, or when cultural norms also restrict interaction with non-family members.

Concentration in such areas, which are in any event typified as having (even in white populations) a higher prevalence of schizophrenia (Giggs, 1986), may have its own effects – especially, perhaps, if a viral agent, one posited cause of schizophrenia, should prove to be implicated.

Racism as stress

A unique cause of stress, however, for ethnic minority populations is the increasing level of racist abuse and harassment – a more direct and immediate threat than the institutional racism referred to above. While this abuse was hitherto rarely life-threatening, a number of murders whose motivation was unquestionably racist have been recorded, and attacks involving arson or actual bodily harm are apparently on the increase. Such attacks are usually accompanied by racist taunts, or the daubing of graffiti, whose multiplication (and encounter) around the inner-city environment must increase the fear and stress in the minority communities (Johnson, 1993).

Thoughtless use of language, over-intrusive questioning as to citizenship status and rights to services (demands for passports as proof of entitlement), and culturally insensitive approaches reinforce this sense of marginalisation and threat, and create additional barriers to the receipt of services designed to counter those stresses.

Other models

Other key factors normally discussed include the 'migrant selection' and 'migrant stress' models, which appear to operate in opposite directions (Cochrane & Bal, 1987). If migration is a rational reponse to hardship, and survival of the group is best assured by dispersion or movement to better opportunity, then 'migrant selection' should mean that those who migrate are drawn from the fittest in society. Certainly, migration requires some determination and ability to negotiate successfully, as well as other resources. On the other hand, the process of migration itself is stressful, and those who undergo it may suffer subsequently, thereby off-setting the 'beneficial' effects of the change in environment.

There is also an argument that migrant populations (and perhaps those descended from that origin) may consist of two groups: those disposed to migrate because of inherent mental instability and those who attempt and cope with migration because of better than average mental health. This smacks of having one's cake and eating it (Cochrane & Bal, 1987). Nor does it answer the problem that while those of Afro-Caribbean background are over-represented in mental health care, an opposite finding is found in relation to British populations of Asian origin – that is, of lower than expected reported mental illness. There is no suggestion possible that continent of origin affects mental health – the more usual supposition is that all populations should show some equivalence! The solution, therefore, is likely to be found in the description and diagnosis of the state of illness.

As Littlewood & Lipsedge (1989) observe, reviewing the development of transcultural psychiatry since 1982, most research has continued to be culture-blind, and to consist of statistical accounts of numbers treated, or at least processed. We have already commented upon the desire of the professions to seek 'scientific' and universalistic explanations for the phenomena they treat. Consequently, the literature is full of uncritical and colour-blind assumptions.

The new practitioner will have to make up his or her own mind regarding the appropriateness of 'emic' and 'etic' perspectives. It may indeed be useful to consider that certain syndromes or collections of symptoms fall naturally into culture-bound, 'indigenous' (or emic) groups while others are cross-culturally (etic) valid (Mumford *et al*, 1991). It may be that such differences can be explained in terms of culturally preferred metaphor, or religious belief. We now live in a multi-faith community, and each faith suggests its own explanations of 'reality', and the degree to which individuals are responsible for their actions and health in this (or a previous and future) life. The attribution of a locus of control is surely as much a part of the cultural resources of explanation as the availability of counselling through religious hierarchies. Equally, I am not prepared to assert unequivocally that one model or another is essentially 'Asian' or Muslim, or otherwise determined by an ethnic origin. If we are to assert the notion of free will, the individual must remain free to select his or her explanations and cultural supports from the range available in the wider, multicultural society which they (and we) inhabit. If that causes confusion – and indeed a potential for tensions which may themselves generate mental distress – then that is part of the price we pay for having the choice.

Migration and mental health

The role of migration as a process affecting mental health itself is not fully understood. While the original definition of the disorder labelled 'nostalgia' was a feeling of loss of homeland, which clearly can be related to the migrant state, few observers nowadays would use this as a clinical diagnosis, or regard the nostalgic as mentally ill. For many, indeed, travel (and even permanent migration, which is clearly a distinct state) is seen as beneficial.

Observers disagree as to whether one needs to be more stable, competent, and aspiring to undertake a successful migration, or whether it is the unstable and incapable of coping 'at home' who form the bulk of migrants and settlers. Furthermore, the experience of 'return' may itself create greater tensions and be far from providing a 'cure' (Burke, 1972).

Current debate appears to favour the conclusion that populations of migrants are composed perhaps equally of those who are 'super-fit' mentally, and those who are essentially predisposed to mental instability. Unfortunately for the practitioner, and perhaps also for the officials charged with migration control who are expected to exclude those who will become a charge upon the 'host' society or a threat to its smooth ordering, there is no way of telling these two groups apart in advance. Nor, for the British (and increasingly the mainland European) practitioner, is the term 'migrant' necessarily an appropriate label to apply to the ethnic minority population: hence, neither can mental distress be ascribed to the migration process.

Nevertheless, the situation of migrants must be considered, and their sojourner or settler status itself has considerable implications for their health. As Gupta (1991) reminds us, migrants comprise a variety of highly heterogeneous groups – about whom it is unwise to overgeneralise. Still, the majority

> "are over-represented in the more socially deprived sectors of the population, and tend to suffer from poor living and working conditions, unemployment and the effects of social prejudice" (Gupta, 1991, p. 1).

The transformation from migrant with expectations of return to a remembered homeland with wealth and honour, to that of settler, reunited with family in the alien setting, perhaps after considerable struggle and with children growing up 'between two cultures', brings its own stresses. To these may be added the strains of racial harassment, and culturally insensitive services, as well as the effects of ignorance or prejudice among those seeking to extend those supposedly beneficial services to the minority client.

Increasingly, we are seeing also a recognition that these stresses may in fact become worse in subsequent generations (there is no such thing as a 'second-generation migrant', but there are descendants of migrants).

With this in mind, it is perhaps more useful to move forwards to a consideration of ways in which mental health services might become more sensitive and appropriate, and thereby more able both to serve the client population and to understand the prevalence and causes of mental illness.

Service provision in a multicultural society

What is required to provide an adequate and appropriate service for mental health in a multicultural society?

(1) The extirpation of racism, either in attitudes of practitioners and population or in the practice of society.

(2) The development of a high level of 'multicultural' awareness and knowledge which will enable cultural differences to be valued, and not misunderstood and used as excuses for discriminatory practice.

It has been argued that racism itself, as well as a cause of mental disease, is a form of mental illness. Until a cure is found for that, there are some clear steps which may be taken to promote more appropriate and effective services, as described above, and as suggested in good practice leaflets from the Commission for Racial Equality (forthcoming) and others (e.g. Renshaw, 1988).

Education and outreach

Key points which arise in all prescriptions for change include both an improvement in the accessibility of the service to minority clients, and a transformation of the service itself. Education is required, both of the population as to what services are available and how they may be reached, and of the practitioners. Without a greater awareness among psychiatrists and psychologists of the needs and nature of minority groups, they will continue to be handicapped in their ability to offer a professional service. This will include an ability to understand the effect of racism in their clients' lives. Once this is achieved, and practices are rendered culturally aware and sensitive, an appropriate service may be made available: initially at least, this will require special forms of outreach. It may well be that innovation here – for example, by developing new ways of working in and with communities and through existing community facilities such as temples – will prove the spur to wider improvements in practice, benefiting the majority community as much as the minority community.

Monitoring need and use

It appears that at present there is little knowledge of the actual levels of use (or types of need expressed) by minority groups. This will require the operation of monitoring procedures – which will fall under the requirements of the new National Health Service information systems that insist on the inclusion of ethnic origin in the 'minimum data set' which accompanies each patient around the health service. The same reforms have led to guidance circulars which, among other things, insist that hospitals take explicit steps to "ensure respect for the religious and cultural beliefs of each patient" (National Health Service Management Executive, 1992, p. 1). This may include the monitoring of the patient's religious persuasion.

Advice and 'good practice' on ethnic monitoring in the health service is still in its infancy, but when it is properly implemented, along with data on religion and language, it will provide a powerful tool for epidemiology and service planning, as well as useful immediate guidance for the informed practitioner.

There are innovative and valuable projects in operation throughout Britain, designed to develop good practice in mental health care for ethnic minorities.

Staff

Black staff play an important part in the provision of mental health services nationally – although this role is rarely recognised. Indeed, it may be seen as a problem, perhaps relating to the effects of discriminatory recruitment and promotion practices in the past which led black staff to be concentrated in lower grades and less popular specialties. It has not, however, seemed to have prevented the same black staff being used to provide a generic service to the white community and expected at the same time to provide additional services (for which they have not been trained or graded), such as interpretation and 'expert advice' on minority culture. It might be appropriate to consider the need for new generic training to be explicitly 'multicultural', as well as adopting an anti-racist stance.

National Health Service legislation

It is worth considering the implications of the reforms of the National Health Service (NHS) for the provision of services which are 'ethnically sensitive'. It is now no longer true that the main legislative provision affecting the rights of ethnic minorities to receive non-discriminatory and appropriate care is laid out in the Race Relations Act 1976. The provisions of the NHS and Community Care Act 1989, the Patients' Charter, and the guidance circulars of the National Health Service Management Executive, have all directed attention to the needs of racial, religious, ethnic, and cultural minorities. Indeed, they have changed this from a need to a statutory requirement. Increasingly, planning documents and community-care plans contain sentences such as the following (drawn from the City of Coventry Community Care Plan (Coventry Health Authority, 1991)):

"The stresses within black people's lives caused by racism and discrimination must be recognised and acknowledged as a causative factor of many black people's mental health problems. We must be sensitive to this in our planning, assessment and delivery of services .... We are increasingly aware that our services do not meet the needs of black people. We will continue our efforts to develop services which are more appropriate, including looking at the process of assessment, treatment and aftercare, support services, working with the Coventry Black Mental Health Group, access to information, the use of interpreters, and training about the effects of racism".

"Everyone should have ready access to the services they need, when they need them. People with different needs (eg. those from a different culture or who speak a different language) should not be put at any disadvantage" (Coventry Health Authority, 1991, pp. 6, 16).

Conclusions

Those who suffer from mental illnesses are already disadvantaged in society: there can be no justification for increasing that disadvantage, especially along lines which may have caused the mental distress in the first place. These needs, however, are not 'special' in such a way that they should be fenced off from normal, everyday consideration, any more than people with mental illnesses should be regarded as 'lunatics' first and as people only latterly.

The needs of black and ethnic minority clients may be the same as, or different from, those of white clients from the majority culture: they deserve, and are entitled to, equal and equitable consideration. Competent and professional practitioners will ensure that they are educated and trained, ready and able to provide that.

Further reading

Browne, D. (1990) *Black People, Mental Health and the Courts.* London: National Association for the Care and Resettlement of Offenders with the Afro-Caribbean Mental Health Association and Commission for Racial Equality.

Cox, J. L. (ed.) (1986) *Transcultural Psychiatry.* Beckenham: Croom Helm.

Harrison, G., Owens, D., Holton, A., *et al* (1988) A prospective study of severe mental disorder in Afro-Caribbean patients. *Psychological Medicine,* **18**, 643–657.

Kleinman, A. (1986) *The Social Origins of Distress and Disease.* New Haven, CT: Yale University Press.

Leff, J. (1990) The 'new cross-cultural psychiatry': a case of the baby and the bathwater. *British Journal of Psychiatry,* **156**, 305–307.

Littlewood, R. (1986) Ethnic minorities and the Mental Health Act: patterns of explanation. *Bulletin of the Royal College of Psychiatrists,* **10**, 306–308.

—— (1990) From categories to contexts: a decade of the 'new cross-cultural psychiatry'. *British Journal of Psychiatry,* **156**, 308–327.

Stevens, K. A. & Fletcher, R. F. (1989) Communicating with Asian patients. *British Medical Journal,* **299**, 905–906.

References

Bennett, M. & Rutledge, J. (1989) Self-disclosure in a clinical context by Asian and British psychiatric out-patients. *British Journal of Clinical Psychology,* **28**, 155–163.

Burke, A. W. (1972) Physical illness in psychiatric hospital patients in Jamaica. *British Journal of Psychiatry,* **121**, 321–322.

—— (1989) Psychiatric practice and ethnic minorities. In *Ethnic Factors in Health and Disease* (eds J. K. Cruickshank & D. G. Beevers), pp. 178–189. Guildford: Wright.

Cochrane, R. & Bal, S. (1987) Migration and schizophrenia: an examination of five hypotheses. *Social Psychiatry,* **22**, 181–191.

Commission for Racial Equality (1994) *Race Relations Code of Practice for the Elimination of Racial Discrimination and the Promotion of Equal Opportunity in the Provision of Mental Health Services.* London: CRE.

Cope, R. (1989) The compulsory detention of Afro-Caribbeans under the Mental Health Act. *New Community* **15**, 343–356.

Coventry Health Authority, City Council & Family Health Services Authority (1991) *Community Care Plan 1991 (Draft Summary).* Coventry Health Authority; City Council & Family Health Services Authority.

Cruickshank, J. K. & Beevers, D. G. (1989) *Ethnic Factors in Health and Disease.* Guildford: Wright.

Fernando, S. (1991) *Mental Health, Race and Culture.* London: Macmillan/Mind.

Fuller, J. H. S. & Toon, P. D. (1988) *Medical Practice in a Multicultural Society.* London: Heinemann Medical.

Giggs, J. (1986) Ethnic status and mental illness in urban areas.In *Health Race and Ethnicity* (eds T. Rathwell & D. Phillips), pp. 137–167. Beckenham: Croom Helm.

Gupta, S. (1991) *The Mental Health of Migrants: Report from Six European Countries.* Copenhagen: World Health Organisation Regional Office

Harrison, G. (1989) Ethnic factors in psychoses: a perspective from Nottingham, UK. In *Ethnic Factors in Health and Disease* (eds J. K. Cruickshank & D. G. Beevers), pp. 194–200. Guildford: Wright.

Helman, C. (1984) *Culture, Health and Illness.* Guildford: Wright.

Ineichen, B. (1989) Afro-Caribbeans and the incidence of schizophrenia: a review. *New Community,* **15**, 335–341.

Johnson, M. R. D. (1993) *The Prevention of Racist Attacks* (New Monograph Series). Coventry: Centre for Research in Ethnic Relations.

Jones, S. (1991) *The 1991 Reith Lectures.* London: BBC Radio 4 (extract taken from broadcast 11 December, reprinted in *The Independent,* 12 December 1991, p. 14).

Krause, I. B. (1989) Sinking heart: a Punjabi communication of distress. *Social Science and Medicine,* **29**, 563–575.

Littlewood, R. & Lipsedge, M. (1989) *Aliens and Alienists: Ethnic Minorities and Psychiatry* (2nd edn). London: Unwin Hyman.

McGovern, D. (1989) Ethnic factors in psychoses: a picture from Birmingham, UK. In *Ethnic Factors in Health and Disease* (eds J. K. Cruickshank & D.G. Beevers), pp. 190–194. Guildford: Wright.

Mumford, D. B. Bavington, J. T. Bhatnagar, K. S. *et al* (1991) The Bradford somatic inventory – a multi-ethnic inventory of somatic symptoms reported by anxious and depressed patients in Britain and the Indo-Pakistan sub-continent. *British Journal of Psychiatry,* **158**, 379 – 386.

National Health Service Management Executive (1992) *Meeting the Spiritual Needs of Patients and Staff* (HSG(92)2). London: National Health Service Management Executive.

Ranger, C. (1989) Race, culture and 'cannabis psychosis': the role of social factors in the construction of a disease category. *New Community*, **15**, 357–370.

Rathwell, T. & Phillips, D. (1986) *Health, Race and Ethnicity*. Beckenham: Croom Helm.

Renshaw, J. (1988) *Mental Health Care for Ethnic Minority Groups*. London: Good Practices in Mental Health.

17 The sociology of illness and deviance

Joan Busfield

Concepts of illness and deviance • The distribution of illness and deviance • Explaining illness and deviance • Conclusions

---

Sociology offers us ways of thinking about illness and deviance that differ from the approaches derived from the natural sciences which inform much of medical and psychiatric practice. Conventionally defined as 'the study of society' or 'the science of society', sociology is a discipline with its own intellectual concerns and traditions. These direct attention first and foremost to social structures – that is, institutionalised social arrangements – and to social relations – the relations between persons and groups – examining them in a critical, analytical manner.

Taking as their starting-point the assumption that both illness and deviance are, whatever else they may also be, social phenomena, sociological approaches and theories often complement and supplement ways of thinking about illness and deviance that are more common among medical practitioners. Less often, however, sociological theorising calls other ways of thinking into question, making claims that may contradict those made by other disciplinary specialists, either on matters of empirical fact or because of conflicting values. Such disputes often involve competing professional interests, and may be difficult to settle.

This chapter shows how sociology can illuminate and enhance our understanding of illness and deviance. The material is divided into three sections. The first deals with concepts of illness and deviance; the second raises issues concerning their social distribution; and the third examines social explanations of both illness and deviance.

Concepts of illness and deviance

Conceptual clarification is fundamental to the sociological enterprise – clarification both of its own conceptual apparatus and of lay concepts and understandings to which its own theorisations refer. In certain respects, the concepts of illness and deviance are an ill-assorted pair, for illness has a lay provenance and deviance academic origins. However, in both lay and academic parlance they commonly embody a distinction between two broad types of phenomena: disturbances of bodily function that happen to a person, and actions that break some social rule, be it the criminal law or some civil, religious, or moral code. In everyday terms, the distinction is between 'illness' and 'wrong-doing', the latter term highlighting the moral connotations that usually attach to rule-breaking.

Since illness can be analysed both as a subjective experience (the symptoms of illness) and as an objective state (the signs that are observed and measured by others), some sociologists reserve the term 'illness' for the subjective dimension, using the term 'disease' to refer to objective bodily changes. More commonly, however, 'illness' is used quite loosely to cover either the subjective or the objective aspects of illness, whereas 'disease' is used more restrictively to refer to identifiable biological changes.

The binary divide between illness and deviance is further complicated by the division of illnesses into two types: physical and mental – a contrast that follows the everyday, though contested, distinction between body and mind. Mental illnesses are conditions, modelled on physical illnesses, whose symptoms involve disturbances of mental functioning; they may or may not also involve bodily malfunction. The shared characteristic of these three concepts of physical illness, mental illness, and deviance is that they all identify some dimension of human functioning as problematic – as a departure from the normal – not just statistically (although this may be the case) but also, more importantly, in terms of what is considered desirable. The distinction between the three lies in their referents: body, mind, and behaviour, respectively.

The social construction of illness and deviance

Awareness of their evaluative dimension is central to any sociological understanding of the concepts of illness and deviance. In the first place it requires us to accept that, whatever their biological or physical basis, both illness and wrong-doing are 'social constructs'; that is, the phenomena to which they refer are categorised and given meaning through human thought and action. This is as true of the biological processes we term illnesses as of the behavioural processes we term delinquency. Peter Sedgwick (1973, p. 211) puts it like this:

> "Outside the significances that man voluntarily attaches to certain
> conditions, there are no illnesses or diseases in nature .... The fracture
> of a septuagenarian's femur has, within the world of nature, no more
> significance than the snapping of an autumn leaf from its twig: and
> the invasion of the human organism by cholera germs carries with
> it no more the stamp of illness than does the souring of milk by other
> forms of bacteria."

One corollary of this point is that the boundaries and precise meaning of the concepts of illness and deviance are very likely to change over time, and to be culturally and socially variable. What is deemed undesirable functioning of body, mind, or behaviour at one time, or by one group, will not necessarily be the same as at or by another.

Such an idea is a commonplace in our thinking about wrong-doing. We recognise that religious, legal, and moral codes do, in practice, vary, even if we argue for the absolute validity of our own ethical code. The same idea is less widely recognised in relation to illness or disease, which tend to be viewed as having a universal character. We need, however, to distinguish the medical claim that, for example, cholera as a set of biological processes exists and is identifiable across time and place, from the sociological claim that which conditions are identified as illnesses and how they are interpreted are not constant. The material reality of the biological processes is not called into question by the claim that illnesses are socially constructed.

Another corollary is that the scientific understandings of illness and deviance with which professional practice is associated represent only one among a number of understandings of the phenomena in question. Lay and scientific understandings compete with one another, often creating problems for effective communication between practitioner and client.

Drawing the boundaries

Acceptance of the evaluative component of the concepts of illness and deviance directs our attention to a related point: that the boundaries between the concepts may be and often are contested, by both professionals and lay people. This applies both to assessments of someone's actions, and to assessments of types of behaviour.

If we consider, for example, the concept of deviance, there is not only the question of where we draw the line between socially acceptable and socially unacceptable conduct, a distinction which may be difficult in relation to judging either people's behaviour (are they mad or bad?) or a type or class of behaviour (is smoking socially acceptable, and what of abortion?). There is also the problem of determining the boundaries between deviance and mental illness, as well as determining the boundaries between deviance and physical illness. The potential boundary disputes are portrayed graphically in Fig. 17.1, which places deviance as the central concept whose boundaries are open to dispute.

Of the boundaries, that between deviance and mental illness (badness and madness) is perhaps the most contested. This applies both to judging individual cases and to allocating types of behaviour to one or the other category. Is 'problem drinking' a form of deviance or a type of mental illness? Is homosexuality a form of mental pathology (albeit largely manifest in behaviour) or a form of deviance, or is it normal, acceptable behaviour? What of suicide?

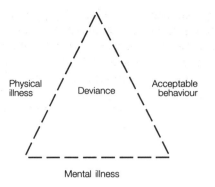

Fig. 17.1 Deviance as the central concept whose boundaries are open to dispute

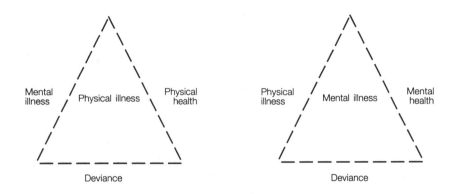

Fig. 17.2 Physical illness and mental illness as the central concepts whose boundaries are open to dispute

Such boundary disputes are especially obvious in debates between the legal and medical professions over issues such as diminished responsibility – issues over which public sentiment often has a definite voice. Was the Yorkshire Ripper either evil or insane?

Similarly, we can put physical or mental illness centre stage, as Fig. 17.2 shows. The same boundary disputes remain, although the focus of normality differs in each case: acceptable conduct (normal behaviour), physical health (normal bodily functioning), and mental health (normal mental functioning).

These boundary disputes involve both lay people and professionals – for instance, neurologists and psychiatrists dispute the boundary between physical illness and mental illness. Such disputes are not, however, simply matters of scientific fact, but of social and cultural values and of professional interests. Indeed, an important contribution of sociology in this area has been to examine the way in which professional interests help to shape the form and content of medical, legal, and police practice (see Freidson, 1970; Johnson, 1972), and, consequently, the boundaries between physical illness, mental illness, deviance, and normality.

Social control

Awareness of the evaluative component of concepts of illness and deviance directs our attention to the social control that is involved in their use. Again, this is more widely accepted in relation to deviance than it is to illness. Indeed, the dimension of control in the activities of the police and the legal profession or of those who try to encourage and maintain conformity to rules and regulations, be they parents, teachers, workplace managers, or whoever, is typically juxtaposed to the care, help, and support provided for the sick. However, care, help, and support, while humanitarian, are also regulatory, since they involve controlling and monitoring sick people's behaviour with a view to facilitating their return to the responsibilities and demands of normal life.

The sick role

The social regulation of sickness has been effectively illuminated in Talcot Parsons' discussion of the sick role. Parsons (1951) argues that while disease implies biological dysfunction, being ill ('sick') – that is, being identified and accepted as ill – is a social role, and the diseased person is always also a potential patient.

As a social role, illness is governed by certain key social expectations. Parsons (pp. 436–437) delineates four.

(1) Since illness is identified with incapacities, there is the expectation of "exemption from normal social role responsibilities". This is "relative to the nature and severity of the illness". This exemption is not, however, automatic, but has to be legitimised and, in advanced societies, the medical profession is a key arbiter in this legitimisation.
(2) Ill people are also "exempted from responsibility – they are in a condition that must 'be taken care of'. . . while the illness lasts they 'can't help it'".

(3) Since the state of being ill is defined as undesirable, the ill person is under an "obligation to want to 'get well'".

(4) There is also the obligation, again related to the severity of the condition, "to seek *technically competent* help, namely, in the most usual case, that of a physician and to *cooperate* . . . in the process of trying to get well".

These expectations constitute a mechanism for the regulation of illness in which the medical profession plays an important role. According to Parsons, this regulation is necessary to the smooth functioning of society, which can tolerate only so much illness – too high an incidence can be dysfunctional because it undermines role performance.

The requirements of the 'sick role' facilitate sick people's return to health, helping to ensure their compliance when they are ill. The requirements also help to ensure that only those who are genuinely ill are exempt from social obligations. Indeed, Parsons, influenced by Freudian theorising, argues that illness often, even if not always, involves motivational factors – wishes and feelings that are often unconscious. It can, therefore, be analysed as a particular form of deviance – a form in which a person withdraws into dependency and "is asking to be 'taken care of'" (1951, p. 285).

Viewed in the light of Parsons' critique, illness may be an alternative to other forms of deviant action, and one which has certain advantages for the social system, since the ill do not group together and attempt to establish an alternative collectivity that challenges agreed values and tries to secure its own legitimacy.

Parsons' analysis is not without its problems (see Turner, 1987, pp. 45–49). We can question what proportion of illness is motivated, as well as the focus on what is functional or dysfunctional for the social system as a whole, rather than for specific groups within it. We can question, too, the relevance of his analysis to long-term illness. Nonetheless, viewing illness as a social role undoubtedly generates important insights which direct our attention to:

(1) the social expectations shaping the behaviour of the ill
(2) the relationship between doctor and patient
(3) issues of regulation and control.

The distribution of illness and deviance

Neither illness nor deviance is randomly distributed across society, and a major sociological concern is to determine their distribution in relation to key dimensions of society, such as age, sex, social class, and race or ethnicity (see Chapters 11, 15, and 16). These matters provide an important foundation for examination of sociological explanations of illness and deviance.

Determining the distribution of illness (often termed 'morbidity' in the epidemiological literature) and of deviance is no easy task, not least because the boundaries of the phenomena we wish to measure are not always precisely drawn. The first task is to produce an agreed definition of the phenomena under study; the next is to find reliable and valid measures.

Researchers draw on two main sources of data. The first and most readily available are official statistics that monitor and measure population changes and service use. These include statistics on use of health services (the numbers of operations performed and cases dealt with) various criminal statistics (crimes committed, detection levels, numbers imprisoned), as well as mortality statistics. The second source of data is surveys screening for illness and deviance in the community, largely on the basis of 'self-reports' – that is, people's responses to questions concerning symptoms of illnesses, or criminal or other deviant activities.

Official statistics

Each type of data has its own limitations. Official statistics of sickness or deviance deal only with identified or reported cases – with persons who have had contact with the health services, or with crimes reported to the police or persons apprehended. There is often a large pool of illness or deviance that is not identified – for instance, cases of rape or burglaries which are not reported to the police, or aches, pains, and incapacities which are not brought to medical attention.

Moreover, official statistics are inevitably shaped by the nature of service provision: introduce a particular form of service and you are likely to increase the numbers of identified cases, whether it is a special unit to deal with rape victims or a special unit to deal with alcoholism, venereal disease, or arthritis.

Statistics are also shaped by the values, attitudes, and perceptions of people and their willingness to report problems to officials (the police or health services). In the sphere of health, these differences in response to illness, including the assessment of symptoms and patterns of help-seeking, are termed 'illness behaviour' – a concept that has proved to be of considerable value in the sociological analysis of illness (see Mechanic, 1978). Because of the influence of such factors, official statistics are defective as measures of underlying illness or deviance, although the under-reporting is generally, but not necessarily, related to the severity of illness or crime.

In the case of illness, mortality statistics represent an important and more reliable source of data, since in advanced societies official data on deaths are comprehensive (although a few infant deaths may go unreported). Moreover, as most deaths result from what can be regarded as degenerative conditions, death rates arguably provide a good summary measure of lifetime bodily health in industrial societies.

Mortality data are, therefore, widely used for comparative purposes, even though they do not tell us about much of the illness people have experienced during their lives.

Self-report surveys

Surveys designed to assess illness and deviance in community samples have the advantage of the potential for identifying cases that have not been reported to any official agency. However, they rely on self-reports and do not usually involve professional assessments. Consequently, there are problems about the validity of the measures they generate. Is someone who reports a range of symptoms necessarily very ill, or one reporting few necessarily healthy? Is someone who denies all deviant activity necessarily one who commits no crime or other form of deviant action? Certainly, surveys of illness and deviance in the community tend to identify far higher rates than official statistics, and people are apparently willing to report many undetected deviant actions. However, especially when it comes to assessing the social distribution of cases, self-reports cannot be used on their own, since factors such as age, sex, class, and race affect people's perceptions of illness and deviance, and, consequently, their answers to questions posed in these types of surveys.

Empirical findings

Given these limitations, as well as those associated with official statistics, we have to try to build up a picture from a variety of sources, looking for confirmation of any potential generalisation from a range of data. What generalisations can be made about the social distribution of sickness and deviance from the range of available data? Let us look at age, sex, class, and ethnicity in turn.

Age

There can be little doubt that both illness and deviance are closely related to age, but the respective relations are very different. The precise pattern varies from society to society. However, in industrial societies, there are some common patterns.

On the one hand, overall illness rates and death rates show a curvilinear relationship with age, with high rates in infancy, a decline in childhood, and then increasing rates with middle and old age, especially once retirement age is reached.

On the other hand, deviance, at least in the form of reported criminal activity, has the reverse relation to age. It is far more common among the young – adolescents and young adults – than among children or older people.

Sex

In industrial societies, women tend to live longer than men and engage in less criminal activity. In contrast, they report more ill health and make more use of health services. An important component of this greater use is linked to medical involvement in reproduction. Women also report more minor psychiatric disorder, especially depression and anxiety.

Women's criminal activity is largely concentrated in certain areas, especially shoplifting, although even here women's rates are lower than men's (Box, 1983, p. 167).

Social class

Ill-health, especially that leading to premature death, is more common among those of a lower social class (Townsend & Davidson, 1988) than among those higher up the social scale, although if we control for differences in state of health, the middle class make more use of the health services (Tudor-Hart, 1975).

Data on the relationship between class and deviance is less clear-cut. There is a marked link between identified criminal activity and class, with higher rates at the bottom of the social structure; nonetheless, self-report studies tend to suggest that, criminal statistics notwithstanding, there is no clear association between class and crime over a broad range of criminal activities (Box, 1981, p. 80).

Ethnicity

Official statistics indicate a uniform picture, in which Afro-Americans and Afro-Caribbeans in Western societies tend to have higher mortality and morbidity rates and are over-represented among psychiatric residents and prison inmates (Mercer, 1986). However, a range of evidence suggests that this over-representation may be affected by selection biases, and that the distribution of mental disorder and deviance may be far less different than these figures suggest. There is also evidence of lower rates of mental disorder and deviance in some groups, such as those originating in India and Pakistan. However, such findings may also be due to selection biases (see Chapter 15).

Explaining illness and deviance

Illness

We have seen how a sociological approach to illness emphasises not only the way in which illness is socially constructed (its boundaries and meaning vary across time and place), but also the fact that illness is a social role governed by social expectations. Illness is, however, not only a social construct – it is also a social product, since social factors are involved in the causation of illness as well as in the way it is defined and interpreted.

Sociological analyses of causation focus on the way in which the organisation of society – its social structures and social relations – sustains and facilitates health or generate illness by impinging on biological and psychological processes, with different theorists arguing about the significance of different factors.

Marxist theorists, who emphasise the significance of the way production is organised, have long argued that capitalist production is not conducive to health, while recognising that the different stages of capitalist development will be more or less deleterious to health.

Historical perspective

We do not have to accept the details of Marxist theorising to allow that the way in which the productive process is organised can have detrimental consequences for health. Marxist writers have pointed to the way in which, in the early stages of industrialisation, the capitalist organisation of work, with its labour-intensive production involving a high proportion of relatively unskilled workers who could be easily replaced, was very costly to the health of workers (see Doyal, 1979). Levels of pollution were high, safety standards were low, and workers were poorly protected from noise, dust, and dangerous machinery. In addition, they worked long hours, often away from sunlight. Their health suffered, as did that of their wives and children, even when their wives were not directly involved in production. Much of the illness was not formally recognised as occupational sickness, which remained a narrow though contested category, since it was not in the interests of either owners or managers to recognise the effect of the organisation of work on their workers' health.

The picture is in some respects like the one that has more recently been visible in Eastern Europe and the former Soviet Union, suggesting that it is the exploitation associated with intensive industrialisation, not capitalism *per se*, that is decisive.

In 19th-century Britain, the illness of workers and their families did not result only from the direct impact of the productive process. Low wages, the rapid growth of towns, and poor sanitation resulted in a poorly housed, often ill-nourished population living in overcrowded, unsanitary conditions.

Table 17.1 Average age of death (in years) in a rural area and an urban area, 1842

	In Manchester	In Rutlandshire
Professional persons & gentry, & their families	38	52
Tradesmen & their families, (in Rutlandshire, farmers & Graziers are included with shopkeepers)	20	41
Mechanics, labourers & their families	17	38

Source: E. Chadwick, *Report on the Sanitary Condition of the Labouring Population of Great Britain* (1842).

As a result, athough the health of the labouring population was far worse than that of the upper classes, all suffered from the high level of infectious diseases which was the predominant cause of premature mortality (infant mortality was especially high). Table 17.1, which is taken from Edwin Chadwick's *Report on the Sanitary Condition of the Labouring Population* (1842), highlights both the rural–urban contrast in mortality and the very marked class differences.

The current situation

With the shift from early capitalism to late or monopoly capitalism and the associated economic growth, together with advances in technology, workplace safety has been increased, pollution levels have been reduced, wage rates have improved, sanitary standards have been raised, and overall standards of living have increased. As a result, there have been marked declines in death rates and increased life expectancy. Some writers have consequently argued, against Marxist theorists, that capitalism is actually good for your health. However, just as Marxists tend to conflate capitalism and industrialisation, so these writers tend to conflate different stages of capitalism. What seems to be true is that late capitalism has marked advantages for health over early capitalism, especially in relation to manufacturing. However, even under late capitalism, sickness arising from poor conditions of work remains, and within the context of aggregate improvements there are still very marked class and sex differences in life expectancy. Those at the bottom of the social structure, who have fewer resources and lower standards of living, have comparatively low life expectancies (Townsend & Davidson, 1988).

'Lifestyle' factors

Instead of focusing on the social conditions of life and on social deprivation, doctors and policy makers often focus on behaviour, concentrating on the so-called 'lifestyle' factors. The lifestyle factors most frequently mentioned are diet, smoking, alcohol, and exercise. These factors are typically analysed at the individual rather than the social level, both in biological or in behavioural terms. They are viewed as individual patterns of behaviour which are within the control of the individual, the preventive task being to change individual behaviour.

Yet diet, smoking, alcohol consumption, and exercise are also influenced by social factors. They are shaped by material circumstances – a healthy diet is more expensive – and the perception and significance attached to those material circumstances, as well as by other cultural factors, such as habits and customs. There is, for instance, evidence to suggest that the consumption of tobacco and alcohol are related to status and esteem – and to the stresses of people's daily lives – to feelings of alienation and dissatisfaction, and to feelings of exclusion from consumer society. If we want to change lifestyles, we need to move beyond education, to analyse and change the wider structural features of society.

Deviance

Sociological explanations of deviance tend to take Emile Durkheim's ideas about deviance as their starting-point.

Durkheim

Durkheim, one of the founders of sociological theory, writing in 1895, argued that deviance is an inevitable feature of any society and is linked with issues of social order. There could be no society without rules and regulations, and if people were generally law-abiding, standards would inevitably be raised. As a result, there would still be some deviants even in this apparently well-regulated society:

> "Imagine a society of souls, a perfect cloister of exemplary individuals. Crimes, properly so called, will there be unknown, but faults which appear venal to the layman will create there the same scandal that the ordinary offence does in ordinary consciousness. If, then, this society has the power to judge and punish, it will define these acts as criminal and will treat them as such." (Durkheim, 1964, pp. 68–69)

The existence of rules, which are essential to social order, always creates the possibility of deviance. Indeed, in Durkheim's view, deviance actually facilitates social integration. In an earlier study, *The Division of Labour* (1893), Durkheim commented:

> "Crime brings together upright consciences and concentrates them. We have only to notice what happens, particularly in a small town when some moral scandal has been committed, they stop each other on the street, they visit each other, they seek to come together to talk of the event and wax indignant in common." (quoted in Box, 1981, p. 26).

Deviance, by clarifying and maintaining social rules, contributes to what Durkheim called the conscience collective, which is so essential to the solidarity of society.

In his classic study, *Suicide* (1897), Durkheim developed his ideas about social solidarity and deviance through a comparative examination of different rates of suicide in different societies and social groups. For him, suicide was "the antithesis of social solidarity and a high suicide rate was an index of the ineffectiveness of social bonds" (Lukes, 1975, p. 206).

Durkheim distinguished three main types of suicide. In egoistic suicide the bonds between the individual and society (and so to life) "are slackened or broken, because society is not sufficiently integrated at the points at which he is in contact with it" (quoted in Lukes, 1975, p. 206). Conversely, in altruistic suicide the individual is too strongly integrated, and the self has too little autonomy. Finally, in anomic suicide – anomie referring to a state of normlessness – the problem is the lack of regulation, not the links to society or lack of them. Durkheim expresses the contrast like this:

> "Egoistic suicide occurs because men no longer see any justification for life; altruistic suicide because that justification seems to them to be beyond life itself; [anomic] suicide ... because their activity lacks regulation and they therefore suffer" (Lukes, 1975, p. 207).

Anomie, Durkheim argued, increased not only in periods of economic recession and unemployment, but also in circumstances of sudden economic prosperity – what has been called the 'anomie of affluence' (Simon & Gagnon, 1977). Anomie also increased among those whose marriages broke down – a form of 'domestic anomie'.

Merton

Durkheim's ideas were developed and modified by the sociologist Robert K. Merton in the 1930s. Merton (1957) offered an analysis of deviance which distinguished between:

(1) the cultural values or goals of a society
(2) the culturally accepted means for achieving those values – the norms
(3) the distribution of opportunities for achieving the goals in a normative manner – the institutionalised means.

Table 17.2   A typology of modes of adaptation

Modes of adaptation	Cultural goals	Institutionalised means
Conformity	+	+
Innovation	+	−
Ritualism	−	+
Retreatism	−	−
Rebellion	±	±

Key: + = acceptance; - = rejection; ± = rejection of prevailing values and substitution of new values.

He regarded the relationship between these elements as decisive in understanding deviance, arguing that strain arises where there is a disjunction between cultural goals and institutionalised means, as when, for instance, material objects such as cars are highly valued, but some people do not have the resources to acquire them. In this situation there is a weakening of commitment both to the accepted goals and to the institutionalised means – a state of anomie. Merton identifies the various outcomes, or modes of adaptation that can arise in the situation. One is conformity; the others constitute different types of deviance. They are listed in Table 17.2.

Merton's analysis provides important insights into the criminal behaviour of those who are materially deprived in a society placing great value on material resources. As such, it is consistent with and provides an account of the class distribution of crime detected in official statistics. However, as we have seen, self-report studies suggest important areas of crime and delinquency undetected in official statistics – white-collar, middle-class, and corporate crimes to which the Mertonian analysis was not directed (Box, 1983, pp. 34–43). Nonetheless, as we shall see, some of the features of Merton's analysis can be extended to cover corporate crime.

Labelling theory

In the 1960s the structural-functional type of analysis of Durkheim was largely superseded by work derived from the symbolic interactionist tradition within sociology.

On the one hand, there was a range of attention to the emergence and development of delinquent subcultures and to a systematic examination of the extent to which cultural values were rejected or temporarily neutralised, an idea that has considerable relevance in understanding all forms of deviant activity (Matza, 1969).

Table 17.3 Deviance in labelling theory

	Action	
	rule-breaking	not rule-breaking
Reaction labelled rule-breaking	*a*	*b*
not labelled rule-breaking	*d*	*c*

$a + b$, not $a + d$ constitute deviance.

On the other hand, labelling theories of deviance were developed. Labelling theorists argue that it is the 'societal reaction' to deviance – the nature of the response to an action – that is decisive. Indeed, deviance should be defined not as rule breaking *per se,* but as labelled rule breaking, that is, as actions identified as deviant (see Becker, 1963) – a difference in definition that is shown in Table 17.3. According to labelling theorists, it is $a + b$, not $a + d$, that constitutes deviance.

Underpinning this approach to deviance is the belief that rule-breaking is routine. Therefore it is the reaction to the rule-breaking that makes the difference and is likely to lead someone to take on a deviant identity. This emphasis on the salience of societal reaction in defining what constitutes deviance, and also in determining subsequent deviance, needs to be distinguished from the wider sociological point that deviance is a social construct. This latter contention makes no claims about the consequences of being identified as deviant.

Mental illness

The labelling approach has been applied to mental illness by Thomas Scheff in his controversial study *Being Mentally Ill* (1967). Scheff argued that chronic or stable mental illness is a social role whose stereotypical behaviour we learn to recognise in childhood – everyone learns what it is like to be mad.

Entry into the role of the mentally ill person is primarily a function of the reaction to routine 'residual rule-breaking', residual rules being those rules 'left over' when those which lead to labels of 'bad mannered', delinquent, and so on have been specified.

The reaction to this rule-breaking is determined by a range of factors, such as the visibility of the rule-breaking, the power of the rule-breaker, the power of the person who is doing the labelling, and so forth. Following

Lemert's (1976) formulation, Scheff distinguishes the initial rule-breaking, identified as primary deviance, from the rule-breaking that follows, that is, secondary deviance.

Scheff suggests that his analysis of mental illness as a form of deviance should be viewed as complementary to analysis at an individual level, whether in physical or psychological terms, and the focus on societal reaction helps to illuminate aspects of the stigmatisation and marginalisation of the mentally ill. However, his claim that societal reaction is the single most important factor determining entry into a stable mental illness is not entirely consistent with such accounts, and a range of authors have seen it as directly contradicting traditional psychiatric ideas (see Gove, 1975).

Critics have attacked the basic proposition that mental illness can be viewed as a form of deviance on the grounds that it ignores the suffering experienced by the sick person (the reality of their sickness) and that it assumes they have control over their symptoms, suggesting that their behaviour is mere 'performance' (but see the discussion above of Parsons' view that all illness can be viewed as a form of deviance). These critics have also questioned the idea that mental illness constitutes some form of 'residual' category, as well as the primacy given to societal reaction in understanding the causation of mental illness.

Power

From a sociological point of view, one of the limitations of the labelling perspective is the relative lack of attention to the structural features of society – in particular, to the distribution of power within society and the way in which it shapes the development and application of deviant labels. A range of sociological theorising about deviance since the 1960s, including Marxist and feminist, has drawn attention to the way in which what is defined as deviant is related to the distribution of power and resources within society. Consequently, the functions of deviance that Durkheim identified – clarifying and maintaining rules – may benefit some groups at the expense of others (Box, 1983).

Historically, the relative lack of attention and under-resourcing of attempts to pursue white-collar and corporate crime are indicative of the way we often pay more attention to the crimes of the powerless than to the crimes of the powerful. In a similar fashion, crimes *against* the powerless have often been ignored, as with sexual abuse, domestic violence, child abuse, and so forth.

Recent analyses of white-collar and corporate crime have paid especial attention to two factors: first, after Merton, to the way in which the values of capitalist businesses, with their focus on money and profit-making, are themselves potentially crimogenic; second, to the opportunity provided within the business world – and the workplace more generally – for criminal activity. In the case of crimes such as sexual and child abuse, studies have focused on the dimension of power, seeing abuse as an assertion of power over the powerless. Such analyses offer fruitful ways of understanding crime and deviance in a broad range of social contexts.

Conclusions

It is always individuals who become ill and individuals who act in deviant ways, even when they do so as members of some business or corporation. Yet both illness and deviance need to be analysed at the social as well as the individual level if we are to have a clear understanding of their multiple origins and their complex place in society. The way in which people are integrated into society, the character of social relationships, and the distribution of material resources and of social statuses and rankings, as well as ideas, values, and culture, must be studied in detail in seeking to analyse and comprehend illness and deviance in their full diversity and complexity.

References

Becker, H. (1963) *Outsiders.* New York: The Free Press.

Box, S. (1981) *Deviance, Reality and Society* (2nd edn). London: Holt, Rinehart and Winston.

—— (1983) *Power, Crime and Mystification.* London: Tavistock.

Doyal, L. (1979) *The Political Economy of Health.* London: Pluto Press.

Durkheim, E. (1964) *The Rules of Sociological Method.* New York: Free Press.

Freidson, E. (1970) *Profession of Medicine.* New York: Dodd, Mead.

Gove, W. R. (ed.) (1975) *The Labeling of Deviance.* New York: Halsted.

Johnson, T. J. (1972) *Professions and Power.* London: Macmillan.

Lemert, E. (1976) *Human Deviance, Social Problems and Social Control.* Englewood Cliffs, NJ: Prentice-Hall.

Lukes, S. (1975) *Emile Durkheim.* Harmondsworth: Penguin.

Matza, D. (1969) *Becoming Deviant.* Englewood Cliffs, NJ: Prentice-Hall.

Mechanic, D. (1978) *Medical Sociology* (2nd edn). New York: Free Press.

Mercer, K. (1986) Racism and transcultural psychiatry. In *The Power of Psychiatry* (eds N. Rose & P. Miller). Cambridge: Polity Press.

Merton, R. K. (1957) *Theory and Social Structure.* New York: Free Press.

Parsons, T. (1951) *The Social System.* London: Routledge and Kegan Paul.

Scheff, T. J. (1967) *Being Mentally Ill.* London: Weidenfeld and Nicholson.

Sedgwick, P. (1973) Mental illness is illness. *Salmagundi*, **20**, 196–244.

Simon, W. & Gagnon, J. H. (1977) The anomie of affluence: a post-Mertonian conception. *American Journal of Sociology*, **82**, 356–378.

Townsend, P. & Davidson, N. (1988) *Inequalities in Health: The Black Report.*
    Harmondsworth: Penguin.
Tudor-Hart, J. L. (1975) The inverse care law. In *A Society of Medical Practice* (eds
    C. Cox & A. Mead). London: Collier-Macmillan.
Turner, B. (1987) *Medical Power and Social Knowledge.* London: Sage.

18   Health services and institutions

Ellen Annandale

Understanding organisational structure • Frameworks for understanding formal organisations • Mental health services and institutions in transition • Community care policy • Concluding remarks: the social organisation of services and the health care division of labour

The organisation of institutions and services is an important influence upon the experience of patients, health-care workers, and the interaction between them; as such, it should be of central concern to psychiatrists and others working in the mental health field. This chapter outlines and assesses the various ways in which social scientists have sought to understand formal institutions. Particular attention is given to the interplay between organisational structure and the division of labour within institutions and services. It is suggested that the historical organisation of professional knowledge and the constellation of power relationships in health care influence the organisation of services, but that the social organisation in its turn sets particular limits upon the work roles of psychiatrists and other occupational groups.

The chapter begins by explaining the different theories of institutional structure that have been put forward by social scientists, with particular reference to hospitals. It then turns to consider mental health institutions and services in transition, considering deinstitutionalisation and community care and their implications for the division of labour in mental health care.

Understanding organisational structure

The social scientific study of mental health settings goes back to the 1930s and 1940s. As part of an ascendant 'humanist' critique, several anthropologically orientated US studies claimed that, far from providing treatment, mental hospitals might be seen to inhibit effective therapy.

For example, Stanton & Schwartz's (1954) classic three-year sociopsychiatric study concluded that the rigid organisational structure of the hospital encouraged custodialism. A vivid picture was presented of a static and routine organisation, within which patients had little autonomy and where the bulk of care fell upon less qualified staff and ward attendants, who essentially exercised social control.

In addition to describing the environment as impoverished and standardised, a link was made in these early reports between organisation and patient behaviour, with suggestions that lack of autonomy, confusion, and conflict on the part of staff, as well as periodic explosions of tension generally, were associated with clinical deterioration (Szurek, 1947).

Thus, from the early days, research has pointed out that the organisational structure is not just a backdrop, but can have a role in determining the therapeutic interaction of staff and patients. This theme was taken into the 1960s by Erving Goffman (1968), whose work on 'total institutions' continued both the humanist critique and the concern for the association between organisational structure and the behaviour of staff and patients.

Focusing on the intricate details of hospital life and developing an explicitly moral stance, Goffman suggested that the power of the institution over the life of 'inmates' derived from the fact that normally separate spheres of life (such as home life, work life, and leisure time) were collapsed into one entity – the total institution. Patients, cut off from their social world on the 'outside', construct a new identity on the 'inside'. This process of change in social relationships is conceptualised by Goffman as a 'moral career'; as the person becomes a patient, previous identities, statuses, and social relationships are fundamentally altered. Depicted in this way, the total institution as an organisational structure appears to exert a forceful influence upon the people within it. Yet at the same time, Goffman attempts to present the individual not in a passive way, but as thoughtful and resisting. This has led some commentators, such as Williams (1987, p. 147), to remark that "in Goffman's scheme of imagery man [*sic*] is at one and the same time a determined and determining being".

It is useful to bear in mind the relationship between people (staff and patients) and the organisations within which they live and work, since the manner in which this relationship is depicted is one important way of distinguishing between the theories discussed below.

Frameworks for understanding formal organisations

Three approaches to understanding the mental hospital as an organisation are discussed:

(1) positivist
(2) interactionist or negotiated
(3) radical.

This tripartite framework (although not the detailed discussion of it) is drawn from Morgan *et al*'s (1988) discussion of the hospital as an organisation.

The positivist framework

Weber

The positivist approach to hospital organisation has its origin in Max Weber's (1978) classic work *Economy and Society* (written in the early 1920s), in which a bureaucracy (such as a hospital) was portrayed as a hierarchical system of authority based on a set of rational and explicit rules. Weber argued that a rational/legal bureaucratic structure is best suited to modern society, since it guarantees that activities such as patient care and administration of the hospital are reliably carried out.

In a rational bureaucracy, the tasks that people are expected to perform are clearly specified, and the individual is subject to a unified control and disciplinary system. This is defined as rational because means are expressly designed to achieve certain goals (such as the rehabilitation of patients). It is evident that in Weber's model, the focus is upon the formal structure of the hospital as a determinant of individual behaviour – the individual doctor, nurse, or manager involved in the running of the hospital is an incumbent of an office constrained by a set of rules and regulations which define the limits of official behaviour.

Perrow

Perrow (1965, p. 913) also stresses the hospital as a unit which functions independently of any one person or set of group. However, in distinction from Weber, he views

> "organisations in terms of the *work* performed on the basic material which is to be altered [i.e., patients], rather than focusing upon the interaction of organisational members" (my emphasis).

In his view, hospital organisation is influenced by three interdependent factors, which he describes as:

(1) the cultural system (which sets legitimate goals)
(2) technology (which determines the means to achieve goals)
(3) social structure (the organisation in which techniques are embedded such that they permit goal achievement).

The relative influence of these factors on the nature of the hospital varies according to the time frame adopted: in the long-range view, the cultural system seems determinate; in the medium-range view, technology seems determinate; and in the short term, the social structure (of the hospital) may seem most important.

Given his central focus on the work that is performed as the major feature of organisations, Perrow's work has often been characterised as 'technologically determinist'. This is exemplified in his discussion of the state of mental hospitals at the time he was writing. He remarks that

> "the reasons for the depressing conditions do not lie in the structure, processes, and goal commitments, but in the limitations of the available technology" (Perrow, 1965, p. 925).

The concept of technology is broadly defined, referring not to equipment, but to knowledge:

> "Equipment is a tool of technology, but technology rests upon knowledge of the nature of raw material" (p. 916).

Consequently, changes in the technology of care 'permit' a particular kind of organisational structure to develop. For example, we could argue, in Perrow's terms, that doctors dominate the hospital when complex, high-technology medicine is in vogue, but that a more complex hierarchy will emerge when mental health care is characterised by a competing system of technology/knowledge which does not necessarily rely upon surgical or drug intervention.

Criticisms of the positivist framework

Several criticisms have been levied against these broadly positivistic approaches. Firstly, there has been considerable discussion of whether hospitals do, in fact, conform to Weber's ideal typical presentation of a rational/legal bureaucracy. It has been pointed out that professions such as psychiatry are not organised along bureaucratic lines and, consequently, it is not possible to specify all possibilities for action. Furthermore, modern hospitals are typically characterised by a dual system of authority linked to doctors on the one hand and managers on the other.
   Turner (1987, p. 160) remarks that

> "the hospital authority structure is fractured around the difference between the rational bureaucratic system and the professional autonomy of the doctor through a system of medical domination".

Conflict between doctors and management characterises the recent history of general hospitals in particular, and it has been suggested that the introduction of 'general management' in the 1980s was primarily motivated by an intent to undermine medical syndicalism (Strong & Robinson, 1990). This dual system of authority has been particularly problematic for nurses, who are typically subject to both medical and bureaucratic management (Turner, 1987).
   A second criticism of the positivistic framework is that it tends to underplay the influence of powerful groups such as doctors and

management in determining both goals within the hospital and the means of achieving them. Historically, the very development of the hospital was inextricably linked with the growth of medical dominance and professional power, although it has been suggested that recent shifts in mental health care policy (discussed, below) have been intended at least in part to disaggregate the psychiatric profession and to bring it closer to the mainstream of ordinary medicine (Baruch & Treacher, 1978).

The main point to bear in mind, then, is that the positivist model tends to consider the perspective of powerful interests (such as doctors and management) in a rather uncritical manner and, for this reason, disregards their relative influence in developing an organisational structure which bests suits their own particular interests. (This point will be taken up further when we discuss the radical framework for understanding the hospital as a formal organisation.)

A third criticism must be mentioned. This is that given the conflicting lines of authority in the hospital and the possibly conflicting interests of various groups (such as doctors, nurses, managers, and patients), it is appropriate to see the hospital not as a goal-orientated, independent, and rational structure, but as a 'negotiated order'. This criticism is put forward by the second approach to understanding the organisation of the hospital and is best considered through a discussion of that framework.

The interactionist or negotiated framework

The central proposition of this framework is that the hospital is best understood by focusing not on the formal, but on the informal organisation; rather than see the work of doctors and nurses and the experience of patients as a product of the formal organisation, it is argued that the organisation itself is a product of the actions and meanings of the people within it. Consequently, it is not taken as a 'given' (as in the positivist framework) but as a "more flexible and uncertain phenomenon [*sic*]" (Morgan *et al*, 1988, p. 149).

A number of authors are closely associated with this approach, including Goffman, whose work was discussed earlier. It is perhaps best exemplified, however, by the work of Anselm Strauss and his colleagues (cf. Strauss *et al*, 1981). Distinguishing their approach from the earlier rational framework, the authors explain:

> "We began our research not by looking at hospitals *per se*, but by thinking of them as sites where the ideological battles characterising the mental health arena were being fought, implemented, critiqued, modified and transformed" (Strauss *et al*, 1981, p. vi).

They reject what they see as the two principal conceptions of the more positivist hospital studies of the time (their study was originally published in 1964, before the process of deinstitutionalisation):

(1) that the hospital is a more or less efficient organisation for the attainment of stated purposes
(2) that the hospital has covert functions which are not perceived by its personnel.

A response to these points was developed during an anthropological study which involved detailed observation of three psychiatric settings in Chicago, USA: two consisted of the 'chronic custodial services' and 'treatment services' at the state mental hospital, and the third was a private hospital. The last two settings were described by the authors as psychotherapeutic in orientation. A picture emerges of a network of social relationships, leading Strauss *et al* (1981, p. 16) to describe the social structure (organisation) of the hospital

> "at any point in time as the total of all its rules, agreements, and understandings – of whatever kind".

In this way the hospital is conceptualised as a 'negotiated order'.

At the empirical level, this framework has generated interesting insights into the daily life of staff and patients in mental hospitals, therapeutic communities, and out-patient facilities. For example, Goffman's (1968) work highlights the ways in which people who appear not to be powerful, such as paramedical staff, visitors, and patients, can influence the formal organisation through bargaining and negotiation. Goffman vividly portrays the 'underlife' of the hospital, showing the ways in which patients work the system and 'get by' within established routines.

A further illustration of the usefulness of this approach is found in studies which reveal the way in which clinical decision-making is influenced by a series of organisational constraints and conflicts. Brown (1987) studied psychiatric diagnosis in a walk-in clinic in the USA, and revealed the disparity between the ideal DSM–III (American Psychiatric Association, 1980) and the actual process of diagnostic work. He remarks (Brown, 1987, p. 47) that DSM–III

> "has attempted to make diagnostic categories objective and behavioural, rather than subjective and psychodynamic".

These categories are held by many to be reliable. In fact, he found the diagnostic process to be characterised by uncertainty, ambiguity, and conflict. By observing the interactions of psychiatrists and their clients over 18 months, the author observed that

> "Clinicians and supervisors, in the course of routine diagnostic evaluations, engage in many conflicting and ambivalent behaviours. These include humour and sarcasm about diagnostic categorisation, real or imagined alternatives to the diagnostic schema, evading diagnosis, minimalization of severity for some patients, and critiques of the various diagnostic models" (p. 37).

A range of broad organisational factors are put forward to account for this situation, including conflict between an ascendant biopsychiatric model and the everyday work of a therapeutic service, the tensions involved in providing a service to clients while servicing the needs of public agencies (such as social services), and the mixed agendas which surround diagnosis.

In terms of the theoretical framework of interactionism, the significant points to apprehend are:

(1) that the organisation which surrounds the everyday work of psychiatry is often characterised by ambiguity and conflict (not by the straightforward implementation of rules and procedures)
(2) that this can create problems for staff and patients alike, such that they must "play an active, self-conscious role in the shaping of the social order" (Day & Day, 1977, p. 132).

Earlier, it was noted that the depiction of the relationship between people (staff and patients) and the organisations within which they live and work is one way of distinguishing between different theories of hospital organisation. The positivist framework presents a fairly deterministic model, whereby individual behaviour is a product of the formal organisation. The interactionist framework, in contrast, emphasises the fluidity of organisational structure and people's creative roles as they live and work in the hospital and other mental health settings.

Criticisms of the interactionist framework

It is apparent that the focus of much research within the interactionist framework is at the 'micro' level of institutional life. That is, it concentrates upon immediate, usually observable experience. It has been quite widely criticised for giving little attention to how the world outside the hospital impinges upon what goes on inside it. This criticism is more valid for some theorists broadly within the interactionist framework than others. It has, for example, been levied, in particular, against the work of Goffman and of Strauss. When these theorists fail to take explicit account of external influences upon individual behaviour in the hospital,

"the end result is the failure of the negotiated order theorists ... to critically examine the hard realities of power and politics and the influence they exert upon the negotiative process" (Day & Day, 1977, p. 134).

The radical framework

The issue of power and control over resources is at the heart of the radical model of the hospital, where attention is focused on an alliance between the economic structure of society and an organisational structure in the hospital which is dominated by powerful medical and economic interests.

Vicente Navarro (1975), for example, discusses the fragmented and hierarchical division of labour in hospitals, arguing that they are determined primarily by social class and sex divisions existent in society more broadly. Power and status elide such that authority resides in the hands of consultants and managers, who are typically white, male, and of middle-class origin, and who exercise social control in providing care to patients.

Economic imperatives often drive the explanatory framework of the radical model. This is evident, for instance, in the work of Scull (1977), who gives an economic interpretation of the development of community care which, he argues,

> "must be viewed as dependent upon and a reflection of more extensive and deep-seated changes in the social organisation of advanced capitalist societies. In particular, it reflects the structural pressures to curtail sharply the costly system of segregative control once welfare payments . . . make available a viable [cheaper] alternative to management in an institution" (p. 152).

Thus, although doctors may exercise power in determining the particular hospital organisation, this power is available only insofar as it coincides with the economic needs of an advanced industrial economy.

Combing the interactionist and radical frameworks

Even though the interactionist and radical frameworks seem to conflict, since one focuses on the 'micro' level of interaction and the other on the 'macro' structures of power which influence the organisational structure, they are not necessarily incompatible. A more complete approach to understanding the organisation of hospitals might combine a concern with the microprocesses of everyday work and experience in the hospital with an equal concern for wider factors which might influence these processes. Brown's (1987) study of diagnostic conflict, mentioned earlier, approximates such an approach, since the conflict observed in the walk-in clinic is detailed and then analysed in light of broader conflict and division within psychiatry (concerning the psychotherapeutic and biopsychiatric models) and within society concerning reforms in mental health care and the place of psychiatry within them.

As we now turn to consider the organisation of contemporary mental health services, it is appropriate that the relationship between wider socio-economic structures of society and microprocesses such as the division of labour within mental health care be kept in mind. Taken together, the interactionist and radical frameworks that have been described point to countervailing lines of authority in the hospital. Historically, it may be apposite to view the medical profession as the most influential (in the last instance) in determining the organisation of services. However, as Prior

(1991, p. 484) has stated, during the last 25 years "the medical monopoly on mental illness has been effectively weakened", and we may be witnessing "a fundamental realignment of the organisational structures which surround the mentally ill in the contemporary western world".

This chapter next considers the movement from hospital to community care, the organisation of community care services, and the division of labour between psychiatrists and other occupations involved in the provision of care to patients.

Mental health services and institutions in transition

Towell & Kingsley (1988, p. 170) remark that

> "reform in psychiatric services necessarily emerges from the complex interplay of bureaucratic, professional and community pressures, within the wider economic, social and political context".

Despite the veracity of this statement and general agreement that dramatic changes are taking place, it is evident that controversy surrounds explanations of the transition of mental health care from the hospital to the community. Humanitarian and economic factors have been emphasised, as have changes in the knowledge base of psychiatry. Before we go on to consider the explanations that have been put forward, it is worth briefly outlining the changes that were taking place in the organisation of hospitals in the period before the ideology of community care gained momentum.

Paving the way for community care

A constellation of factors may be seen to have paved the way for community care, beginning with the developing humanitarian critique and the development of scientific and medical knowledge. By the 1930s, mental hospitals were beginning to move from primarily exercising a social welfare function to providing therapy. Thus, the mid-1900s saw the development of somatic treatments such as insulin coma, electroconvulsive therapy, and advances in pharmacology and surgery. World War II and the post-war period saw significant changes in hospitals, such as open and unlocked wards, the increased use of occupational therapy, and the setting up of therapeutic communities. The 1930s witnessed a growth in out-patient clinics and acute wards in general hospitals.

In their case study of the closure of the Darenth Park Hospital (a mental handicap hospital which closed in the late 1980s), Korman & Glennerster (1990, p. 7) note that "from the late 1950s, 'community care' became a bipartisan political objective"; it began largely as ideology and has taken many years to translate into practice.

Deinstitutionalisation may also have been spurred on by a series of inquiries which were set up in the 1970s to investigate alleged ill-treatment in hospitals (the Ely Hospital Inquiry, for example, was much publicised). Building in part on the humanitarian critique stemming from social science (particularly social policy) and from inside the health-care sector, such inquiries tended to conclude that failures in care were embedded in the social organisation of the hospital, and that reform was long overdue (Butler, 1993).

The 1970s were also characterised by much publicised fiscal stress and the onset of a continuing series of administrative reforms in the broader structure of the National Health Service (NHS), which, it has been argued, were also largely motivated by need to cut costs. In the context of mental health provision, it is evident that many institutions were now between 80 and 100 years old and were (or soon would be) in need of major renovation or rebuilding, and, consequently, carried a potentially large burden of cost.

Thus, by the late 1970s, a cluster of factors together suggested that the time was ripe for radical change in the organisation of mental health services in Britain. As noted earlier, however, commentators have placed their emphases on quite different factors in an attempt to provide an explanation for deinstitutionalisation and the implementation of community care: humanitarian, economic (political economy), and knowledge/technological factors.

The humanitarian factor

Aspects of the humanitarian explanation have been outlined earlier. Essentially, it is suggested that after the development of the welfare state, advances in medicine, and criticisms growing out of social scientific research, governmental inquiry, the anti-psychiatry movement, and the patients' rights movement, both professionals and public recognised that the mental institution was causing more problems than it was solving for patients. The concept of 'institutionalisation' – which referred to the dependency of long-stay patients on the institution and accompanying inability to function 'normally' in the community – fuelled calls for reforms in the provision of mental health services on broadly humanitarian grounds. Although the recognition of such reasons undoubtedly played a role, they probably are not sufficient to explain of deinstitutionalisation by themselves. Commentators often draw also upon economic explanations and changes in the knowledge base of psychiatry.

The economic factor

The negative effects of institutions have been apparent since the 1870s, but this did not begin to stimulate policy changes until the 1960s. Citing this and other evidence, Scull (1977) argues that the ideology of deinstitutionalisation only became popular during a time of fiscal stress. Refurbishment of old hospitals would be costly, while closing them and selling their sites would raise substantial capital revenues.

Staffing of large hospitals had also become problematic in a period of a relatively short supply of labour. In the south of England, in particular, vacancies could only be filled by attracting domestic and nursing staff from overseas (Korman & Glennerster, 1990).

The combined result was that the government recognised that financial pressures in the NHS could be reduced by shifting the burden of cost onto the local authorities, which were responsible for community care, or onto the families of the mentally ill.

Shifting the cost burden has been incrementalist in form. In the 1950s, 1960s, and early 1970s, community care consisted of the provision of domiciliary services by the staff of local authorities. By the mid-1970s, it was expanded to include other services, such as day hospitals, hostels, and residential homes, with an emphasis on formal care in the community. After 1979,

> "There was a far greater emphasis in policy documents on an ideal of care *by* the community; that is, care by family, relatives, neighbours and friends and by voluntary organisations" (Mays, 1991, p. 237; my emphasis).

Cognisant of the somewhat overlapping roles of health authorities and local authority social services departments, the Griffiths review of community care in the late 1980s recommended that local authorities be given prime responsibility for community care. The response of the government to this report, subsequent policy documents, and the implications for the division of labour in mental health care are discussed in some detail below.

Commentators vary in the extent to which they put economic imperatives at the centre of explanations for the change in mental health services. Prior (1991, p. 484) contends that in its crude form this argument

> "sees in the hospital/community transition nothing more complicated than an ideal opportunity to offload health expenditure onto social security budgets".

In response to this, he asks whether deinstitutionalisation was consciously planned as a cost-cutting exercise, and remarks that it is not readily apparent that community care is cheaper than hospital care. While recognising that economic factors clearly have some relevance, he remarks further that within a Marxist economic framework in particular (such as that adopted by Scull) it is difficult to explain why community care "was adopted as the most appropriate medium for the expression of capitalist welfare policies in the first instance" (Prior, 1991, p. 485).

The knowledge/technology factor

In proposing an economic model of change in mental health provision, Scull (1977) explicitly argues against the position that improvements in medical treatment have been the major cause of change. He cites evidence to suggest that modern treatments are not very effective and that, in any case, the reduction in the number of patients in hospitals began before such treatments became prevalent in the 1950s. Medical knowledge, therefore, simply provides a rationalisation for other, economic changes.

Others, however, emphasise developments in knowledge, especially advances in pharmacology (notably the introduction of neuroleptics) to explain the decline in the in-patient population. Murphy (1991) affirms that it was widely believed that hospitals could be run down in the light of the perceived successes of antipsychotic drugs. Thus, in 1971, the Minister of Health (Keith Joseph) justified government policy of closing mental hospitals in the following terms:

> "The treatment of psychosis, neurosis and schizophrenia have been entirely changed by the drug revolution. People go into hospital with mental disorders and they are cured, and that is why we want to bring this branch of medicine into the scope of the 230 district general hospitals that are planned for England and Wales" (Joseph, quoted in Murphy, 1991, p. 50).

Several counter-arguments are made by, among others, Scull (1977), Prior (1991), and Butler (1993). First of all, as a policy, deinstitutionalisation also applied to disorders which were not susceptible to treatment with neuroleptics (the elderly, the mentally handicapped). Secondly, Prior argues that a technologically determinist approach such as this divorces change from the organisational context in which knowledge is embedded.

The direction of the relationship between knowledge and the organisation of services is difficult to establish. It seems sensible to suggest that the development of new forms of knowledge about mental health care is influential in steering the development of services in a particular direction. In addition, particular forms of knowledge are facilitated by particular forms of service. We can identify various changes in the knowledge base of mental health care provision in the 1960s, 1970s, and 1980s, not all of which are necessarily compatible.

The implication of developments in pharmacology has already been discussed. In addition, we can point to (among other things) changes in psychiatric practice in the mid-20th century, such as the development of group therapy and of ideas which led to therapeutic communities. The therapeutic community movement is characterised by a fair degree of diversity, but the assumption that mental illness is a product of unsatisfactory social relations is typically central to its philosophy. The 'solution' to mental problems is thereby sought in restructuring social relationships which, in turn, are taken as the focus of therapeutic intervention. Rapoport (cited in Morgan *et al*, 1988, p. 163) identifies four objectives which serve as a vehicle for social rehabilitation in therapeutic communities. These are the following: the democratisation of the hospital; ensuring that the hospital is very permissive of 'deviant' behaviour; the establishment of a real community; and providing the conditions for communal reflection (a form of group therapy).

A second change in the practice base of psychiatry was evident in the anti-psychiatry movement. Goffman's (1968) work on the total institution is often considered part of this movement, but it is more aptly associated with the two schools represented by Thomas Szasz (1961) and R. D. Laing (1960). In Szasz' work, psychiatrists are interpreted as acting as agents of social control on behalf of the state, by applying the label of 'mental illness' to behaviour which does not conform to the norm. In this way he argues that medical labels (which define mental health problems as an illness rather than as problems in living) mask the moral and political character of human behaviour. Less polemical in some ways, Laing's work focused specifically upon mental illness as a product of a disturbing social environment, particularly associated with the family, which was defined as an oppressive institution for many people. Laing's theories inspired a number of treatment centres which adopted the principle that "a laissez-faire ethos and a style of communal living would see people through their madness" (Murphy, 1991, p. 56).

Taken together, the therapeutic community and anti-psychiatry movements engendered a form of 'practice' which was at direct variance with the 'medical model' of mental illness. In retrospect, it is clear that these have failed to develop as independent mainstream alternatives but, culturally, they may have contributed to the climate of change away from a traditional, institution-based approach to mental illness.

A third change in the practice base of psychiatry came from the more behaviourally based approaches to patient care associated with reforms in nursing practice within institutions. Once again a counter to a strictly medical or illness model, behavioural approaches may provide an impetus for community care.

This argument is put forward by Prior (1991) in his interesting case study of psychiatric services in a Northern Irish hospital. Referring specifically to nursing policy and the assessment of patients, he highlights the focus upon activities of daily living (ADL) as a centre of therapeutic practice. The ADL approach was aimed at 'normalisation' of the patient and countering institutionalisation. Crucially, however, 'normal' behaviour cannot be judged in abnormal settings (such as the hospital ward) and 'behaviour' is not something that can be effectively monopolised by nursing and psychiatry. Drawing these points together, Prior (1991, p. 487) states

> "that in choosing behaviour as an object of therapeutic focus, psychiatry and psychiatric nursing have lost the rationale they once had for confining themselves within the grounds of a psychiatric hospital . . . . It is in this sense that I argue that the old asylums have been destroyed from within rather than from without the walls."

Community care policy

The foregoing discussion shows that a range of often competing explanations have been put forward to account for the impetus towards community care. With this in mind it behoves us to consider the actual nature of contemporary community provision for the mentally ill.

It would seem sensible at the outset to provide a definition of community care, but this is by no means a straightforward task. The problem is summed up in rather evocative language in the following comment:

> "To the politician it is a useful piece of rhetoric; to the sociologist it is a stick to beat institutional care with; to the civil servant it is a cheap alternative to institutional care which can be passed on to the Local Authorities for action or inaction; to the visionary it is a dream of a new society in which people really do care; to the social services departments it is a nightmare of heightened public expectations and inadequate resources to meet them. We are only just beginning to find out what it means to the old, the chronic sick and the handicapped" (Jones *et al*, quoted in Mays, 1991, p. 236).

There is, then, no one definition of the term 'community care'. Nonetheless, there are two points which are fairly consistently made in the literature on community care: that it is largely fragmented and relatively uncoordinated, and that there is a clear gap between policy statements and the reality of everyday provision.

The 1962 Hospital Plan serves as a useful starting-point from which to outline government policy on community care. This plan called for the NHS to provide a mental health service based in district general hospital psychiatric units and for local authority social services to provide residential and day-care support in the community (Murphy, 1991). Murphy states that by 1974 there were around 60 000 fewer people in the old hospitals than in 1954, but that very few actual services had been set up in the community.

In recognition of this, community care policy was restated in a 1975 White Paper entitled *Better Services for the Mentally Ill.* After the first major reorganisation in the NHS (in 1974), the exhortations contained in the paper had minimal overall impact, and there was little further impetus until the late 1980s, which saw a series of reports on the financing and organisation of community care. Murphy (1991) notes that the two most influential of these were the Audit Commission report of 1986 and the Griffiths report of 1988.

The Audit Commission report, *Making a Reality of Community Care*, argued that major changes were required to provide a suitable environment for a community-based and integrated service. Three points were emphasised (see Murphy, 1991, pp. 124–125): that local authorities be responsible for long-term care of the vast majority of the elderly and mentally handicapped; that a single budget be set up for the care of the elderly in the community with a budget manager who would act as purchaser of services; and that the NHS retain prime responsibility for mental health care.

The Griffiths report and the Conservative government's response in the report *Caring for People* (1989) formed the basis of the 1990 NHS and Community Care Act (which was to have been launched in April 1991, but was delayed until 1993). The Act brings together health authorities and local authority social service departments to determine community care plans, both in terms of organisational functioning and the care of individual clients, in an attempt to reduce the fragmentation of care. At the centre is the care or case manager, whom Butler (1993, pp. 101–102) describes as the

> "fulcrum of the reformed system of care in the community as the task is to bring together social and health care services to meet the assessed needs of individual patients and clients".

The care manager is frequently located in social services departments, although it is possible for other care providers to take on the role. As Butler (1993) points out, while attractive in principle, the care manager's job may be fraught with difficulties and ambiguities stemming from the remit simultaneously to assess need and allocate scarce resources.

The organisation of community care needs to be understood in the context of the market culture of purchasers and providers introduced by the 1989 White Paper *Working for Patients*. District health authorities are responsible for identifying the health needs of the local population and for purchasing the appropriate services from a range of providers, such as directly managed units (in the hospital or community), self-governing trusts, or the independent sector.

Thus, many mental health care practitioners now work in either directly managed units or trusts which are contracted to provide services. This will almost certainly result in a changed practice environment, as attention is directed towards the integration of the traditionally separate areas of clinical and management activity, the setting up of new organisational structures, and the introduction of clinical and budgetary audit. A useful discussion of the evolution of a new service structure is provided in Tom Butler's (1993) case study of central Manchester.

Despite legislative delays in the implementation of formalised community care, and a hybrid period as new service structures are developed, care is, and for a long time has been, taking place in the community. Ramon (1988, p. 261) notes that over half of hospital in-patients stay no longer than a month. This, taken with the fact that "the majority of the clientele of the psychiatric services lives . . . outside the hospital for most of the time", means that "deinstitutionalisation has already taken place".

Barriers to normalisation

Ramon (1988) highlights the barriers to 'normalisation' (defined as "leading an ordinary, unmarginalized life", p. 262) including:

(1) the conceptual frameworks of most psychiatrists and nurses (which, she argues, are still rooted in a disease model)
(2) the lack of knowledge and skill of professionals who do work in the community
(3) cuts in local authority spending
(4) the chaos of the social security system
(5) the lack of coordination between health authority and local authority services
(6) the lack of support for informal carers
(7) the attitudes of local neighbourhoods in which 'ex-patients' live
(8) relapses on the part of some patients
(9) fears of an incipient and poorly regulated private-sector involvement in community care.

One particular point to be stressed from this broad list is the assumption in policy documents that the bulk of care in the community will be provided informally a policy which, given sex divisions in society, puts a clear burden on unpaid female carers.

Concluding remarks: the social organisation of services and the health care division of labour

When we discuss the organisation of the mental hospital and/or the structure of community services, we need to take into account the interplay between the wider socio-economic structure of society and microprocesses such as the division of labour in health care. In the first part of this chapter it was suggested that the hospital is characterised by a certain amount of conflict, deriving from factors such as countervailing lines of authority and the existence of a range of treatment modalities. It is evident that similar problems exist in the community services.

It has been suggested that, historically, the medical profession has been pivotal in the division of labour, but that in recent times (particularly from the late 1980s onwards) its ability to direct services has been reduced because of stemming from managerial reforms. From the point of view of health-care providers, the current climate may generate a sense of opportunity, coupled with particular concern for the medical profession's place in a turbulent health-care system.

Ramon (1988, p. 267) depicts the system as characterised by polarisation:

> "polarization in thinking about it, in form and content of services, among the providers, the direct and indirect users, among policy makers, and in the message expressed by the media".

Polarisation tends to generate both overt and covert conflict, manifest in competition for power outside the hospital. There has been a massive increase in the number of specialists involved in the mental health field since World War II, such as psychologists, nurses, occupational therapists, and social workers. The role of these specialists has changed both within and outside the hospital in recent years, and several commentators suggest that new patterns of interprofessional relationships herald a new era in which the psychiatrist no longer occupies the pivotal role (Ramon, 1988).

Discussing reforms in mental health knowledge, Prior (1991, p. 488) talks of the "demedicalisation of psychiatry" rather than the "psychiatrisation of normality" in community care, and Baruch & Treacher (1978) contend that the desegregation of the psychiatric profession has a latent function of shifts in social policy in the post-war period.

It may be that some professionals, comfortable within the hospital environment, feel unprepared to work outside it, and others feel that their power base is left behind in the hospital. Mental health institutions and services are clearly in a state of flux. The organisation that emerges in the immediate future will be a product of the many factors which have been stressed in this chapter, as we have outlined 'the story to date'. The future script is certainly constrained by socio-economic factors and the particular knowledge base of psychiatry, psychiatric nursing, and other occupational groups. The health-care division of labour that emerges, however, will also be influenced by active negotiation between the various groups involved in the provision of care to patients.

Further reading

Murphy, E. (1991) *After the Asylums.* London: Faber & Faber.
Perrow, C. (1965) Hospitals: technology, structure and goals. In *Handbook of Organisations* (ed. J. G. March), p. 910. Chicago: Rand McNally.
Scull, A. (1977) *Decarceration.* Englewood Cliffs, NJ: Prentice-Hall.
Strauss, A., Schatzman, L., Bucher, R., *et al* (1981) *Psychiatric Ideologies and Institutions.* London: Transaction Books.

References

American Psychiatric Association (1980) *Diagnostic and Statistical Manual of Mental Disorders* (3rd edn). Washington, DC: APA.
Baruch, G. & Treacher, A. (1978) *Psychiatry Observed.* London: Routledge, Kegan Paul.
Brown, P. (1987) Diagnostic conflict and contradiction in psychiatry. *Journal of Health and Social Behavior,* **28,** 37–50.
Butler, T. (1993) *Changing Mental Health Services. The Politics and the Policy.* London: Chapman and Hall.
Day, R. & Day, J. (1977) A review of the current state of negotiated order theory: an appreciation and a critique. *Sociological Quarterly,* **18,** 126–142.
Goffman, E. (1968) *Asylums: Essays on the Social Situation of Mental Patients and Other Inmates.* Harmondsworth: Penguin.
Korman, N. & Glennerster, H. (1990) *Hospital Closure: A Political and Economic Study.* Milton Keynes: Open University Press.
Laing, R. D. (1960) *The Divided Self.* London: Tavistock.
Mays, N. (1991) Community care. In *Sociology as Applied to Medicine* (3rd edn) (ed. G. Scambler), pp. 236–248. London: Baillière Tindall.
Morgan, M., Calnan, M. & Manning, N. (1988) *Sociological Approaches to Health and Medicine.* London: Routledge.
Murphy, E. (1991) *After the Asylums.* London: Faber & Faber.
Navarro, V. (1975) The industrialization of fetishism or the fetishism of Ivan Illich. *Social Science and Medicine,* **9,** 351–363.
Perrow, C. (1965) Hospitals: technology, structure and goals. In *Handbook of Organisations* (ed. J. G. March), p. 910. Chicago: Rand McNally.
Prior, L. (1991) Community versus hospital care: the crisis in psychiatric provision. *Social Science and Medicine,* **32,** 483–489.
Ramon, S. (1988) Towards normalization: polarization and change in Britain. In *Psychiatry in Transition* (ed. S. Ramon), pp. 261–272. London: Pluto Press.
Scull, A. (1977) *Decarceration.* Englewood Cliffs, NJ: Prentice-Hall.
Stanton, A. H. & Schwartz, M. S. (1954) *The Mental Hospital.* New York: Basic Books.
Strauss, A., Schatzman, L., Bucher, R., *et al* (1981) *Psychiatric Ideologies and Institutions.* London: Transaction Books.
Strong, P. & Robinson, J. (1990) *The NHS – Under New Management.* Milton Keynes: Open University Press.
Szasz, T. (1961) *The Myth of Mental Illness.* New York: Harper & Row.

Szurek, S. A. (1947) Dynamics of staff interaction in hospital psychiatric treatment. *American Journal of Orthopsychiatry*, **17**, 652–664.

Towell, D. & Kingsley, S. (1988) Changing psychiatric services in Britain. In *Psychiatry in Transition* (ed. S. Ramon), pp. 170–181. London: Pluto Press.

Turner, B. (1987) *Medical Power and Social Knowledge.* London: Sage.

Weber, M. (1978) *Economy and Society.* Berkeley, CA: University of California Press.

Williams, S. (1987) Goffman, interactionism, and the management of stigma in everyday life. In *Sociological Theory and Medical Sociology* (ed. G. Scambler), pp. 134–164. London: Tavistock.

Index

Compiled by Linda English

352